ART & COURT OF JAMES VI & I

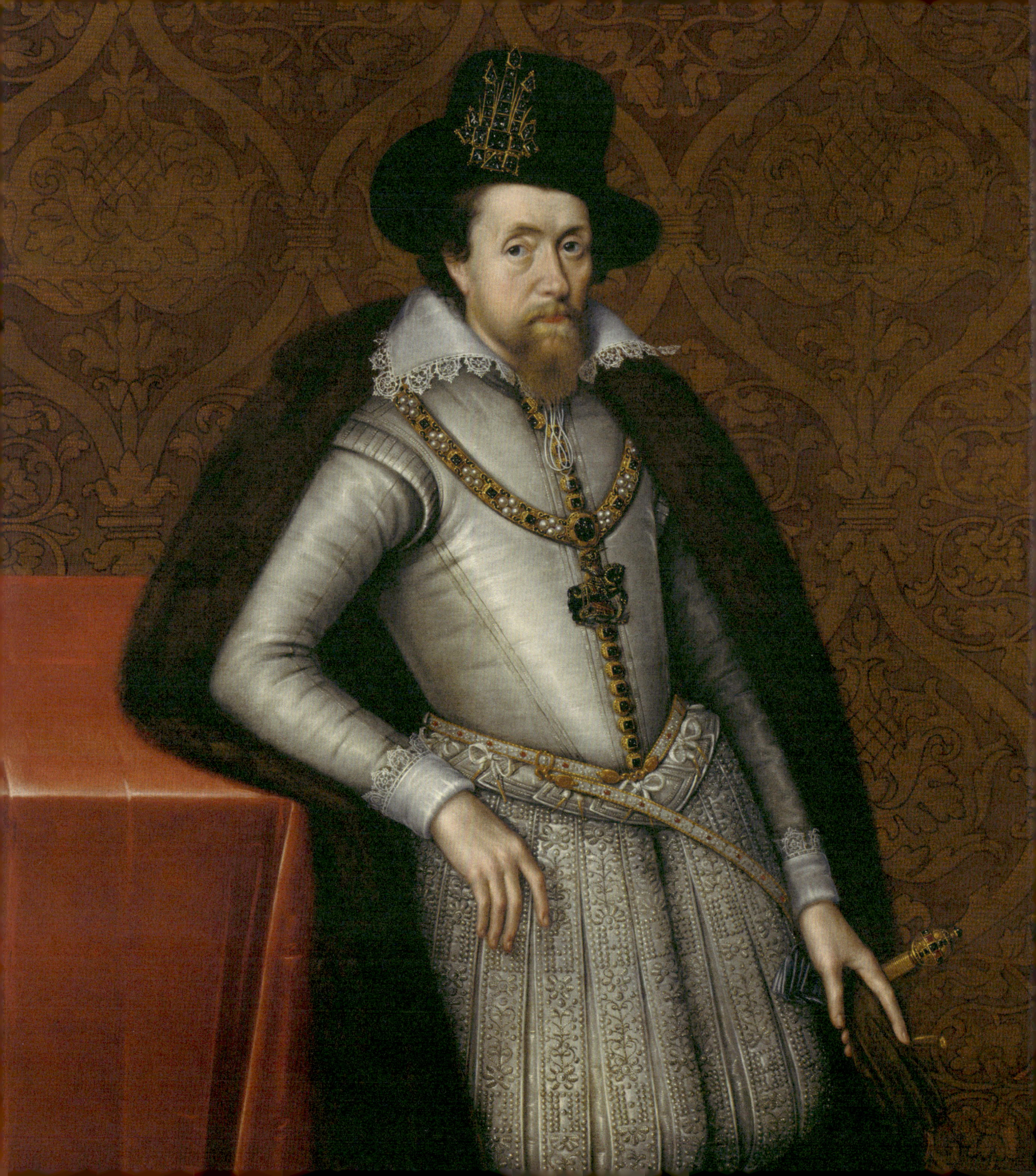

ART & COURT
OF JAMES VI & I

Kate Anderson
with Catriona Murray, Jemma Field,
Anna Groundwater, Karen Hearn
and Liz Louis

NATIONAL GALLERIES OF SCOTLAND, EDINBURGH

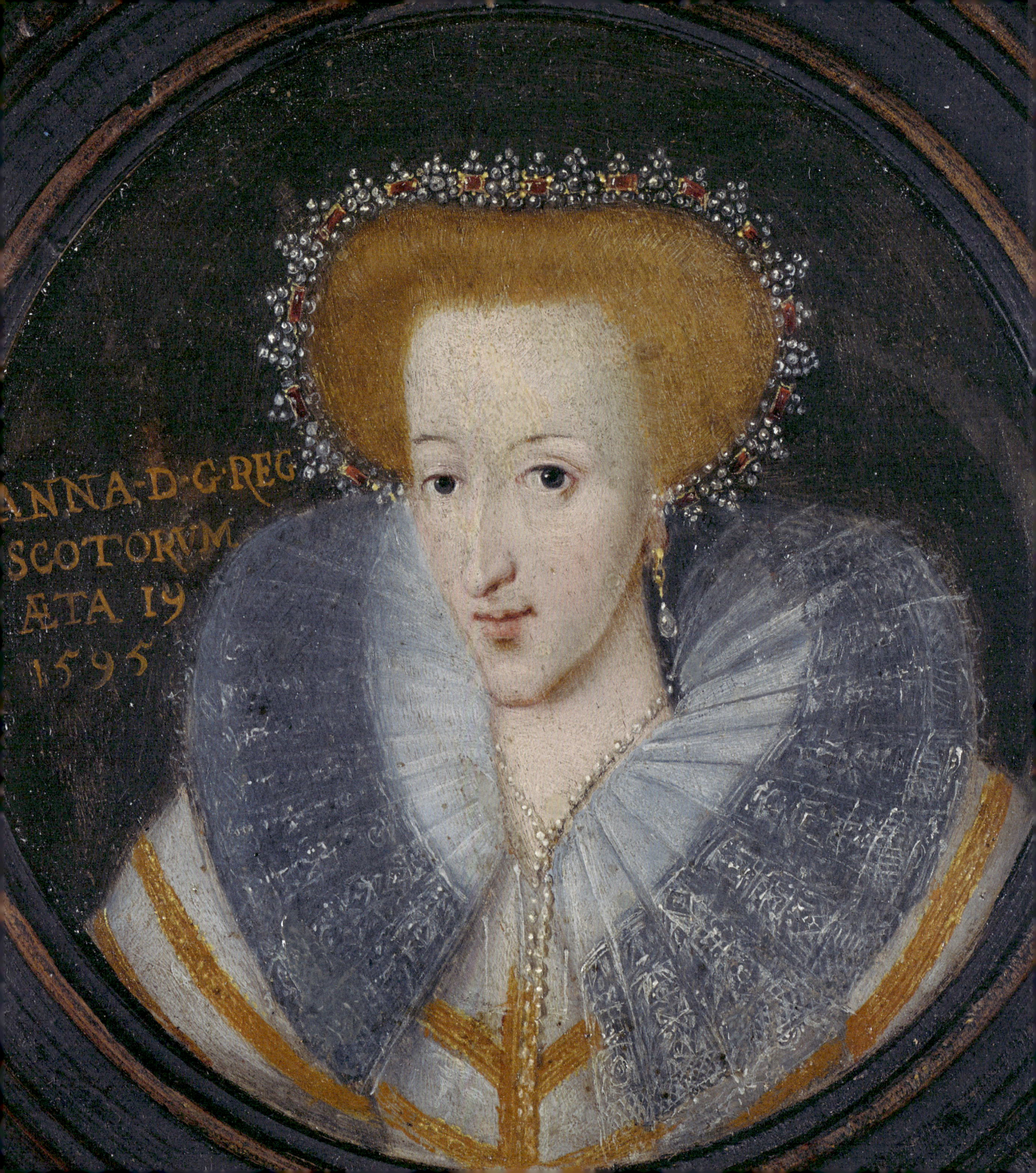

ANNA·D·G·REG
SCOTORVM
ÆTA 19
1595

CONTENTS

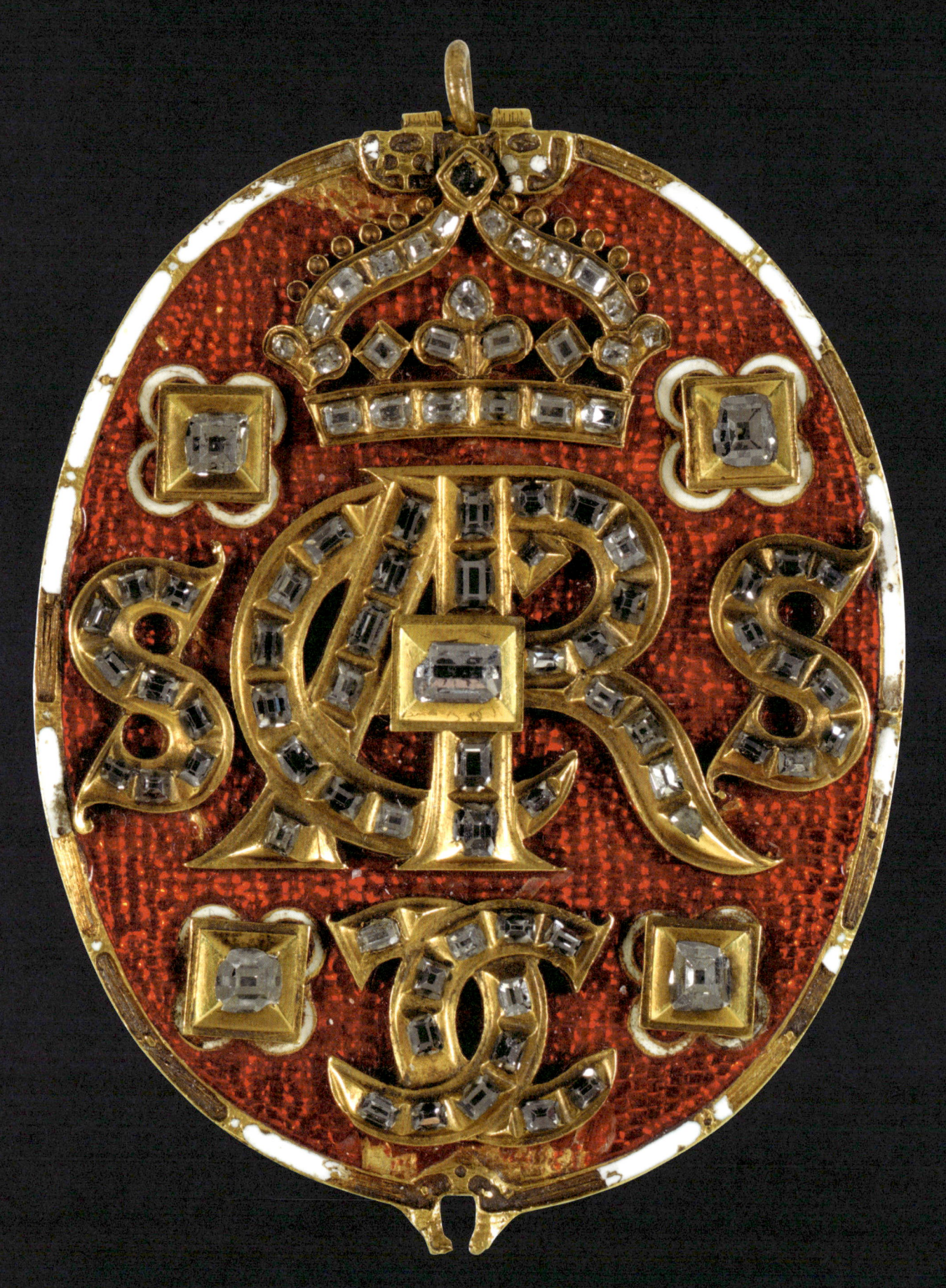

DIRECTOR'S FOREWORD

Detail of cat.15 (opposite)
Detail of cat.4 (previous spread)

KING JAMES VI & I WAS A COMPLEX, INTRIGUING AND PROVOCATIVE figure in both Scottish and British history of the late sixteenth and early seventeenth centuries. To some extent, he has been overshadowed by the reputations of his mother, Mary, Queen of Scots, and son, Charles I, whose lives and stories have been exhaustively studied. A reappraisal of James is however of great interest in its own right, and timely because of the fascinating historical context it provides for current debates about questions of nationhood, identity and international connections.

When James arrived in London in 1603, he unified the kingdoms of Scotland, England and Ireland for the first time and was described as the 'Bright Star of the North'. This book and the ambitious exhibition it accompanies, *The World of King James VI and I*, set out to consider the reality behind such rhetoric, and to explore James's life, family, court and connections – as such it is the first major project to address this subject in nearly five decades. The approach taken is broadly chronological, with emphasis being placed on the remarkable art and objects that survive which give us insight into the king, those closest to him, and the world he lived in. A key theme that emerges is the quality and variety of the art, objects, literature and performance that resulted from the patronage of James's courts in Scotland and England, as illustrated by splendid paintings, miniatures, drawings, prints, dress and textiles, jewellery, books, manuscripts and coins. Outstanding works, by artists such as John de Critz, Nicholas Hilliard, and Sir Peter Paul Rubens, exemplify the splendour and sophistication of the Jacobean age.

We are especially grateful to Kate Anderson, Senior Curator, Portraiture, at the National Galleries of Scotland for devising this groundbreaking exhibition and the dedication and care and insight she has brought to every aspect of it. Among other colleagues special thanks are also due to Imogen Gibbon, Liz Louis, Kim Macpherson, Elinor McMonagle and Louise Rowlands. The challenge of the complex design has been met with great skill by Smith-Gordon Design, while the installation and promotion of the project is thanks to many specialists across the Galleries' Conservation, Collection Management, Art Handling, Retail and Communications teams.

This beautiful book will continue to disseminate the scholarship that the exhibition has created beyond its run. We are incredibly grateful indeed to the distinguished contributors: Dr Catriona Murray, Dr Jemma Field, Dr Anna Groundwater and Professor Karen Hearn. Thanks are also due to the Publishing Team at the National Galleries of Scotland, in particular Catherine Aitken and Ann Crawford for expertly bringing the catalogue to publication.

Projects of this ambition can only be realised through two key forms of generosity: that of lenders and financial supporters. In this case both institutional and private lenders have been exceptionally supportive and we are most grateful to them all: His Majesty The King and The Royal Collection Trust; The Duke of Hamilton and Brandon; The Duke of Atholl and The Collection at Blair Castle, Perthshire; The Earl of Mar & Kellie; The Buchanan Society; Alexander McCall Smith; The National Museum of Scotland; The National Library of Scotland; The National Records of Scotland; Glasgow Life; George Heriot's Trust; The University of Edinburgh Heritage Collections; The National Portrait Gallery, London; Dulwich Picture Gallery; The Victoria and Albert Museum; The Fitzwilliam Museum, University of Cambridge; The Fashion Museum Bath, and The Blackie House Library and Museum, and a number of private collections, which wish to remain anonymous.

In terms of financial support, we would like to express our sincere thanks to the Friends and the Patrons of the National Galleries of Scotland. It is only because of their belief in the importance of the work of the National Galleries of Scotland that it has been possible to create *The World of King James VI and I*, which will, we hope, inspire its many visitors over the spring and summer of 2025.

Anne Lyden
Director-General, National Galleries of Scotland

NOTES ON THE TEXT

Naming conventions for individuals
Names of individuals are those used when the individuals were alive. For example, Anne of Denmark is the anglicised form of James's wife's name, but she was born and referred to as Anna while in Denmark and Scotland. Titles of artworks appear as they do in their respective collections.

Individuals frequently mentioned throughout the book
Mary, Queen of Scots (1542–1587)
James VI & I (1566–1625)
Anna of Denmark (1574–1619)
Prince Henry Frederick (1594–1612)
Princess Elizabeth, Electress Palatine, Queen of Bohemia (1596–1662)
Frederick V, Elector Palatine, King of Bohemia (1596–1632)
Charles I (1600–1649)

Denmark-Norway
Denmark-Norway is the term used to describe the dual monarchy or real union of the Kingdoms of Denmark and Norway and their territories (1536/7–1814). The term Denmark is used on its own when referring to the geographical location or when commonly used in an individual's title, e.g. Anna of Denmark.

Language
When quoting seventeenth-century prose, spellings, punctuation and grammar have been modernised.

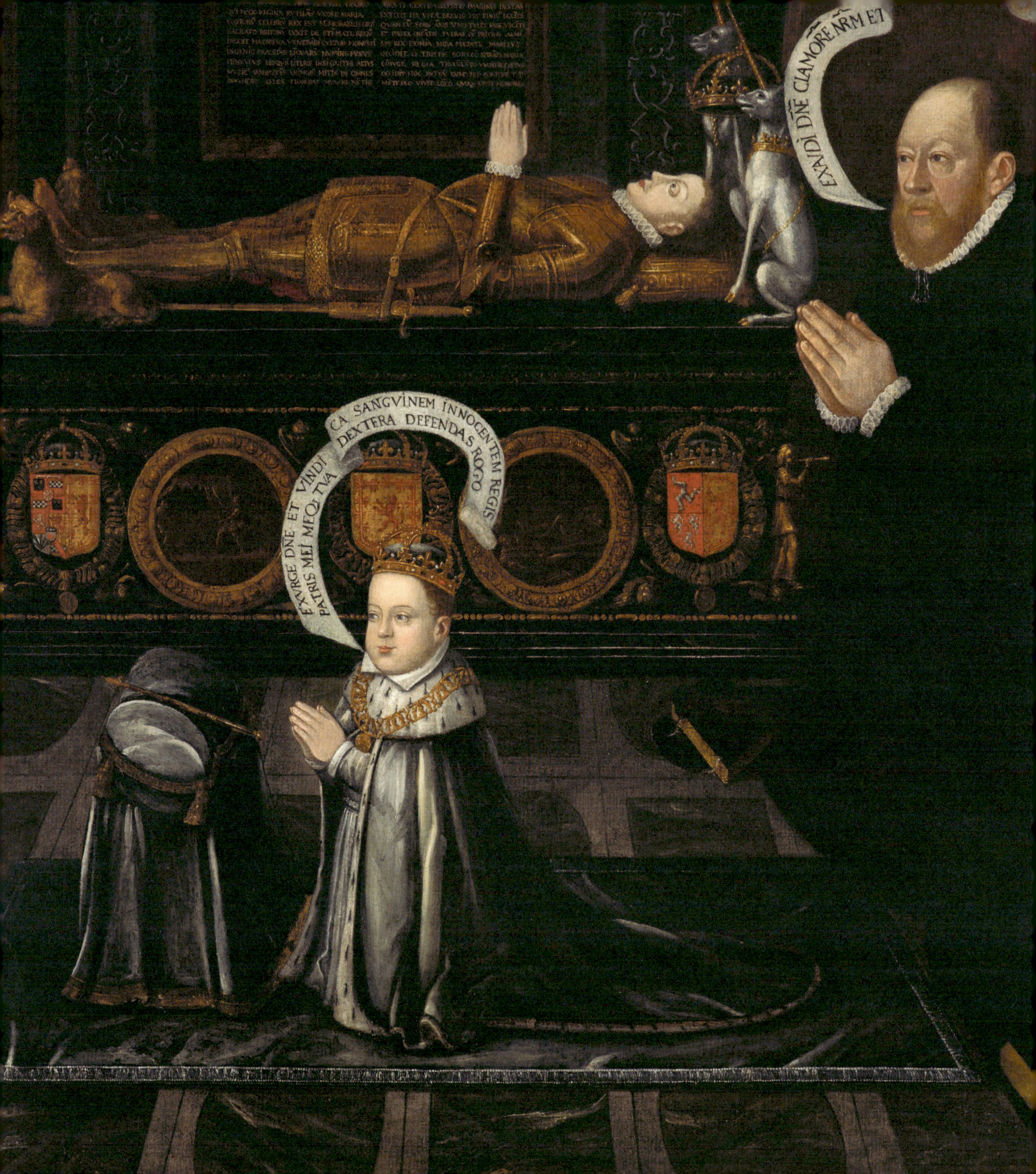

INTRODUCTION

Kate Anderson

HISTORY HAS NOT BEEN KIND TO JAMES VI of Scotland and I of England and Ireland. For many, he has fallen between the cracks of the reigns of his mother, Mary, Queen of Scots, and his son Charles I, overshadowed by their contentious and heavily romanticised legacies. Both James's reign and character were heavily criticised in the seventeenth century by writers, notably Sir Anthony Weldon. Published posthumously in 1650, the pejorative account of James's physical appearance claimed that the king's tongue was too big for his mouth, that he possessed weak legs and constantly fidgeted with his codpiece.[1] Weldon was a former English courtier who had been dismissed from his position, and the memoir was anti-Scottish in sentiment and full of scandal and unfounded rumour. However, its legacy continued to impact on subsequent histories of the king for centuries. While recent scholarship has revised some of these inaccuracies and prejudices, misconceptions about James and his reign still exist. One of the aims of this book, and the exhibition it accompanies, is to reframe

James and consider his life and reign in a wider context; they also seek to explore the extraordinary art, objects and culture that were produced during this period, and demonstrate how James, his family and members of the court used them to promote messages of status, power and allegiance.

This is not a detailed biography of James. His reign and character are incredibly complex, and while the narrative here is multi-layered, it does not set out to comprehensively examine the historical context of Scotland, England and Europe during this time. Instead, an object-based approach has been taken, with the visual and material culture of the Jacobean period being placed at the centre of this study, alongside an overview of some of the key individuals and events that shaped the king.

In an attempt to address the imbalance of scholarly attention that the Scottish and English courts have received over the years, a concerted effort has been made to highlight James's Scottish period. However, it is too simplistic to directly compare the artistic quality and output of the two

Detail of cat.30

courts, as the political, religious and economic climate in Scotland during James's early life had a major impact on the development of the country's cultural productivity.

This book has been published to accompany the exhibition *The World of King James VI and I*. It is hoped, however, that the essays and catalogue will have a legacy beyond the exhibition. Many of the artworks and objects in the exhibition are published here for the first time.

The Cradle King

James was born at Edinburgh Castle on 19 June 1566 and was baptised Charles James in December of that year, the only son of Mary, Queen of Scots (cat.32), and her second husband Henry Stuart, Lord Darnley (1545/6–1567, cat.29), who like Mary was a great-grandchild of King Henry VII of England (1457–1509). His parents' union in 1565 had strengthened Mary's claim to the English throne, alarming Elizabeth I (1533–1603). The birth of a male heir fuelled the English queen's hostility towards her cousin. James was born into one of the most turbulent periods of Scottish history, which was dominated by radical religious reform, persistent feuding between noble factions and power struggles for the position of regent. Within a year of James's birth, his father had been murdered, his mother had been forced to abdicate, and he was crowned king at just thirteen months old on 29 July 1567. In line with Scottish royal tradition, James was brought up at Stirling Castle (cat.46) and was placed under the care of John Erskine, 1st Earl of Mar (d.1572, cat.48) and Annabella Murray, Countess of Mar (1536–1603). James was effectively an orphan, and while his early childhood environment at Stirling was relatively secure and comfortable, the loss of his parents and lack of immediate family had a lasting impact that would go on to define his character into adulthood. In his later years, he famously lamented that as a child he was 'alone, without father, mother, brother or sister'.[2]

The portrait of *James VI with a Sparrow Hawk*, *c.*1574 (cat.1), by an unknown Netherlandish artist, is believed to show James at around eight years old. The artist has sensitively captured the boy king wearing adult dress of a black doublet, black hat with jewelled hatband and white feather plume. He

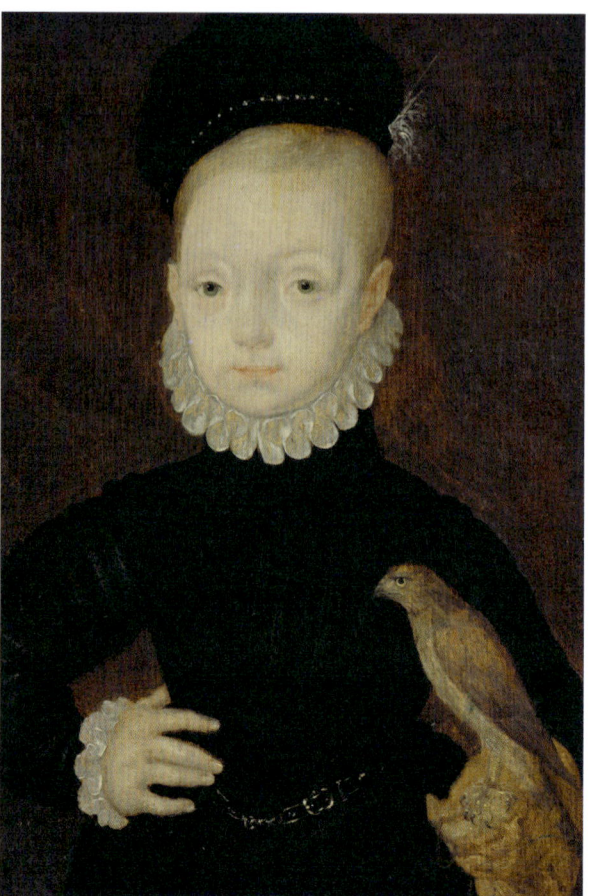

Cat.1
Unknown Netherlandish artist
James VI with a Sparrow Hawk,
c.1574
Oil on panel, 45.7 × 30.6 cm
National Galleries of Scotland,
Edinburgh (PG 992)

PROVENANCE: Sir Peter Young; gifted by him to Charles I; sold 23 October 1651 but recovered at the Restoration; Breadalbane Collection, with R. Baillie-Hamilton at Langton House, Duns by 1889; sold by Lieut.-Col. Thomas Breadalbane Morgan-Grenville-Gavin at Christie's, London, 27 March 1925, lot 12 and purchased by the Scottish National Portrait Gallery.

REFERENCES: London 1889, cat.57, p.27; Edinburgh 1959, cat.79, p.30; Millar 1960, p.65; Auerbach 1961, p.269; Millar 1963a, p.14; Strong 1969a, plate 341; Strong 1969b, p.137, no.92; Millar 1972, p.317; Thomson 1974, p.45, no.8; Thomson 1975, p.23, no.8; Thomas 2013, pp.100–01; Allerston 2023, no.1, p.28

holds a small sparrow hawk which alludes to the princely pastime of falconry, a pursuit which, along with hunting, would develop into one of James's great passions. In this period of great political uncertainty, the aim of a portrait such as this was to reassure contemporary audiences by showing the young king healthy and active. Part of the Royal Collection in the seventeenth century, the painting has the brand of Charles I on the reverse, and is recorded in the inventory created by Abraham van der Doort in 1633 where it is listed as 'given to the King by Sir Peter Young (1544–1628), one of James's tutors'.[3]

At Stirling Castle, the focus of James's early years was his education. The two tutors who were responsible for this were the humanist scholar George Buchanan (1506–1582, cat.18) and the aforementioned Sir Peter Young. Buchanan provided James with a strong Protestant education that focused on a mastery of Latin and Hebrew,

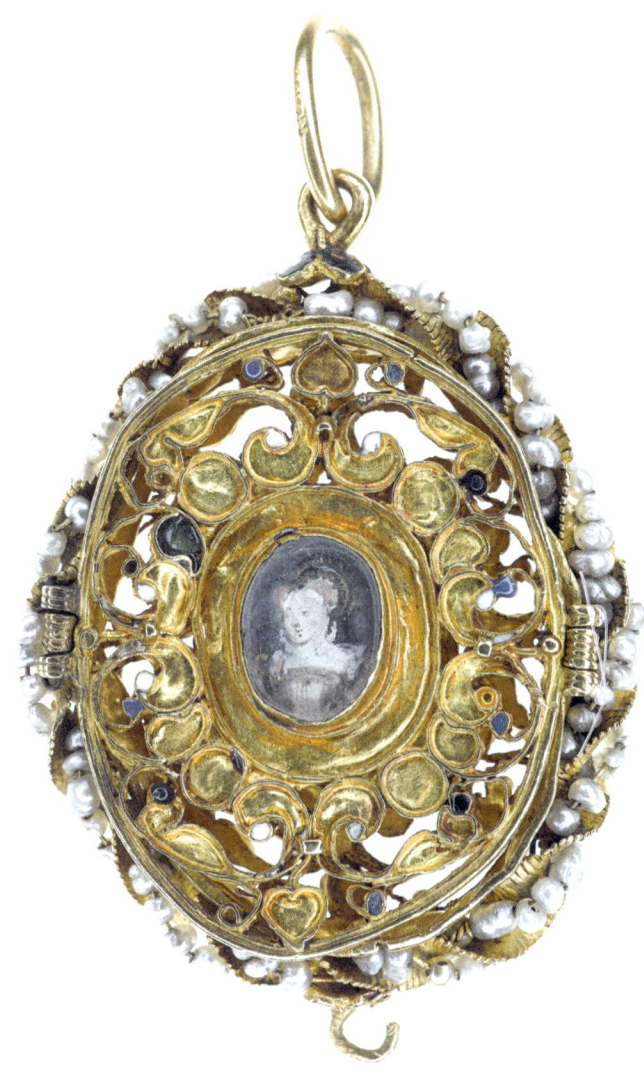

Cat.2
Unknown Scottish goldsmith and artist
Pendant locket set with miniature portraits of Mary, Queen of Scots and James VI, part of 'The Penicuik Jewels', late sixteenth century
Gold, enamel and seed pearls with watercolour miniatures, 6.4 × 3.4 × 0.7 cm
National Museums Scotland, Edinburgh (H.NA 422)

PROVENANCE: The Clerks of Penicuik.

REFERENCES: Edinburgh 1990, cat.44, p.58; Edinburgh 1991, cat.7, p.19; Edinburgh 2013, cat.93, p.84; London 2021, cat. 126, pp.232–33; Groundwater 2024, p.111

assassination in 1570, James's grandfather, Matthew Stewart, 4th Earl of Lennox (1516–1571), held the title, followed by James's governor, the Earl of Mar. The fourth and final regent was James Douglas, 4th Earl of Morton (c.1516–1581, cat.33), who ruled Scotland from November 1572 to March 1578.

The political and religious upheavals of these years account for the relative dearth of art and fine objects from this period in Scotland. An important survival is an exquisite piece of jewellery: an intricate gold, enamel and pearl locket which contains two tiny miniature portraits, thought to be of Mary and James (cat.2). The locket not only gives us insight into the style of gold and enamel work that was fashionable in sixteenth-century Scotland, but also demonstrates how jewellery and portrait miniatures were highly emotive objects that could be used to communicate messages of status, allegiance and even affection.

There are tantalising glimpses of the artistic activity at court as the 1570s progressed. In the exchequer records of 1573, a 'French painter' was paid £10 Scots to make a pattern for the king's portrait.[4] This may have been the pattern used for a small portrait of James VI from which a few other versions survive. There is also a small group of portraits of members of the royal household, including the Earl of Morton (cat.33), George Buchanan (cat.18) and James Hamilton, 2nd Earl of Arran which, like *James VI with a Sparrow Hawk*, have all in the past been attributed to the Netherlandish émigré artist Arnold Bronckorst (active 1565–1583).[5] Following technical analysis, it is now believed that the portraits, with the exception of Buchanan, are by a different and as yet unidentified hand.[6] The Buchanan one is after a portrait perhaps originally by Bronckorst.[7] This group of works demonstrates that there were artists working at the Scottish court about whom we have much to discover.

James, King of Scots

With the end of the Morton regency in 1578, James, aged twelve, assumed personal rule, and his formal ceremonial entry into Edinburgh took place on 19 October 1579.[8] The spectacle took the form of a Renaissance pageant with allegorical and religious imagery, speeches, music and performance,

in addition to history, political theory, theology and mathematics. While he instilled in James a great thirst for learning, which he would retain throughout his life, the boy was terrified of his master and was subjected to frequent beatings. Young on the other hand was a far gentler tutor, and the two would remain close once James reached his majority, with Young accompanying the king to London in 1603.

While James experienced relative stability in the schoolroom, life in the outside world was increasingly volatile. During James's minority, a succession of regents ruled Scotland. The first, in 1567, was Mary's half-brother, James Stewart, 1st Earl of Moray (1531/2–1570), who had defeated her at the battle of Langside in May 1568 before her ill-fated flight to England. Following Moray's and tapestries hanging in the streets. Accounts record that James was met at the Over Bow by Cupid, a young boy descending in a globe from the heavens to present the king with the keys to the burgh.[9] At the Salt Tron, the king passed paintings representing the genealogy of the kings of Scots going back to the mythological King Fergus I, who appeared as 'The First King of Scots' in chronologies written by the Scottish historians Hector Boece and George Buchanan, and was said to have lived around 330–305 BC. It is possible that a series of portraits depicting the Scottish kings from James I to James V (cats 92–95) may have been part of this decorative scheme.[10]

Symbolically, the entry marked the ceremonial commencement of James's personal rule, and it is estimated that over 3,000 nobility and gentlemen were called on to attend the event.[11] However, historians suggest the period of 1578 to 1585 can be viewed as an apprenticeship for the king, with his true ascendancy occurring in the latter year.[12] Around that seven-year period, the development of a Renaissance court at Holyroodhouse emerged, which corresponded with the arrival of James's second cousin Esmé Stewart (1542–1583) from France in 1579. James was quickly drawn to the handsome, cultured Esmé, who was to become the first in a series of royal favourites that were intimately linked with the king. Unlike other European princes, James had not grown up in a court setting, and with the exception of his baptism at Stirling – a triumphant Renaissance pageant orchestrated by his mother, of which he would have no recollection – there had been no precedent for a cultural programme at court for James to follow.

Esmé inspired his cousin to develop such interests, and soon there was a flourishing circle of poets at court, including Patrick Hume of Polwarth, Alexander Montgomerie and William Fowler, who were commissioned to compose prose and speeches for performances such as court masques.[13] Masques were spectacles that combined dance, music and the spoken word, and were highly symbolic, being imbued with messages about dynasty, personal alliances and political developments. They were normally held at New Year or for birthdays or weddings, and James both composed and performed in them. In 1581 the English ambassador recalled a 'strange masque' being performed at Holyroodhouse, and later that year the English court musician William Hudson received the huge sum of £100 Scots for his 'extrardinar pains in teitching of his grace to dance'.[14] James also promoted the advancement of music at court and in October 1589 granted a pension to Andrew Blackhall and his son to encourage their study of music.[15]

In tandem with this expansion of cultural patronage, James's future was being discussed. In 1587, his mother Mary had been executed – the death warrant was signed by Elizabeth I (cat.49). Despite this tragic event, around the same time James's marriage became a matter of national interest. It would not only be crucial to secure the succession, but also bring a much-needed dowry to the cash-strapped country. Proposals for brides from Europe had been considered earlier in the decade, including two French candidates, Christine of Lorraine, granddaughter of Catherine de' Medici, and Catherine de Bourbon, Protestant sister of Henri III of Navarre. Esmé favoured Christine and arranged for his agent to go to France to collect her portrait for James. In return, Bronckorst was paid for a portrait of James to be sent to the princess.[16] Portraits played a significant role in marriage negotiations and international diplomacy.

While discussions around a French marriage had deteriorated, a match with a Danish princess, one of the two daughters of Frederick II, King of Denmark-Norway, Elizabeth or Anna, progressed – and, following protracted negotiations, in 1589 the match was finally agreed between Princess Anna and James (cats 3 and 4). The couple were married by proxy on 20 August at Kronborg Castle, north of Copenhagen, with George Keith, 5th Earl Marischal, standing in for James.[17] Anna's journey to Scotland was thwarted by storms – and, eager to meet his new bride, James took the extraordinary decision to fetch Anna himself. He sailed from Leith, Edinburgh, on 22 October and arrived in Norwegian waters one week later. A church ceremony took place on 23 November, and the royal couple undertook an extended honeymoon travelling through Norway and Sweden by sledge, finally arriving in Denmark the following January, where they were welcomed by Anna's family at Kronborg Castle.

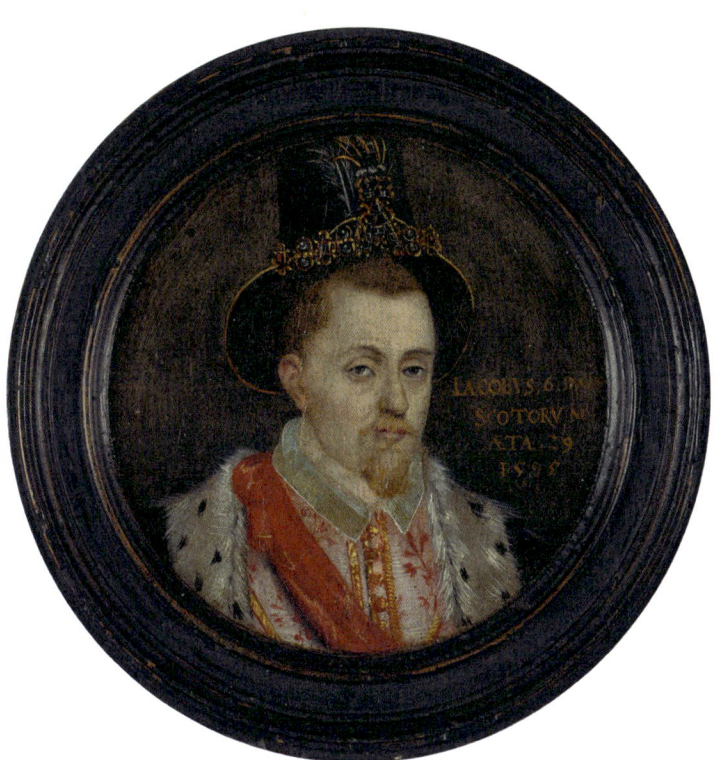 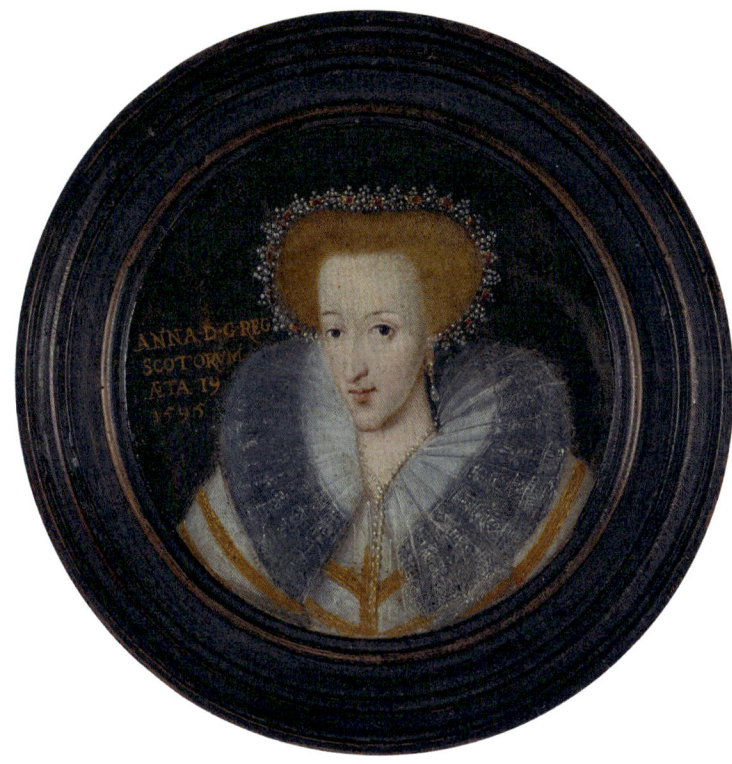

Cat.3 (above left)
Attributed to Adrian Vanson
(active 1581–1603)
James VI, 1595
Oil on panel, diameter 11.9 cm
National Galleries of Scotland,
Edinburgh (PG 1109)

PROVENANCE: Bequeathed by
A.W. Inglis, 1929.

REFERENCES: Edinburgh 1959,
cat.67, p.26; Thomson 1975,
no.15, pp.28–29; Edinburgh 1990,
pp.53–54, cat.52; Edinburgh 1998,
p.32

Cat.4 (above right)
Attributed to Adrian Vanson
(active 1581–1603)
Anna of Denmark, 1595
Oil on panel, diameter 11.4 cm
National Galleries of Scotland,
Edinburgh (PG 1110)

PROVENANCE: Bequeathed by
A.W. Inglis, 1929.

REFERENCES: Edinburgh 1959,
cat.67, p.26; Thomson 1975,
no.16, pp.28–29; Edinburgh 1990,
pp.53–54, cat.52; Edinburgh 1998,
p.32

In Denmark, James toured the royal palaces, met with famous Scandinavian theologians, scientists and professors and enjoyed the company of Anna's close-knit family, enthusiastically participating in the drinking culture for which the Danes were notorious. James's experience in Denmark had a profound impact on him and influenced the cultural and intellectual direction of his court back in Scotland; on a more personal level it also inspired his future role as an involved and attentive father.

On their return to Scotland in the spring, James and Anna's journey was hampered yet again by the perilous weather. This time the storms were to have far-reaching consequences that went beyond the delay of the royal couple's sea voyage as accusations turned towards witches, who were blamed for conjuring up the storms to kill the newlyweds. James himself accused a group of supposed witches at North Berwick of conspiring with the devil. In the third essay in this book, Anna Groundwater explores James's publication *Daemonologie* (1597), which was in part written as a response to these events.

Scottish Court Culture

Arriving in Edinburgh, the newlyweds were met with both ceremony and festivity; and Anna, aged fifteen, was crowned at Holyrood Abbey on 17 May 1590. Two days later she made her formal entry into the city, an event that was even more spectacular and politically charged than James's entry in 1579 – there had been no entry of a queen consort in Scotland since Margaret Tudor in 1503.[18]

James attempted to emulate the type of Renaissance court he had experienced during his time in Denmark. The Palace of Holyroodhouse (fig.1) was the centre of court life, and at this time there were around 600 people living and working there.[19] In a letter to James from Anna's brother, Christian, the Danish king made a request for portraits of Anna and James to be sent to him.[20] This portrait exchange would no doubt have been reciprocal; and, while no artist is mentioned in the correspondence, Adrian Vanson (active 1581–1603) was official court painter from 1584 to 1603. He was responsible for painting the pendant portraits of James VI, 1595 (cat.13), and presumably the accompanying pendant of Anna, now lost. Vanson is

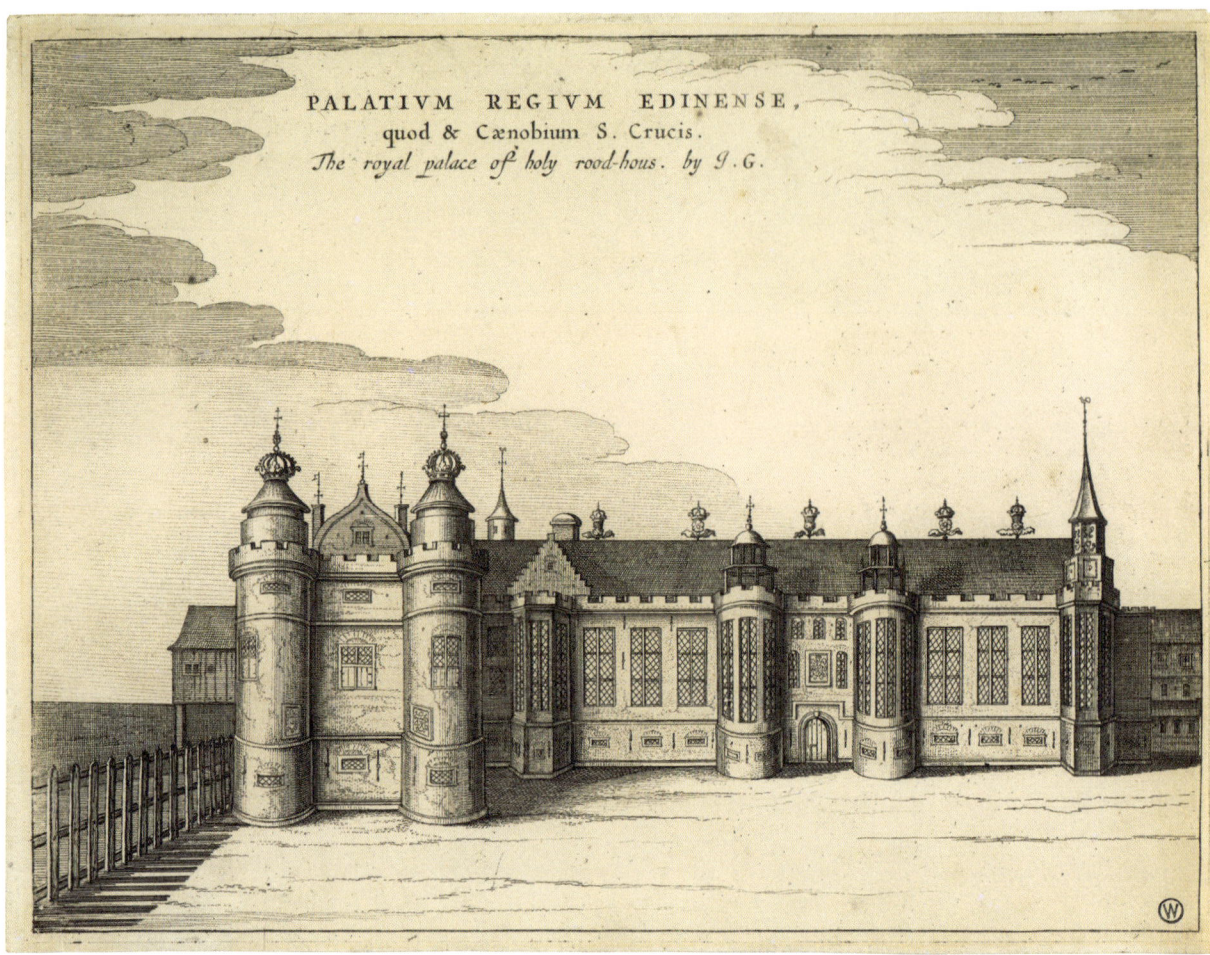

PALATIVM REGIVM EDINENSE,
quod & Cænobium S. Crucis.

The royal palace of holy rood-hous. by I.G.

Fig.1 (left)
James Gordon of Rothiemay
(*c*.1615–1686)
The Palace of Holyroodhouse,
seventeenth century
Engraving on paper, 20.7 × 27.4 cm
National Galleries of Scotland,
Edinburgh (SP II 176.1)

Cat.5 (opposite)
Unknown artist
Esther Inglis (1569–1624), 1595
Oil on panel, 74.6 × 63.2 cm
National Galleries of Scotland,
Edinburgh (PG 3556)

PROVENANCE: In the collection
of David Laing until his death in
1878; bequeathed to the Society of
Antiquaries of Scotland; on long-
term loan to the Scottish National
Portrait Gallery (SNPG) from
1885, then gifted by the Society
of Antiquaries of Scotland to the
SNPG, 2009.

REFERENCES: Edinburgh 1959,
cat.97, p.36; London 2013a, cat.70,
pp.178–79; SNPG 2014, p.16;
Leighton 2015, p.39; Allerston
2023, no.2, p.29

also associated with the portrait miniatures of James VI, 1595 and Anna of Denmark, 1595 (cats 3 and 4).[21]

A portrait of the calligrapher *Esther Inglis* (1569–1624), 1595, by an unknown artist (cat.5), provides another insight into the type of cultural activity in Edinburgh in the late sixteenth century. Inglis had come to London as an infant with her Huguenot parents, who had fled religious persecution in France, and subsequently settled in Edinburgh. Learning her art from her mother, a handwriting teacher, Inglis went on to become an exceptionally skilled calligrapher, illustrator and embroiderer and dedicated some of her work to James and his family. She wrote in Latin, Scots and French, and her manuscripts also include tiny self-portraits which promoted her authorship and talent (cat.50).

Intriguing accounts of 'Inglische commedianis' (English comedians) visiting Edinburgh and Aberdeen present an opportunity to discuss the

cultural exchange between Scotland and England before 1603. Lawrence Fletcher, an English actor, was in Edinburgh with a group of players (actors) in November 1599, and their presence created discontent in the Presbyterian Kirk. The episode forced the king to issue a warrant defending the players and granting the use of a property on Blackfriars Wynd for public performances.[22] Fletcher appears again in 1601, the head of a troupe of players who had journeyed to Aberdeen with a letter of recommendation from the king.[23] Fletcher is also listed in a warrant commissioned by James in 1603 appointing the group of actors, known as the 'Lord Chamberlain's Men', to which William Shakespeare belonged, as the 'King's Men'.[24] The group would be part of the royal procession for James's official entry into London on 14 March 1604, and Fletcher's name appears alongside Shakespeare's in a document granting

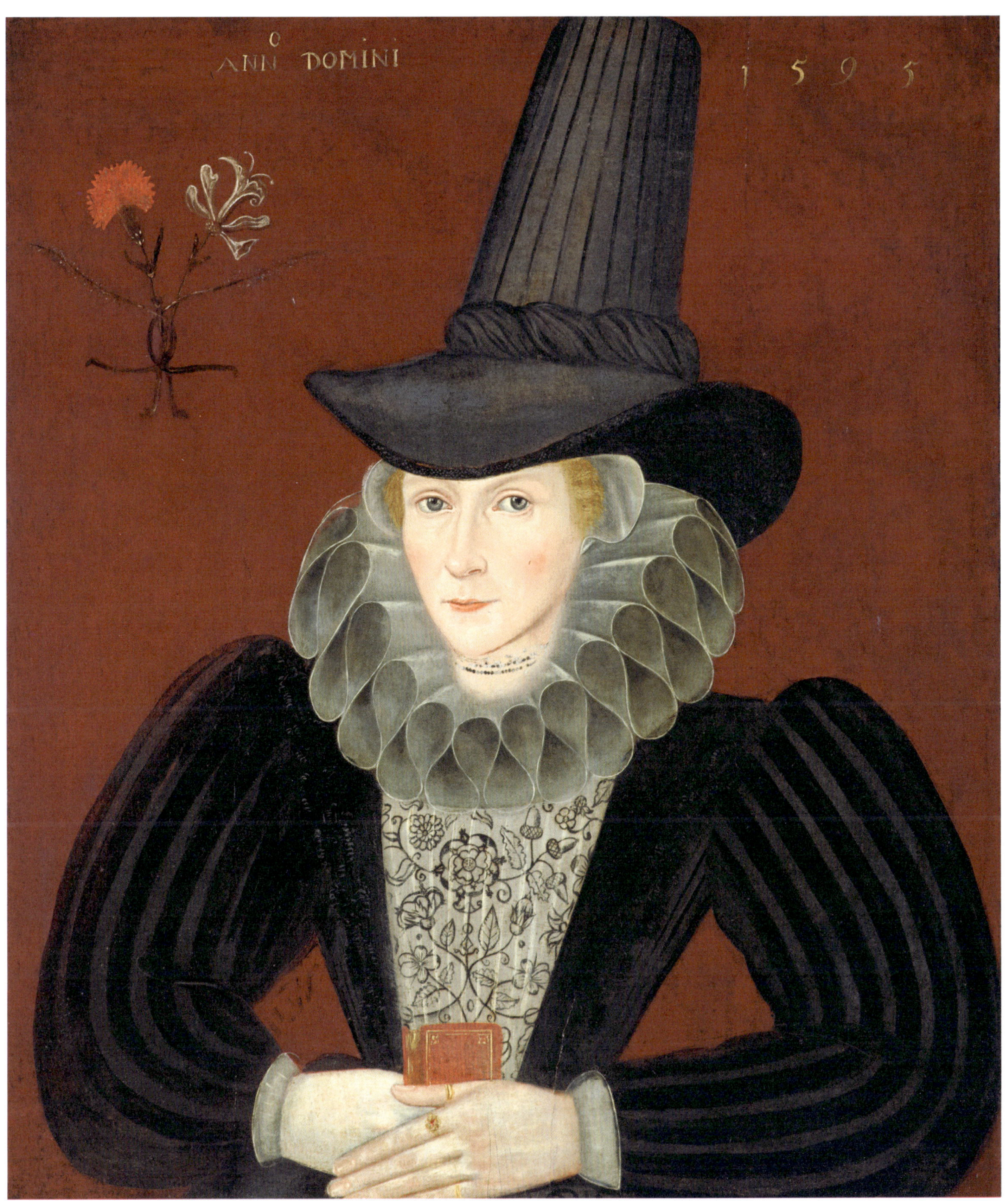

them red cloth for livery for the ceremony.[25] These references illustrate that James was engaged in the promotion of stage performances while in Scotland and continued his patronage immediately after his accession in London.

James's patronage was also extended to those making luxury goods, including jewellery, clothing and other precious objects such as timepieces. In her essay, Jemma Field discusses the role of two key figures at court: the merchant Robert Joussie (d.1610), responsible for sourcing the expensive and luxurious fabrics for the royal wardrobe, and George Heriot (1563–1624, cat.47), the Edinburgh-based jeweller who supplied the Stuart household with hundreds of thousands of pounds worth of jewels. The surviving accounts give us invaluable insights into the vast expenditure that was required to clothe and decorate the royal body.[26]

Fatherhood and Family

James was a father to seven children in all, although only three survived to adulthood. Having successfully secured the Stuart succession, James embraced an ideology which promoted him as father of the state. These concepts of fatherhood are explored in detail in the essays by Catriona Murray and Anna Groundwater. The latter considers James's writings, notably *Basilikon Doron*, 1599, the manual on kingship he wrote for his heir and first-born son Henry Frederick, who was born in 1594 (fig.5, cat.36).

James and Anna's second child Elizabeth, later Electress of the Palatine and Queen of Bohemia (fig.6, cat.39), was born in August 1596. Their third child, Margaret, was born in December 1598, but died before she was two years old. In November 1600, Charles, the future Charles I, was born; and in January 1602 another son, Robert, was delivered, only to die four months later. In England, Anna gave birth to two more royal children, Mary in April 1605 and Sophia in June 1606. Tragically, both girls also died, Mary aged two and Sophia when she was only one day old. These births and deaths illustrate the reality of pregnancy and infant mortality in the early modern period and attest to why some of the most elaborate and costly examples of courtly display and patronage, particularly Henry's baptism in

1594 and Elizabeth's wedding in 1613 to Frederick V, Elector Palatine (cat.89), were focused around the surviving royal children. The significance of these performances is discussed in detail in Catriona Murray's essay.

James certainly held his family in high esteem; and, unlike many monarchs, his correspondence with his wife and children is marked by interest and affection. He used Anna's prestigious lineage, as a Princess of Denmark from the House of Oldenburg, as well as her religion (she secretly converted to Catholicism in 1593) for political and diplomatic advantage.[27] The close relationship between Scotland and Denmark-Norway was significant and reflects the broader European connections cultivated by the Scottish court. This emphasis on dynasty, lineage and European standing was to become central to James's image in the lead-up to the Union of the Crowns in 1603 and throughout his reign as King of Great Britain.[28]

Bright Star of the North: The Stuarts in England

Elizabeth I died on 24 March 1603 and James was named her successor, becoming the first Stuart monarch of England, Scotland, Ireland and the principality of Wales. When he reached the outskirts of the city of London on 7 May 1603, James was welcomed by the lawyer and orator Richard Martin, who praised the king as the 'Bright Star of the North'. James's arrival was met with mixed feelings – on the one hand he represented the patriarchal model of a monarch, as unlike his predecessor he was married with a young healthy family, an heir, a spare and an eligible daughter. With this came stability and continuity for the future. On the other hand, many saw the Stuarts as an unknown prospect, and anti-Scottish sentiment had been growing in England since the 1580s. To complicate things further, James was the son of Mary, Queen of Scots, the woman Elizabeth had condemned to death as a traitor in 1587.

James did little to alleviate these concerns, and he appointed many Scots in his retinue to key posts within the royal household and lavished honours and affection on his favourites, notably Robert Carr, 1st Earl of Somerset (1585/6–1645, cat.57), Ludovic Stuart, 2nd Duke of Lennox and Duke of

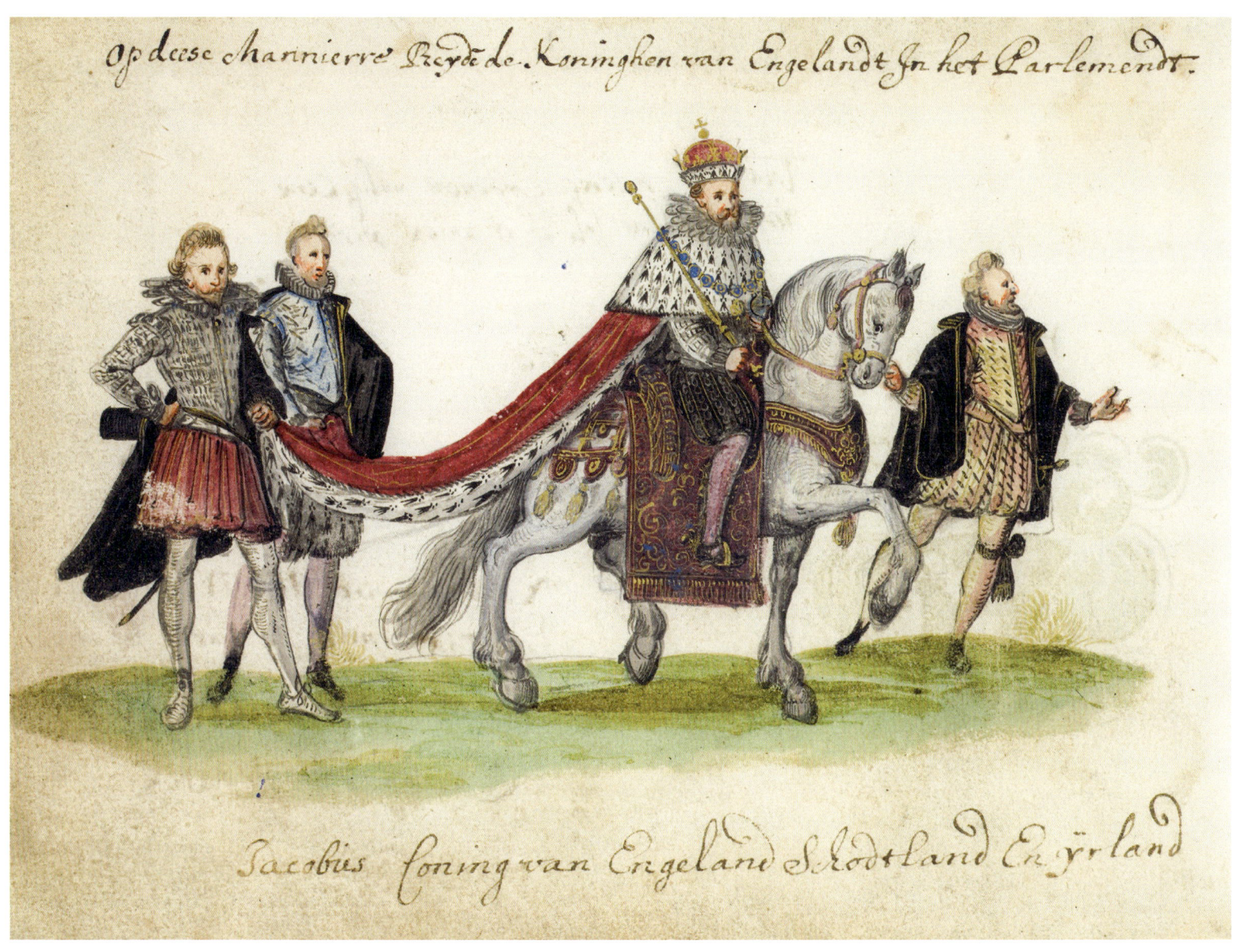

Op deese Manniere Reyde de Koninghen van Engelandt In het Parlement.

Jacobus Coning van Engeland Schodtland En ÿrland

Cat.6
Unknown artist
King James riding to Parliament with three noblemen, **from an**
Album Amicorum **owned by**
Michael van Meer, 1614–48
Ink and watercolour on paper, bound in leather, 13 × 19 cm
The University of Edinburgh Heritage Collections (La.III.283, f.159v)

PROVENANCE: David Laing Bequest, 1878.

REFERENCES: Edinburgh 1975, p.9, cat.10; Laroque 1993, pp.66–67; Schlueter 2006, pp.301–14

Richmond (1574–1624, cat.43), and the Englishman George Villiers, 1st Duke of Buckingham (1592–1628, cat.28). The nature of these relationships and James's sexuality has been debated over the years. However, current scholarship is starting to take a more nuanced approach and considers the problems with interpreting early modern terms of affection and forms of relationships through a contemporary lens.[29]

As the early years of James's reign progressed, there were concerns about his style of kingship, which centred on the ideology of the Divine Right of Kings and created uneasiness among his councillors. In her essay, Anna Groundwater considers James's prolific literary output by examining key texts which presented James's views on monarchy and government. She also explores his diverse writings on the subjects of religion, witchcraft and tobacco.

A unique object that gives us some insight into the ceremonial and recreational activities of James and Anna is the Van Meer *Album Amicorum* (friendship album), of 1614–48, in the University of Edinburgh Special Collections. Such friendship albums were the equivalent of modern-day

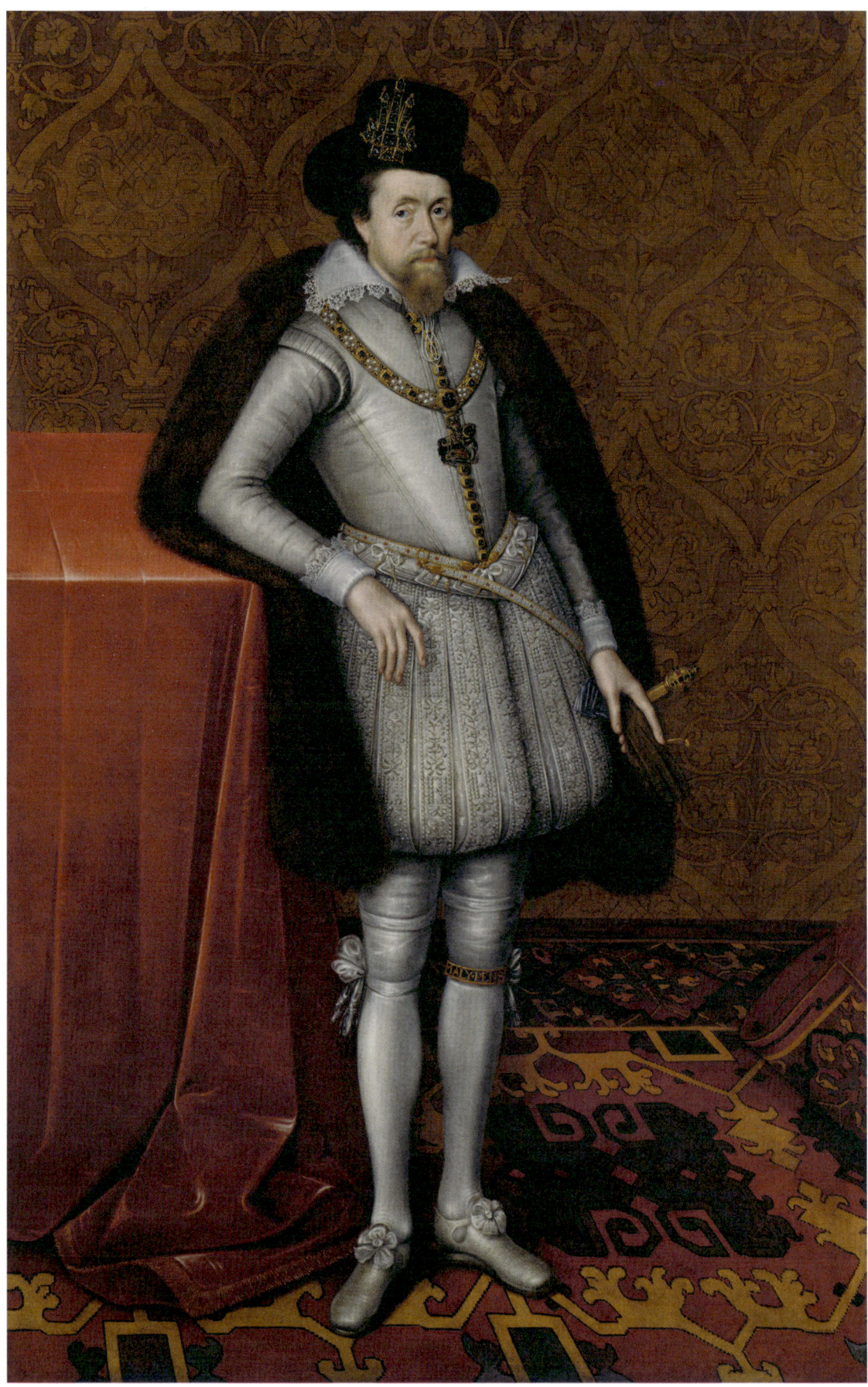

Cat.7
**Attributed to John de Critz
the Elder (c.1550–1642)**
*James VI & I, c.*1606
Oil on canvas, 200.5 × 129.5 cm
Dulwich Picture Gallery, London
(DPG548)

PROVENANCE: Countess of
Warwick of Holland House, who
married Joseph Addison of Bilton
Hall, Warwickshire in 1716; Miss
Addison (d.1797); bequeathed
to the Hon. John Simpson; by
descent to the Rev. Bridgeman-
Simpson at Bilton Hall; Bilton Sale,
Christie's, London, 28 June 1898;
bought by Henry Yates Thompson
and gifted by him to Dulwich
Picture Gallery, London, 1898.

REFERENCES: Strong 1969a, p.179;
Ingamells 2008, p.200; Rae &
Burnstock 2014, pp.59–64

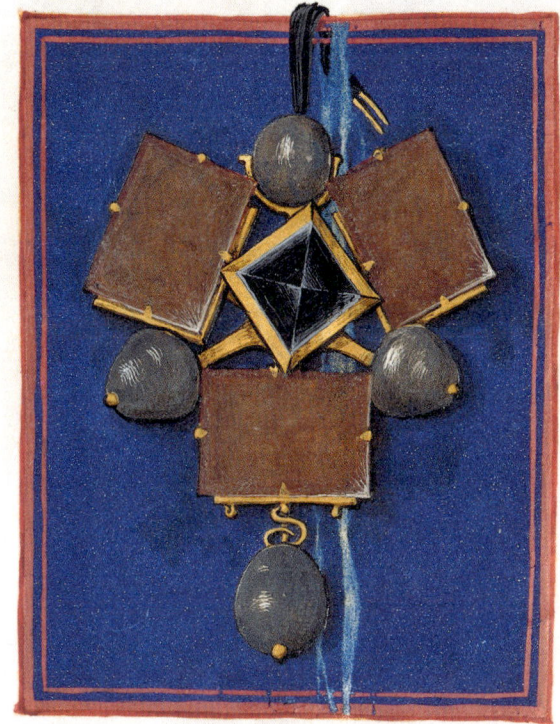

Fig.2
Unknown artist
The Three Brothers Jewel,
between 1476 and 1504
Watercolour on paper, 17 × 13 cm
Historisches Museum Basel
(Inv.1916.475)

autograph books, with their owners collecting signatures, coats of arms and illustrations in a personal book. This album, which belonged to the German Lieutenant Michael van Meer, includes fascinating scenes featuring James and Anna, including *King James riding to Parliament with three noblemen* (cat.6), *James attending a Cockfight*, and *King James and Anna of Denmark with a Venetian Goblet* (cat.52) as well as people and scenes of seventeenth-century London, including *Eiakintomino, in St James's Park* (cat.9).

James's personal programme of artistic patronage was somewhat conservative in England, and he retained court artists who had served under Elizabeth, such as Nicholas Hilliard (1547–1619) and Robert Peake the Elder (*c*.1551–1619). This could be viewed as a deliberate tactic to retain some visual consistency between his reign and that of Elizabeth. The patronage of Netherlandish and Flemish artists by members of the Jacobean court is explored in detail in Karen Hearn's essay.

The artist responsible for creating the official image of the royal couple in the early years following the English accession was the Flemish painter John de Critz the Elder (*c*.1550–1642). In 1605, De Critz was granted the office of Serjeant Painter (painter to the royal court) to James for life and commissioned to paint a series of full-length pendant portraits of James and Anna which were disseminated around the country and presented as gifts to European rulers.[30] The portraits take the standard European format for royal portraiture at this time, but are especially interesting for James's conspicuous display of jewels.

In terms of artistic patronage, James was a far more enthusiastic collector of jewellery than of paintings, and he used jewels for communicating political messages about the Stuart dynasty and the Union of the Crowns. The first of these magnificent jewels is depicted in a portrait of James of about 1606, attributed to De Critz, now in the Dulwich Picture Gallery (cat.7); worn as a hat jewel, it is known as the 'Feather'. It was made up of twenty-six large diamonds, which may have been sourced from Elizabeth I's collection, that were set into points to mimic a feather. The 'Mirror of Great Britain', which is depicted in the 1604 portrait of James that is now in the National Galleries Scotland (cat.8), was created specifically to commemorate the Union of the Crowns and takes the form of a rhombus constructed from three diamonds, two pearls, a large ruby and, as a pendant drop, the magnificent 55-carat Sancy diamond.[31] The final jewel in this category, the 'Three Brothers', is recorded in a watercolour (fig.2) in the Basel Historisches Museum collection and combined three balas rubies, four large pearls and a pointed diamond. In 1623, this jewel was sent to the royal jeweller George Heriot – who, like many Scottish craftsmen and artists, had made the move south to the English court from Edinburgh in 1603 – to be remounted in preparation for Prince Charles's trip to Madrid to woo the Spanish Infanta, Maria Anna (1606–1646). James was acutely aware of the currency that jewellery held, and it was his chosen medium for promoting the message of his power as ruler of a united Great Britain.

King of Peace

One of James's first major achievements after 1603 was the successful negotiation that secured

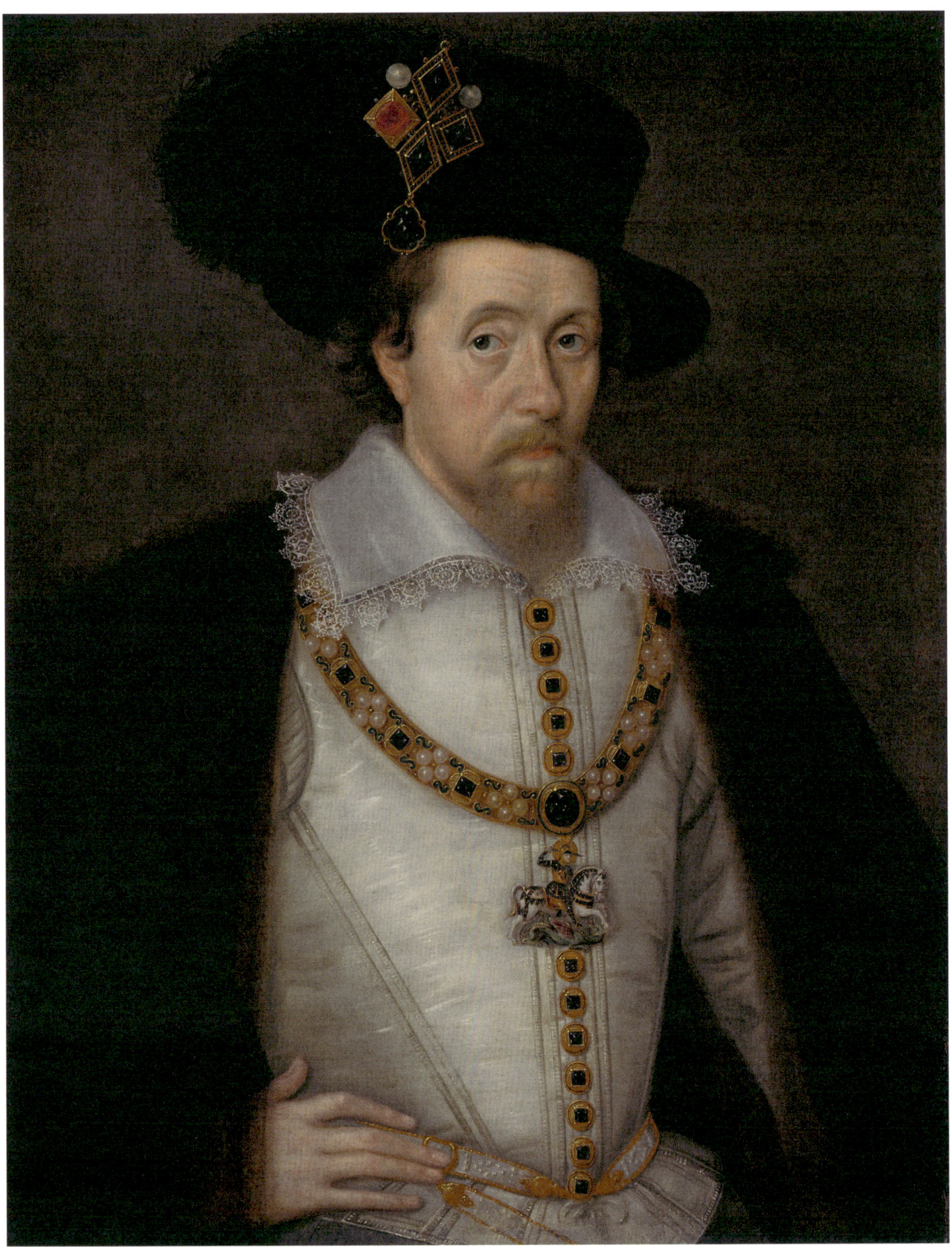

peace with Spain, ending the Anglo–Spanish war that had consumed much of Elizabeth's reign and coffers. Those involved in the discussions are recorded in the large group portrait *The Somerset House Conference*, 1604 (fig.20). This painting, and the context in which it was made, is examined in the final essay.

James's moderating position in the religious and political wars in Europe is illustrated further in a fascinating painting, *Fishing for Souls*, 1614, by Adriaen Pietersz van de Venne (1589–1662) (fig.3). The painting represents the Protestant and Catholic nations with their respective leaders on either side of the river. James appears on the left next to his son-in-law Frederick, Elector Palatine and other Protestant European rulers. In the river, Protestant ministers and Catholic archbishops are in boats vying to save as many souls as possible. The painting is a visual commentary on the way in which religion and politics were inextricably linked at this time, dividing Europe along confessional lines.

Global Ambitions

James's interests and projects extended beyond Europe to North America and Asia. The king and his government were outward looking and ambitious in their attempts to increase international trade and territorial expansion,

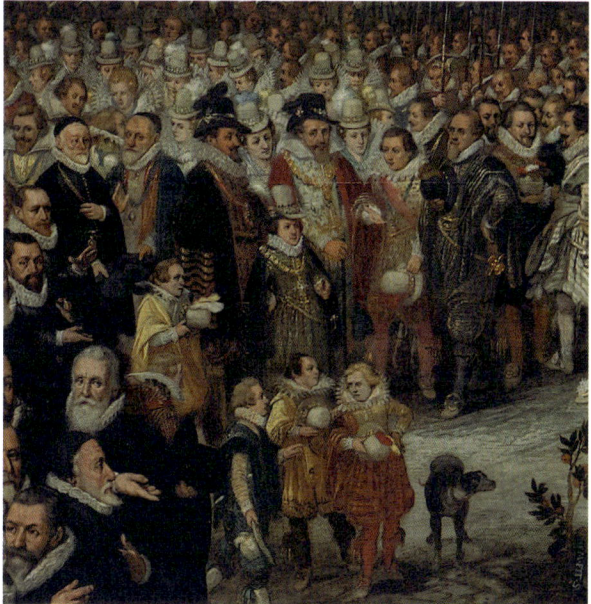

however with this came colonial attitudes, behaviours and oppression.

The establishment of Britain's first permanent settlement on North American soil took place under James's reign. In 1606 the king granted The Virginia Company of London a royal charter and the following year the 'Virginia Colony' was established. The settlement, named 'James Fort', later called Jamestown, was built on Indigenous lands called Tsenacommacah, which were home to the Powhatans. A map of 'Virginia', marking Jamestown, as recounted by Captain John Smith (1580–1631), *Virginia: Discovered and Discribed* (fig.4) was engraved by William Hole (before 1600–1624) and first published in 1612. It presents the English account of the topography of the wider area including Chesapeake Bay, four major rivers and 200 place names, alongside representations of the Algonquian peoples who lived on these lands.[32]

A fascinating illustration from the Van Meer *Album Amicorum* (cat.9) shows a depiction of a Powhatan man, probably Eiakintomino (dates unknown), who migrated from Virginia to England.[33] In the watercolour painting we see the man in Indigenous dress, holding his bow, surrounded by North American birds, a sheep and a ram. The inscription records that he was 'in St. James Park in the zoo by Westminster before the City of London'.[34] While the watercolour survives as a unique and extraordinary representation of an Indigenous American in the early seventeenth century, it also reminds us of the realities of colonialism which frequently saw Indigenous peoples displaced, objectified and, as in this case, exhibited to the public.

Eiakintomino was just one of a number of Indigenous Americans linked to the Virginia Colony who made the journey to England. Pocahontas (about 1595–1617), whose given names were Amonute and Matoaka, was the daughter of Wahunsenaca (about 1547–1618), known as Powhatan, the leader of the Powhatan nation.[35] In 1613 when hostilities between the colonists and the Powhatans escalated, she was kidnapped and during her captivity converted to Christianity. The following year she married one of the English colonists, John Rolfe (about 1585–1622) who

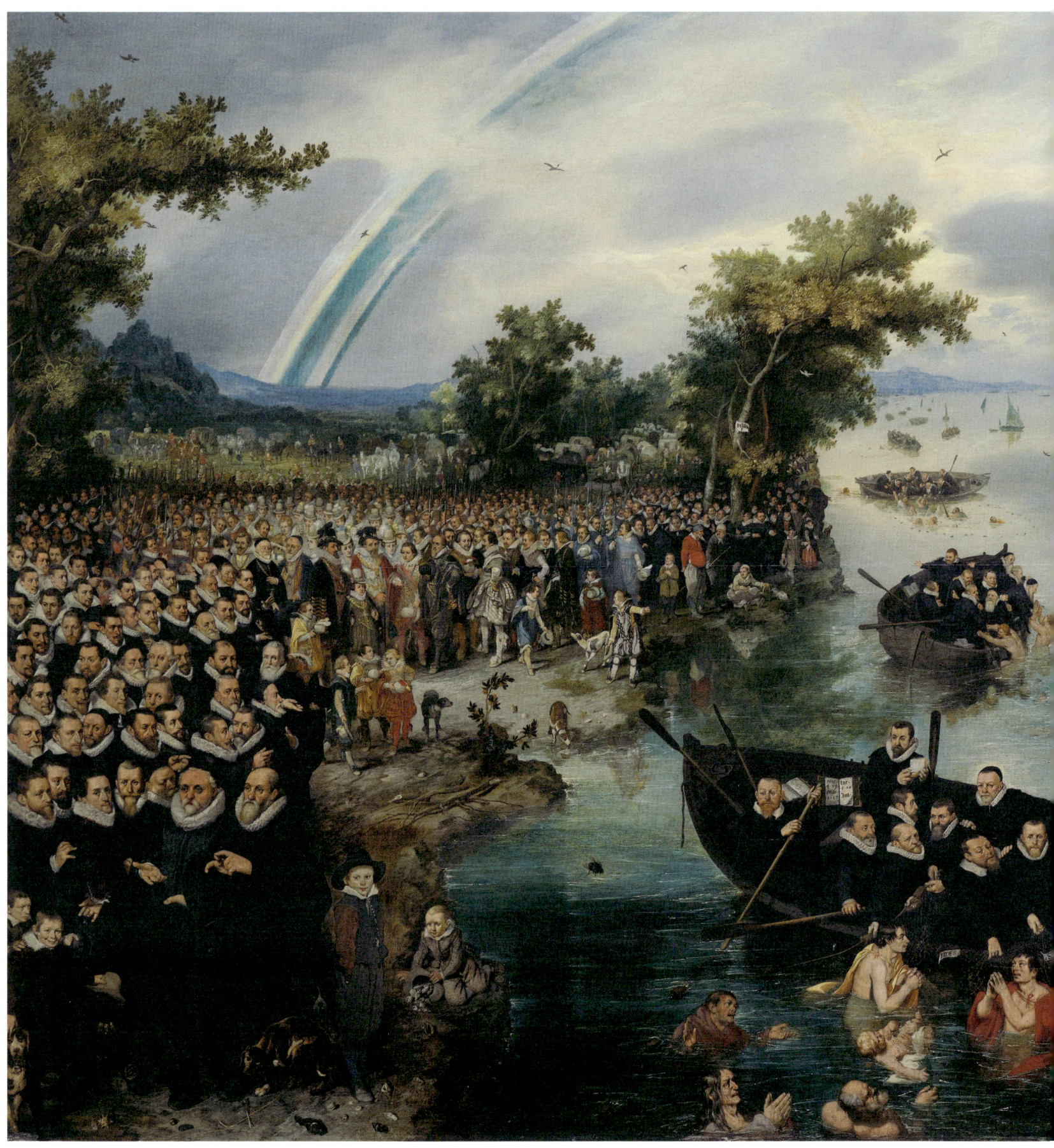

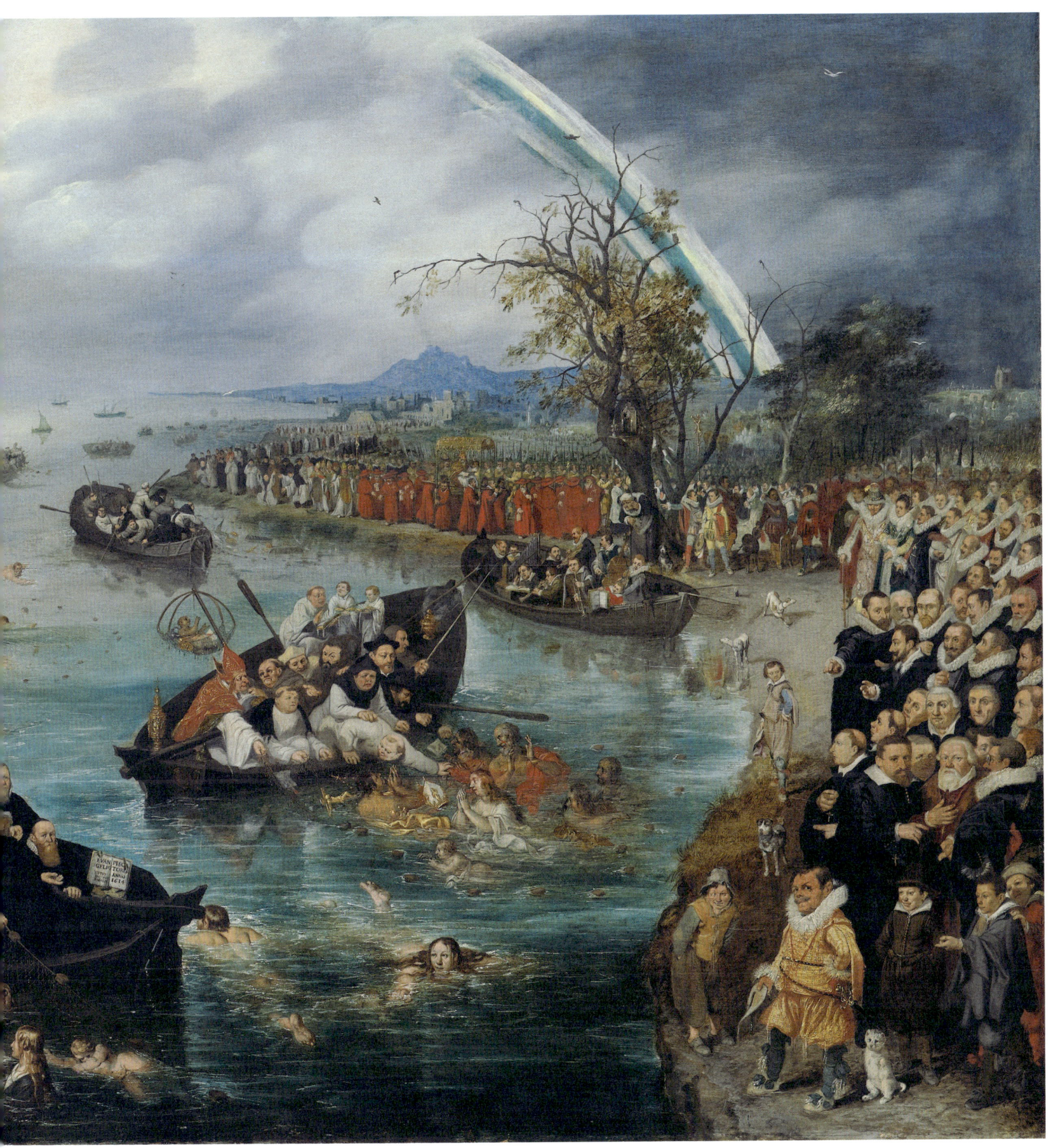

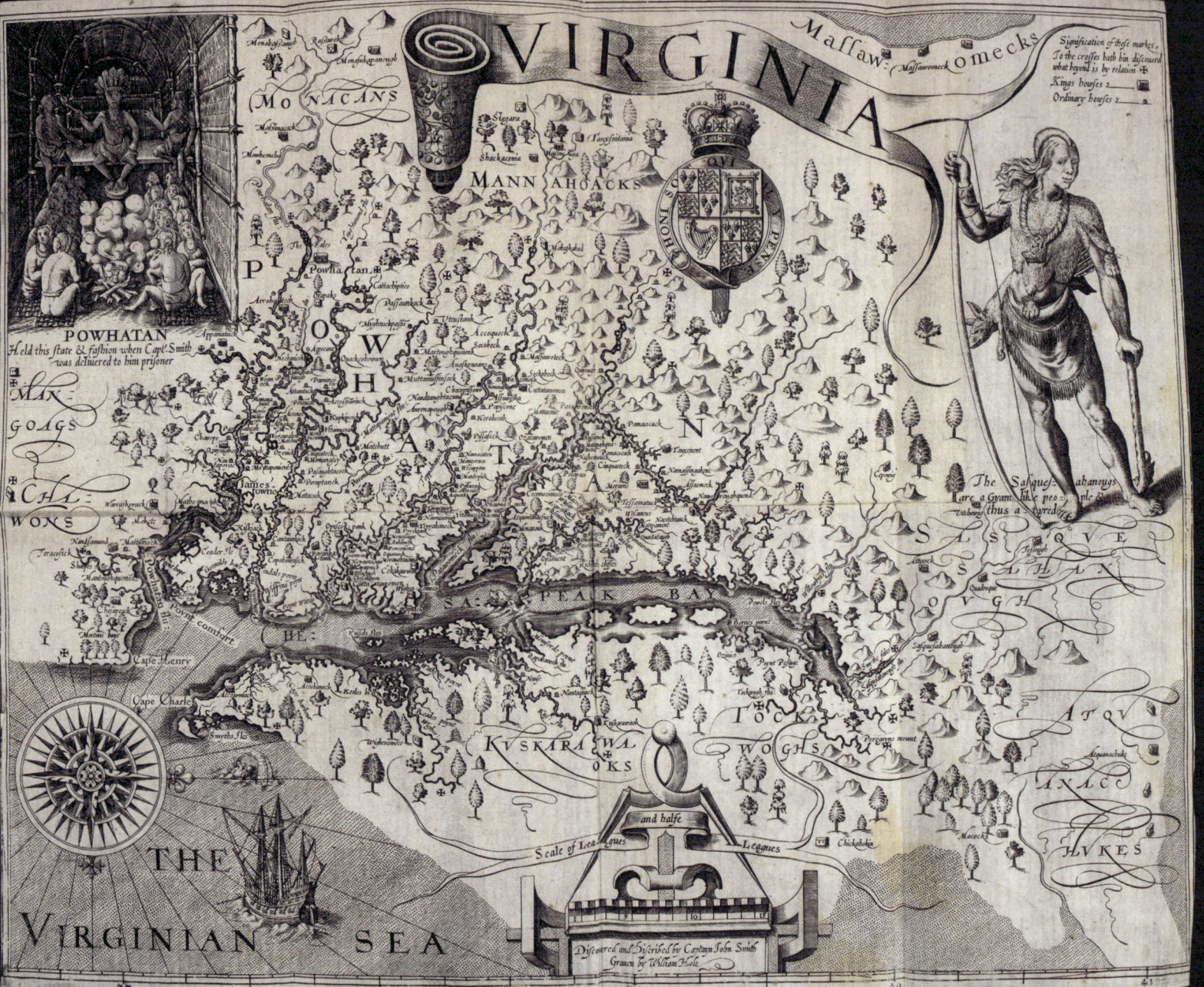

Fig.4
William Hole (before 1600–1624)
Map of Viriginia, discovered and
described by John Smith, 1612
Engraving, 41.5 × 33.5 cm
British Library, London
(Maps 75005(9))

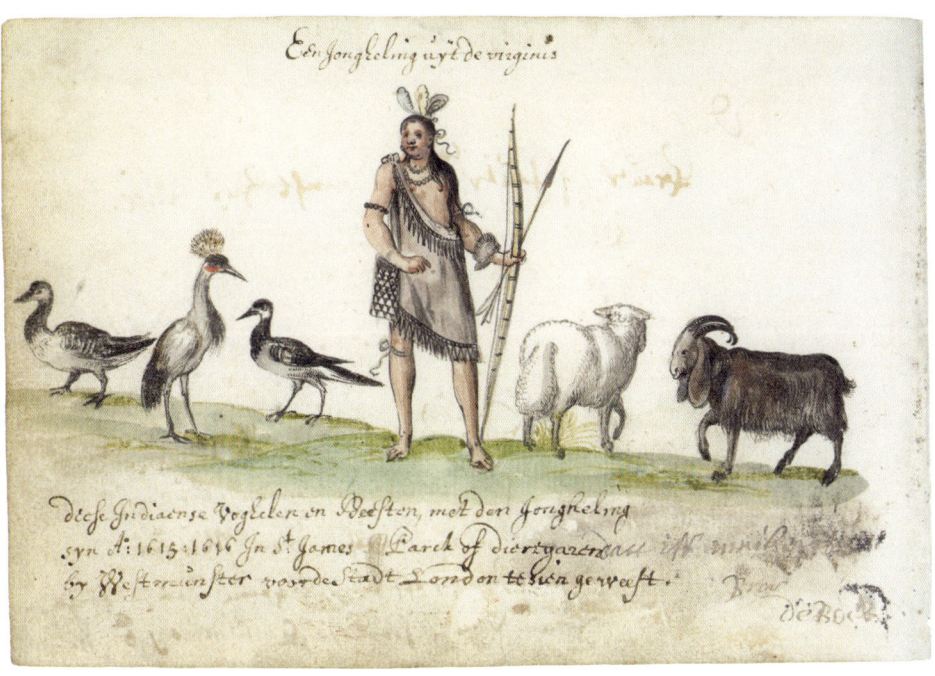

Cat.9
Unknown artist
*Eiakintomino, in St James's
Park*, from an *Album Amicorum*
owned by Michael van Meer,
1614–48
Ink and watercolour on paper,
bound in leather, 13 × 19 cm
The University of Edinburgh
Heritage Collections (La.III.283,
f.264v)

PROVENANCE: David Laing
Bequest, 1878.
REFERENCES: Edinburgh 1975, p.9,
cat.10; Laroque 1993, pp.66–67;
Schlueter 2006, pp.301–14

was a farmer and tobacco merchant. According to contemporary English accounts the marriage was a diplomatic one and symbolised the truce between the Powhatans and the English. In 1616 the couple and their infant son Thomas journeyed to England to promote interest and investment in Jamestown and the tobacco trade. An engraving made in the same year by Simon van de Passe (1595–1647) (cat.91) shows Pocahontas aged twenty-one, in fashionable Jacobean dress – the type of clothing she may have worn when she was presented at court to King James and Queen Anna. The inscription which runs around the oval records both her Indigenous and Christian names; Matoaka and Rebecca, a reminder of her dual identity.

As well as occupying the ancestral lands of the Indigenous Americans, in 1619 the colony received a group of enslaved African people, who had been seized from a captured Portuguese ship, to work on the tobacco plantations on the settlement. Significantly this was the first transatlantic movement of enslaved Africans to North America.

Alongside the Virginia project, James sought to strengthen trade relations with South Asia and appointed Sir Thomas Roe (about 1551–1644) as English ambassador to the Mughal court of Jahangir (1569–1627) at Agra, India from 1615 to 1618.[36] Representing not only the king, but the East India Company, part of Roe's diplomatic mission was to negotiate permission and protection for the founding of an East India Company factory based at Surat. A vividly coloured watercolour (cat.51) represents Jahangir, Ruler of the Mughal Empire, investing a courtier, with Roe depicted mid-left of the composition wearing an orange doublet, hose and lace cuffs and collar. Non-western depictions of Elizabethan and Jacobean people are exceptionally rare, and the painted portrayal of Roe situates him in the international context in which he, and James, were operating.

Conclusion

James returned to Scotland only once following his accession to the English throne. His much-anticipated visit in 1617 was commemorated in the panegyric *Forth Feasting*, 1617 (cat.141), by the Scottish poet William Drummond of Hawthornden (1585–1649, cat.40). Anna did not accompany James on this progress due to her rapidly declining health, and in March 1619 she died of dropsy. Her death had a profound impact on James; he became physically and mentally unwell. The remaining years of his life were dominated by ill-health and war. Despite his reluctance to involve Britain in the Thirty Years' War (1618–48) which dominated Europe, James was soon to be intimately linked to the conflict through his son-in-law's ill-judged decision to accept the crown of Bohemia, which had devastating consequences.[37]

As he entered a new decade, James became increasingly disillusioned with Parliament, the Church and the political situation in Europe. Concurrently his health was deteriorating – he suffered from kidney problems and arthritis. Following a stroke and a case of serious dysentery, he passed away on 27 March 1625 at his country estate, Theobolds in Hertfordshire. He was buried in the Henry VII Chapel at Westminster Abbey (cat.90).

The four essays that follow combine to provide a vivid exploration of the cultural activity that flourished under the reign of James VI & I, and reassess his life and rich legacy.

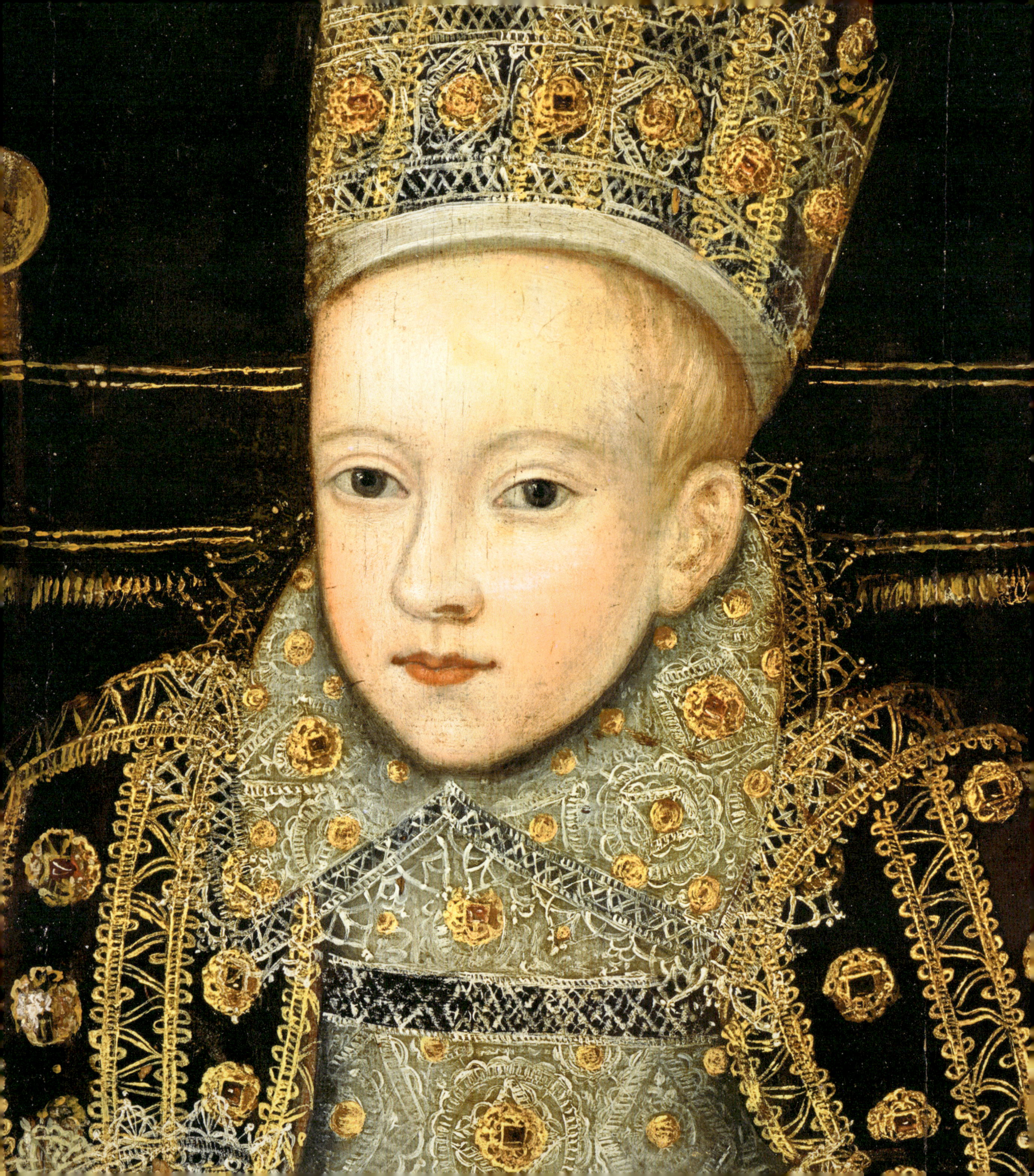

JAMES VI & I AND THE PAGEANTRY OF FATHERHOOD

Catriona Murray

WHEN JAMES VI, KING OF SCOTS, ACCEDED to the English throne in 1603, he was both a husband and a father. Indeed, as heir and then successor to Elizabeth I (1533–1603), the Virgin Queen, James's family was central to his representation. Whereas Elizabeth's celibacy had gradually become a fundamental part of a public image that exalted her as pure and untainted, James's portrayal instead prioritised the fulfilment of his kingly duties to take a wife and to produce children. Texts and images referenced both his ancestry and his offspring, articulating reassuring messages about the stability and continuity of the Stuart dynasty, while presenting the king's authority in patriarchal terms (cat.10). James's spousal and paternal standing was also central to his ritual representation, and he consistently promoted his wife and children through elaborate court and public celebrations. James was keenly aware of the impact of public performance, counselling his elder son, Henry Frederick: 'a King is as one set on a scaffold, whose smallest actions & gestures all the people gazing do behold'.[1] Indeed, the most important presentation of monarchy was the king himself – his appearance, bearing and behaviour.[2]

If James had to act the part of king, then his principal stage was the court. Additional lustre could be added to his day-to-day appearance through spectacle: grand ceremonial, theatrical and martial events which marked key moments in the life of the royal household. The promotion of James's family complemented his image and contributed yet more glamour to this regal display. His queen, Anna, was a major sponsor of the arts, whose literary, artistic and architectural patronage offered balance to James's more scholarly pursuits. Public interest, however, focused on the Stuart offspring. The royal marriage produced seven children, of whom three survived to adulthood.[3] This essay will explore James's paternal propaganda, the pageantry of fatherhood, through a series of entertainments that promoted those surviving children. Focusing on the baptism of his first-born son, Prince Henry Frederick, the marriage of his

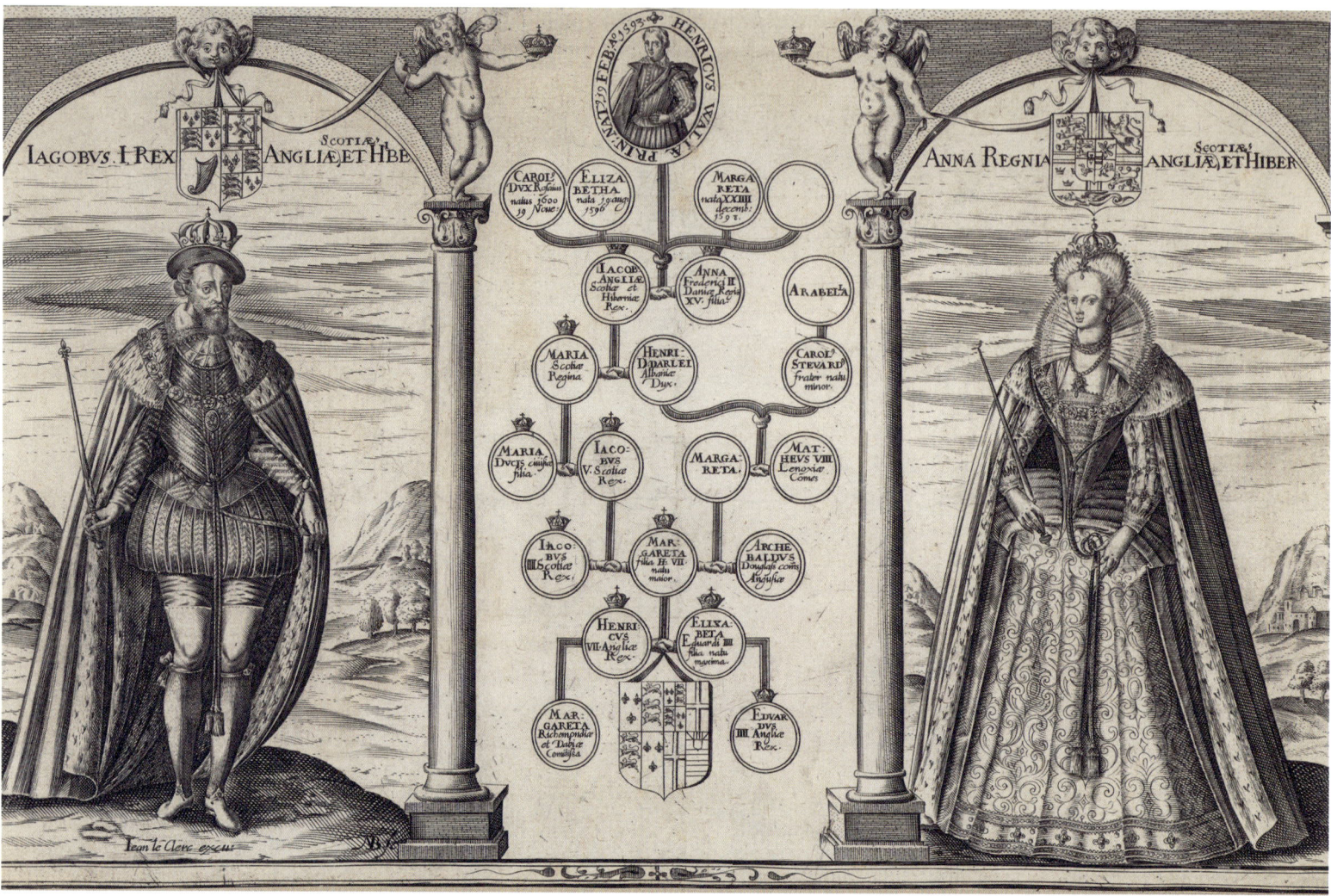

Labels within the genealogical tree engraving:

IAGOBVS · I · REX · · SCOTIÆ / ANGLIÆ ET HIBE

ANNA REGINA · · SCOTIÆ / ANGLIÆ ET HIBER

HENRICVS WALLIÆ PRIN: NAT: 19 FEBR: 1593

CAROL· DVX Roſaiun natus 1600 19 Noue:
ELIZA BETHA nata 19 aug 1596 C
MARGA RETA nata XXIIII decemb: 1598

IACOB: ANGLIÆ Scotiæ et Hiberniæ Rex:
ANNA Frederici II Daniæ Regis XV: filia:
ARABELA

MARIA Scotiæ Regina
HENRI: D: DARLEI Albaniæ Dux:
CAROL° STEVARD° frater natu minor:

MARIA Dvcis cuiuſd: filia
IACO: BVS V. Scotiæ Rex:
MARGA RETA:
MAT: HEVS VIII Lenoxiæ Comes

IACO: BVS Scotiæ Rex:
MAR: GARETA filia H: VIII nati maior:
ARCHE BALDVS Douglaſs com: Anguſiæ

HENRI CVS VII Angliæ Rex:
ELISA BETA Eduardi IIII filia natu maxima:

MAR: GARETA Richemondiæ et Darbiæ Comitiſsa
EDVAR DVS IIII Angliæ Rex:

Jean le Clerc excus

---

daughter, Princess Elizabeth, and the coming-of-age of his eventual heir, Prince Charles, it will argue that James shrewdly exploited these events to support his representation as a father king. He recognised that monarchy was an institution and, in celebrating his children, those festivities also celebrated Stuart government and its future. James basked in the reflected glory of a thriving royal line.

Celebrating a Stuart Prince

After four years of marriage, the twenty-seven-year-old king and nineteen-year-old queen of Scots finally produced an heir. To the relief of both his parents and his subjects, Prince Henry Frederick was born on 19 February 1594. Almost immediately, James set about organising a magnificent baptism that would celebrate the next generation of Stuart rule and extol the achievements of the royal parents. The vast sum of £100,000 Scots was secured to fund the event, which would take place at Stirling Castle that August.[4] Henry Frederick's birth strengthened both James's position upon the Scottish throne and his claim to the English one. As the closest living relative to the childless and aged Elizabeth I, he now offered the English people the security of a stable succession. It was an achievement he was keen to advertise. Ambassadors were sent to the courts of England, France, Denmark-Norway and the Dutch Republic, as well as to the German princes, the Dukes of Brunswick and of Magdeburg, to announce the arrival of a Scottish prince and to invite their

Cat.10
Nicolaes de Bruyn (1571–1656)
Genealogical Tree with James VI and I, Anna of Denmark and Prince Henry Frederick, 1604
Engraving, trimmed, 22.2 × 34.9 cm
National Galleries of Scotland, Edinburgh (SP II 53.4)

PROVENANCE: Bequeathed by William Finlay Watson, 1886.

representatives to the celebrations.[5] The king intended to project an image of an affluent and cultured Renaissance court to his international audience. Accordingly, Stirling Castle underwent extensive refurbishment and its Chapel was demolished and rebuilt. Even the royal household was given a makeover, with royals, courtiers and servants alike receiving splendid new apparel.[6]

After several delays, the festivities began with a royal tournament, during which the king and his followers competed at martial exercises on horseback. The champion of the day was judged to be Ludovic Stuart, 2nd Duke of Lennox (1574–1624), the king's cousin, who received a 'rich Ring of Diamonds' for his efforts.[7] Two days later, on 30 August, the baptism itself was performed. The English ambassador, Robert Radclyffe, 5th Earl of Sussex (1573–1629), acting as proxy for Henry Frederick's godmother, Elizabeth I, carried the infant prince to the Chapel Royal beneath a crimson velvet canopy, edged with gold. After the service, the little prince's titles were proclaimed by the principal herald, Lord Lyon King of Arms: 'The right Excellent, High and Magnanimous, FREDERICK HENRIE, HENRIE FREDERICK, by the Grace of God, Knight and Baron of Renfrew: Lord of the Isles, Earl of Carrick, Duke of Rothesay, Prince and great Steward of Scotland'.[8]

Although the ceremony had been magnificent – the Chapel decked with tapestries, cloth of gold and multicoloured taffetas and velvets – the centrepiece of the celebrations was undoubtedly that evening's banquet. Half indulgent feast, half dramatic tableaux, the banquet was a display of both regal munificence and dynastic ambition. The climax was the arrival of the third course on a massive ship, some 12 metres tall, loaded with fruits of the sea – herrings, whiting, flounders, oysters, limpets, lobsters, crabs, razor fish and clams – all modelled in sugar.[9] A crew of seven accompanied the ship, as well as the classical sea deities Neptune, Thetis and Triton, and a host of mermaids. The ship's sails were white taffeta, the mainsail adorned with the arms of Scotland and Denmark-Norway (denoting the royal marriage), the tops, flags and streamers in the king's colours of gold and red. The ship's foresail was painted with a compass, pointing to the North Star and a Latin motto, which proclaimed

the king's clear course through rough waters.[10] The significance of these elaborate devices was specific, referencing the young king's voyage in 1589, through stormy winter seas, to meet his new Danish bride and her stranded fleet in Norway. James, it was said, had heroically triumphed over the foul plots of witches to bring his queen safely to Scotland's shores.[11] Now, at last, the royal couple's courage and perseverance had been rewarded. Their match had been blessed twice over; first in the consummation of their union, despite maleficent forces, and then in the production of a healthy male heir.

The special status of the infant prince was reflected in the presents bestowed upon him. The Danish embassy gifted a great silver cup, a gold chain and a jewel, while the English gave a silver gilt cupboard 'curiously wrought'.[12] Nevertheless, the most impressive present was from the Dutch delegation, who presented two gold cups and a gold box containing a charter, which granted the prince a pension of £5,000 Scots a year.[13] Like his gifts, Henry Frederick too was richly adorned, decked in a purple velvet robe covered with pearls.[14] Although miniature paintings of him were commissioned for the occasion, the earliest surviving portrait dates from two years later (fig.5) and similarly demonstrates how the prince was visually presented as a precious treasure. Enthroned on a gilded chair, he is dressed in black fabric, richly embroidered with gold and embellished with jewels. His cuffs, collar and apron are ornate white lace. In one hand he holds cherries, symbolic of God's blessing, and in the other a gold rattle, perhaps an allusion to the sceptre he will one day sway.

The royal toddler is literally the ornament of his parents' marriage. Representations of Henry Frederick, therefore, were also celebrations of his father and mother. His baptism was no different. Of course, royal spectacle was short-lived. King James, however, ensured that the baptism's imagery reached beyond the diplomats and courtiers assembled at Stirling Castle. He preserved its magnificence in print. William Fowler's *A True Reportarie of the Most Triumphant, and Royal Accomplishment of the Babtisme of the most Excellent, right High, and mightie Prince, Frederik Henry* (cat.11) was published in Edinburgh and London

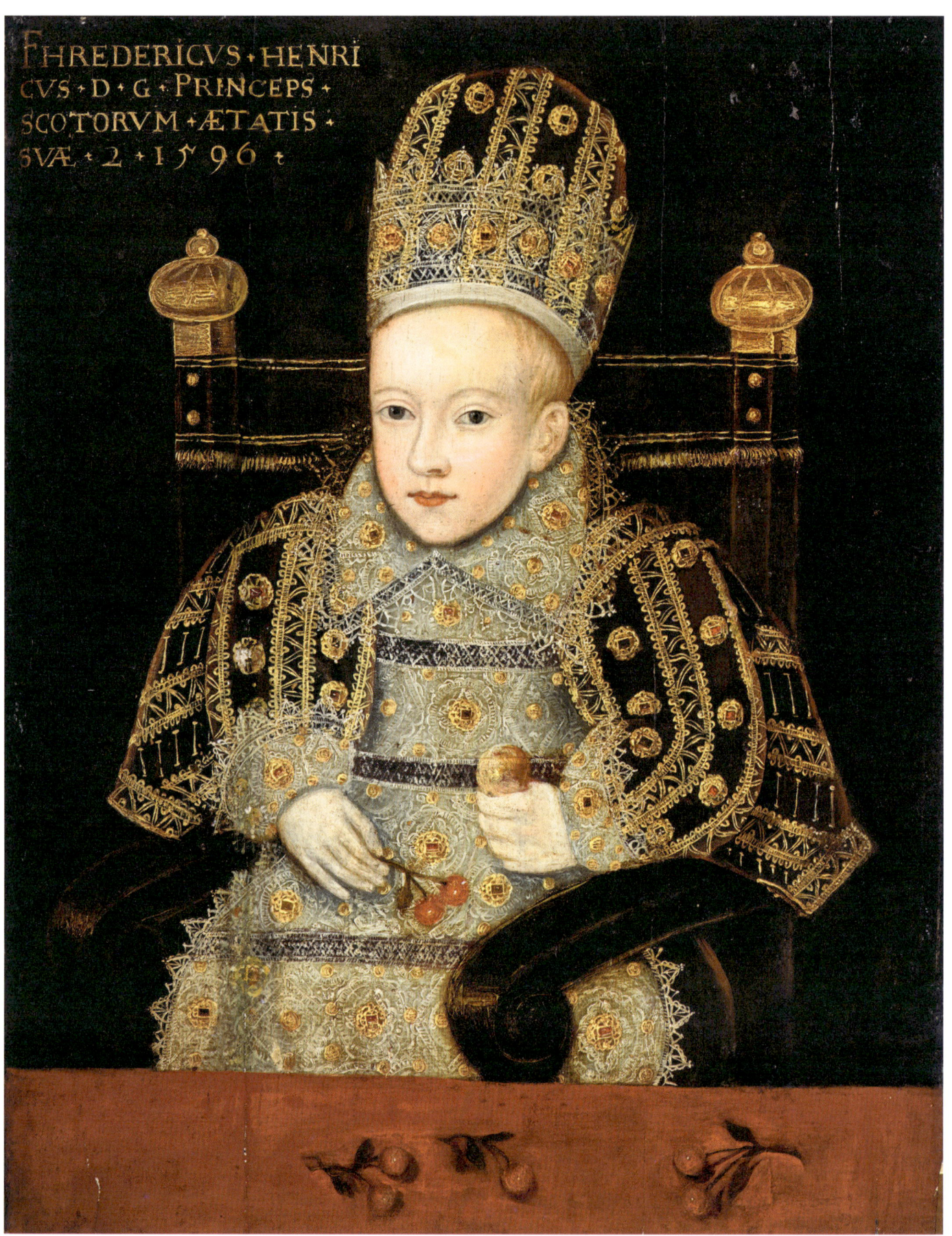

FHREDERICVS·HENRI
CVS·D·G·PRINCEPS·
SCOTORVM·ÆTATIS·
SVÆ·2·1596

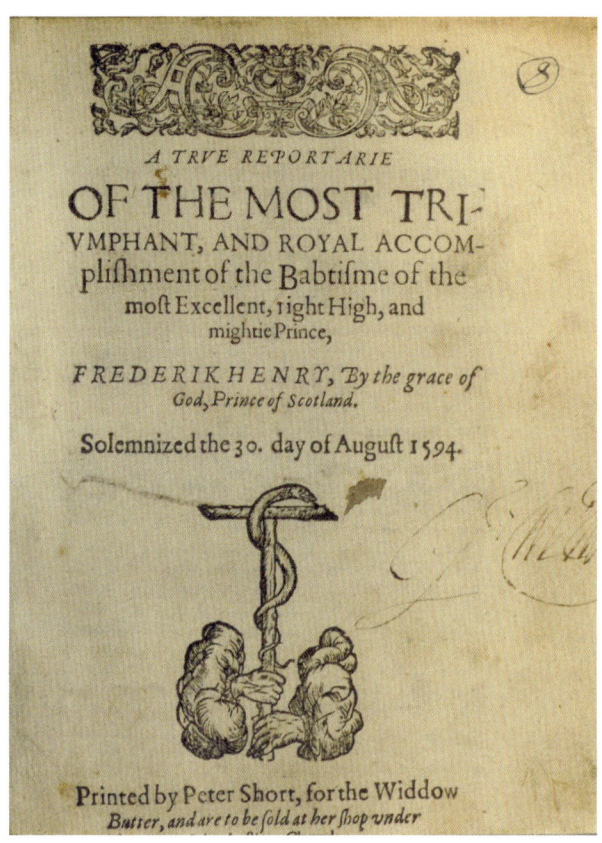

before the year was out. Through the text's detailed descriptions of the lavish christening festivities, news of Stuart dynastic achievements and aspirations spread to a popular readership. James shrewdly broadcast his fatherhood to both his present and future subjects.

Staging a Royal Wedding

On 6 November 1612 at the age of eighteen, Henry Frederick died after a short illness, probably typhoid fever. His tragic loss sparked a wave of public grief. The damage and distress of this wholly unexpected blow, however, was tempered by the forthcoming marriage of his younger sister, Princess Elizabeth. Elizabeth was born at Falkland Palace on 19 August 1596 and baptised a few months later with little fanfare. She had lived a relatively quiet life, first at Linlithgow Palace and then, following her father's accession to the English throne in 1603, at Coombe Abbey near Coventry. When she turned twelve, Elizabeth took up residence at court in London, but it was not until

the matter of her marriage became pressing that she was cast into the limelight. The celebrations surrounding her nuptials offered a magnificent counter-attraction to the solemn mourning which had accompanied the death of her brother. Amid dynastic rupture, her match fortuitously shifted focus onto the future of the line, rather than its recent loss.

The bridegroom was the sixteen-year-old German prince, Frederick, Elector Palatine. Like most seventeenth-century princely marriages, this match was arranged by the couple's parents: Elizabeth's father, James VI & I, and Frederick's mother, Louisa Juliana, the dowager Electress Palatine (1576–1644). Elizabeth and Frederick's first meeting was on 18 October 1612 before a courtly audience at the Great Chamber of Whitehall Palace. Thereafter, the couple met regularly without such ceremony, and soon a fondness developed between them. It was noted that the prince took 'delight in nothing but her company'.[15] They were eventually married at Whitehall on St Valentine's Day, 14 February 1613. In common with modern royal weddings, there was intense public interest in the proceedings. On the day itself, vast crowds gathered to catch a glimpse of the bride and groom, while in the following months a number of pamphlets were published describing the pomp. Together the Stuart parents had cut a dashing figure. James was dressed in black, with a great diamond in his hat, while the queen wore an embroidered white satin gown, arrayed with diamonds.[16] The newlyweds, however, stole the show. Placed upon a specially erected stage in the centre of the chapel, they wore matching suits of cloth of silver, richly embroidered with silver thread. Elizabeth's auburn hair was let down in plaits to her waist, dressed with strings of gold spangles, pearls, rich stones and diamonds and crowned with a gold coronet, covered with gems and pearls.[17]

An anonymous portrait of the princess (fig.6) probably depicts her in her wedding dress, although her hair is styled, as it was for her betrothal ceremony, with a 'plume of white feathers'.[18] As well as the intricate opulence of her gown, Elizabeth's attire also features coded messages about her family and marriage. Most noticeably, her lace collar is patterned with the royal Stuart coat of arms, fleurs-de-lis and the heraldic supporters of lion and unicorn. Stuart and even Tudor connections are further underlined by the long strands of pearls she wears, likely those that had belonged to her grandmother, Mary, Queen of Scots, and that were bought by Elizabeth I after Mary's forced abdication. James had inherited the pearls upon his accession to the English crown; and, following his death in 1625, they would be passed on to his daughter.[19] More intimate associations are marked by her black armband and the jet miniature locket tied to her breast, signifiers of her continued grief at her brother's death. Finally, the earrings that she wears are probably those gifted to her by her husband: 'two pearls for bigness, fashion and beauty esteemed the rarest that are to be found in Christendom'.[20] A short lock of Frederick's hair is tied to her left earring as a token of devotion. Overall then, as well as communicating magnificence, the bride's dress and accessories articulate both her new status as wife and her enduring dynastic ties. Elizabeth may have become a Palatine consort but, significantly, she remained a Stuart princess.

The spectacle surrounding the match encompassed more than simply the wedding ceremony. Both before and after the marriage, there were extravagant public and court events. Firework displays, water pageants, dramatic masques and martial tournaments were all staged to promote the match as a strengthening force for pan-European Protestantism (fig.7). With reference to those public festivities performed beyond the court, it has been argued that both James and his daughter were 'passive spectators', with no influence over the narratives at play.[21] However, the fireworks performed upon the Thames were, in fact, 'invented and wrought' by His Majesty's Gunners; the powders and salts taken from the king's store.[22] It is not unreasonable then to assume that the form and meaning of the pyrotechnics had royal assent. Indeed, the survival of an illustrated manuscript booklet, detailing the Gunners' intentions for the display, suggests that their proposals were subject to scrutiny and approval.[23]

The principal conceit for the fireworks show was a simple one, rendered remarkable by its execution. Amid shot, rockets, mortars, breakers

and fire-balls, a distressed maiden appeared, taking refuge in a burning tower. Her hero, St George, like a 'fiery vision', rode forth to fight a dragon, which roared and belched flames (fig.8).[24] Next, the champion vanquished a terrible giant, their battle resounding like 'thunder claps', with lightning and 'fiery exhalations' which sparkled in the air.[25] Finally, George encountered the enchanter, who had imprisoned the lady, tying him to a pillar. As the magician burned, lights, fires and rockets were released.

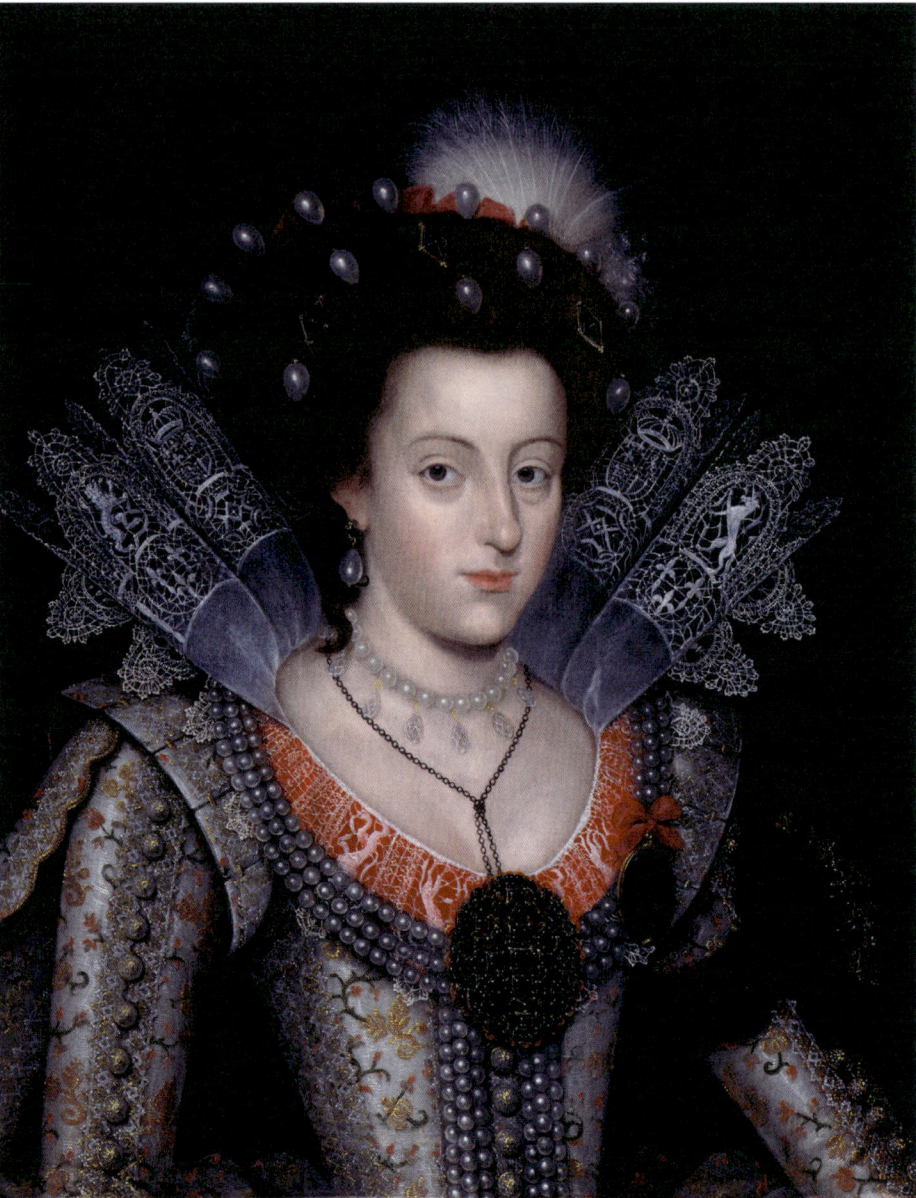

Fig.6
Unknown artist
Princess Elizabeth, Electress Palatine and Queen of Bohemia, 1613
Oil on panel, 78.4 × 62.2 cm
National Portrait Gallery, London (NPG 5529)

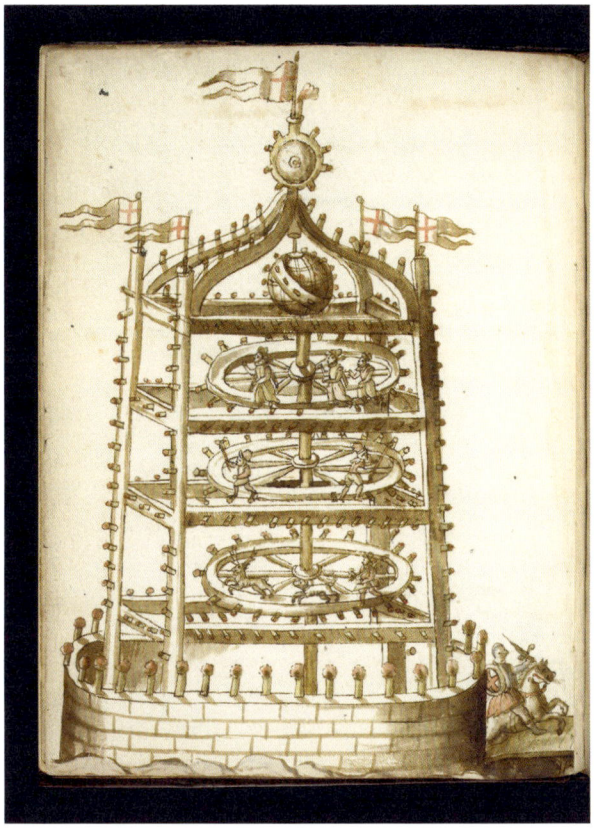

We should not underestimate the impact that such a show would have had on the thousands of spectators gathered to behold it. The uninitiated viewer might experience both wonder and terror at the bellows, flashes and glimmers.[26] Of course, Saint George was England's heroic patron saint, but he had also come to signify Protestant virtue. What is more, the tale of a hero triumphing against supernatural forces to save his lady had resonance. As we have seen, the king's own mythology featured a similar romance. He too had struggled against malevolent powers to rescue his queen. It is possible then that, here, St George and King James are symbolically connected. After all, James had arranged a match for his daughter that promised to bolster European Protestantism and to secure the Stuart succession. As such, he had assumed the mantle of England's saviour. Once more, then, the king promoted his child to support his fatherly authority. Elizabeth's marriage was testament to the care he took both for his offspring and for his subjects.

Presenting a New Heir

The newlyweds left England for Frederick's seat in Heidelberg on 26 April 1613. With their departure, only one Stuart sibling remained, the twelve-year-old heir to the throne, Prince Charles (cat.38). Charles had been born in Dunfermline Palace on 19 November 1600. A poorly infant, the prince was afflicted with early impairments of his speech and mobility. After James's accession to the English throne, when Charles's mother, brother and sister departed for London, he was left behind. He remained at Dunfermline under the care of his guardian, Alexander Seton, Lord Fyvie, later 1st Earl of Dunfermline (1555–1622, cat.25) until, in the summer of 1604, he was deemed strong enough to complete the journey. Charles's life at the English court was sheltered. With the death of Henry Frederick, however, his status was transformed. The shy, sensitive prince suddenly became the focus of popular attention. Nevertheless, Charles's upbringing remained closely guarded and, when he came of age, the prince's public image was indistinct and lacklustre. Unlike the spectacles surrounding his siblings, those public celebrations held in his honour often failed to dazzle.

Certainly, part of the problem was the shadow of Henry Frederick. Indeed, his spectre loomed large over Charles's public debut – his creation as Prince of Wales. The festivities surrounding the elder brother's installation in 1610 had been magnificent, with colourful water triumphs, solemn ceremonial pomp and fantastical military games. Whereas Henry Frederick was conducted to Whitehall by two sea monsters, Charles had to content himself with a less impressive retinue.[27] As he passed through Chelsea, the prince was greeted by an actor, personifying London, who addressed him as a 'Treasure of hope'.[28] In the speeches which followed, however, it was Charles's father who was singled out for praise. The personification of London continues:

> The loves of many thousands speak in me:
> Who from the blessing of our peaceful store
> The Royal Father, has received most free …[29]

Indeed, despite his absence at this stage in the events, the king's influence was conspicuous. His pacific policies and the nation's 'calm Security' were repeatedly acclaimed.[30] The prince himself was relegated to a supporting character. As the celebrations continued, negative comparisons with his brother's installation persisted. The ceremonial creation, where Charles was invested with his symbols of office – the purple mantle, sword, cap, coronet, rod and ring of the Prince of Wales – was performed at Whitehall's great hall rather than the much larger Court of Requests at Parliament House, which had hosted Henry Frederick.[31] Since James had dissolved Parliament in 1614, the younger brother's investiture was performed before a restricted court audience rather than in the presence of the Commons and the Lords. The ceremony surrounding Charles's creation, therefore, was performed with limited public show. Even the tournaments held over the following days were disappointing, with the prince observing rather than competing in the martial sports as his brother had.

Perhaps we can gauge a little more of the prince's image and interests through a later portrait of him (fig.9), attributed to Daniel Mytens the Elder (*c*.1590–1647) and Hendrick van Steenwijck the Younger (*c*.1580–1649). Dressed in his parliamentary robes and holding the rod of the Prince of Wales, Charles sits upon an elaborate gilt throne, supported by the figures of two sphinxes. The canopy of state above is embellished with his dignities, including the badges of the Earl of Chester and Duke of Cornwall. The fact that Charles is wearing parliamentary robes may help date the painting to 1621, when James finally recalled Parliament after a seven-year interval. The king's hand had been forced by events on the Continent. His son-in-law, Frederick, had controversially accepted the crown of Bohemia only to lose his new kingdom and his hereditary lands to the Holy Roman Emperor, Ferdinand II. Money was desperately needed to restore the Palatine family. In many ways, the Parliament of 1621 served as a political training ground for Charles, who regularly attended the debates. He was deeply committed to supporting his sister and brother-in-law, although Parliament was again dissolved before any major financial support for the exiles could be approved. With this avenue of recourse closed, Charles was observed to shut himself away with

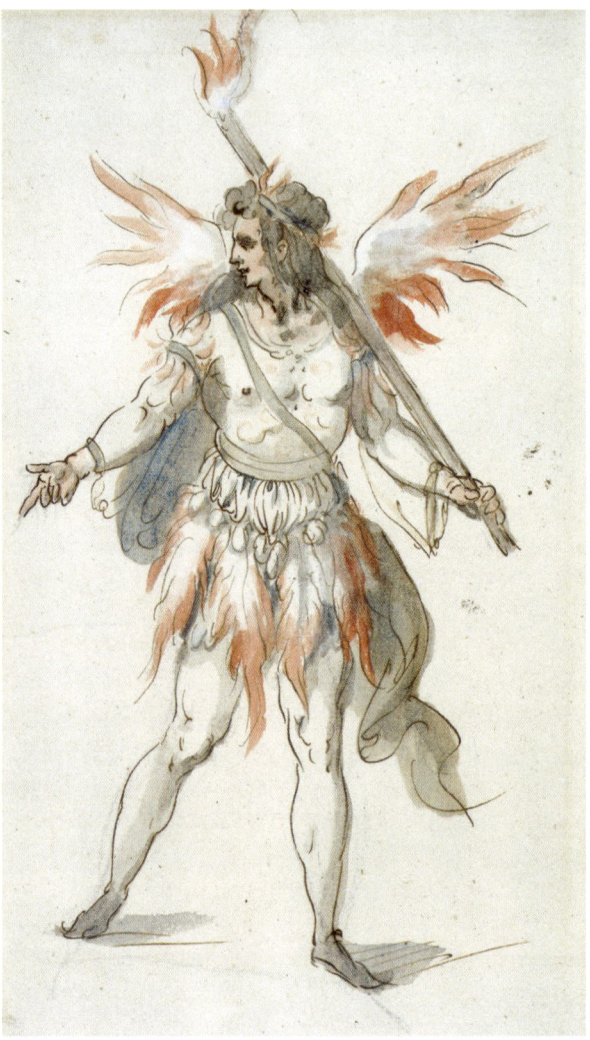

his collections of model war engines and model armies, playing out campaign strategies.[32] The open mechanism and military ground plan resting on the table beside him in this portrait hint at these activities. The prince's martial support for his brother-in-law was, for now, theoretical rather than practical. This portrait, then, presents a statement of intent rather than achievement. Even the grand, classicised architectural setting may allude to another of Charles's unrealised designs, a possible redevelopment of Whitehall Palace.[33] He has thus been portrayed as a Prince of Wales preparing for his future, with promise and ambition, even if both are, as yet, contained or even frustrated.

Ironically, it was another frustrated venture which actually placed Charles centre-stage. In

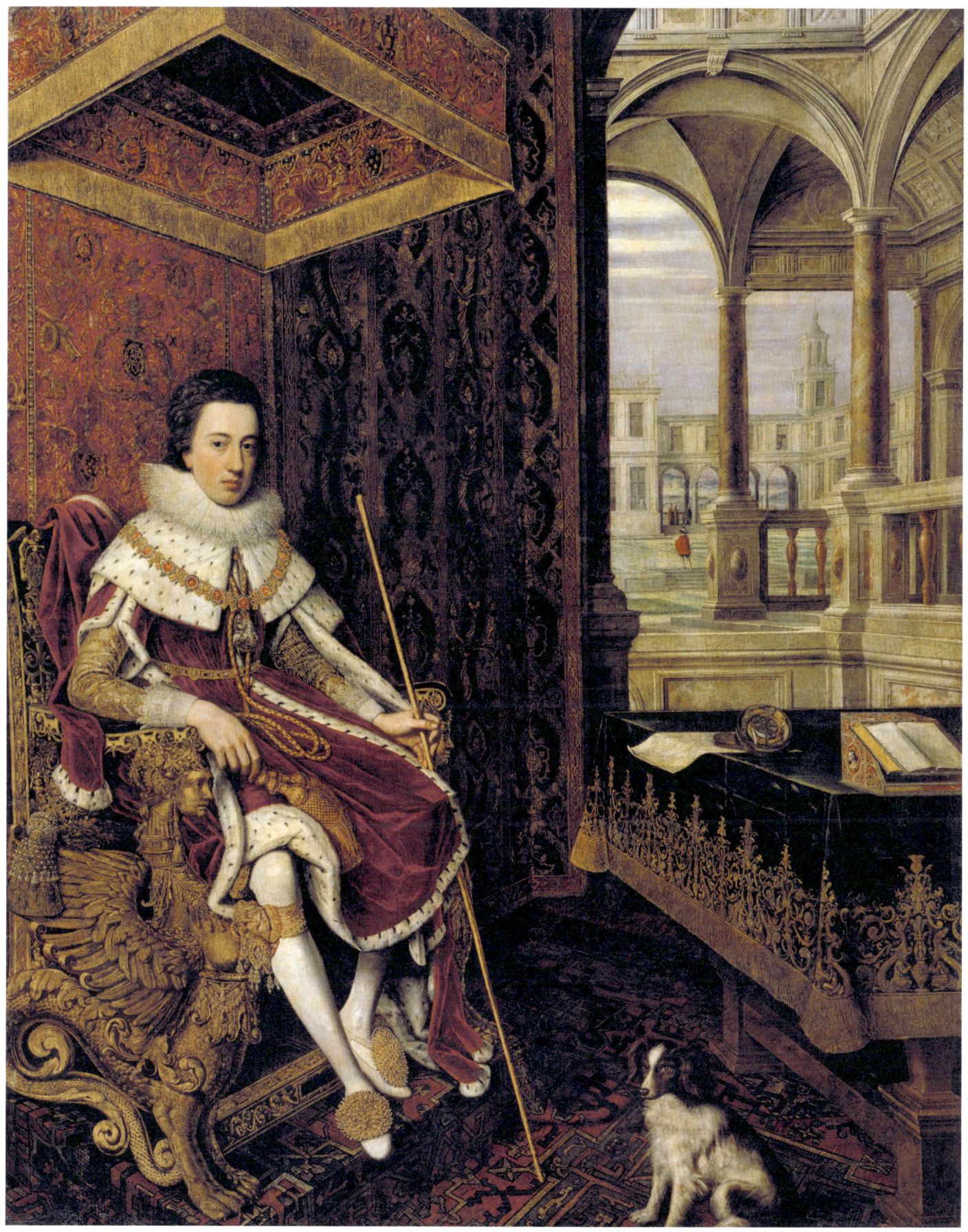

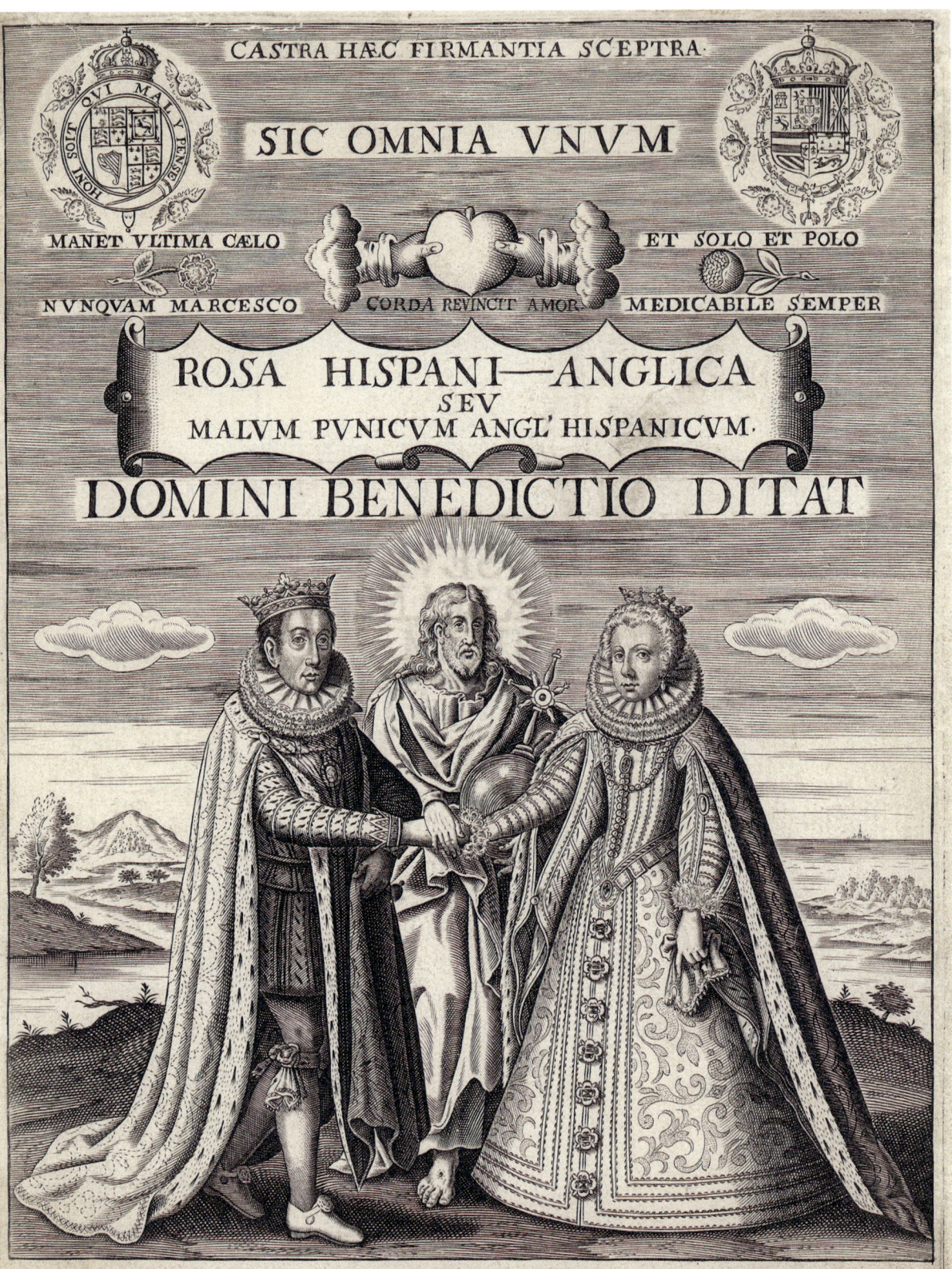

CASTRA HÆC FIRMANTIA SCEPTRA.

SIC OMNIA VNVM

MANET VLTIMA CÆLO   ET SOLO ET POLO

NVNQVAM MARCESCO   CORDA REVINCIT AMOR   MEDICABILE SEMPER

ROSA HISPANI — ANGLICA
SEV
MALVM PVNICVM ANGL' HISPANICVM.

DOMINI BENEDICTIO DITAT

Austriaca est virgo Regum Decus, Alma MARIA,
Deliciæ superum: CAROLVS, Orbis Amor:
Sydera, sol, phœbe, sic CAROLVS atq MARIA,
Illa polo, ista solo, fœdere Cuncta beant.

Cat.12
Unknown artist
The Betrothal of Charles I, when Prince of Wales, with the Infanta Maria Anna of Spain, 1622
Engraving, 21.9 × 15.2 cm
National Portrait Gallery, London
(NPG D10622)

PROVENANCE: Unknown.

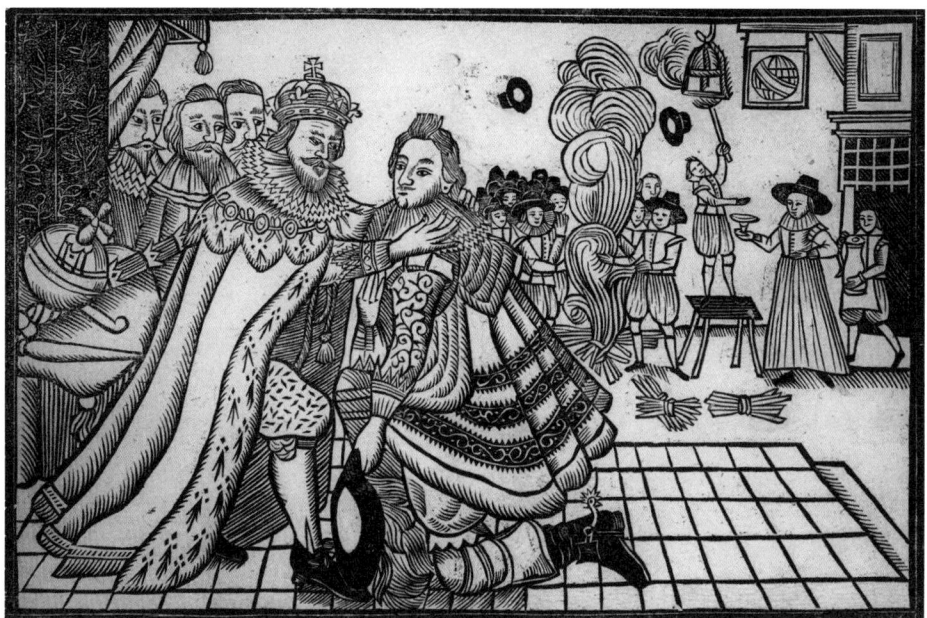

Fig.10
Unknown artist
James VI & I Embracing Charles,
Prince of Wales, 1623
Woodcut, 27.6 × 15 cm
Society of Antiquaries of London

prince and the duke rushed to greet the king, who kissed and held both young men as they all wept.[37] A woodcut (fig.10), illustrating verses on Charles's Spanish journey, depicts this royal reunion. Here, the prince kneels for his father's blessing, receiving the king's warm embrace, while in the background their subjects gather by a bonfire, throwing their hats, ringing bells and toasting the happy occasion. The accompanying poem describes the clamour which marked Charles's return but also indicates the roots of the celebrations:

> Yet it's not enough high fires in streets to frame,
> Unless the fire of zeal your hearts enflame;
> And that in Churches Psalms of thanks be singing,
> As well as in Steeples Bells a ringing.
> You have prayed, your prayer's heard; now this is done,
> Laud God, and Love your King and Kingdom's Son.[38]

February 1623, the prince and his father's favourite, George Villiers, 1st Duke of Buckingham, undertook a journey which, they hoped, would finally settle the prince's marriage negotiations. For seven years, a match with Spain had been deliberated over to no firm conclusion. Now the two young men proposed to make a secret journey to the court in Madrid to claim the bride (cat.12). Charles was following in his father's footsteps, embarking on a romantic voyage to collect his queen. The escapade, however, was naïve and ill-considered. The Infanta Maria Anna (1606–1646) was far from delighted with her over-amorous suitor and not inclined to marry a Protestant.[34] Her brother, Philip IV (1605–1665), stalled and demanded seemingly unacceptable terms.[35] The result was that weak promises were made on both sides but, when Charles returned to England in September, he returned without a wife. Despite this embarrassing and fruitless outcome, the prince's homecoming was greeted with spontaneous public festivity. Hundreds of bonfires blazed across London in celebration. One correspondent quipped: 'We are no less merry here, I assure you, and have made Bonfires, that might well have hazarded our streets, had not the heat been well allayed with London Liquor.'[36] Having reached the capital, the

Although the demise of the marriage plans was not yet official, many were openly relieved that Charles had come back empty-handed. A Catholic bride, it was feared, would threaten Protestantism at home and undermine the efforts to restore Frederick and Elizabeth, still in exile, abroad.[39] The failure of the Spanish match, therefore, was recast as a triumph, which fortified true religion. Both father and son were credited with standing firm against Catholic tyranny.[40] Compared to his older siblings, then, the pageantry surrounding Charles was restrained and the bombast of James's paternal propaganda more subdued. Still, occasions which fêted the Prince of Wales also celebrated the king, proclaiming his provision of a secure Stuart succession.

Throughout his reign as king of Scots and later as king of England and Ireland, James keenly comprehended the power of spectacular display. Rich pageantry and performance elevated the monarchy, imbuing the king and his family with magnificence. Although noted for his robust and noble bearing, the figure of James alone was limited in its impact.[41] Together, however, the Stuarts were impressively splendid. James exploited the glamour of his children to bolster his throne. The glory cast onto the Stuart offspring through court and public festivity was, in turn, directed onto their father.

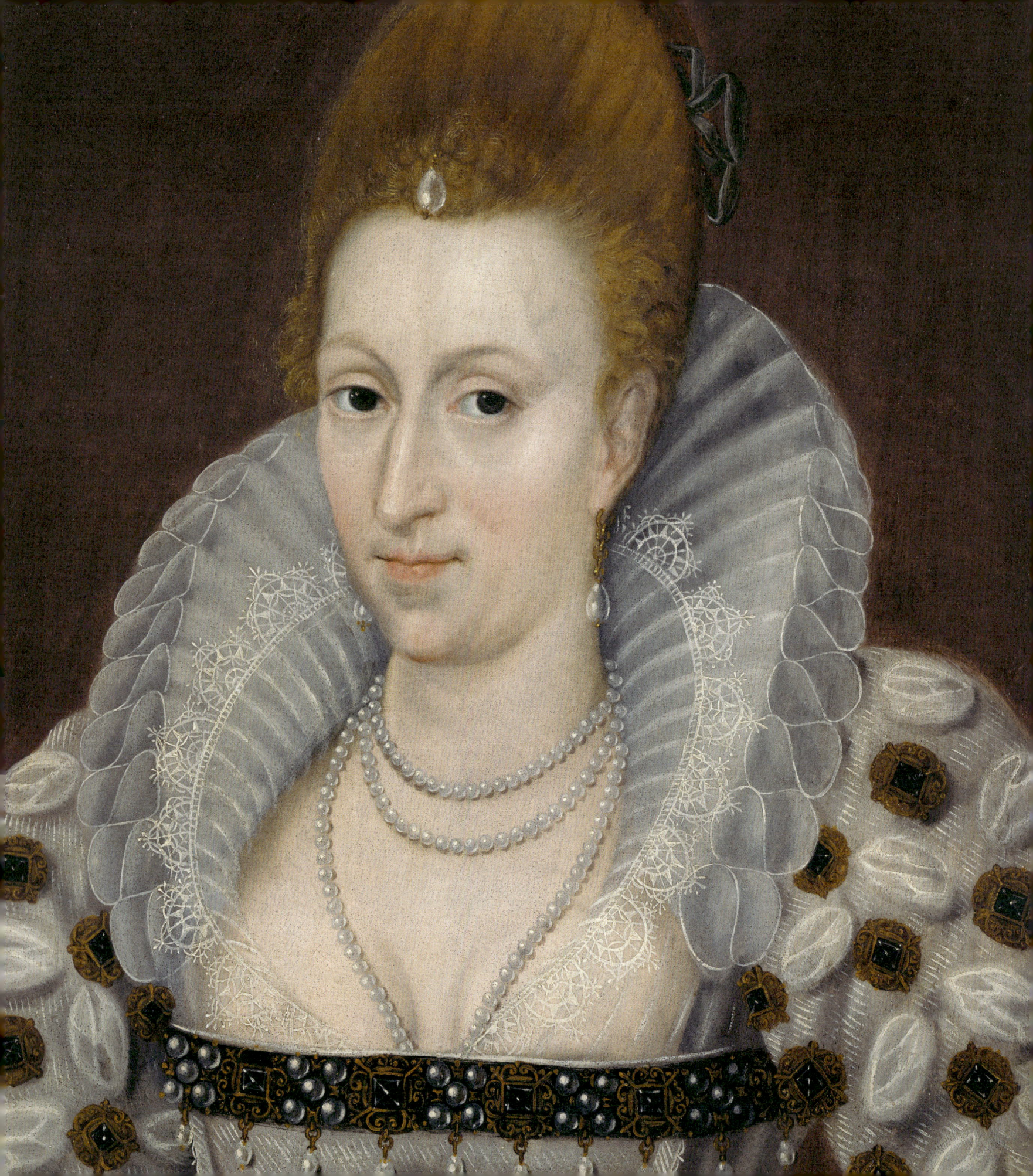

DRESSING THE STUART COURT

Jemma Field

IN OCTOBER 1612, THE STUART COURT began readying itself to receive Frederick V, Elector Palatine, in 'great state' ahead of his marriage to Princess Elizabeth Stuart.[1] The following months saw banquets, masques, barriers, jousts and 'water frolicks' that showed the court to its best advantage as eyewitnesses admired 'the number of lords and ladies, the richness of their robes and liveries' and marvelled over the garments and jewels 'of inestimable value' worn by the royal family. Such display ensured that guests 'could hardly grasp the spectacle' and were left to conclude that the event was 'successful beyond expectation'.[2]

Although the wedding was a special, extraordinary event, seeing the Stuarts wearing priceless gems and luxurious fabrics was a regular feature of court life in Scotland and England, and it was an element that frequently drew comment. Yet significantly, as made clear in a report by Antonio Foscarini, the Venetian ambassador in London (*c*.1570–1622), contemporaries rarely viewed such expenditure as signs of vanity or frivolity but interpreted them in highly politic terms as evidence of the strength, status and sophistication of the monarchy. This essay discusses some of the specifics of dress and jewellery worn by the Stuarts in Scotland and England. The two are combined in this essay, as they were a crucial and commonplace pairing in Jacobean England and Scotland, where jewels were frequently incorporated into apparel, or were carefully chosen to complement and aggrandise the splendour of the wearer's clothing. Mention is made of those garments required for extraordinary events such as the baptism of Prince Henry Frederick, and the jewels required for diplomatic gifts, but focus is also given to the garments used in everyday wear and during those common courtly activities such as riding and hunting. The relationship between finance and dress is discussed, and new archival evidence shows that any economic strictures faced by the crown (even in Scotland) did not significantly impact the royal wardrobe or jewellers. Ultimately, investing in James and Anna's bodily display was

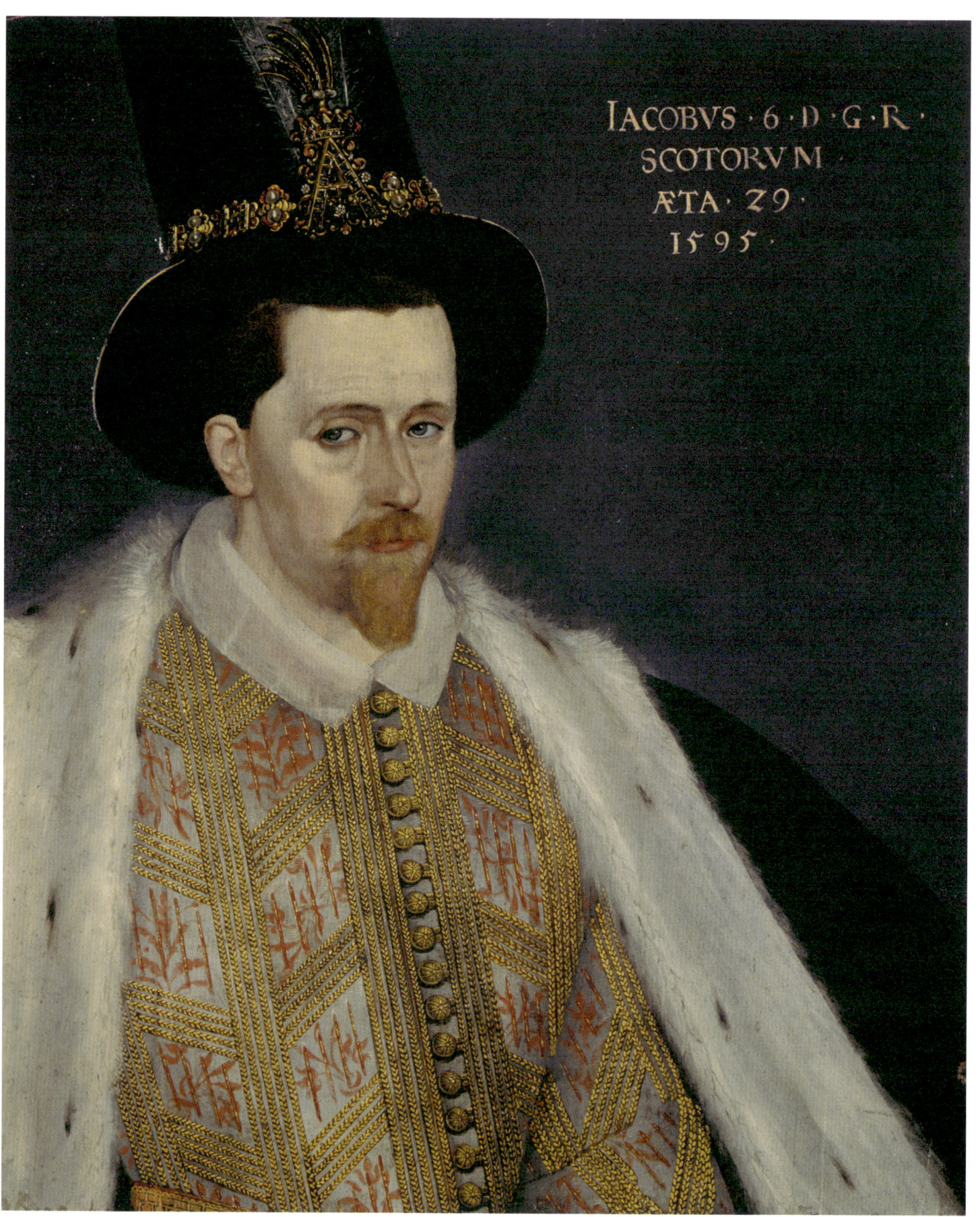

IACOBVS · 6 · D · G · R ·
SCOTORVM ·
ÆTA · 29 ·
1595 ·

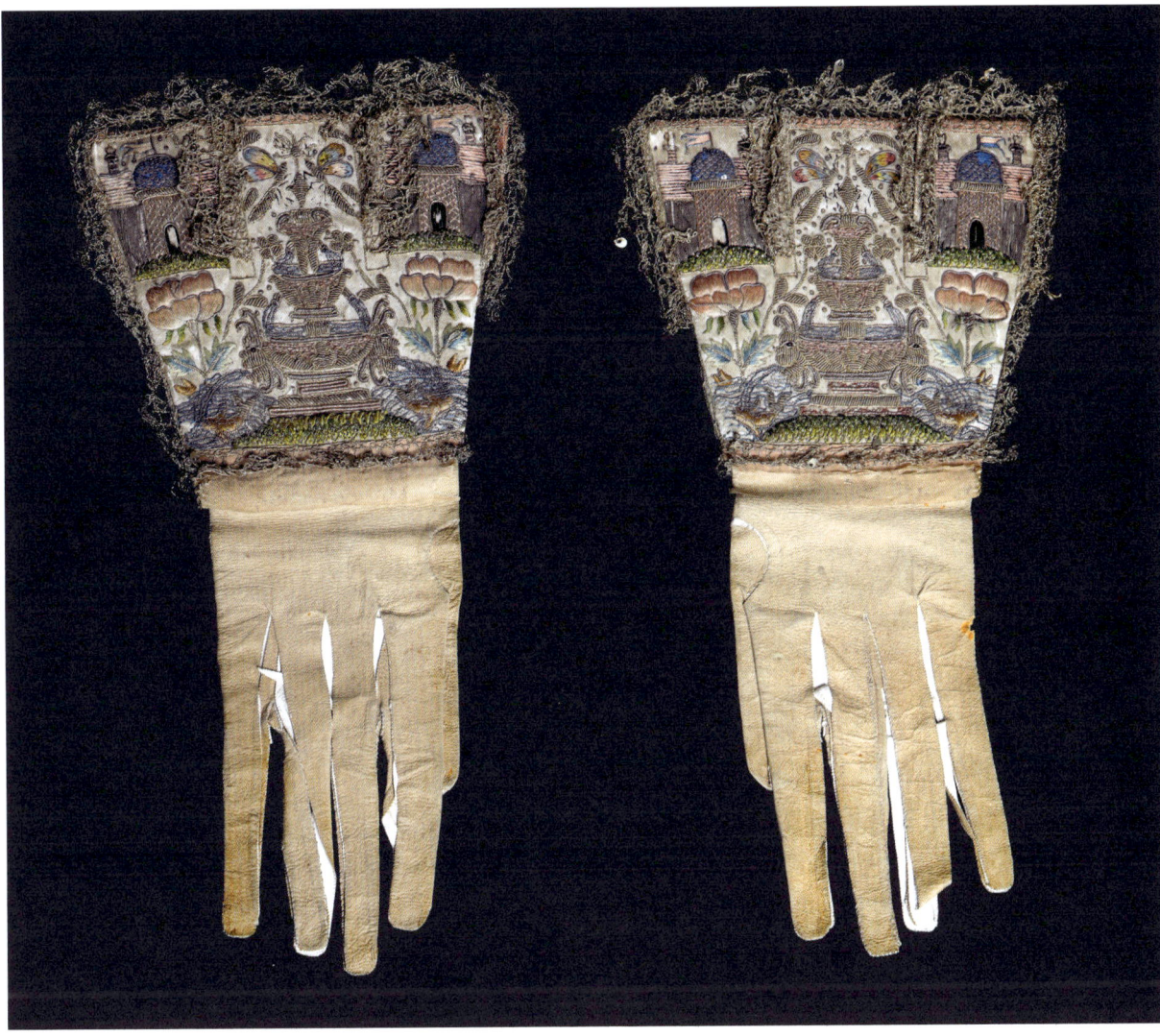

a matter of political importance: it was a physical demonstration of the wealth, power and stability of the Stuart monarchy.

Scotland: Court Finances and the Royal Wardrobe

The financial difficulties faced by the Scottish crown under James VI have been well documented by historians but, significantly, the political premium placed on sartorial display protected the royal wardrobe from shortfalls in central finance. This is most emphatically demonstrated by the accounts of the Scottish merchant and financier Robert Joussie (d.1610), one of the main suppliers of fabric to the royal wardrobe throughout the

1590s. Joussie's accounts from this decade tell us much about the colours, styles and fabrics favoured at court. A consistent demand for imported European fabrics resulted in large quantities of taffeta being brought in from Spain, with smaller amounts secured from Naples, Florence and Genoa. Spain was also a common source for silk – together with Genoa and Lucca – while velvet was preferably brought from Lucca; ribbon mainly came from Florence but was supplemented by lengths from Milan; and rare accounts of plush from Genoa and damask from Bologna are also recorded. A striking example of the fabric type – and the associated expense – includes the precept issued, on 29 October 1590, for Anna to have a new gown, petticoat, sleeves and bodice of imported cloth of silver figured with 'incarnadine' (probably carnation) at £25 Scots per ell (a Scottish ell is just under a metre). The ensemble was covered in extremely large quantities of passementerie (decorative trimmings) – some 440 ells – and fabric costs exceeded £1,340 Scots.[3] However, this paled in comparison to the 'napped cloth of gold and silver' which came into Scotland at £50 per ell, with Joussie securing 40 ells for the queen in January 1596 at a total cost of £2,000 Scots.[4] Given these high rates of expenditure, it is not surprising that when Joussie accounted for his outstanding bills with the queen, on 1 February 1596, he declared that in just under six years he had 'spent and disbursed to the queen's majesty for her apparel' the astonishing sum of £71,513 0s 14d Scots; this was just one of several accounts for the Stuarts.[5] Aware of the censure that such spending would incur, but also aware of the need to communicate power and status through bodily display, James sought alternative streams of revenue to circumvent the exchequer: he paid Joussie from his English annuity and with sums borrowed from John Maitland of Thirlestane, Lord Chancellor of Scotland (1537–1595).[6]

Clothing for Ceremony: The First Stuart Baptism

Many of the most expensive garments ordered by James and Anna were for extraordinary events – births, baptisms, weddings and funerals – when they were literally on show to local and foreign dignitaries and elites. A notable example of Scottish court ceremonial is the 1594 baptism of Prince Henry. The birth of the Stuarts' first child – a healthy son, and legitimate heir – was crucial to the longevity and position of the dynasty, and the baptism was accordingly marked by a resplendence of pageantry and formalised ritual. The royal couple required suitable garments for 'the time of the baptism', with the great wardrobe ordering fourteen new suites of apparel. Those for the king were fashioned from sumptuous imported fabrics of plush, satin and taffeta from Genoa, velvet from Lucca, cloth of gold and cloth of silver. The fabrics were ordered in a wide array of colours including violet, columbine (dove-coloured),

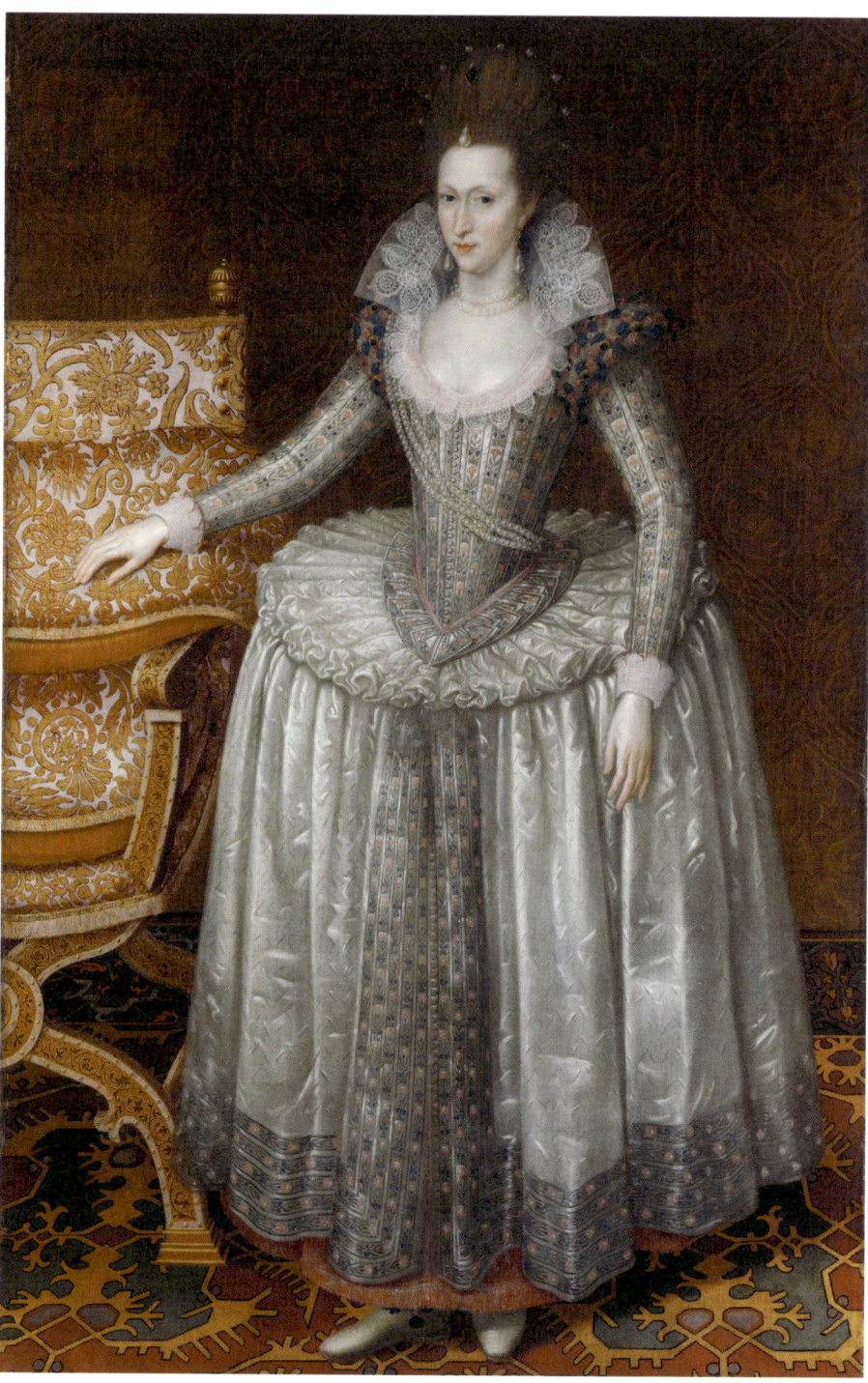

Fig.12
John de Critz the Elder
(c.1550–1642)
Anne of Denmark, 1605–10
Oil on canvas, 201.6 × 126.5 cm
National Portrait Gallery, London
(NPG 6918)

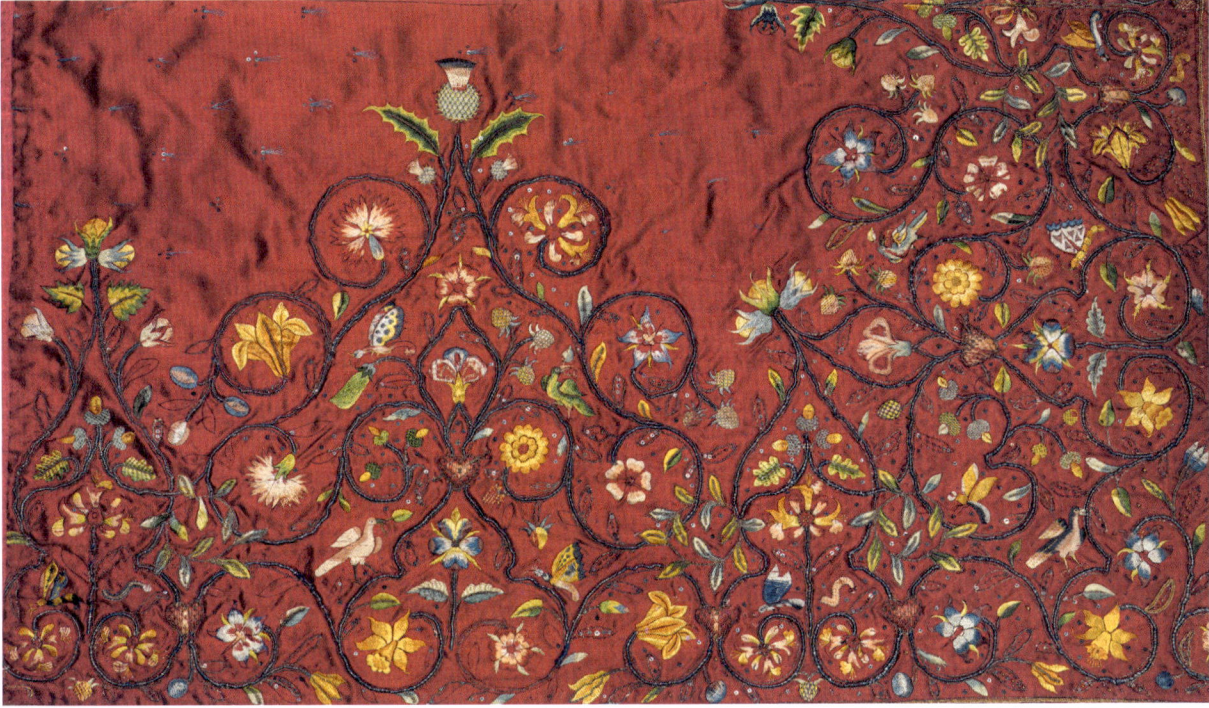

Fig. 13
Unknown maker
Petticoat possibly linked to Anna of Denmark, c.1610–20
Silk and metal, hand-stitched, 91 × 313 cm
The Burrell Collection, Glasgow (29.314)

orange, feuillemorte (dead-leaf colour), grey and peach, and were accompanied by liberal amounts of passementerie, points, buttons and loops made from precious metal and silk. The king's outfits were extremely expensive – the majority exceeding £1,000 Scots each – with one satin ensemble generously covered in silver cordons and embroidered work that alone cost £465 Scots.[7] Expenditure for the queen was only slightly less as lengths of similar types of fabrics – and in similarly varied shades of violet, peach, columbine, parrot-green, sky-colour, crimson and dried rose – were secured for her seven gowns and seven petticoats.[8] Throughout the baptismal celebrations, this sartorial privilege actively transformed the royal bodies into signs of wealth, power and prerogative. It is this standard of dress that is repeatedly commemorated in formal court portraits, wherein it helped to communicate the sitter's social and financial status that were then preserved for posterity (cats 4 and 13).

Riding and Hunting

The royal wardrobe reflected James's itinerant style of kingship – fuelled by his passion for the hunt and buttressed by a keen understanding of the political benefits of mobility – as provisions were regularly made for riding and hunting apparel. In Scotland, James rarely stayed in one place for more than three weeks at a time, constantly moving between the royal palaces of Stirling, Linlithgow, Falkland, Holyroodhouse and Dunfermline.[9] He also frequented a large number of noble residences (the most commonly visited being Dalkeith), and in the summer months covered large parts of the country while hunting or on progress, with his usual route encompassing Inverness, Fortrose and Cromarty in the north, to Carlisle and Dumfries in the south, and as far west as Dumbarton.[10] This pattern continued after the Stuarts moved to England, where, in any given year, James was absent from London for between six and nine months, choosing to spend time at his favoured residences of Royston, Newmarket, Thetford and Theobalds.[11] Anna occasionally accompanied James hunting, and she frequently joined him on the summer progress as well as completing her own progresses, although she did not travel or hunt as often as the king.[12]

The journey between residences provided opportunities for James and Anna to be visible among their subjects, which, in turn, aided the popularity and support of the monarchy. Visibility was often heightened through apparel, for the Stuarts often wore bright garments decorated with precious metal threadwork and fastenings that would have sparkled in the sunlight. On 29 September 1590, for example, orders were given for James to have a new set of 'winter riding clothes', costing just over £200 Scots. Fashioned from columbine-coloured cloth, the 'thick' cloak was lined with red velvet and embellished with gold passements. Both cloak and breeches were worked with cordons of gold, while fifty-four gold buttons were affixed to the doublet. The outfit was finished off with brown silk points and Florentine ribbons together with a pair of long hair-coloured silk hose from Naples.[13] At the same time, scented Spanish taffeta and three ounces of 'gold and silver passements' were ordered for lining and decorating three pairs of gloves for the king.[14] An extant pair of gloves, dating to between 1600 and 1630, offers an evocative example of the type that would have been worn by the king (fig.11). As well as providing warmth and protection, gloves played a decorative role completing outfits that were patterned in silk and silver-gilt thread, and garnished with passages of lace, spangles and purls (cat.60).

The queen likewise wore gloves while riding, and particular care was taken over her complexion with the use of hats, hoods, head coverings or masks.[15] Anna's riding clothes were coordinated ensembles that included a gown or skirt with a long train, a cloak and a safeguard.[16] Thus, on 9 July 1590, the queen's tailor received 15 ells of Spanish incarnadine (crimson) satin to make her 'one riding cloak and one riding safeguard', which were to be lined with incarnadine Spanish taffeta. These pieces were then trimmed with incarnadine Florentine ribbons and enriched with 62.5 ounces (1.8 kilograms) of braided gold passementerie at a significant cost of £312 Scots.[17]

In addition to riding, the princely pastime of the hunt brought specific – and frequent – requirements of dress. Anna had been a keen huntress in Denmark-Norway, and continued this elite activity in Scotland in the company of James, although bills for her hunting attire have not survived.[18] Fortunately, accounts for James's

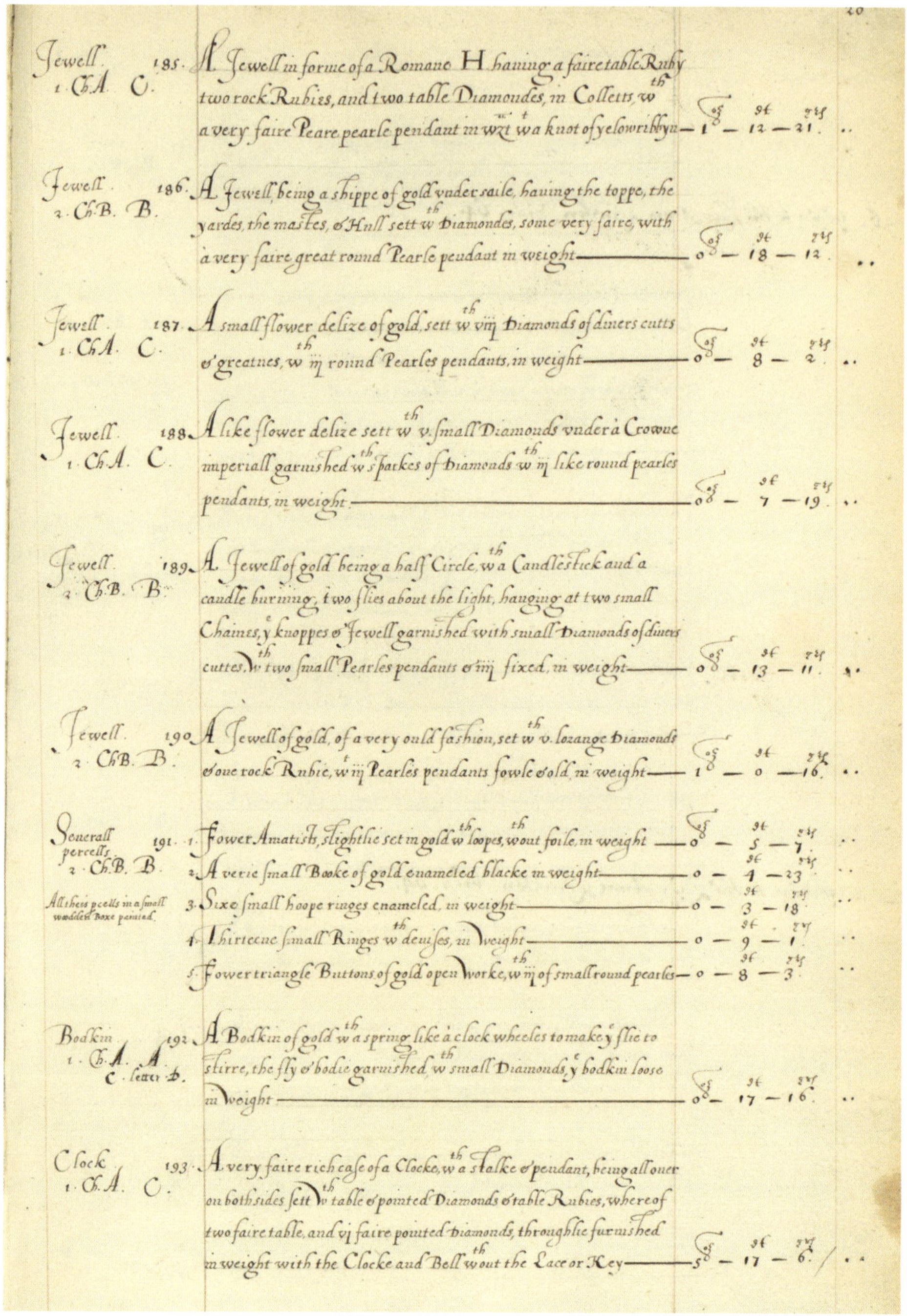

Fig.14
Unknown author
Anne of Denmark's Jewellery Inventory, 1606–07, with later notes dating up to 1612
Ink on paper, 51 × 39 cm
National Library of Scotland, Edinburgh (Adv.MS 31.1.10)

hunting clothes – and those ordered for his chosen servitors – are extant. Unlike the conspicuous outfits worn while riding, the bills for hunting dress evidence a desire for camouflage, with clothing following the seasonal colour palette: those worn in spring/summer were typically green (sometimes decorated with silver), while those worn in autumn/winter were commonly brown (sometimes decorated with gold).

One example, from August 1590, records lengths of 'green satin' being delivered to the tailor, 'to be his majesty's hunting clothes'. The outfit was lined with green taffeta imported from Spain, finished with a pair of long green silk hose from Naples, and a green castor hat with green strings. Decorative trimmings extended to green passementerie, green ribbons and green silk points, while silver lace was used to edge the pockets of the breeches, and forty-eight silver buttons fastened the doublet.[19] When orders were later given, in October 1592, for James to have new 'winter riding clothes', the cloak, coat and breeches were fashioned from 'London brown cloth'. The cloak was lined with brown velvet and fastened with gold buttons, and the 'thick' coat and breeches were covered with 'broad passements of gold'.[20]

Such camouflaging extended to the apparel that James ordered for his accompanying 'hunting men' and pages, which was allocated annually in both Scotland and England. In July 1600, for example, the king's page of honour, Robert Carr, later Earl of Somerset (1585/6–1645, cat.57) – together with four other pages – was given green frieze (a type of coarse woollen cloth) 'to be his hunting clothes' and green stemming for a pair of socks. At the same time, another gentleman and three huntsmen were issued with garments of green stemming for the hunt.[21] The following summer, Robert Walker, attendant to the hounds, was provided with green stemming for coat, breeches and 'schankis' (stockings).[22] Walker moved south to London with the Stuarts in 1603 and henceforth was given an annual allocation – as were five other huntsmen – for a coat, breeches and a hat 'of green'.[23]

Gifts of Clothing and Jewellery

The political role and value of jewellery and apparel extended beyond those worn by the Stuarts to those exchanged in the heavily ritualised practice of gift-giving that cemented formal and informal networks. It has long been recognised that the giving and receiving of gifts was a key component in the creation and augmentation of the patron–client relationships and kinship bonds that underwrote many early modern court systems – Scotland and England included.[24] Gifts were customarily presented to foreign rulers and their representatives, household and family members, local elites and favourites; they were given away at weddings and christenings; offered as rewards for devoted service; and exchanged on Valentine's Day, New Year's Day and while on progress. They commonly took the form of jewels and plate but also included money, animals, plants, garments, soft furnishings and foodstuffs. Exchanged liberally within the kingdom, the practice extended to foreign diplomats, other rulers and faraway relatives.

The number of courtiers who gave Anna fabrics, carpets or apparel as New Year's gifts indicates the queen's passion for clothing and interior furnishings. White satin petticoats, elaborately embroidered in gold, silver and coloured silks, were a markedly popular choice. For New Year 1608/9, for example, Anna received petticoats from Lady Margaret, Countess of Nottingham, from Mary Gargrave, one of her Maids of Honour, from her Lord Chamberlain, Robert Sidney, Viscount Lisle, from Thomas Howard, Earl of Suffolk, and even from the king.[25] As skirts, or under-skirts, petticoats were meant to be seen, and they are often visible in portraits of the period. In the portrait of Anna from 1605–10 by John de Critz the Elder (c.1550–1642, fig.12), for example, the queen's carnation-coloured fringed petticoat is visible extending below her closed skirts. It is not clear from the portrait, but this garment may well have been akin to the rare surviving petticoat fragment held in the collection of Glasgow Museums, and dating to 1610–20 (fig.13).[26] Fashioned from carnation silk, the piece is elaborately embroidered with figurative devices including pansies, daffodils, carnations, honeysuckle, acorns, leaves, pea pods, strawberries, thistles, birds, butterflies and hearts, all of which are set within an arabesque of curling stems. A surviving inventory of Anna's wardrobe goods, compiled around 1608, confirms that the queen owned at least fifty-two petticoats and that many of these were trimmed with lace and decoratively embroidered with representational motifs including ships, serpents, blossoming trees and elephants.[27]

Anna was also a generous benefactor, and regularly gifted articles of clothing, soft furnishings and pieces of jewellery. The queen often gave gifts to her female servitors when they married, and these were sometimes drawn from her personal possessions. On 22 June 1612, for example, when the Scottish chamberer Anna Livingstone (d.1632) married Alexander Montgomerie, Earl of Eglinton (1588–1661), the queen gave her three of her own jewels.[28] These were drawn from the queen's reserve (perhaps inherited) set of jewels, which was inventoried and annotated over a six-year period from 1606 to 1612 (fig.14).[29] Running to some 406 entries, the collection is marked by a diversity of form, material and design. The precious stones include rubies, sapphires and emeralds along with pearls, crystals, coral and opals. These constituted chains, pendants, bodkins (sharp, pointed hair ornaments), aglets (decorative tags attached to the end of a lace), pomanders (containers, usually of precious metal, holding a mixture of aromatic substances) and fans, as well as a quantity of representational jewels such as swans, sailing ships, fish, suns, keys, birds, bells, spiders and moons. While none of these jewels have been definitively identified, the Cheapside Hoard offers a remarkable number of contemporary pieces that are comparable in workmanship and materials (fig.15). In addition to her reserve collection, Anna ordered jewels – on a large scale – from her principal jeweller, George Heriot (1563–1624, cat.47). While in England, between 1603 and 1615, Heriot supplied the queen with 766 items and billed her for more than £42,000 sterling, which is an astonishingly high sum. Unlike the inventoried collection, the most common stone listed among Heriot's accounts is the diamond, and jewellery most commonly took the form of rings, earrings, pendants and miniature cases. Among Heriot's documents are specific orders from the queen for gifts such as the 'jewel of gold, set with diamonds'

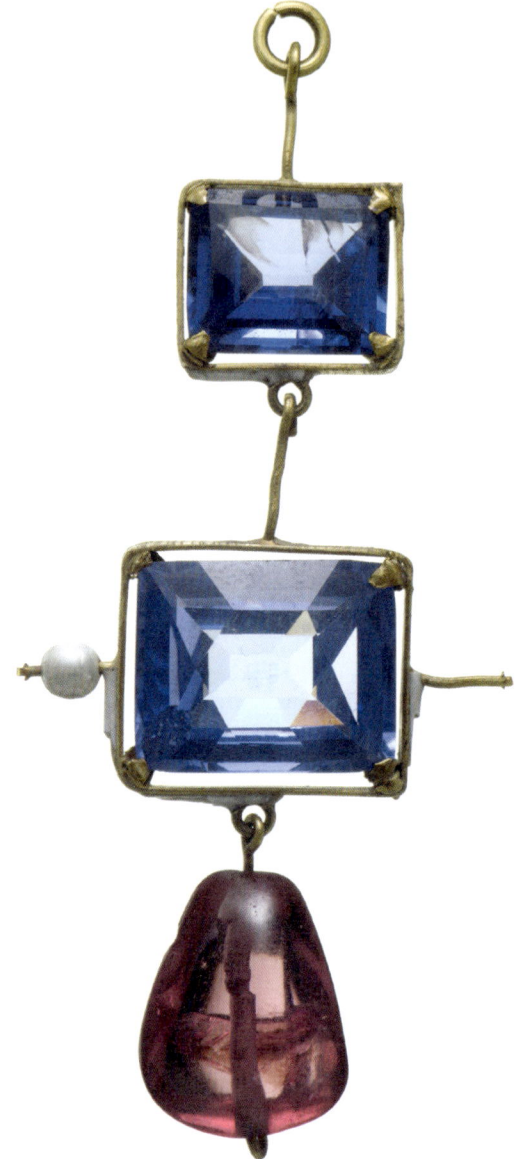

Fig.15
Unknown maker
Sapphire and spinel pendant, late sixteenth to early seventeenth century
Sapphire, spinel, pearl, gold and enamel, 7.2 × 1.5 cm
London Museum, London (A14104)

that she gave to Jane Meautys (c.1580–1659) on her wedding to Sir William Cornwallis of Brome (d.1611) in April 1610.[30]

This pattern of gift-giving was likewise observed in Scotland, and it is well illustrated by the goods that James and Anna lavished on Mary Stewart (c.1582–1644) in celebration of her wedding on 10 December 1592. The wedding was a particularly elite and elaborate affair, for Mary was not just a gentlewoman of the chamber, but the daughter of James's (now deceased) first favourite Esmé Stewart, Duke of Lennox (1542–1583), and she was marrying the extremely powerful John Erskine, 2nd Earl of Mar (c.1562–1634). Mary's bridal attire was provided

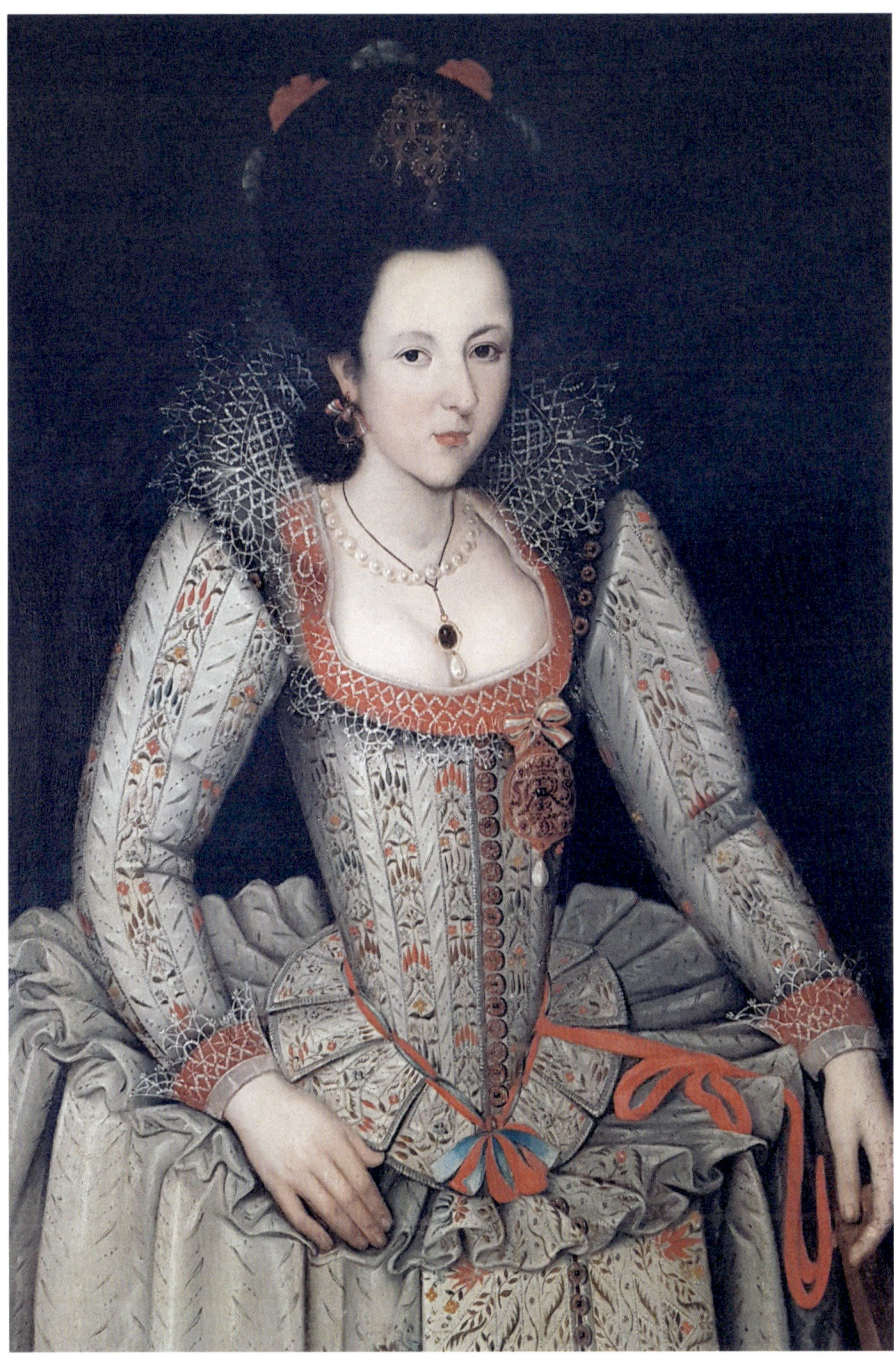

Cat.14
Unknown artist
*Lady Anne Livingstone, Countess
of Eglinton (d.1632), c.1612*
Oil on canvas, 130.5 × 84.5 cm
Scottish Collection (289)

PROVENANCE: Family descent.

REFERENCES: Glasgow 1901, as
'Marion Livingston'; Edinburgh 1991,
pp.22–23; London 2019a, p.185

by the queen, who ordered her a gown of cloth
of gold that was completed by a skirt, sleeves and
bodice in cloth of silver. The ensemble was finished
with 24 ounces (68 grams) of gold passementerie,
resulting in a bride who must have literally shone
and glittered.[31] James, too, bought Mary apparel
'for the time of her marriage', but rather than her
wedding gown, these garments formed part of
her trousseau. On the king's orders, more than
£2,150 Scots was disbursed to equip Mary with four
gowns, four skirts, a pair of 'baleen bodies' (a bodice
strengthened with whalebone), two hoods and two
pairs of silk hose made from costly fabrics such
as Genoese satin, plush and Lucchese double-pile
velvet finished with gold and silver passementerie.[32]
Other female servitors who likewise received costly
apparel at the time of marriage in Scotland included
the Ladies Mary Young, Anna Moray, Jane Stewart
and Margaret Stewart.[33] When Margaret Vinstarr
married, on 26 October 1593, she was presented
with a bed with an expensive set of velvet, damask
and taffeta hangings.[34]

Visual and documentary sources further show
that Anna gave her female chamberers (and her
family members) pieces of personalised jewelled
adornment. Between June and September 1607,
for example, Heriot was commissioned to make
a diamond-encrusted tablet 'to be sent to her
majesty's mother the Queen of Denmark' (Sofie of
Mecklenburg-Güstrow, 1557–1631), which must
have contained a miniature of Anna herself.[35] The
queen also gave jewelled miniatures – decorated
with various configurations of her own letters – to
women in her English court circle. Thus, surviving
portraits of Anna Montgomerie (née Livingstone),
Countess of Eglinton (cat.14), Margaret Seton (née
Hay), Countess of Dunfermline (*c*.1592–1659)
and Elizabeth Grey (née Talbot), Countess of
Kent (1582–1651) show them all wearing jewelled
tablets adorned either with an 'A' or with 'AR' for
Anna Regina.[36] Significantly, the miniature case
depicted in the 1612 portrait of the Countess
of Eglinton survives in the collection of the
Fitzwilliam Museum (cat.15).[37] Most probably a gift
from the queen to the countess on her marriage
to Sir Alexander Seton of Foulstruther, later Earl
of Eglinton, it contains a portrait of the queen by
Nicholas Hilliard (1547–1619) and his workshop.

The richly bejewelled case was made by Heriot and features, on the front cover, the queen's interlinked letters 'AR' spelled out in table diamonds and set beneath a closed imperial crown. Additional letters – 'C' and 'S' – point to the queen's natal identity in referencing her brother, King Christian IV of Denmark (1577–1648), and her mother, Sofie.

These miniatures were intended to be read as signs of allegiance and personal favour, and Anna also used her jewelled letters in matters of international diplomacy. In September 1604, she gave Charles de Ligne, Princely Count of Arenberg (1550–1616), a 'jewel with an A and R' to commemorate the newly formed Anglo–Spanish peace.[38] James likewise lavished the Spanish dignitaries with gifts, delivering the head of the delegation, Juan Fernández de Velasco, Constable of Castile (c.1550–1613), 'a diamond worth six thousand crowns', and distributing £8,000 sterling worth of plate among the other members of the Commission.[39] Like Anna, James too used his portrait and cipher as political currency. Perhaps most famously, in 1610/11, James gifted Sir Thomas Lyte (1568–1638) his miniature, richly set within an elaborately enamelled gold locket (fig.16). The tablet likely shares a history of workmanship with that in the Fitzwilliam (cat.15), for the portrait is attributed to Hilliard, and the bejewelled openwork case – bearing the king's letters 'IR' (*Jacobus Rex*) – is thought to be by Heriot.[40] Subsequently known as the 'Lyte Jewel', it was given in gratitude for Lyte having produced an illuminated document tracing James's lineage back through several lines of descent to the mythic first ruler of Britain, the Trojan prince Brutus. Beyond economic and material worth, these royal gifts held high cultural, personal and political value. With the sovereign readily identifiable through images and letters, the tablet gave visual form to the favour, privilege and influence of the recipient.

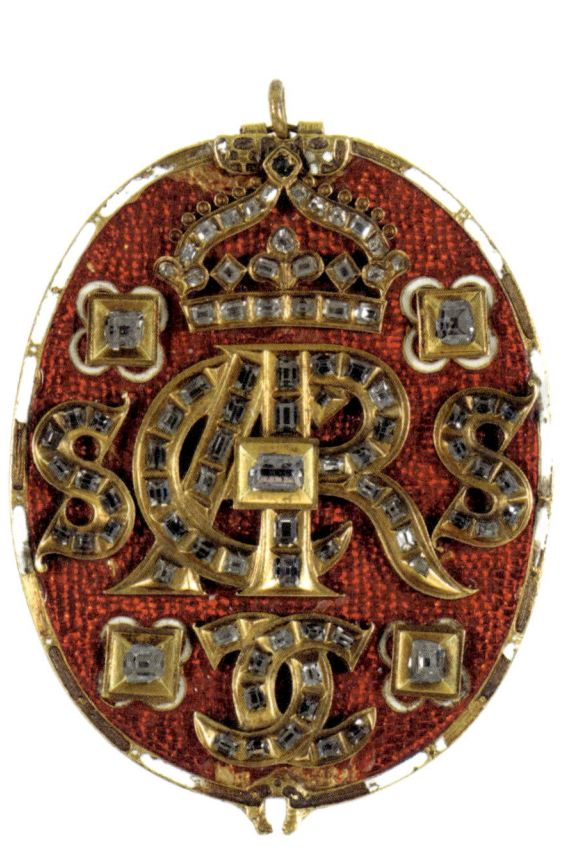

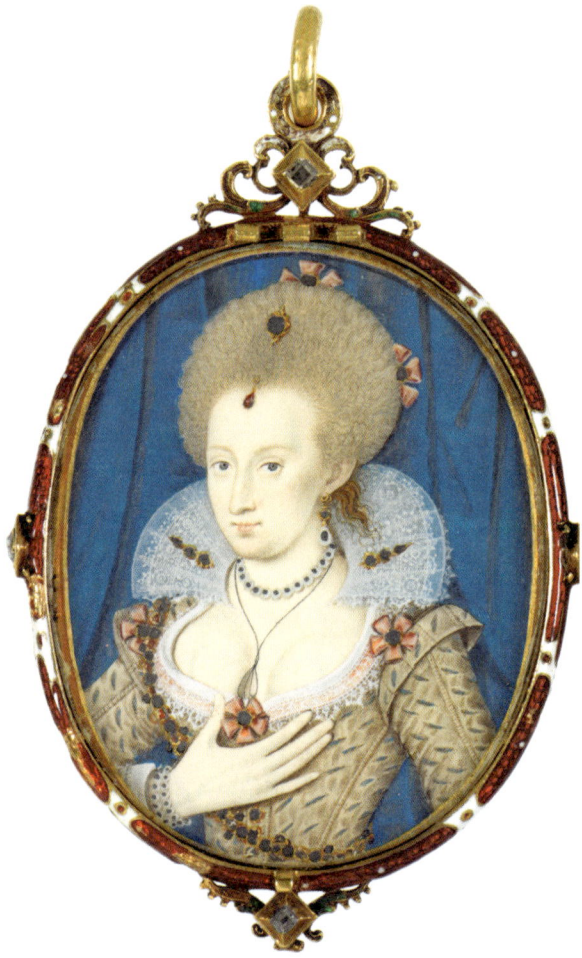

Fig.16 (opposite)
Nicholas Hilliard (1547–1619)
The Lyte Jewel, 1610–11
Vellum, gold, enamel and diamond,
7.9 × 4.8 cm
British Museum, London (WB.167)

Cat.15
**Studio of Nicholas Hilliard
(1547–1619)**
Anne of Denmark 'The Eglinton Jewel', c.1610
Watercolour and body colour with gold and silver on vellum, laid on a playing card (one club visible on reverse), 5.4 × 4.3 cm
Fitzwilliam Museum, Cambridge (3855)

PROVENANCE: Possibly Anna of Denmark; Lady Anne Livingstone, Countess of Eglinton by 1612; by descent to Leonard Daneham, Earl of Eglinton and Winton; his sale, Christie's, London, 13 July 1922, lot 77; bought by L.D. Cunliffe; bequeathed to the Fitzwilliam Museum, 1937.

REFERENCES: Reynolds 1952, p.22; Auerbach 1961, pp.168, 318, no.180; London 1983, pp.147–48, cat.243; Bayne-Powell 1985, pp.118–19; Scarisbrick 1986, p.234; Edinburgh 1991, pp.22–23, cats 10, 11; Hunt, Thornton & Dalgleish 2016, pp.189–92

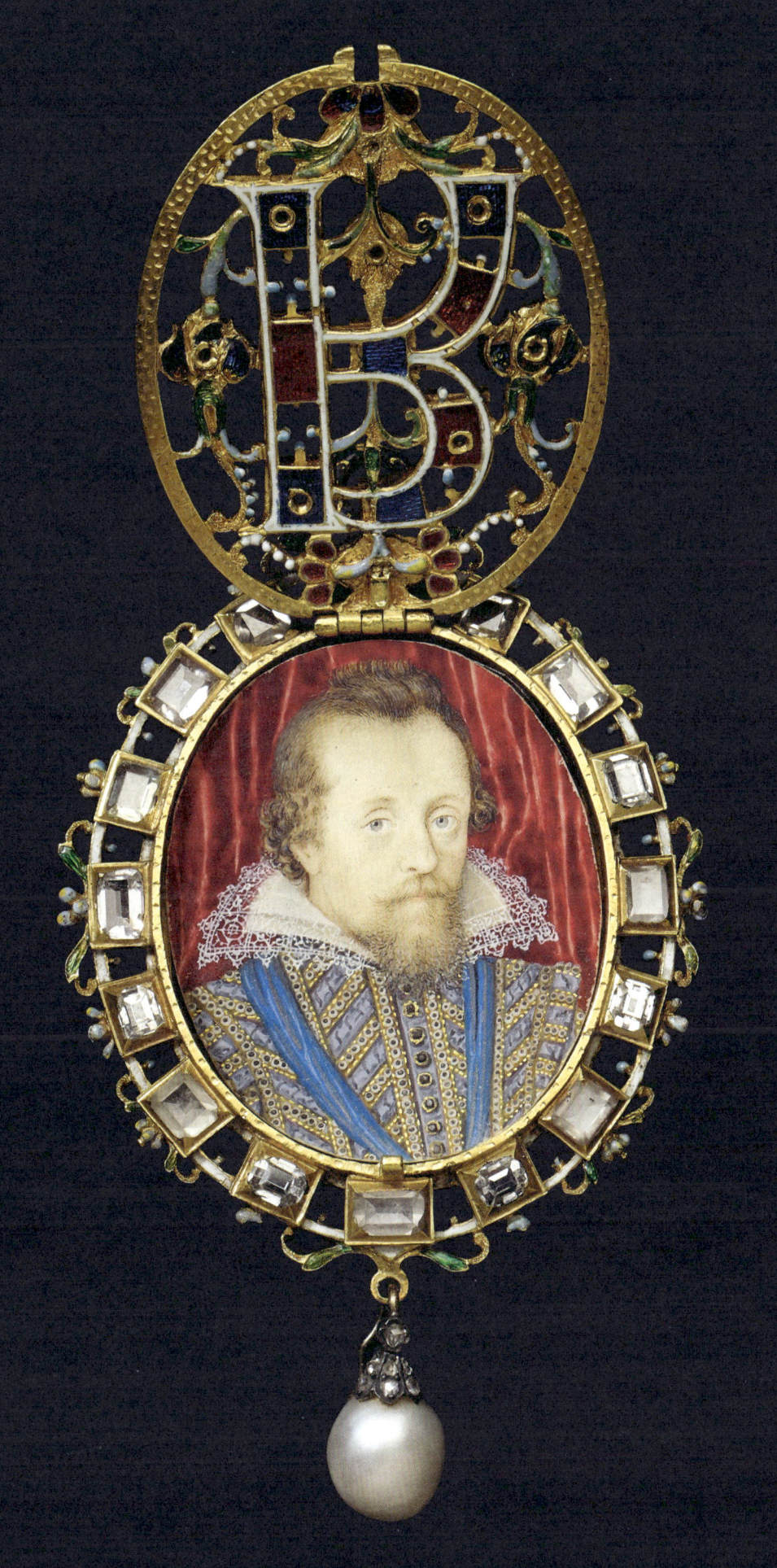

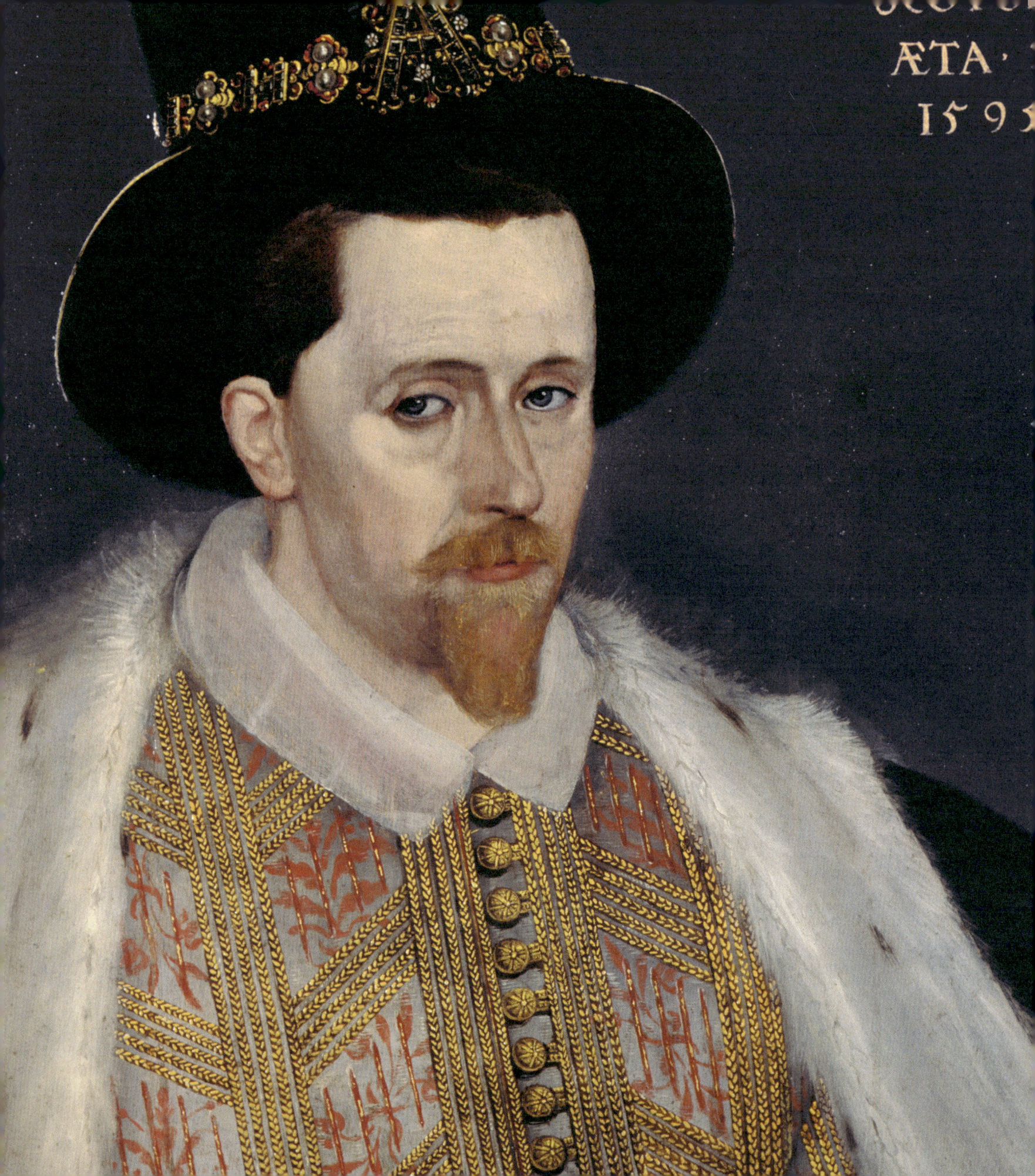

ÆTA·
1595

WRITING MONARCHY, UNION, FATHERHOOD AND TOBACCO

Anna Groundwater

UNLIKE MOST SCOTTISH OR BRITISH monarchs, James VI & I was a prolific author (fig.17). Even more unusually, he was keen to publish those writings, and in 1616 many were brought together in his *Workes* (cat.17). This voluminous book contained nearly 600 pages of his views on kingship, the Anglo–Scottish union and religion, as well as paternal words of advice to his son and heir. It was composed of three important books previously published (*Daemonologie*, *The True Lawe of Free Monarchies* and *Basilikon Doron*), various political and religious tracts and his speeches to parliament. Most presciently, it also included his *A Counterblast to Tobacco*; never has a king been so right about anything.

The *Workes*, though impressive, was not James's full literary outpouring. While it represented what one might expect of a kingly author, other pieces were excluded, most notably his poetry written in Scots, Latin and French. The middle-aged monarch who, in 1610, wrote that kings may 'make and unmake their subjects: they have power of raising,

and casting down: of life, and of death: Judges over all their subjects and in all causes' was also the young man who published several books of poetry, including the *Essayes of a Prentise*, in the *Divine Art of Poesie* in 1585 (cat.129), and his *Poeticall Exercises* in 1591.[1] This essay explores how the combination of all his works reveals the complexity of a thoughtful and erudite man, a king, husband and father, agonising over the future of his newly conjoined kingdoms.

On Absolute Monarchy

But to start with the *Workes*: in its full title, *The Workes of the Most High and Mighty Prince, Iames, By the grace of God, Kinge of Great Brittaine, France & Ireland, Defender of ye Faith &c.* we see a proclamation of the key elements with which the fifty-year-old king framed his monarchy. Firstly, of dynastic union, the Union of the Crowns, a king of two kingdoms (England and Scotland) and one principality (Wales) combined into the imperial Great Britain, with the kingship of Ireland too.

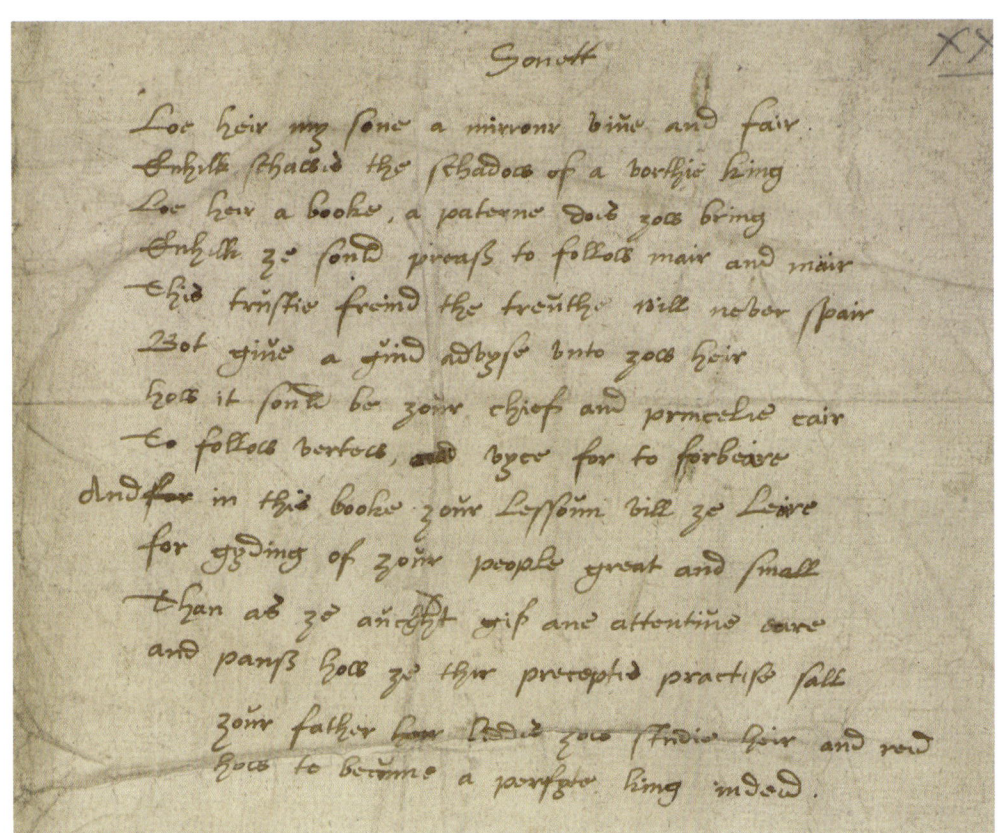

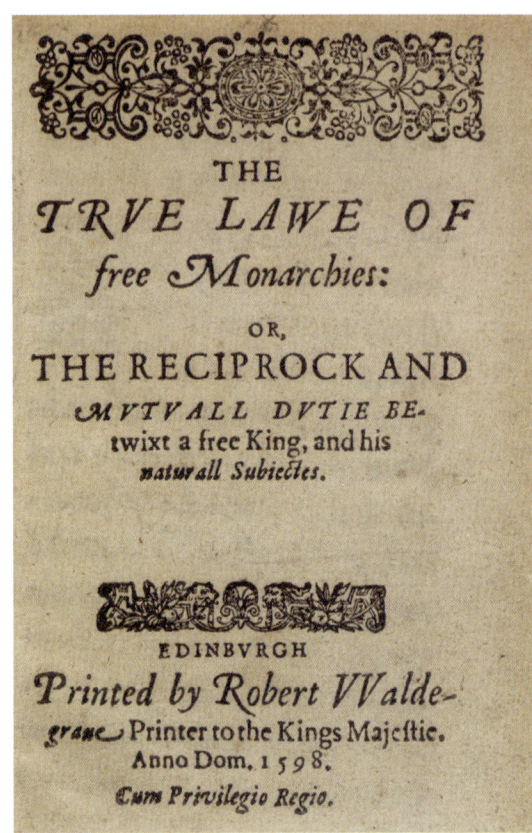

Secondly, he was voicing ancient claims to the French crown and thus the status of a prince in Europe as well. Finally, in the position he claimed as defender of the Protestant faith in both Britain and Europe, James was portraying himself bestriding not only a Scottish or British but a European stage.

The *Workes* were to define James's views on monarchy as they have come down to us today. In the 1600s, for those who could afford the volume, it ostensibly gave an intimate glimpse into the king's mind, a monarch convinced of the divine nature of his sovereignty and of the duty his obedient subjects owed him. But we should not take his words at face value, as mirroring the real extent of his power. They are clever words, steeped in a long education in rhetoric, the classics and the Scriptures. What they express is James's idealised image of kingship, a paternal king with a duty of care to his children, his power a divine gift in order to protect his peoples. Kings, he said, were nothing less than God's representatives on earth: 'Kings are

in the word of GOD itself called Gods, as being his Lieutenants and Vice-regents on earth, and [are thus] so adorned and furnished with some sparkles of the Divinity'.[2] This was James proclaiming an unshakeable belief in the divine right of his kingship, the God-given nature of his power. Therefore, given it was blasphemy to dispute the power of God, 'so it is sedition in Subjects, to dispute what a King may do in the height of his power'.[3] It was the godly duty of a king's people to obey, and not to judge him.

Such an expression of monarchical power has been taken as a claim to absolute monarchy. Indeed, James used the term himself in his clearest statement of the rights of monarchy, in his tract *The True Lawe of Free Monarchies*, published in Edinburgh in 1598 and in London in 1603 (and in *Workes*) (cat.16). Here he set out 'the true grounds of the mutual duty, and allegiance between a free and absolute *Monarch*, and his people'. The power of Scottish kings, he said, was that of 'free Monarchies' and 'not of elective kings', thus

Fig.17 (detail, left)
Written by James VI & I (1566–1625)
Basilikon Doron manuscript, *c.*1598
Ink on paper, in purple velvet binding, 33.3 × 23.8 cm
British Library, London (Royal MS 18 B. xv)

Cat.16 (right)
Written by James VI & I (1566–1625), printed by Robert Waldegrave (*c*.1554–1603/4)
The True Lawe of Free Monarchies, 1598
Printed book in leather binding, 15 × 9 cm, 62 pages
National Library of Scotland, Edinburgh (F.6.f.11)

PROVENANCE: Acquired by the Advocates Library, from the Lauriston Castle fund on 4 October 1943.

Cat.17
Written by James VI & I
(1566–1625), printed by Robert
Barker (1570–1645) and John Bill
(1576–1630)
*The Workes of the Most High
and Mighty Prince, Iames, By
the grace of God, Kinge of Great
Brittaine, France & Ireland,
Defender of ye Faith &c.*, 1616
Printed book, 36 × 21.5 cm,
569 pages
National Library of Scotland,
Edinburgh (Ry.III.a.11)

PROVENANCE: Presented by
Lord Rosebery, 1927.

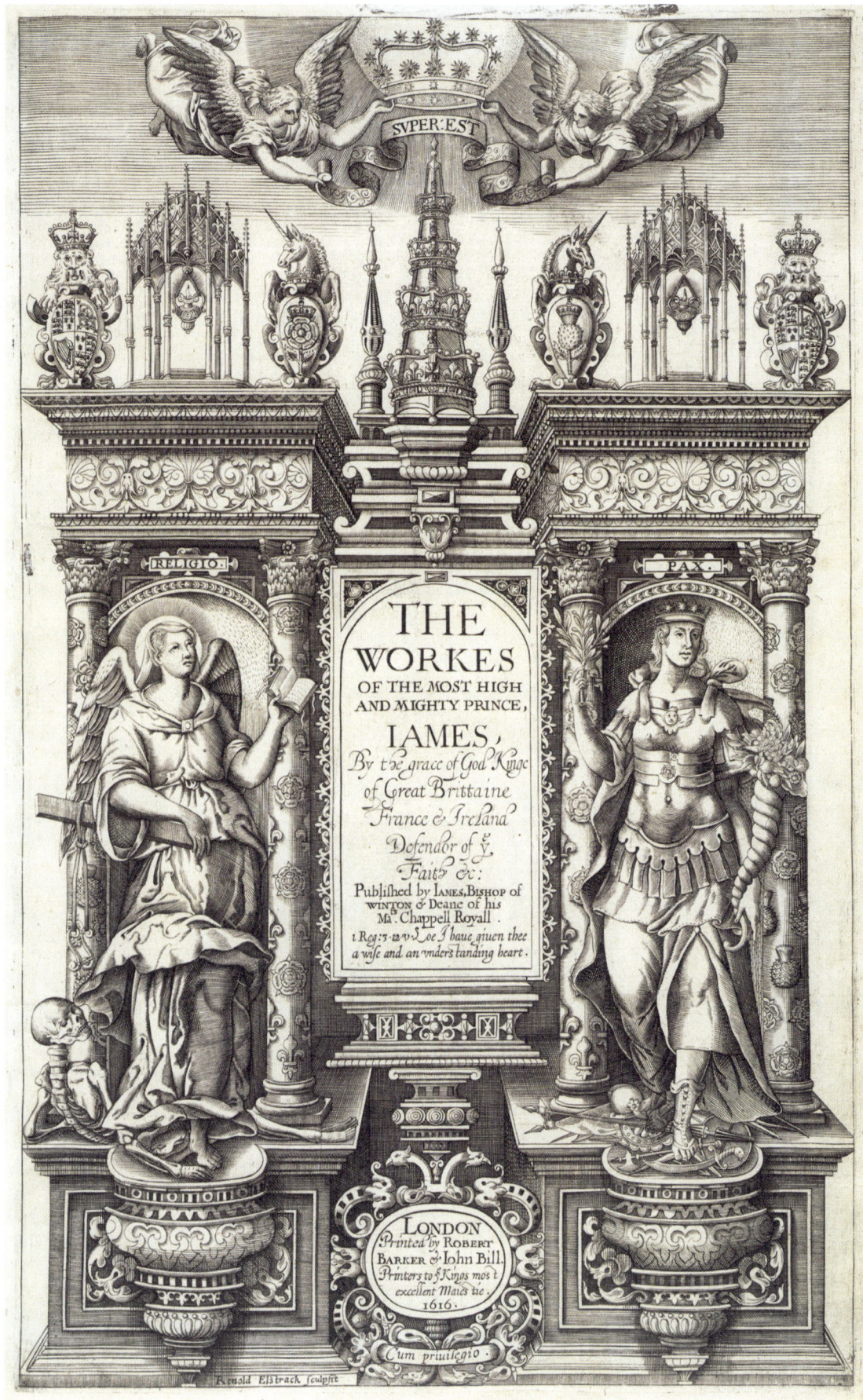

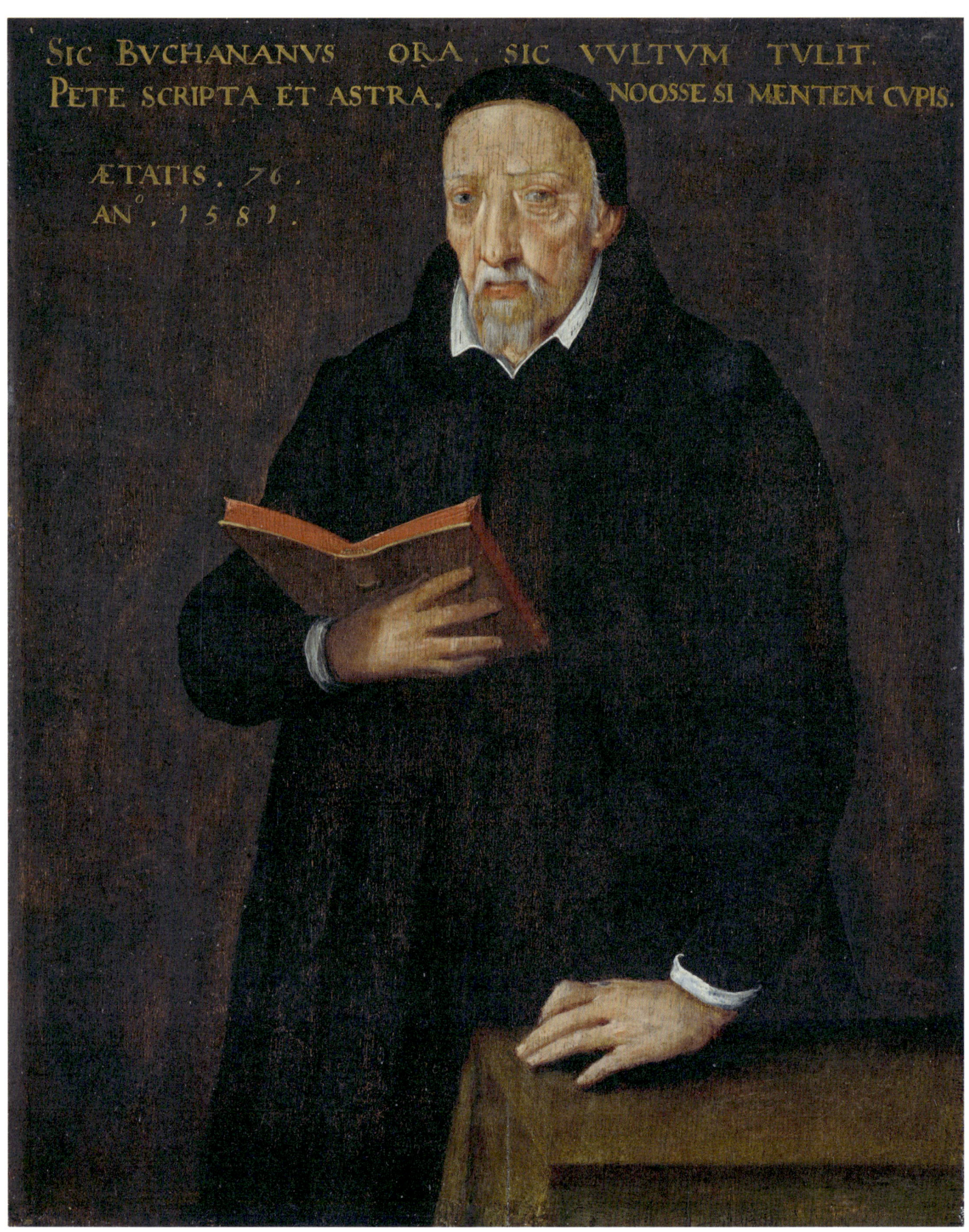

SIC BVCHANANVS ORA. SIC VVLTVM TVLIT.
PETE SCRIPTA ET ASTRA. NOOSSE SI MENTEM CVPIS.

ÆTATIS. 76.
ANº. 1581.

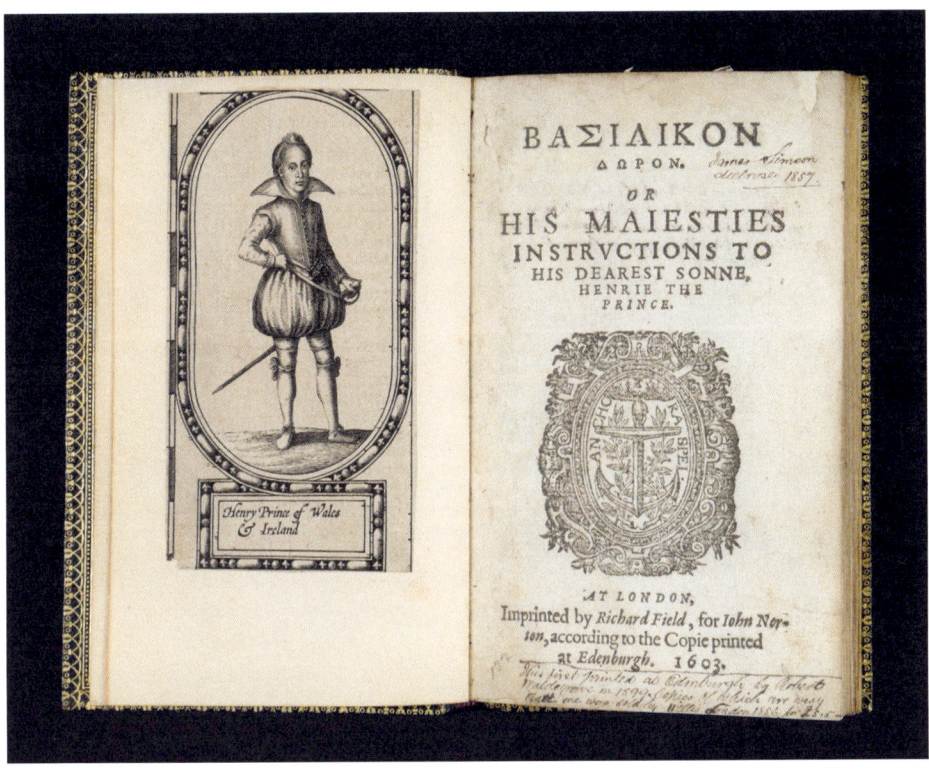

Cat.18 (opposite)
Unknown artist, after Arnold
Bronckorst (active 1565–1583)
*George Buchanan (1506–1582),
Tutor to James VI*, after 1581
Oil on panel, 46.9 × 40.2 cm (framed)
National Galleries of Scotland,
Edinburgh (PG 2678)

PROVENANCE: Purchased at Phillips,
London, 17 December 1985, lot 51.

REFERENCES: Edinburgh 1990,
cat.49, p.51; Macdonald 2000,
pp.40–43, no.28; Edinburgh 2005,
p.21; Thomas 2013, p.167

Cat.19 (above)
Written by James VI & I
(1566–1625), printed by
Richard Field (1561–1624)
*Basilikon Doron Or His Maiesties
instructions to his dearest sonne,
Henrie the prince*, published 1603
(first published 1599)
Paper, goat skin on paste boards,
15.5 × 10 cm
Blackie House Library and Museum
(CAT4290)

PROVENANCE: James Simson,
Melrose (1857); Sold at Bonham's,
'Education: the Book Collection of
John and Monica Lawson' Sale,
1 April 2008, lot 550.

rejecting the limitations of any form of contractual monarchy. So, though a king vowed 'to discharge honorably and truly the office given him by God', if he erred only God could punish him.[4] As a free monarch who was only accountable to God, he denied his subjects the right to resist his actions. He was denying their right to rebel.

You might ask why James felt the need to spell out these potentially divisive opinions. For this we have to look back into his childhood, to understand the circumstances in which his views on kingship were formed. James was crowned king as an infant in the aftermath of the forced abdication of his mother Mary, Queen of Scots. Mary was an anointed queen who had been overthrown by her subjects and replaced by her son. Political writers in Scotland rushed to legitimise these actions, which could have been seen as treason. They did this by claiming the right to overthrow a tyrant, and then set out to portray Mary as such.

Foremost among these critics was the historian and humanist scholar George Buchanan (in his book *De Jure Regni Apud Scotos Dialogus; or, a dialogue, concerning the due priviledge of government*

in the kingdom of Scotland (1579)), the man entrusted with young James's education (cat.18). The exact tenet his pupil would go on to reject, Buchanan spelled out in the right to resist a tyrant: 'if we should obey a good Prince, it will not therefore follow that we should not resist a wicked Prince'.[5] For Buchanan, those in the political community of Scotland had the power 'to bind by Law' their monarchs. Mary had broken that law, he wrote, through alleged adultery and complicity in the murder of James's father, her husband Lord Darnley. It was therefore lawful to replace her.

Partly to refute that interpretation of an unwritten contract between king and people, James put pen to paper. In the *True Lawe*'s preface, bemoaning the turmoils of the past, he tells his readers to behave as 'honest and obedient Subjects to your King' in case they were influenced by any who praised or excused previous rebellions in Scotland.[6] James's own kingship had resulted from rebellion. He, more than anyone, felt the need to legitimise his power – and to educate his people against the evils of revolt.

Kings, he wrote, not parliaments, should be responsible for making laws, since parliament was only 'the head Court of the King'. No parliament, he said, could 'make any kind of Law or Statute, without [a king's] Sceptre' to give it the force of law.[7] The following year, 1599, he was to advise his young heir, Prince Henry Frederick, in the *Basilikon Doron*, to 'hold no Parliaments, but for the necessity of making new Lawes, which would be but seldom' (cat.19). Keep tight control over law-making, he said, 'for few Laws and well put in execution, are best in a well ruled commonwealth'.[8] In other words, do not give parliaments the opportunity to challenge your rule.

Having forcefully reminded his people of his absolute authority, James was also careful to couch it in his paternal affection to them. 'I protest before God, I do it with the fatherly love that I owe to them all', since a 'King towards his people is rightly compared to a father of children, and to a head of a body composed of diverse members'.[9] Since the 'head cares for the body, so does the King for his people', whose 'natural love to his children' spoke of 'the duty that Kings owe to their Subjects'.[10] In a patriarchal society, where accepted notions of

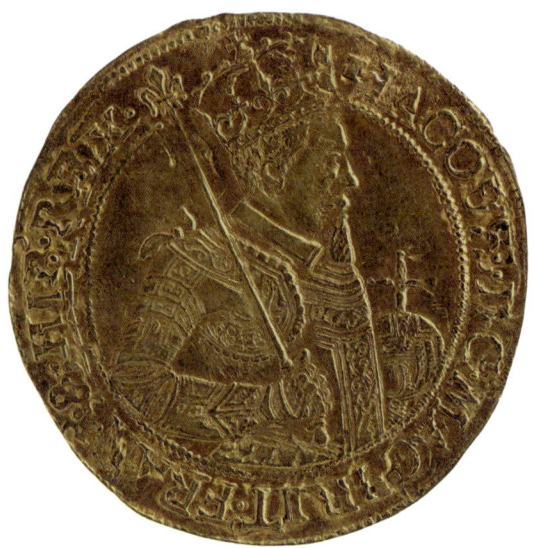
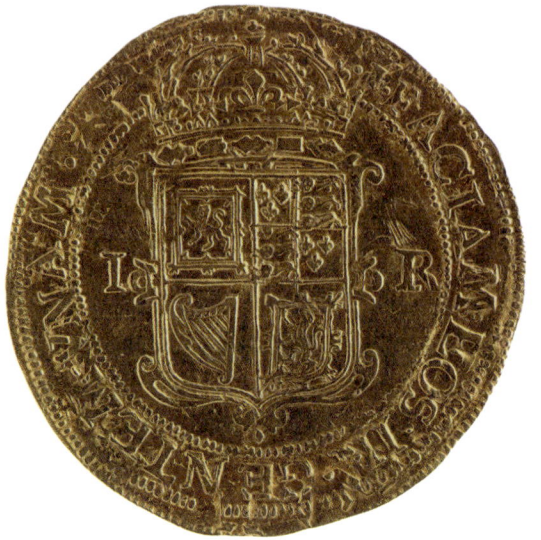

Cat.20
Unknown artist
'Unite' coin, between 1609 and 1625
Gold, 3.9 × 4 cm
National Museums Scotland, Edinburgh (H.C239)

PROVENANCE: Unknown.

REFERENCES: Stewart 1967, cat.204, p.103

the natural, civic and divine order reinforced the dominance of men, such a paternalistic framing of monarchy would have been understood. Presenting himself as the caring father of his subjects offered James a way to validate his power.

On the Anglo–Scottish Union

Nowhere was this imagery of the father as the unifying head of his disparate peoples more evident than in James's writings on Anglo–Scottish union. James's succession to Elizabeth's crowns of England and Ireland and the principality of Wales, in 1603, brought about a dynastic union known as the Union of the Crowns, an event celebrated by the striking of the gold Unite coin (cat.20). This was not full political union, as it would become in 1707. Parliaments, legal systems and churches remained unchanged in 1603. But union had taken place in the body of the king himself, now with three crowns on his one head. Repeatedly, James was to use the allegory of his body to signify the unity of his whole inheritance, a monarchy composed of multiple kingdoms.

James's big project after 1603 was to achieve fuller and amicable union, proposing a political union, yes, but also one of hearts and minds. He asked the Scottish people to accept the English 'as their dearest brethren & friends' and 'to obliterate and remove out of their minds all quarrels' and to pursue a 'universal unanimity of hearts'.[11] Of

both countries, he desired 'a perfect Union of laws and persons' that would 'make one body of both Kingdoms under me your king'.[12]

Union for James was self-evident. England and Scotland were joined together both territorially, and by his kingship of both. 'These two countries being separated neither by Sea, nor great River, Mountain, nor another' were previously divided, he said, only in people's perceptions rather than reality. Britain was one island, and thus 'within itself has almost none but imaginary bounds of separation … making the whole a little world within itself'. Now, under James, the kingdoms were united in his own person. Therefore, as he intoned to the English parliament in 1604, 'What God has joined then let no man separate. I am the husband and the whole isle is my lawful Wife; I am the head and it is my body; I am the shepherd and it is my flock.'[13] Paternal images of his body uniting England and Scotland were used to portray a new Great Britain.

For James, the advantages of such union were obvious. Firstly, it brought peace among former enemies. It was, he said, a 'blessed union', 'the blessings [of] which God hath in my Person bestowed upon you all'.[14] Secondly, a united England and Scotland would be more powerful together than separate. Union was like 'Two snow-balls put together, [which] make the one greater: Two houses joined, make one the larger; two Castle walls made

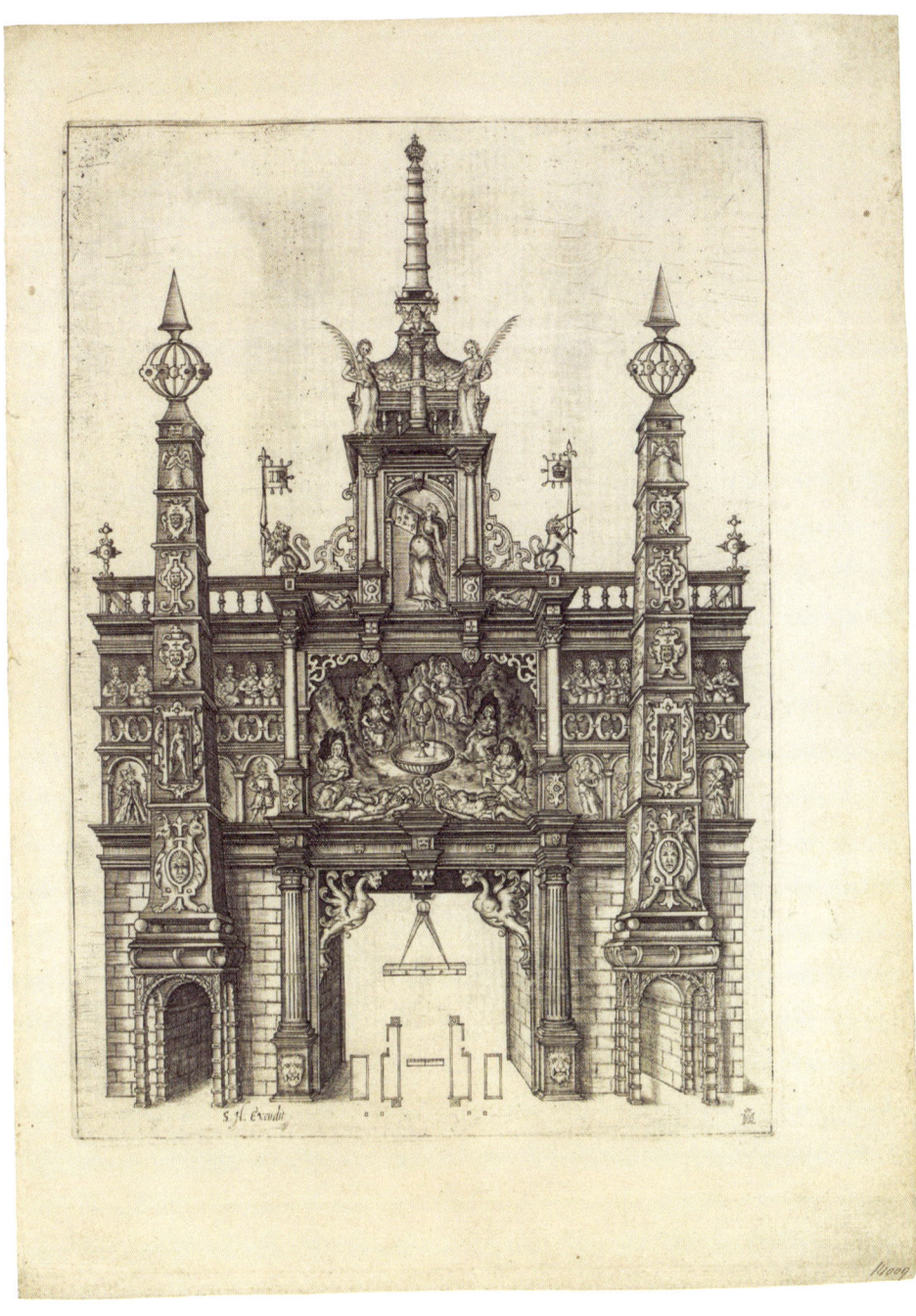

Cat.21
William Kip (active *c*.1598–1635), after Stephen Harrison (active *c*.1603)
The New Arabia from *'The Arch's [sic] of Triumph' Depicting the Series of Temporary Arches Erected in London on the 15th of March 1604, in Honour of James I's Ceremonial Entrance and Passage Through the City to Parliament*, 1604
Engraving, sheet 35.8 × 25.7 cm

Victoria and Albert Museum, London (14009)

PROVENANCE: Purchased in 1856.

REFERENCES: Nichols 1831, p.64; Berlin 1939, cat.2978; Hind 1952–64, vol.II, pp.17–34, 210–11

in one, makes one as thick and strong as both'.[15] And thirdly, it was a union of two similar peoples: 'Has not God first united these two Kingdoms both in Language, Religion, and similitude of manners?', in their experience of a Protestant Reformation, their similar languages and codes of behaviour.[16] The message of unity underlay the triumphal arches on James's royal entry into London (cat.21).

Unfortunately for James's union project, the professed similarity of the two peoples did not convince everyone. The Scots language and English differed significantly, and so did the types of Protestant religions in each kingdom: a stricter Calvinist version in Scotland, and what became the Anglican settlement in England. Successive English parliaments resisted James's attempts at greater political union, and Scottish parliaments were concerned to protect the equality of Scotland's status. No Scottish parliament in the early 1600s would agree to the surrendering of Scots law to English, and no English parliament would allow any tampering with their ancient laws. James claimed to be able to rule Scotland in his absence after 1603: 'Here I sit and I govern it with my pen, I write and it is done … which others could not do by the sword'.[17] But the reality of governing three separate kingdoms was to prove more tricky.

The difficulty of uniting two formerly hostile nations in a supposedly equal partnership was evident in 1604 in the disputed design of the new union flag (cat.22). Here you can see the battle over the representation of each kingdom's status in the differing prominence of Scotland's St Andrew's cross and the English cross of St George. The unity suggested by the Unite coin (cat.20), with the motto on its reverse of 'FACIAM EOS IN GENTEM UNAM' (I will make them one nation), remained more in James's writings than in reality. As a result, in October 1604, he was forced to proclaim himself King of Great Britain, because the English parliament had refused to do so.

As a Father

James wrote about his paternal duties not only to his newly joined nations, but to his children too. Most notable was his fatherly advice on kingship, among other things, in his *Basilikon Doron*, first published privately in 1599 and given

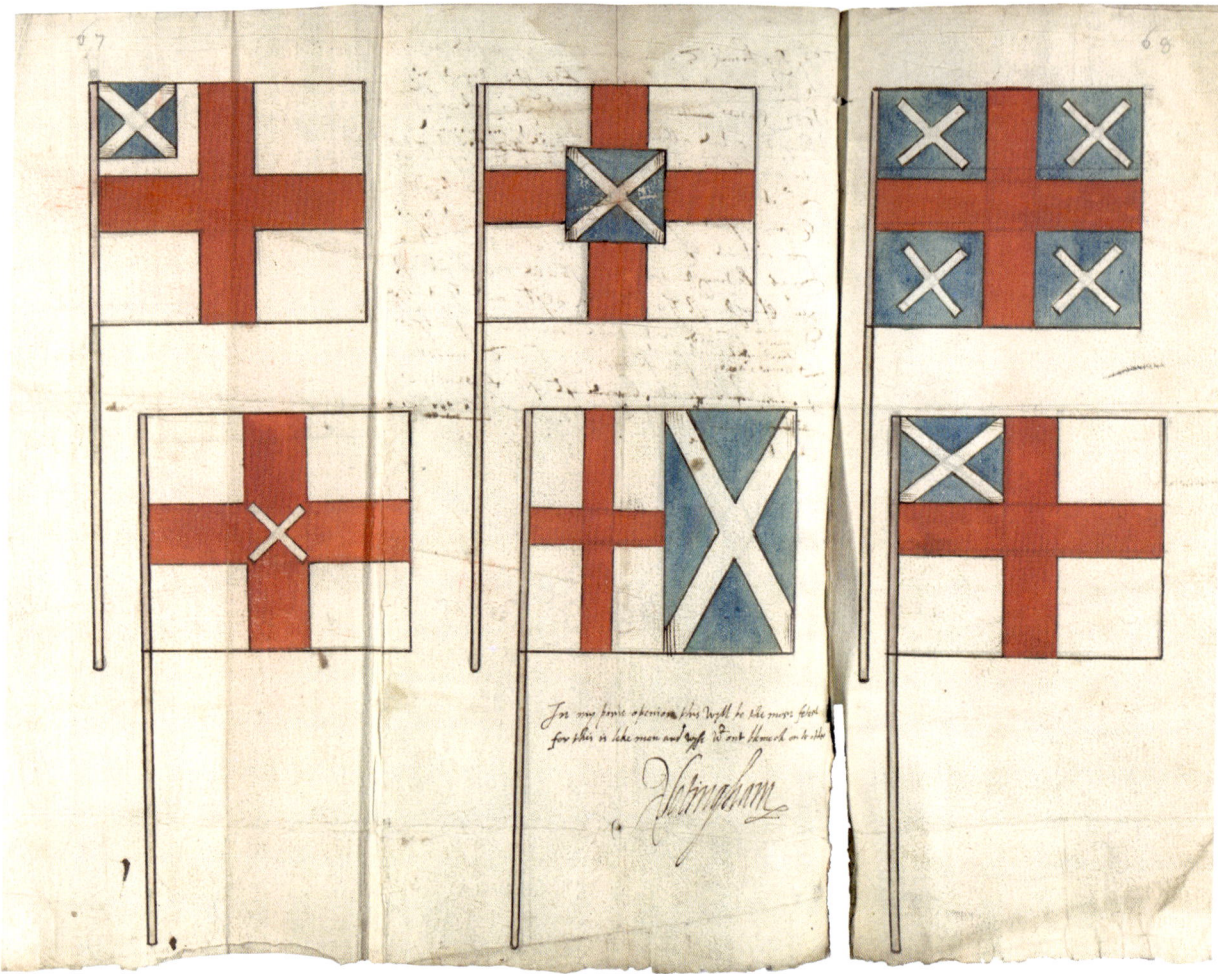

Cat.22
Unknown artist
Designs for the Union Flag, 1604
Ink and watercolour on paper,
40.5 × 53.5 cm
National Library of Scotland,
Edinburgh (MS.2517 ff.67–68)

PROVENANCE: Purchased from
Bernard Quaritch Ltd, 1938.

REFERENCES: Edinburgh 1975,
p.18, cat.98

to five friends, his wife, and his son Prince Henry Frederick. James portrayed himself as a concerned father, protecting the future good rule of his people. As he penned in his dedicatory sonnet to Prince Henry in the first 1599 edition:

> Lo here (my Sonne) a mirror viue and faire,
> Which sheweth the shadow of a worthy King …
> Your father bids you studie here and reede.
> How to become a perfite King indeede.[18]

Kings, James said, should look like kings: 'looking gravely and with a majesty when you sit in judgement, or give audience to Ambassadors; homely when you are private with your own servants; and let your countenance smell of courage and magnamity when you are at war'.

Bodily exercise was important for his son's health, such as running, dancing, wrestling or tennis, but he was to avoid 'rough and violent' exercises such as football. The best form of exercise was on horseback, in jousting and hunting with hounds. He should be cautious in gambling, and only play at cards not dice. He should choose his friends carefully: 'honest persons, not defamed or vicious, mixing filthy talk with merriness'. And he should also be learned, with knowledge of the Scriptures, the classics, of history, mathematics and the laws.[19]

The advice grew ever more intimate. A king should eat modestly and avoid gluttony, maintaining good manners at the table. He should dress as the occasion demanded, and avoid being 'effeminate in your clothes, in perfuming, preening or such like'. Dress modestly, he said, 'not artificially trimmed and decked like a Courtesan, yet not overly sluggish clothed like a country clown; not overly lightly like a Candy soldier, nor a vain young Courtier'. Do not make 'a fool of yourself in wearing long hair or nails'.[20]

Most intimately, James told his son that he should avoid 'the idle company of dames' before marriage. It was his duty to find a good wife, to avoid the temptations of lust and to provide for the succession. In choosing a wife, she should be of similar religion and status, and not have any hereditary defects. Here James perhaps betrayed his own priorities, in counselling that 'if a man will be careful to breed horses and dogs of good kinds, how much more careful should he be' in his own procreations. He should take good care of his wife, who was his to command being of the frailer sex, and he should avoid the 'filthy vice of adultery'.[21] James's own relationship with Anna has come under much scrutiny, and one wonders how much of his own advice he took.

On Religion

James's life was imbued with religion and his religious duty. He is renowned for his commissioning of a new translation of the Bible, the *King James Bible*, published in 1611 and still in use today. His writings included much on religion, on his personal faith, on managing the church, and on doctrine. As a young man, in 1588, he published *Ane Fruitfull Meditatioun [on] … the Reuelatioun in Forme of ane Sermone*, calling for godly behaviour in the face of the threat posed by the Catholic Counter-Reformation. In 1589 another meditation appeared, on the Bible's 'Chronicles of the Kings'. Others were to follow, the *Workes* containing 'A Praemonition to all Christian Monarches, Free Princes and States'. He was positioning himself as the defender of the Protestant faith in Europe, and as a '*Rex Pacificus*', a peacekeeper, in his diplomatic attempts to resolve dangerous confessional enmities.

The most controversial perhaps of his views on religion were related to his homeland, Scotland, and the sterner Presbyterian element of the Scottish kirk. In *Basilikon Doron*, he wrote that they 'fantasise to themselves a Democratic form of government', with 'Parity [equality] in the church', which he described as the 'mother of confusion'

and an 'enemy to Unity'. In this, he advised his son to 'contain them well'.[22] James was writing in the aftermath of an infamous confrontation with the Presbyterian minister Andrew Melville at Falkland Palace in 1596 over the extent of royal authority in the kirk. Here, Melville had grabbed James's sleeve, shaking it, telling him that there were two kingdoms in Scotland: one, the secular, in which James was king; the other, the religious sphere, in which James was but 'God's silly vassal'.

James expended much energy in insisting on his rights as earthly head of the kirk. In 1606, he reintroduced bishops against the will of the Presbyterians, and in 1618, in the face of much opposition, the notorious 'Five Articles of Perth' attempted to reverse the more Presbyterian elements of liturgical practice in the Scottish kirk. In publishing his opinions, he also opened them up to an unprecedentedly wide scrutiny and gave fodder to those who opposed his high-church or Anglican doctrines.

On Demons and Witches

But perhaps of more lasting notoriety was James's work, *Daemonologie*, on the terrors in this life of Satan and his witches, and what one had to do to identify and resist them (cat.23). This book, first published in Edinburgh in 1597, was written in the maelstrom of fear following the prosecution of supposed witches at North Berwick for allegedly stirring up a tempest at sea as James returned from collecting his bride, Queen Anna, from Denmark. James was personally involved in the interrogation and probable torture of the accused, and there is an intense vehemence in his writing on them.

He explained that the 'fearful abounding at this time in this country, of these detestable slaves of the Devil, the Witches or enchanters' had moved him to write *Daemonologie*. Witches, he said, were enticed, either for revenge or worldly riches, to hurt men and their possessions to satisfy their cruel minds. They did this in the service of Satan himself, their 'false Master', 'the devil as God's Ape'.[23] He went on to debate whether witches could fly, how they might be transformed into beasts or birds, and why only a twentieth of witches are male (because the female 'sex is frailer than man is, so it is easier to be entrapped in these gross snares of the devil').[24]

To cure this evil, he wrote that it was necessary to pursue these 'instruments of Satan' to their death, and lawful magistrates should 'be diligent in examining and punishing of them'.[25] He prayed to 'God to purge this country of these devilish practices: for they were never so rife in these parts, as they are now'.[26] If James had not been a king, the significance of these writings would have been limited, but as regal writings they had real-world consequences. There was an immediate wave of witchcraft prosecutions, and a series of witch-hunts followed.

On Gunpowder and Tobacco

If witches and devils had terrified James into print, the immediate physical threat of the Gunpowder Plot of 1605 (cat.84) had a similar effect. Against a violent background of the Counter-Reformation sweeping across Europe, fears of a Catholic uprising at home were inflamed by this attempt to blow up many of England's Protestant ruling elite, including the king at Westminster. Writing in the third person, James described the plot: 'so the earth as it were opened, should have sent forth of the bottom of the *Stygian* lake such sulphured smoke, furious flames, and fearful thunder, as should have by their diabolical *Domesday* destroyed and defaced, in the twinkling of an eye' not only the king, his son and lords, but also parliament and the halls of justice. His gripping account of its discovery offers a curious insight into his awareness of a reputation for paranoia; he feared ridicule if the plot proved only an 'evaporation of an idle brain'. Thus the search party sent to discover the gunpowder 'should be under colour of seeking for Wardrobe stuff'.[27] He did not want to be seen as a cowardly king.

James carefully emphasised the plot's religious motivations, a diabolic Catholic plan intended 'for the utter extinguishing of our true Christian profession'. This was a plot not just to kill the king, he said, but to overthrow the Protestant faith in England, a danger which threatened the entire population. As Guido Fawkes confessed, 'he was moved only for Religion and conscience sake, denying the King to be his lawful Sovereign' since 'he was a Heretic'.[28] James was playing here to a public gallery in order to turn fear of the Catholic

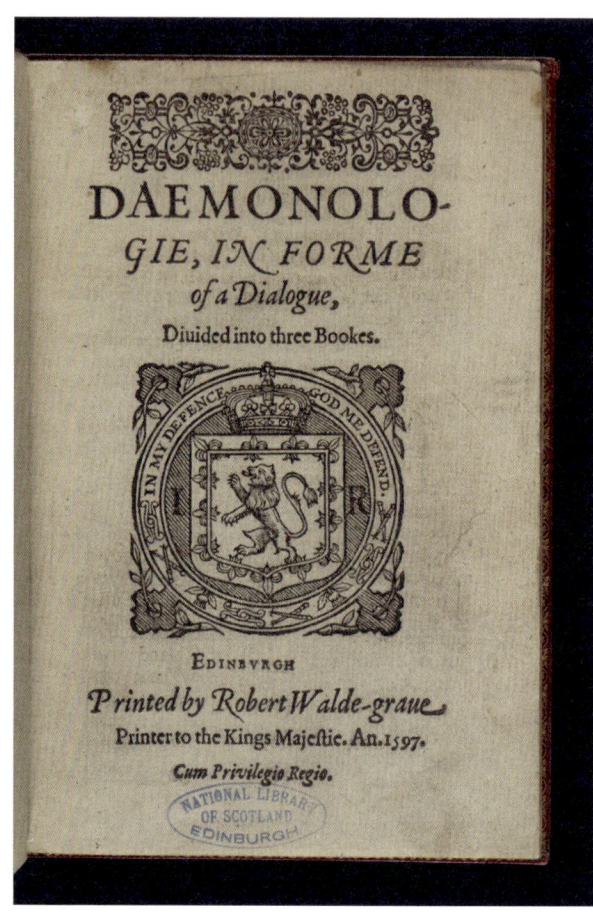

Cat.23
Written by James VI & I (1566–1625)
Daemonologie, 1597
Printed book, 17.5 × 10.5 cm, 81 pages
National Library of Scotland, Edinburgh (L.C.1499)

PROVENANCE: Bequeathed by Mr and Mrs William Robert Reid, 1926.

REFERENCES: Aldis 1904, p.296

'enemy under the bed' into support for him in defence of Protestantism.

In his writings, James presents himself as the protector of his people, their faith, their peace, their justice. In his *A Counterblast to Tobacco* of 1604 (cat.24), he protects their health as well, advising against the 'manifold abuses of this vile custom of *Tobacco* taking' and its 'bewitching quality'. There 'cannot be a more base, and yet hurtful, corruption in a Country, than is the vile use of taking *Tobacco*' which had 'moved me, shortly to discover the abuses thereof'. He described smoking as a 'custom loathsome to the eye, hateful to the Nose, harmful to the brain, dangerous to the Lungs and in the black stinking fume thereof, nearest resembling the horrible Stygian smoke'. He equated his efforts to counter this to good rule more generally: where a kingdom ails, for the 'remedy whereof, it is the *Kings* part (as the proper Physician of his Politic-body) to purge

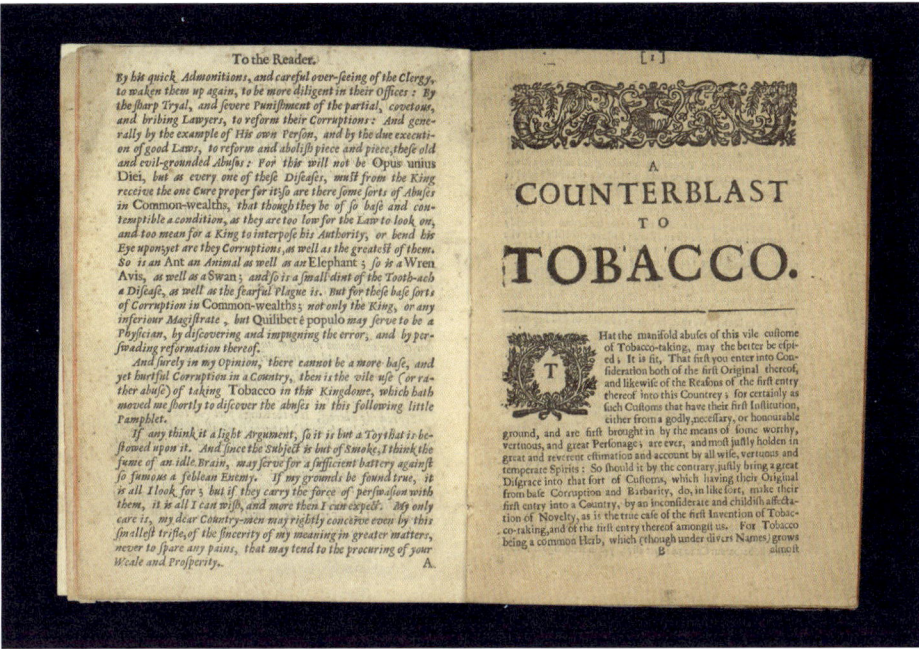

Cat.24
Written by James VI & I
(1566–1625)
A Counterblast to Tobacco,
1604, in a later edition of 1672
Printed book, 19 × 11.5 cm,
72 pages
National Library of Scotland,
Edinburgh (RB.s.1492)

PROVENANCE: Purchased at
Sotheby's, London, 22 July 1988,
lot 273.

it of all those diseases'. In doing so, he would be sure 'never to spare any pain, that may tend to the procuring of your health and prosperity'.[29]

His lengthy argument refuted the alleged restorative properties of tobacco, ranting against the 'hateful smell' that ruined dining, its expense, and its addictive nature: many now had 'such a continual use of taking this unsavoury smoke, as now they are not able to forbear the same, no more than an old drunkard can abide to be long sober'. It was a barbarous habit that would kill you: a man could 'smoke himself to death with it' since it 'makes a kitchen … in the inward parts of men, soiling and infecting them, with an unctuous and oily kind of Soot, as hath been found in some great *Tobacco* takers, that after their death were opened'.[30] James was centuries ahead of his time

on tobacco's evils, his banning of its use at court an early forerunner of the current ban on smoking in public places.

The Dangers of Writing Monarchy

James's publications coincided with an exponential increase in the numbers of manuscripts going into print as handbills, pamphlets or books. Suddenly, works that would have previously only been available in a few circulating handwritten texts were being published for much wider audiences. When James came south in 1603, his *Basilikon Doron* was rushed into mass publication, with an estimated 13,000 to 16,000 copies printed in the first few months of his English reign.[31] Even if you were not literate, you could still hear a king's thoughts when one of the thousands of its owners read it aloud at home, in a tavern, or in a religious meeting. As importantly, you could also form your own opinions on the claims he made, say, for his divine kingly powers.

So, while James used the printing press to promulgate his monarchical authority (and profess his care for his people), ironically he was losing control over how that wider audience received and re-used his words. Publishing mattered to James as a tool of monarchy, but it was a double-edged sword: it left his words open to manipulation by those who disagreed with him. His oeuvre became a problematic legacy for his son Charles I, who took James's advice on the rights of kingship too literally. Unlike James, Charles appeared not to understand that the stated ideals of absolute monarchy were in reality dependent on negotiation and compromise. Four centuries later, we too stand guilty at times of taking James's writings at face value. He said he was an absolute king, but he knew he was not.

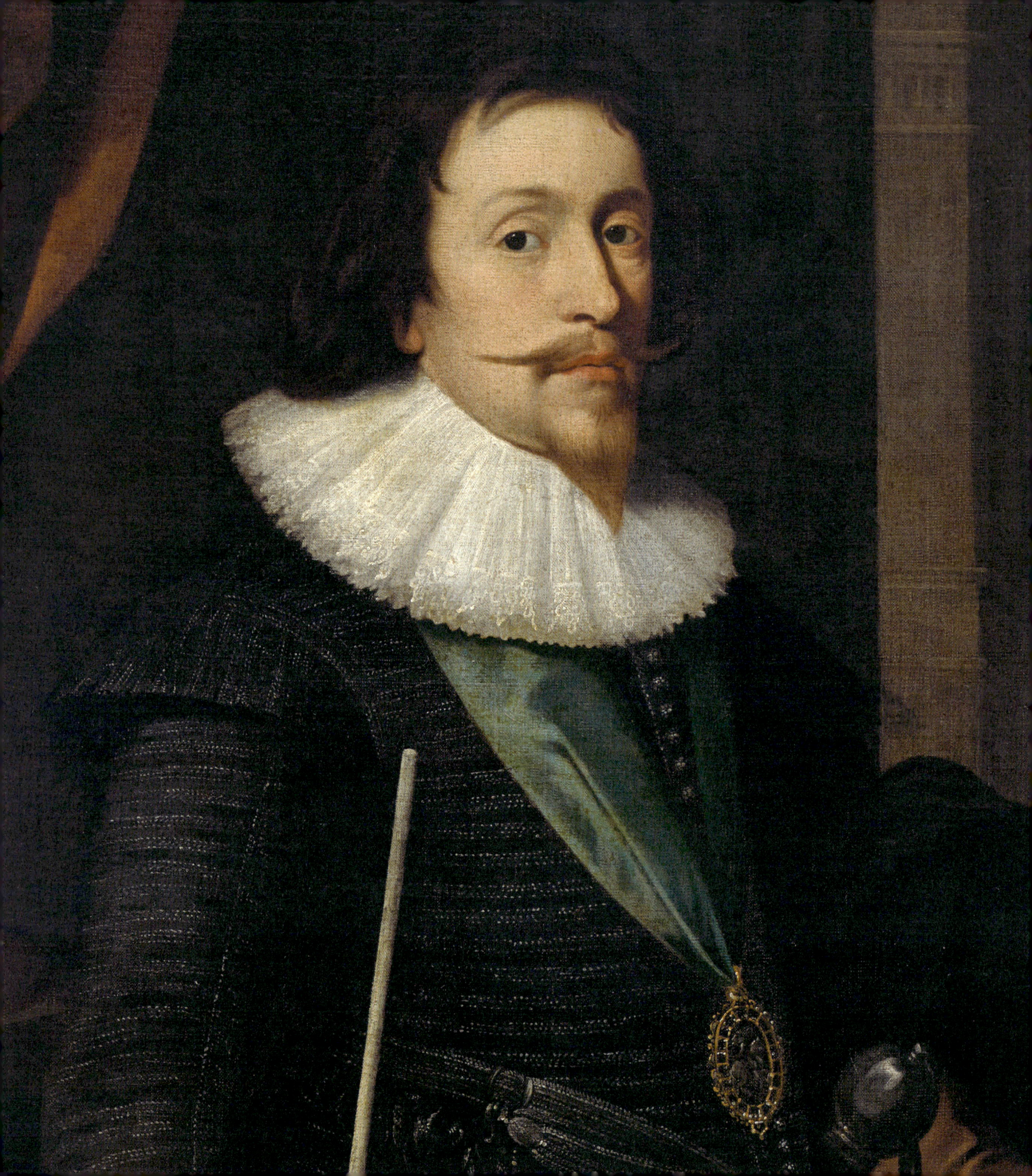

PAINTERS AND SCOTTISH PATRONS AT THE LONDON COURT OF JAMES VI & I, 1603-25

Karen Hearn

THE YEARS OF JAMES VI'S REIGN AS JAMES I of Great Britain have sometimes been viewed by art historians as artistically unadventurous. It is true that, owing to gaps in the documentary record, many facts about art production in Jacobean Britain are not known. Nevertheless, surviving paintings, miniatures and funerary sculpture of the period reveal that it was, in fact, remarkably rich and productive. While much attention has been focused on art patronage and collecting at the court of James's son, Charles I, and his queen Henrietta Maria, many key artistic initiatives took place during James's reign at the royal court in London.[1]

Indeed, it was during James's years as British ruler that the young Anthony van Dyck (1599–1641) first came to work in London from October 1620 to February 1621, and that initial discussions subsequently took place with the Flemish superstar painter Sir Peter Paul Rubens (1577–1640) in Antwerp, about the commission for an immense painted decoration for the ceiling of James's new Banqueting House at Whitehall Palace. On 13 September 1621, Rubens wrote to James's agent in Brussels: 'regarding the hall in the New Palace, I confess that I am, by natural instinct, better fitted to execute very large works than small curiosities'.[2] The commission for Rubens to design and paint this still extant ceiling would finally be clinched in 1629–30, when Rubens visited Charles I in London (fig.18). Moreover, it was under James, and Anna, that a serious interest in art collecting became a marker of elite status at court.[3]

Portraits in Diplomacy

James has often been characterised as reluctant to sit for his portrait, and consequently as uninterested in self-presentation, but the considerable number of versions and copies of certain portraits of James – especially those produced in, or deriving from ones produced in, the London workshop headed by John de Critz the Elder (c.1550–1642) – give the lie to that.[4] The records of payments for royal portraits to be sent abroad for diplomatic purposes make it clear that James perfectly understood the importance of participating in international exchanges of portraits. As Sir Oliver Millar first noted, by the middle of his reign in England, James's palaces displayed numerous and diverse portraits, many of them full-lengths, and English, Scottish, German and French in origin.[5] Among these were also full-length companion portraits of the rulers of the Spanish Netherlands, the Archdukes Albert and Isabella, which the Flemish ambassador Charles de Ligne, Duke of Arenberg, had presented to Anna in 1603;[6] two newly painted full-lengths of Philip III of Spain and his queen, Margaret of Austria (fig.19), produced by Pantoja de la Cruz (1553–1608) in 1605 and delivered to England in 1606 (with a now-lost portrait of the couple's daughter the Infanta Ana);[7] and a full-length of the French king Henri IV, which was sent to London in 1611.[8] There were also 'portraits of the queen's German and Danish relations and of Scots and English courtiers'.[9] Indeed, once James and Anna had come to the throne, the London painters were kept busy, since portraits were now required not simply of a single monarch – Elizabeth I – but of a king and a consort and, increasingly, of their three surviving children, Henry Frederick, Elizabeth and Charles.

This was also the era of the spectacular full-length seated or, more commonly, standing portrait, which proliferated in Britain during James's reign. The format had become fashionable there during Elizabeth I's final decade. On mainland Europe, it was generally reserved for members of the ruling families – as in the international examples cited above – but in England it was adopted by a broader range of members of the British elite.[10]

Moreover, perhaps paradoxically, the tiny portrait miniature, painted in watercolour and gouache on vellum stuck to card, was more popular in Britain than anywhere else in Europe (cats 55–57). Miniatures made easily portable personal and diplomatic gifts, and portrait miniatures of James and members of his family are recorded in international exchanges.[11]

Numerous overseas-trained painters were active among the migrant artisans in Elizabethan London. Following the advance of the Reformation, many

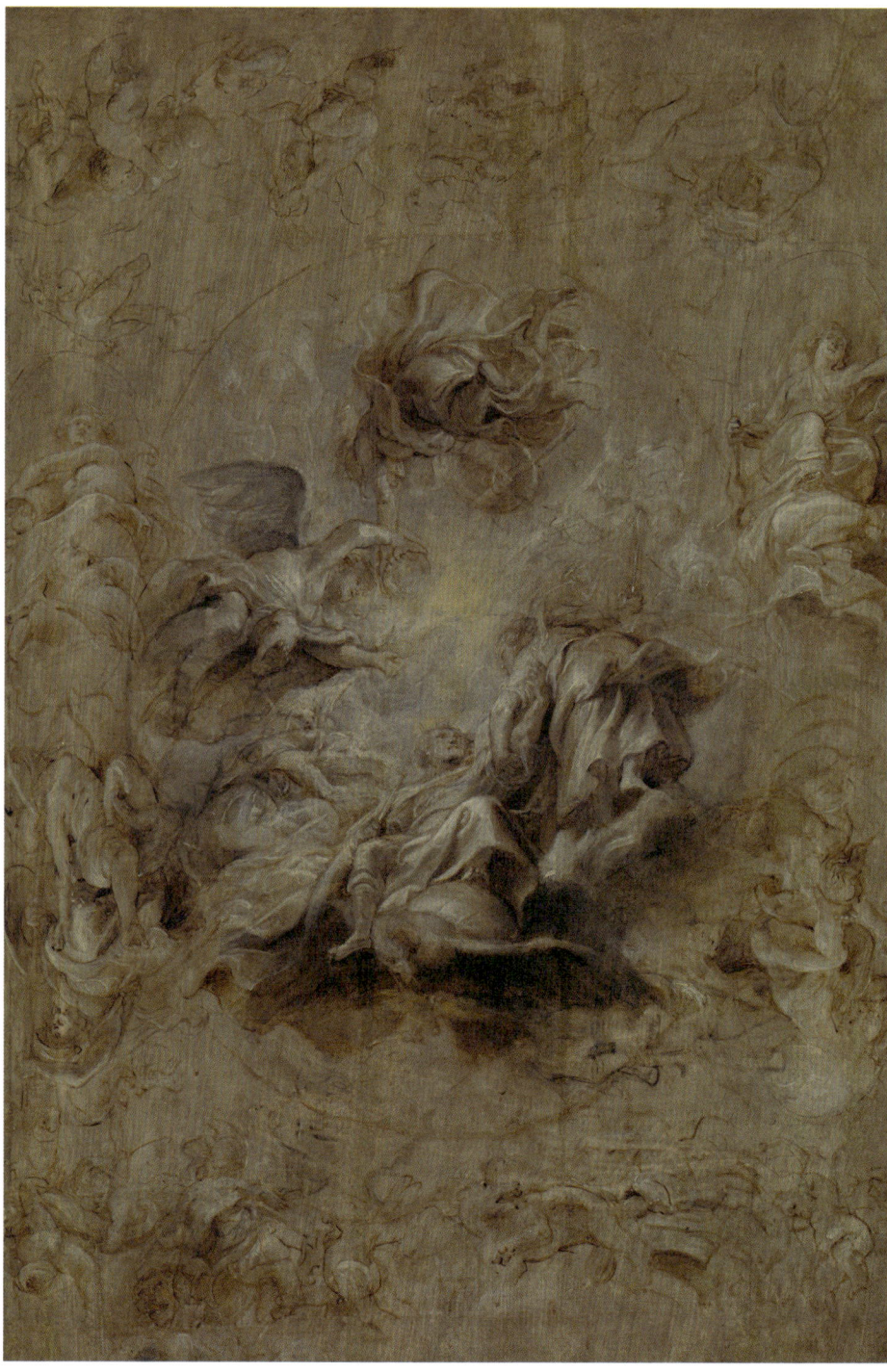

Fig.18
Peter Paul Rubens (1577–1640)
The Apotheosis of James I and Other Studies: Multiple Sketches for the Banqueting House Ceiling, Whitehall, 1628–30
Oil on oak panel, 95 × 63.1 cm
Tate (T12919)

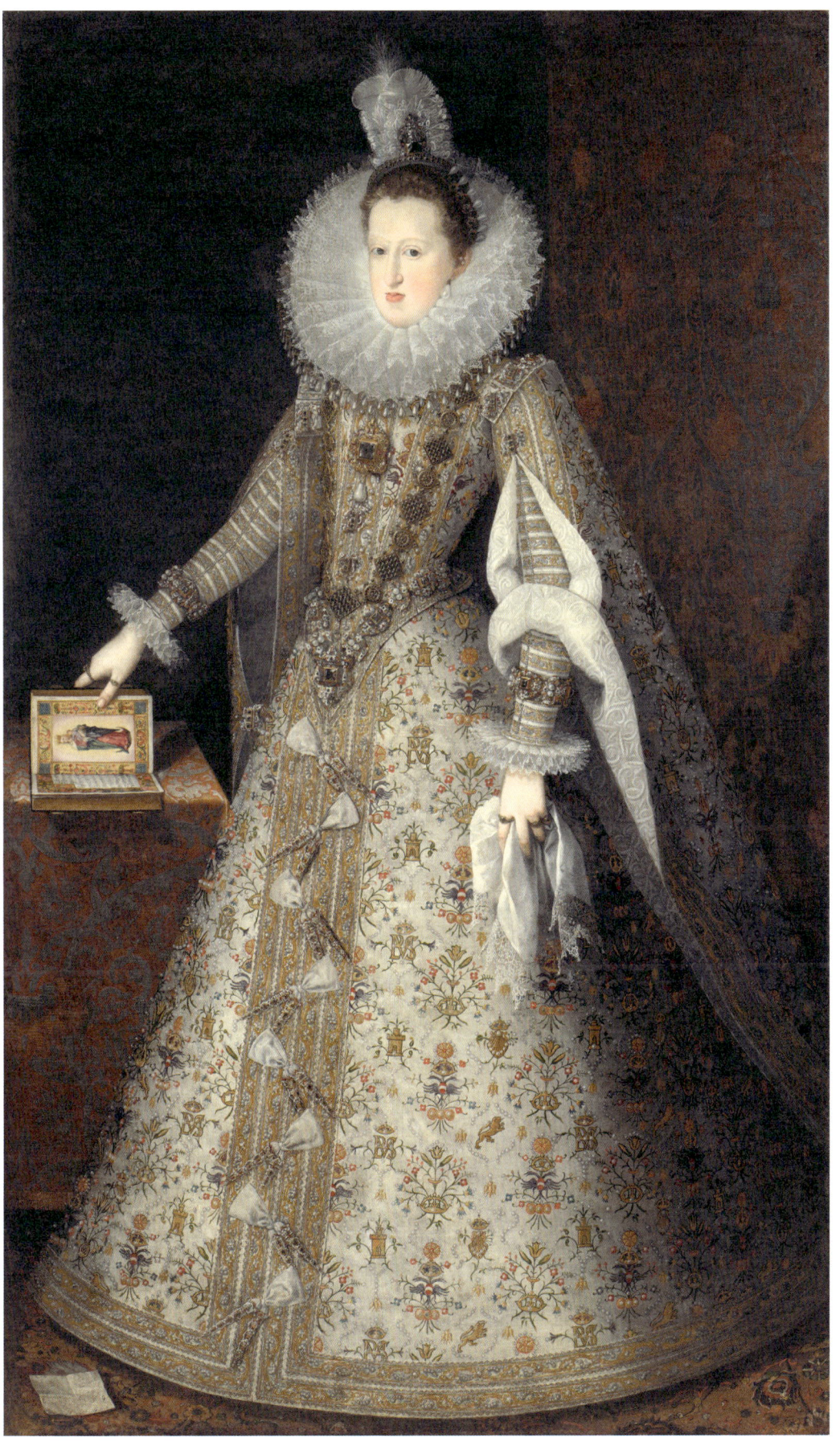

Fig.19
Pantoja de la Cruz (1553–1608)
Margaret of Austria, Consort of Philip III of Spain, 1605
Oil on canvas, 204.6 × 121.2 cm
Royal Collection Trust / His Majesty King Charles III (RCIN 404970)

well-trained peripatetic painters came initially from the Southern Netherlands (which remained Catholic), especially from Antwerp, but as the early seventeenth century advanced, a number also came from the Northern Netherlands (where the majority held Protestant beliefs). Indeed, James's more international outlook, after the comparative political isolation of the latter years of Elizabeth's reign, would in due course mean the arrival in London of a new group of Netherlandish painters in the second decade of his reign as King of Great Britain.[12]

By 1603, the successful portrait-painters of the 1590s were no longer young men. They included John de Critz and Marcus Gheeraerts the Younger (1562–1636), both the sons of Protestant parents who had fled to London from the Southern Netherlands. De Critz had been brought from Antwerp as a baby to London, where he had been trained by the Flemish-born and -trained exiled artist and poet Lucas de Heere (1534–1584).[13] De Critz established a workshop in London in the early 1590s, and gained the powerful patronage of Robert Cecil, later 1st Earl of Salisbury; this is thought to have influenced James's decision to grant him the promise of the key office of Serjeant Painter on 17 September 1603. On 25 April 1604, De Critz applied for denization (a form of naturalisation), and after the death of the in-post Serjeant Painter, Leonard Fryer the Elder, in 1605, he took up the post formally. As early as 1603–04, the London Merchant-Taylors' Company paid De Critz for producing 'pictures' of Elizabeth I, James (cat.7), Anna (fig.12) and Prince Henry Frederick – suggesting that he had hit the ground running in terms of access to the new royal family. However, in 1608 it was reported that De Critz had lost his sight and was no longer able to paint himself.[14]

The *Somerset House Conference* Painting

One of the iconic – and indeed largest – paintings of the early years following James's English accession, *The Somerset House Conference* (fig.20), is also one of the most anomalous and mysterious. There are two versions of this enormous group portrait on canvas, but the National Portrait Gallery (NPG) one includes a small number of *pentimenti* (changes made in the course of producing a painting) which suggests that it is the (or an)

original, while the version in the Royal Museums Greenwich appears to be an early copy of it, probably made in Spain.[15]

Following the deaths of Philip II of Spain in 1598, and of Elizabeth I early in 1603, their royal successors James, Philip III of Spain, and the Archdukes Albert and Isabella in Flanders, driven by financial pressures, decided to discuss peace terms. Accordingly, during the summer of 1604, a group of commissioners came to England for a conference that met in eighteen sessions from late May to mid-July at Somerset House, on the River Thames, which James had lavishly furnished for the purpose. Under discussion were English trade with Spain, the Spanish territories in America and the Netherlands; English support for the Protestant rebels in the Northern (Dutch) Netherlands; religious toleration in England for Roman Catholics; and an easing of the Spanish Inquisition's control of English Protestants abroad. Once agreement had been reached, the absent leader of the Habsburg delegation, Juan Fernández de Velasco, the Constable of Castile, set off from Flanders for London, where the ceremony of swearing the peace treaty took place on Sunday 19 August, followed by a spectacular banquet. The following year, 1605, Charles Howard, 1st Earl of Nottingham, led a delegation to Spain to ratify the treaty in Valladolid with Philip III, amid opulent celebrations there.[16]

Who painted this remarkable group portrait? The 'signature' of the Spanish painter Pantoja de la Cruz on it, bottom left, can be discounted, as it differs from his customary style and wording, and seems to have been added a little later. It must have been painted in Britain, probably by more than one artist in collaboration. The composition has a number of Netherlandish elements. The heads of most of the five British delegation members, seated on the right, are based on known discrete English portraits of them (in the case of the Earl of Nottingham, a portrait miniature).[17] It must have been commissioned by someone connected with the negotiations. The NPG version is first recorded in 1680, when it returned to Britain with the British envoy to Portugal, Francis Parry; by 1698 it was in the collection of the Dukes of Hamilton at Hamilton Palace, where it remained until 1882.

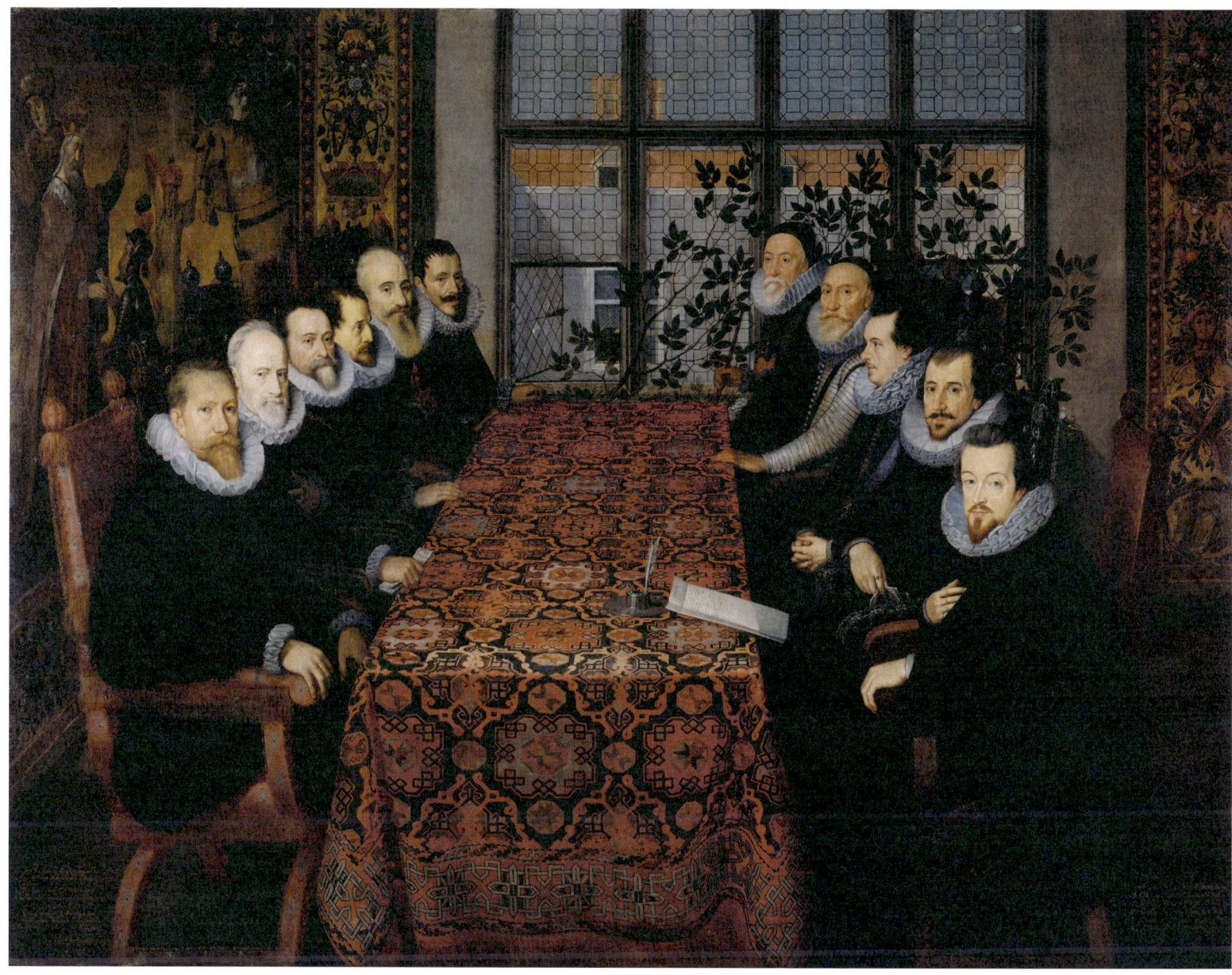

Fig.20
Unknown artist
The Somerset House
Conference, *c*.1604
Oil on canvas, 205.7 × 268 cm
National Portrait Gallery, London
(NPG 665)

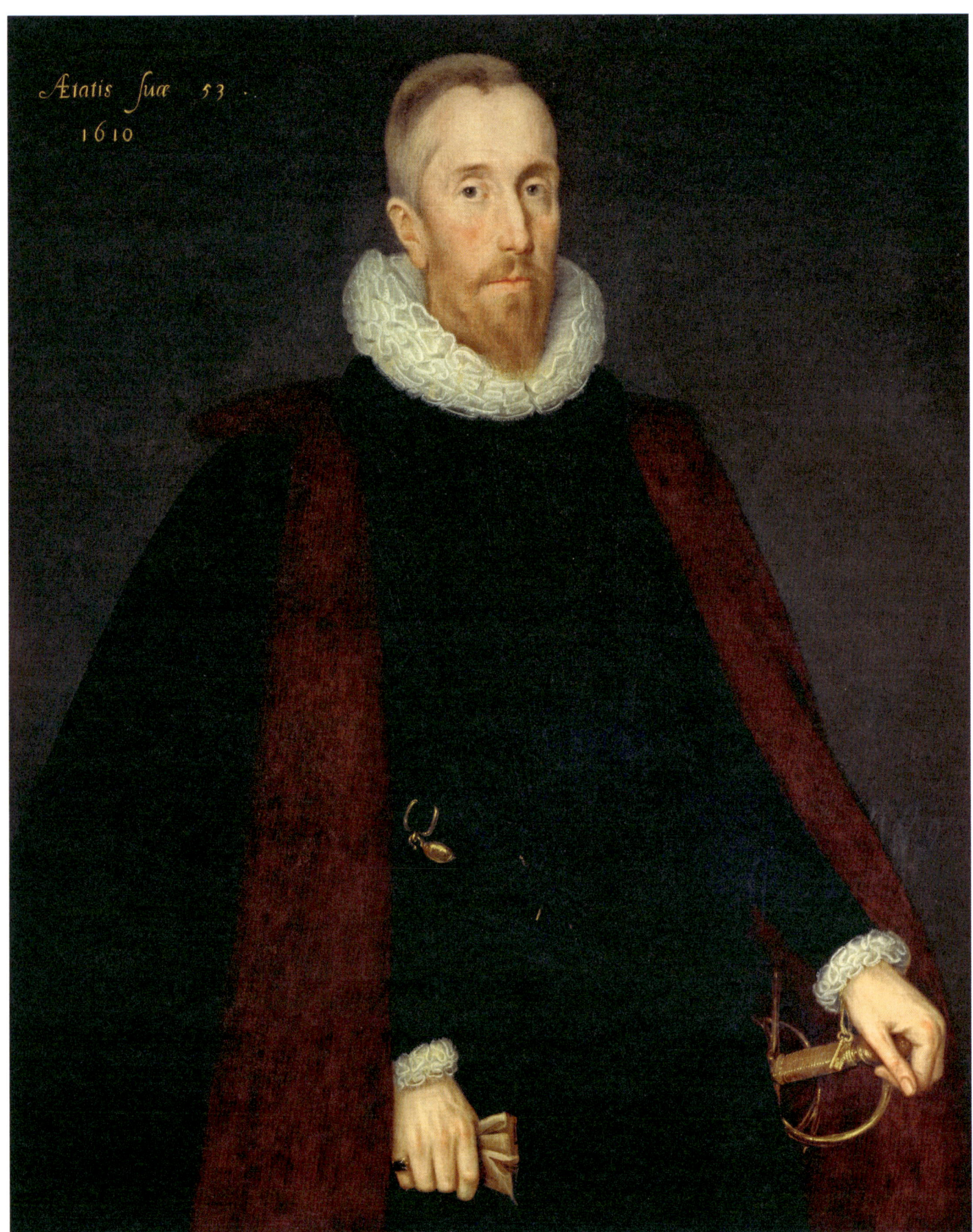

Ætatis ſuæ 53 ·
1610

Evidence suggests that there may at one stage have been more than one other copy of it. In the principal *pentimento* – one that suggests that it was in production around the time that all the delegates were physically present in London – the head of de Velasco (back left), the Habsburg delegation's leader, who only arrived in London on 10 August, has clearly been painted in (using a visibly different paint consistency) after the other heads. The inclusion in the picture of the standard De Critz workshop image of Robert Cecil (front right) has led to the suggestion that the painting may have been produced in that studio, although this is by no means certain. There is no reference to this picture in the royal accounts.

Portrait-painters in London in 1603

Painters who were born in England worked in London, too. Robert Peake the Elder (c.1551–1619) had trained as a goldsmith, and is first recorded working for the Office of Revels in 1576. The earliest documented payments to Peake for portraits were made in 1590. At the start of James's reign, the English 1st Baron Harington of Exton and his wife, who acted as guardians for Princess Elizabeth, seem to have commissioned from Peake a pair of companion full-length portraits of Prince Henry with Sir John Harington (Metropolitan Museum of Art, New York) and of Princess Elizabeth (National Museums Greenwich) in distinctive outdoor country settings. These marked the couple's new roles in the care of Princess Elizabeth; both paintings are dated 1603.[18] In 1607, Peake joined De Critz in the role of Serjeant Painter, and subsequently produced a number of full-length portraits of the royal children (cats 36, 38 and 39), for which payments are recorded in the royal accounts, although he does not seem to have painted either James or Anna.[19]

Marcus Gheeraerts the Younger had moved from Bruges to London with his family, as a child. While his artist father, Marcus Gheeraerts the Elder (c.1520–c.1590), returned to the Netherlands in the late 1580s, Gheeraerts the Younger seems to have remained in London, where he subsequently made his entire career. He painted the mature Elizabeth I about 1592, in the celebrated 'Ditchley' portrait (National Portrait Gallery, London) and

was subsequently employed by Anna of Denmark – as the Latin legend below the 1644 print after his (now lost) self-portrait of 1627 makes clear (in translation): 'Marcus Garrard the painter, in the service of the most illustrious and Serene Princes, Elizabeth and Anna, of blessed memory, Queens of Great Britain, France and Ireland'.[20] Portraits of Anna by Gheeraerts survive from about 1610 onwards.[21] In 1614, he was commissioned to paint a portrait of Tom Derry, or Durie, Anna's 'fool' or jester (cat.26).[22]

Following De Critz's loss of sight, Gheeraerts evidently became the painter of choice for portraits of members of the royal family for dispatch overseas. Records of payments are known for various pictures (some probably, from the size of the payments, full-lengths) that apparently no longer survive: £79 in 1611 for portraits of James, Anna and their daughter Elizabeth to go to the Margrave of Brandenburg; and in 1618, £85 for a set comprising James, Anna, Elizabeth and Charles, to a Polish destination.[23]

There was a healthy market for portraits of the Jacobean elite, both English and Scottish. There were new reasons to be painted, including marking the sitter's participation in a richly costumed court entertainment, or masque. There is evidence that Gheeraerts was especially popular with Scottish clients while they were in London. Alexander Seton, 1st Earl of Dunfermline (1555–1622), had been trusted by James with the education of his son Charles; and, in 1604, James appointed Seton Lord Chancellor in Scotland.[24] Seton remained in Edinburgh, but in September 1610 he visited London, where he was made a member of the English Privy Council, and evidently also took the opportunity to have his portrait painted by Gheeraerts (cat.25); it is inscribed 'Aetatis suae 53 / 1610'). Seton was back in Edinburgh by 4 December, when he presented a letter from James to the Scottish council, so he must have sat for this remarkably penetrating image during that autumn.[25] Seton was a scholar, a patron of writers and an innovative builder who had the ceiling of his long gallery at Pinkie House near Edinburgh painted with a complex programme of emblems, heraldic arms, Latin texts and trompe-l'œil decoration.[26] Also by Marcus

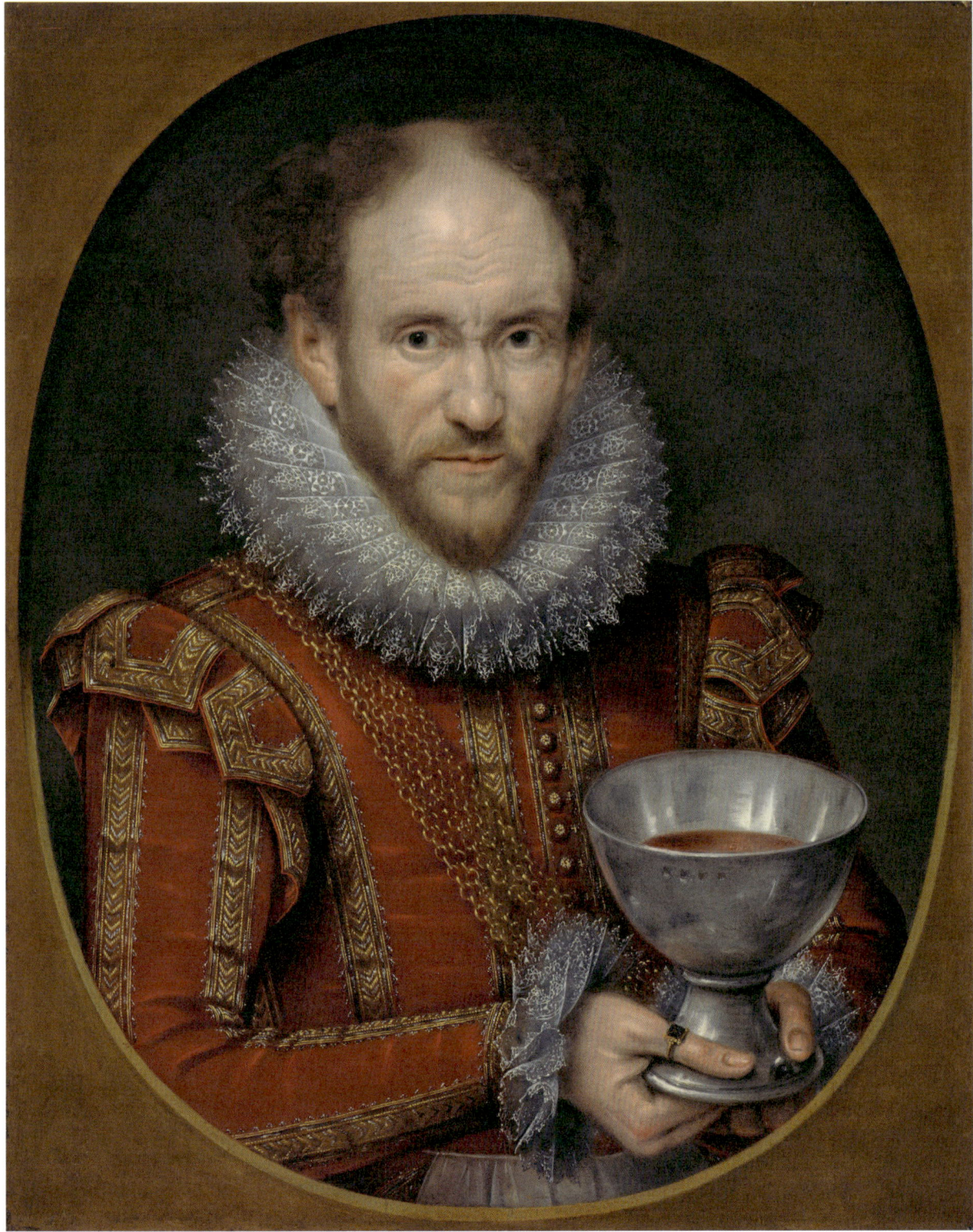

**Marcus Gheeraerts the Younger
(1562–1636)**
*Tom Derry, Jester to Anne
of Denmark*, 1614
Oil on panel, 71.4 × 57.9 cm
National Galleries of Scotland,
Edinburgh (PG 1111)

PROVENANCE: Collection of
Charles I; 18 June 1859 sale by
T. Nisbet, Edinburgh which
included part of the collection
of Colonel Ferguson; Rt Hon.
John Inglis, Edinburgh by 1884;
bequeathed by A.W. Inglis, 1929.

REFERENCES: Edinburgh 1884,
cat.33 (as Sir David Murray,
Viscount Stormont); Edinburgh
1959, p.36, cat.98 (as Sir David
Murray, Viscount Stormont);
Millar 1960, p.197; Millar 1972,
p.67; Edinburgh 1975, cat.22, p.11
(as Sir David Murray, Viscount
Stormont); London 1995, cat.131,
p.194; SNPG 2014, p.20; Leighton
2015, pp.112–13

Fig.21 (opposite)
**Studio of William Larkin
(c.1580–1619)**
*James Hay, 1st Earl of Carlisle
(1580–1636), c.1618–19*
Oil on canvas, 220.5 × 130.5 cm
Weiss Gallery, London

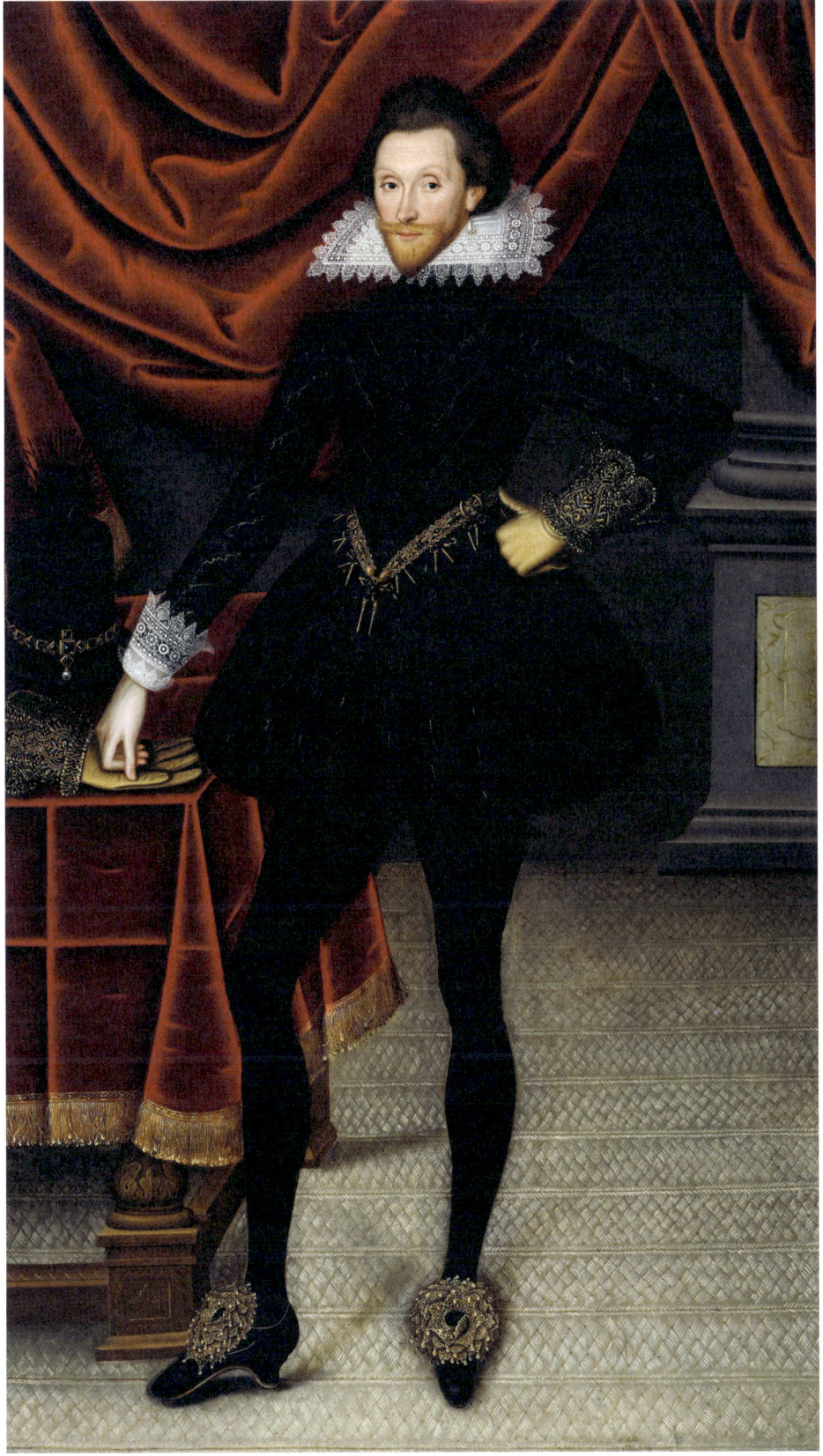

Gheeraerts the Younger, or from his workshop, is a surviving portrait of Seton's wife Margaret Hay, Countess of Dunfermline.

Scots who were based in London and were interested in their own self-presentation included James Hay, Earl of Carlisle (c.1580–1636).[27] Hay had spent some of his early years in France, before James appointed him a Gentleman of the Privy Chamber in May 1603 and in October the same year, at the request of Anna, a Gentleman of the Bedchamber. James's later favourite, Robert Carr, Earl of Somerset (cat.57), first came to court as Hay's page. Hay was knighted, following an embassy to France in March 1604; in December 1605, he was appointed Master of the Robes, and in 1613 Master of the Great Wardrobe. Various portraits of Hay, who became known for the extravagance of his lifestyle, survive: the earliest are two versions of a full-length portrait connected with the workshop of the English painter William Larkin (c.1580–1619) (fig.21). In these, Hay, standing, is attired in black, with a wide-standing lace collar over a piccadil (a rigid under-support). The original image may have been commissioned to mark a title or appointment or relate to a mission to France.[28] While travelling on diplomatic business, Hay took the opportunity to have his portrait painted in the Delft studio of Michiel van Miereveld (1566–1641).[29] After Charles's accession, Hay would commission another full-length from an unidentified artist painted in 1628 (National Portrait Gallery, London), and perhaps a further one from Anthony van Dyck in the 1630s, the original of which is now lost.

Netherlandish Portrait-painters

The initiative in 1611–12 to persuade the Delft-based portrait specialist Van Miereveld to come to England to work for Prince Henry Frederick seems in retrospect to have been a significant, albeit ambitious moment.[30] Negotiations led by Sir Edward Conway, the Governor of Brill, began in late January 1611, but Van Miereveld, who ran an enormous and lucrative portrait-painting workshop in Delft, was unwilling to spend more than three months in England, and by February the following year the project had petered out. Hay was not, however, the only British client to sit to

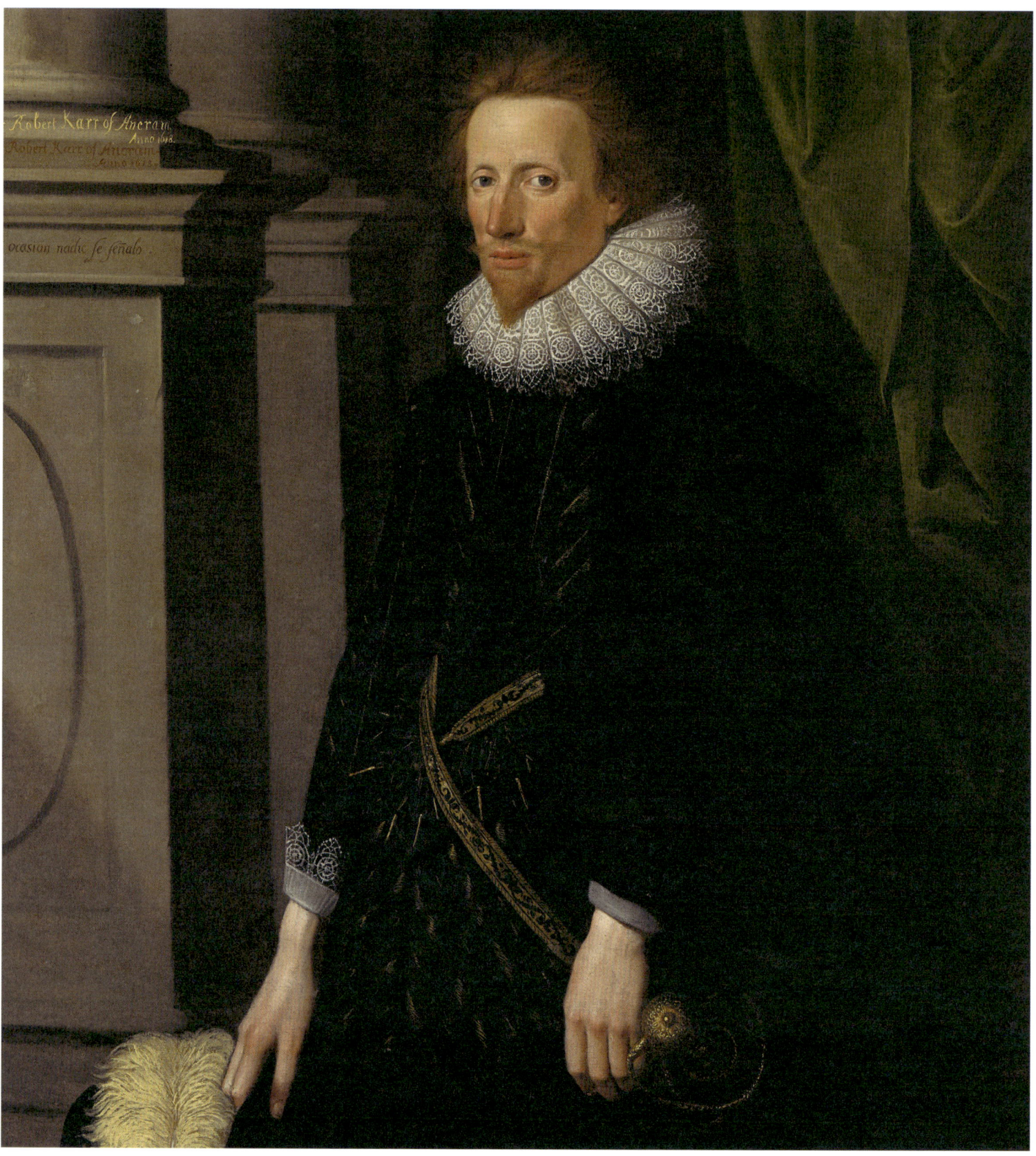

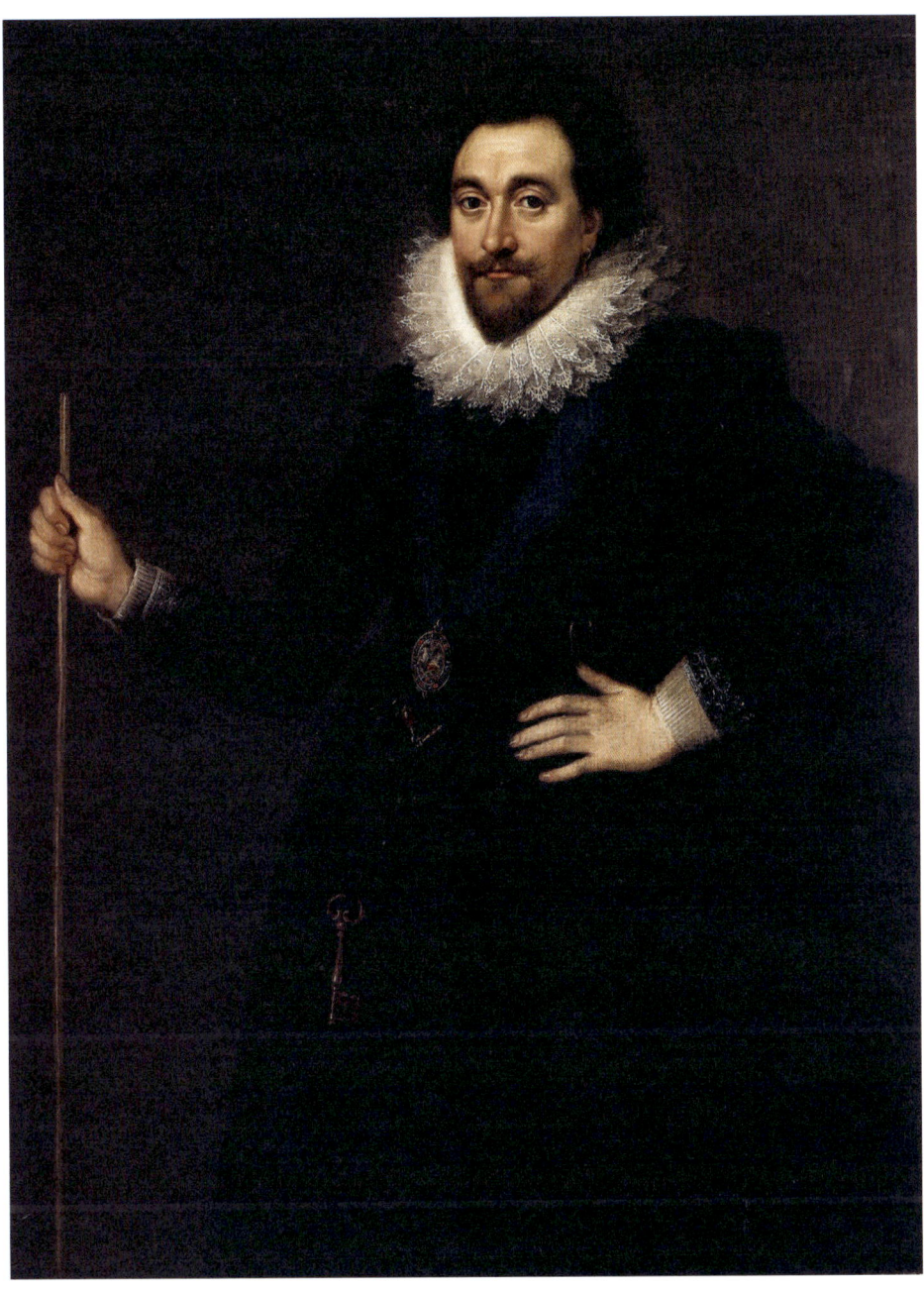

Van Miereveld while visiting the Netherlands.[31] The first seems to have been Edward Cecil, later Lord Wimbledon (1572–1638), in 1610, while other British sitters included the envoy Sir Dudley Carleton. It may have been a legacy of the 1611–12 discussions that prompted other Netherlandish-trained portrait-painters – such as Daniel Mytens the Elder (see below) – to travel to London some years later to take charge of English royal and court portraiture.

Abraham van Blijenberch (or Blyenberch) (1575/6–1624) from Flanders worked between 1617 and 1622 in London, where he is known to have produced designs for tapestries to be woven for Prince Charles. By late 1622, however, he was in Antwerp, where he died two years later.[32] Nevertheless, he had worked for some of the most cutting-edge London clients: portraits by him survive of William Herbert, 3rd Earl of Pembroke (Powis Castle);[33] the Scottish courtier Robert Kerr, later 1st Earl of Ancram (fig.22);[34] and the poet Ben Jonson (National Portrait Gallery, London); while a (now lost) portrait by him of Prince Charles is also documented.[35]

Paul van Somer was born in 1577/8, probably in Antwerp. It is known that he had worked in various cities in the Netherlands in the second decade of the seventeenth century, and had settled in London by December 1616; he was clearly a peripatetic artist who travelled from centre to centre. Although his working life in England was to last only five years – he died around New Year 1621/2 – he worked for the most significant patrons in London.[36] Thus, in 1617 Van Somer painted both William Herbert, 3rd Earl of Pembroke (fig.23) and Anna of Denmark, who was shown in an outdoor setting by her palace of Oatlands, in an innovative full-length (Royal Collection Trust).[37] Both were sitters with a clear interest in their own image. The following year, Van Somer painted James full-length, completely refreshing the official presentation of the king (fig.24); many copies and versions of Van Somer's image of James survive, suggesting that he ran a busy studio. In March 1619, Van Somer attended Anna of Denmark's funeral as her 'picture maker'.[38]

The Dutch incomer Daniel Mytens (or Mijtens) the Elder (c.1590–1647) was born in Delft, and

Fig.22 (opposite)
Abraham van Blijenberch
(1575/6–1624)
Robert Kerr, later 1st Earl
of Ancram, 1618
Oil on canvas, 106.7 × 99 cm
Private collection

Fig.23 (above)
Paul van Somer
(1577/8–1621/2)
William Herbert, 3rd Earl of
Pembroke (1590–1630), 1617
Oil on canvas, 132.1 × 99.1 cm
Royal Collection Trust / His
Majesty King Charles III
(RCIN 405870)

probably trained at The Hague. He was connected by marriage to Paul van Somer and is recorded as working in London from at least August 1618, in which year he probably produced the two celebrated seated paired portraits of the avid collectors, the Earl and Countess of Arundel, depicted in front of works of art and antiquities in their collection (National Portrait Gallery, in situ at Arundel Castle).[39] Mytens began working for the British crown about 1620 and painted the sombre portrait of the by-now-widowed James in 1621. A number of versions from Mytens's workshop, and later copies, exist, including the reduced version at Ham House. In 1623, Mytens was paid for further portraits of James (for the ambassador of the Spanish Netherlands) and of Charles, Prince of Wales (for the Spanish ambassador). On 19 July 1624, James granted Mytens a life pension of £50 a year, on condition that he serve the king and his heirs 'faithfullie and diligently'. Mytens became a British denizen on 22 August 1624, when he was described as 'DANIEL Mittins, painter, born in the parts beyond the seas'; this was apparently 'preceded by a grant of £50, for his better encouragement in the art and skill of picture drawing. Done by direction from the Prince [Charles].' At Charles's accession in 1625, he appointed Mytens one of his 'picture-drawers', for life, at a reduced annuity of £20.[40]

While nothing is known about Mytens's workshop, it must have been extremely productive. He produced numerous portraits of eminent figures at the Jacobean court, including the Scot James Hamilton, 2nd Marquess of Hamilton (1589–1625), whom James appointed a Privy Councillor for Scotland in 1613 and for England in 1617.[41] Hamilton became Lord Steward of the royal household, and also Lord High Commissioner of the Scottish Parliament; he was a documented collector of paintings.[42] There are at least twenty-two known versions or derivations of Mytens's full-length

portrait of Hamilton, including the version in the National Galleries Scotland collection (cat.27).

The young Anthony van Dyck paid a short visit from Antwerp to London from late October 1620 to February 1621, reportedly at the invitation of Lord Purbeck, the brother of George Villiers, later Duke of Buckingham (1592–1628). Buckingham himself – James's favourite after about 1615 – commissioned his own portrait from various painters, including William Larkin, Daniel Mytens, Anthony van Dyck (probably) and Michiel van Miereveld. In Paris, a few weeks after James's death, he met and was sketched by Peter Paul Rubens (cat.28). The Earl of Arundel had also already taken an interest in his work; Lady Arundel had visited Antwerp in summer 1620, and there sat for her portrait to Van Dyck's master, Sir Peter Paul Rubens. While in London, Van Dyck painted Thomas Howard, Earl of Arundel in a highly innovative, and subsequently influential, image.[43] An intriguing record of a payment was made to Van Dyck for 'speciall service by him p[er]formed for his Matie [sic]' (James VI & I), but it is not clear what that was for.[44]

Thus, it is evident that, following the accession of James to the English throne, London offered new opportunities for the royal family and for Scottish courtiers to be painted by a wider and more skilled range of artists than they had previously had access to. There, James and Anna, and in due course their sons, could avail themselves of a range of painters. Meanwhile, some other patrons chose to try out more than one image-maker. After 1619 – the year in which leading English painters such as William Larkin and Robert Peake, as well as miniaturist Nicholas Hilliard (1547–1619) and Anna herself, all died – the market was captured by the more recently arrived Netherlandish painters, particularly Van Somer and Mytens. Indeed, on the basis of the portraits that survive, the most successful and productive artist working during James's period in London was probably Mytens.

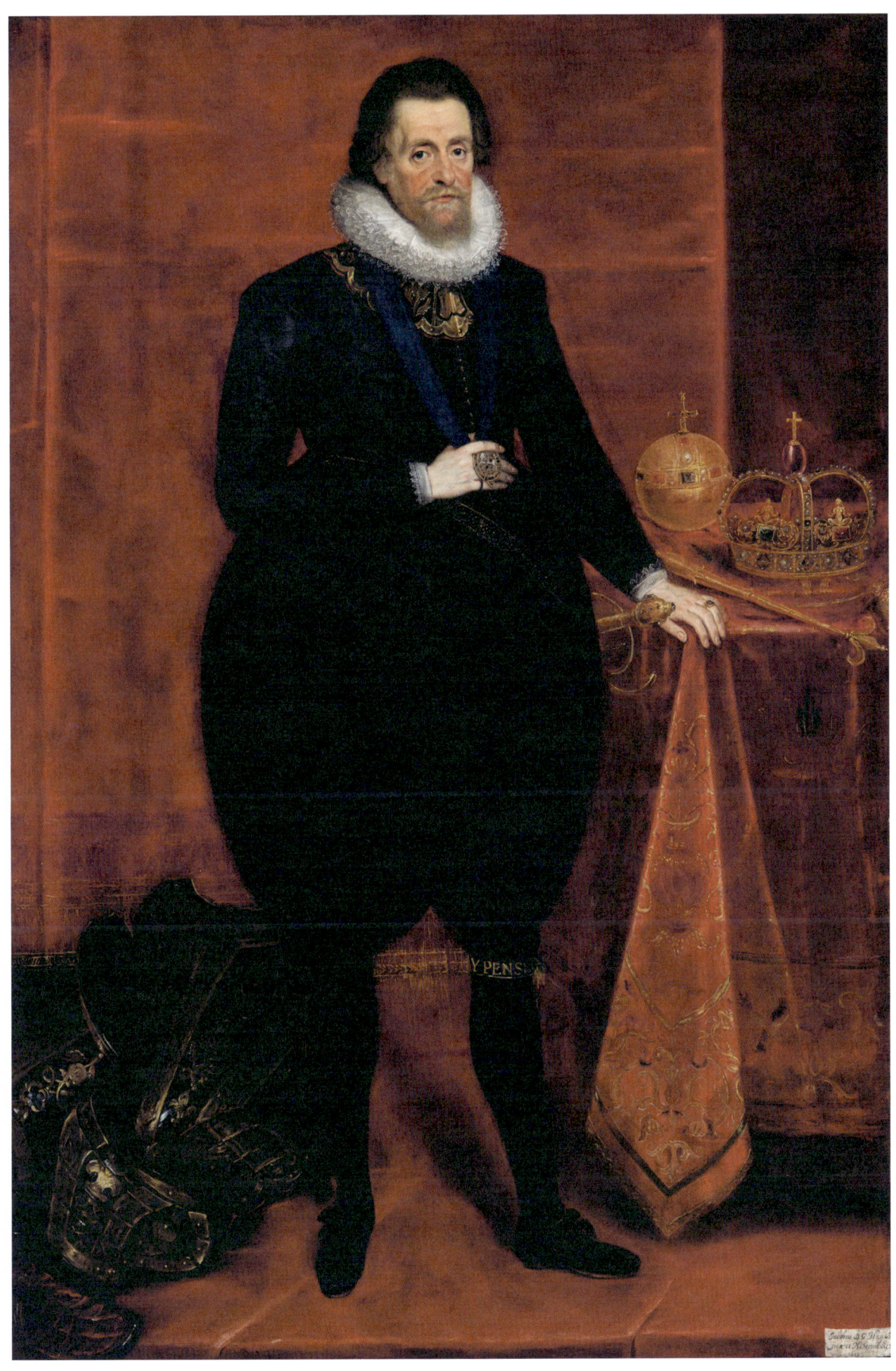

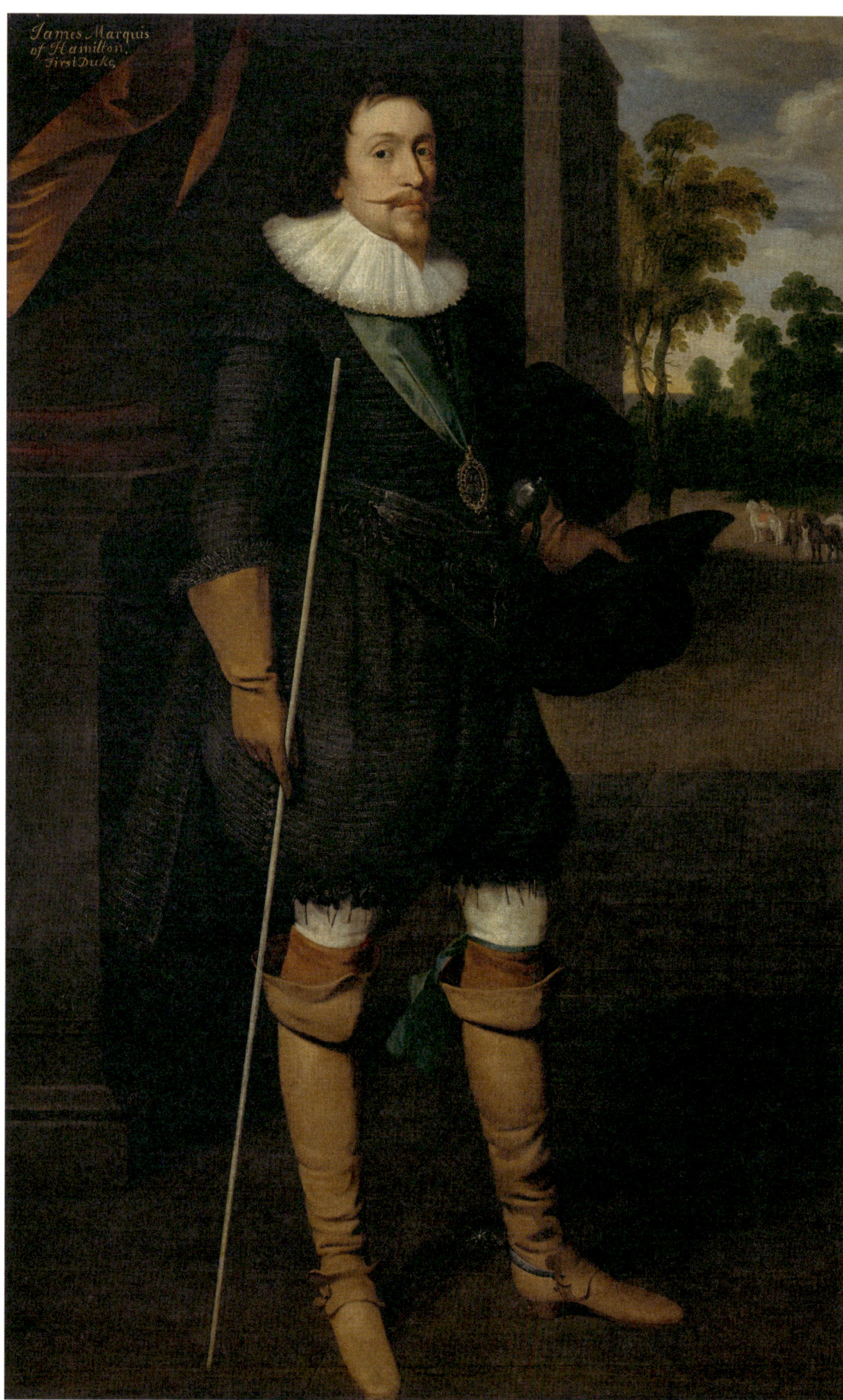

James Marquis
of Hamilton.
First Duke.

Cat.27 (left)
Unknown artist, after Daniel Mytens the Elder (c.1590–1647)
James Hamilton, 2nd Marquess of Hamilton (1589–1625), **1622**
Oil on canvas, 206.4 × 129.5 cm
National Galleries of Scotland, Edinburgh (PG 1056)

PROVENANCE: Bequeathed by Mrs Nisbet Hamilton Ogilvy of Biel, 1921.

Cat.28 (opposite)
Peter Paul Rubens (1577–1640)
George Villiers, 1st Duke of Buckingham (1592–1628), **c.1625**
Oil on panel, 60.9 × 47.3 cm
Glasgow Museum (PC.49)

PROVENANCE: Possibly in the collection of Sir Horace Walpole at Strawberry Hill, seen by George Vertue in *c*.1742, and listed in an inventory of Strawberry Hill, 1774. A painting of the same description was sold at the Strawberry Hill sale, 18 May 1842, lot 55, and bought by Henry Farrer; possibly included in Henry Farrer sale, Christie's, London, 15 June 1886, lot 229 and bought by 'Soloman'; Sir William Stirling Maxwell 9th Bart (1818–1878); by descent to Sir John Stirling Maxwell; gifted by his daughter Anne Maxwell Macdonald to Glasgow City in 1967.

REFERENCES: Dundee 1867, no.306; Caw 1936, no.75; Glasgow c.1968, no.49, p.33, as by Cornelius Johnson

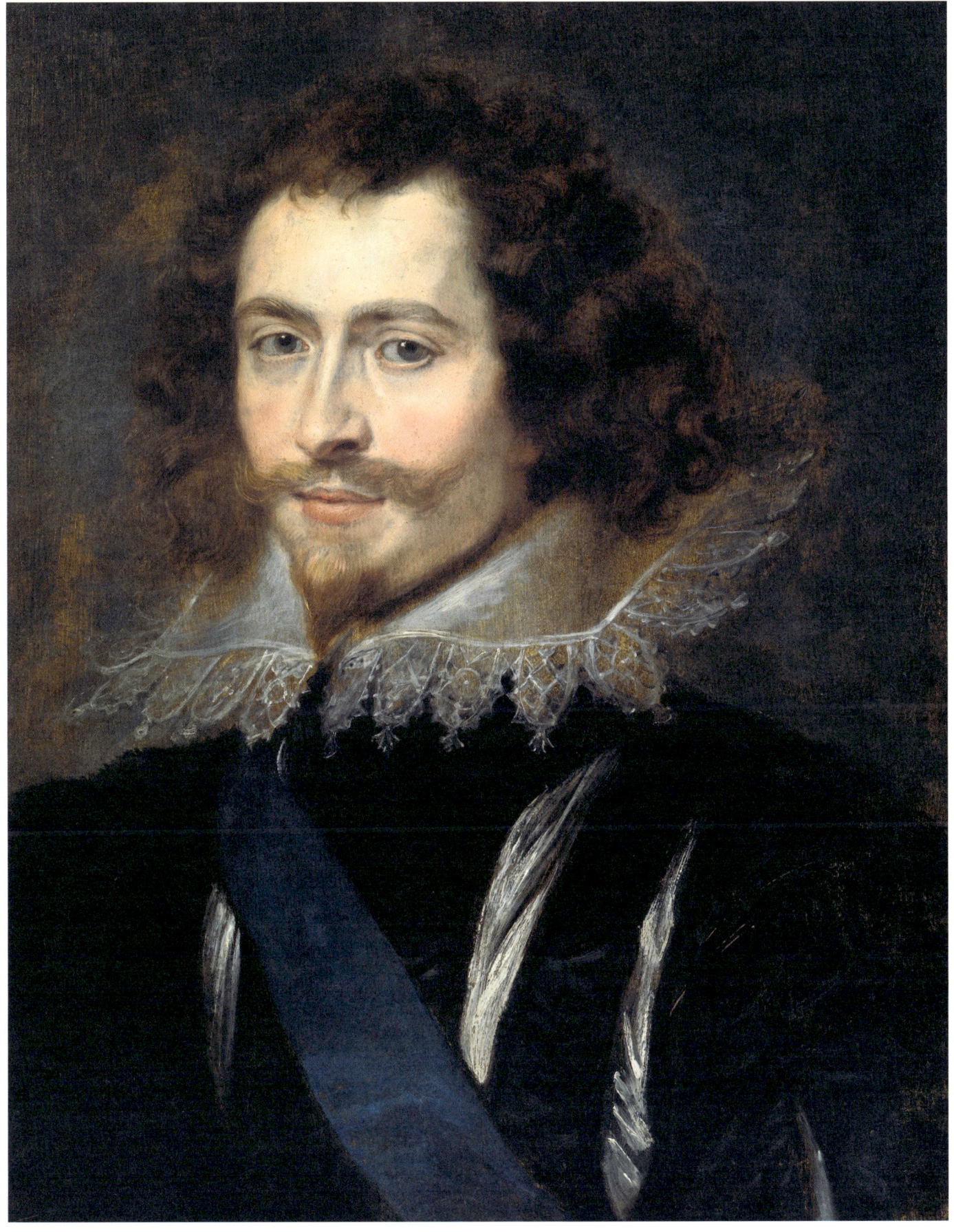

ART & COURT OF JAMES VI & I

CATALOGUE

Kate Anderson and Liz Louis

The following catalogue reflects the content of the exhibition *The World of King James VI and I*, which took place at the National Galleries of Scotland: Portrait, Edinburgh in 2025. The catalogue is divided into two sections: illustrated and unillustrated. In both sections, the entries are grouped by the following media: Paintings; Drawings & Watercolours; Miniatures; Dress & Jewellery; Objects; Prints; Books & Manuscripts. The entries are then structured chronologically within each group. When a work has been illustrated in the essays, the entry is not duplicated in the catalogue. In instances where references are omitted it is because, to date, the work appears to be unpublished.

Detail of cat.41

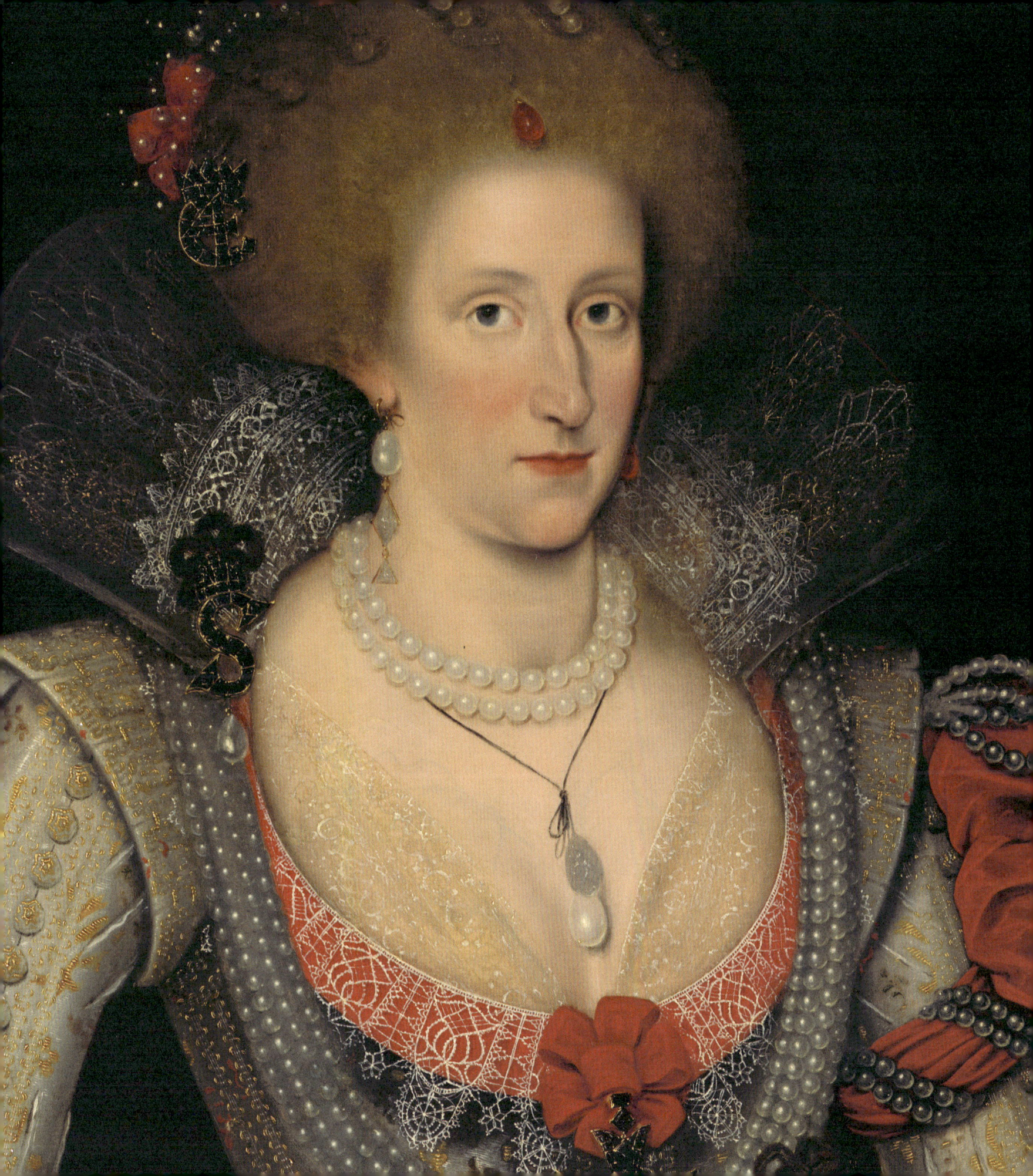

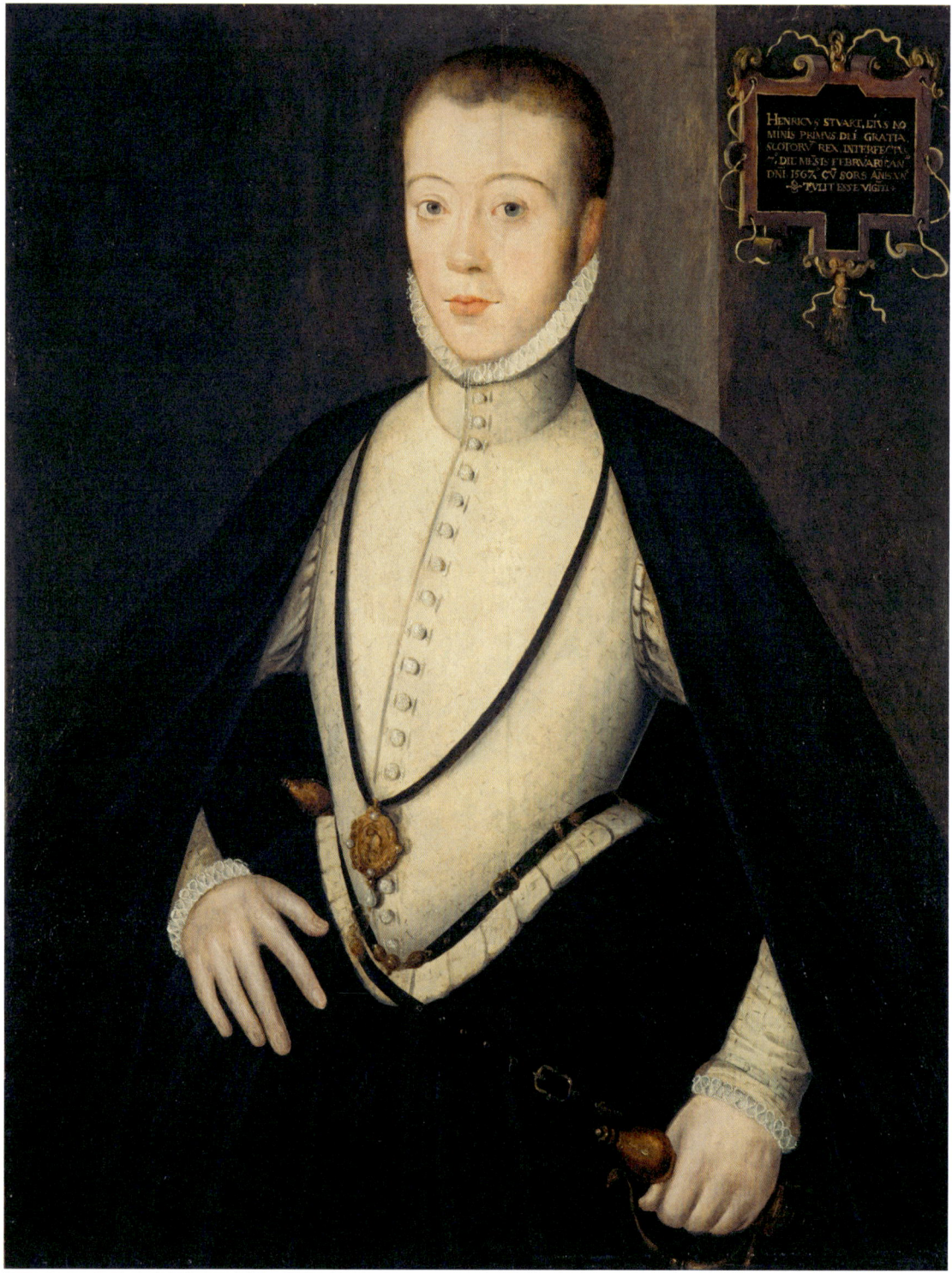

Cat.29
Unknown, possibly English, artist
Henry Stuart, Lord Darnley (1545–1567), c.1564
Oil on panel, 76.20 × 58.40 cm
National Galleries of Scotland, Edinburgh (PG 2279)

PROVENANCE: Purchased at Christie's, London, 21 March 1975, lot 57.

REFERENCES: Edinburgh 1990, cat.38, p.45; Edinburgh 2013, p.31 and cat.141, p.95

PAINTINGS

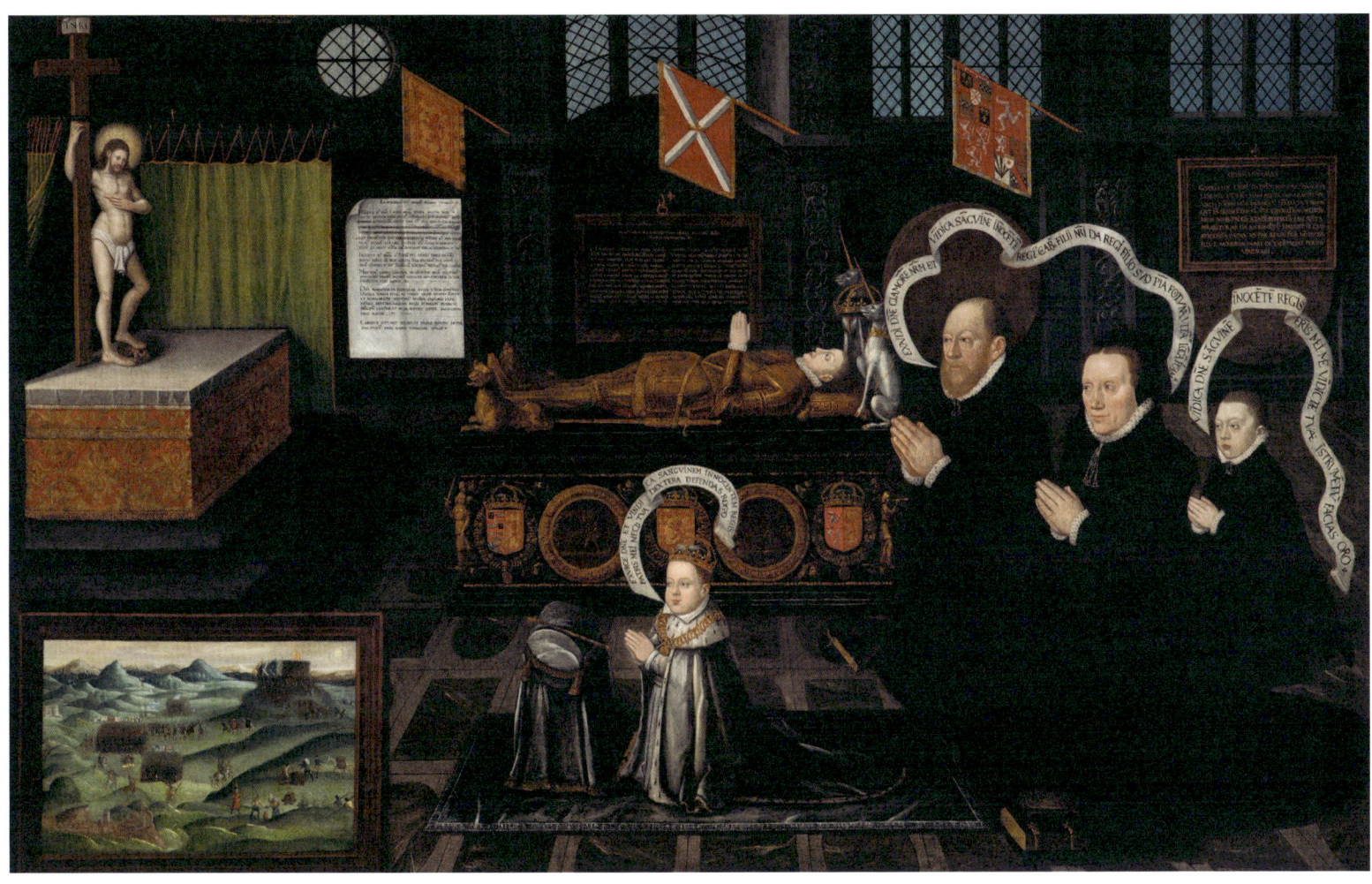

Cat.30
Livinus de Vogelaare
(active 1551–1600)
The Memorial of Lord Darnley,
1567
Oil on canvas, 142.3 × 224 cm
Royal Collection Trust / His
Majesty King Charles III
(RCIN 401230)

PROVENANCE: Commissioned by
the Earl and Countess of Lennox;
presented to Queen Caroline,
consort of George II.

REFERENCES: London 1889, p.23,
cat.46; Edinburgh 1959, cat.72,
pp.27–28; Millar 1963a, no.90,
pp.75–76; Thomson 1975, no.1,
pp.18–19; Edinburgh 2013, pp.50
and 99, cat.158

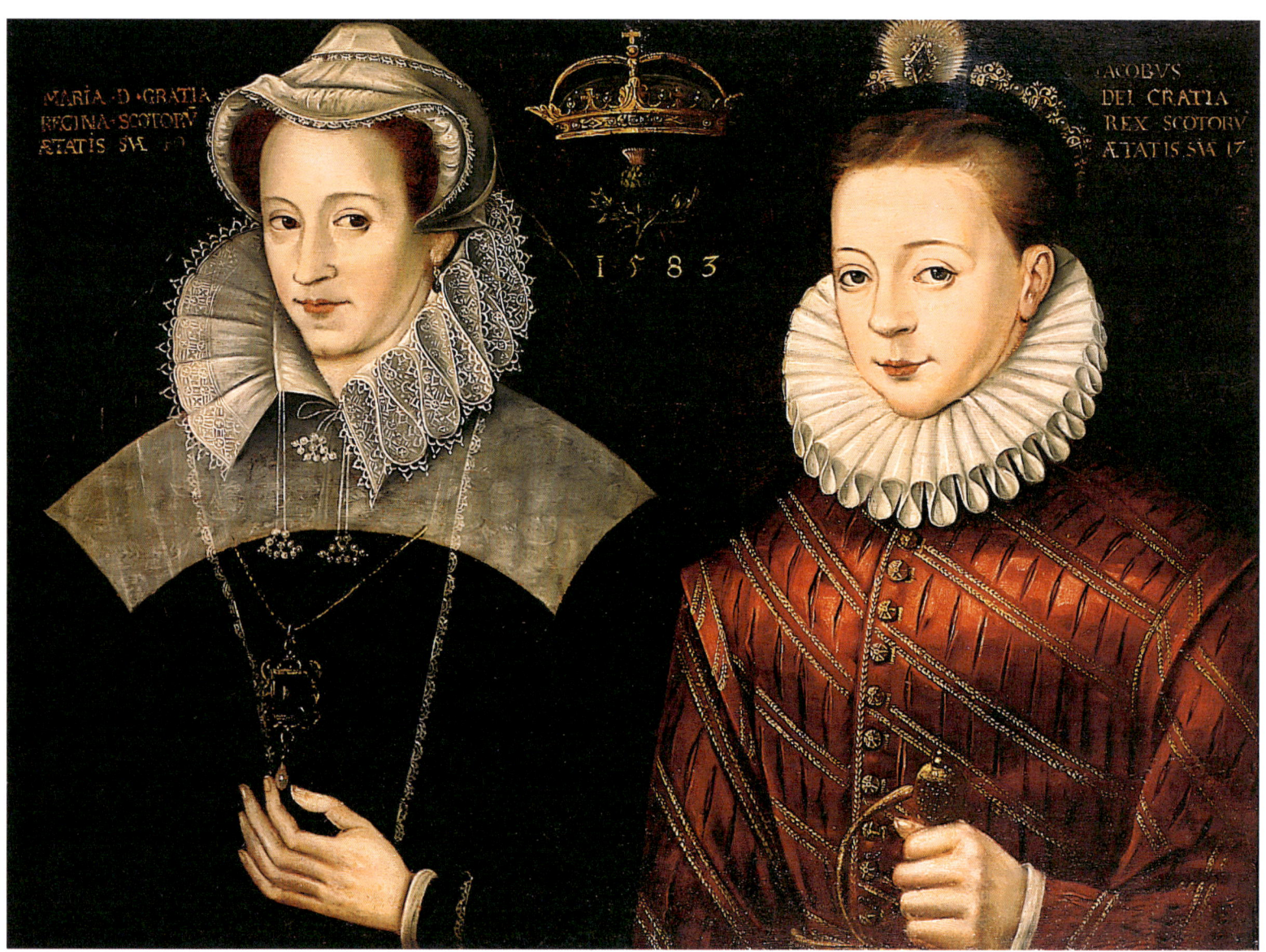

Cat.31
Unknown artist
Double Portrait of Mary, Queen of Scots and James VI, **1580s**
Oil on panel, 62.2 × 83.8 cm
Collection at Blair Castle, Perthshire

PROVENANCE: Traditionally said to have been sent from England, by Mary, Queen of Scots, to Margaret, Countess of Atholl, 2nd wife of John, 4th Earl of Atholl; by descent through the Dukes of Atholl; until 1884 at the family property at Dunkeld.

Cat.32
Unknown artist
*Mary, Queen of Scots
(1542–1587)*, 1610–15,
after an original of 1578
Oil on canvas, 201.5 × 95.7 cm
National Galleries of Scotland,
Edinburgh (PG 1073)

PROVENANCE: Ludovic Stewart,
2nd Duke of Lennox and 1st
Richmond at Cobham Hall;
eighteenth century, Cobham
Hall and contents acquired by
the Earls of Darnley; by descent
to 8th Earl of Darnley until 1925,
when purchased by the Scottish
National Portrait Gallery.

REFERENCES: London 1889, p.19,
cat.36; Strong 1969a, pp.220–21;
Edinburgh 1987, p.53; Edinburgh
1990, p.47; Edinburgh 1991, p.15;
Edinburgh 1998, p.17; SNPG 2014,
p.13; Leighton 2015, no.38, p.108

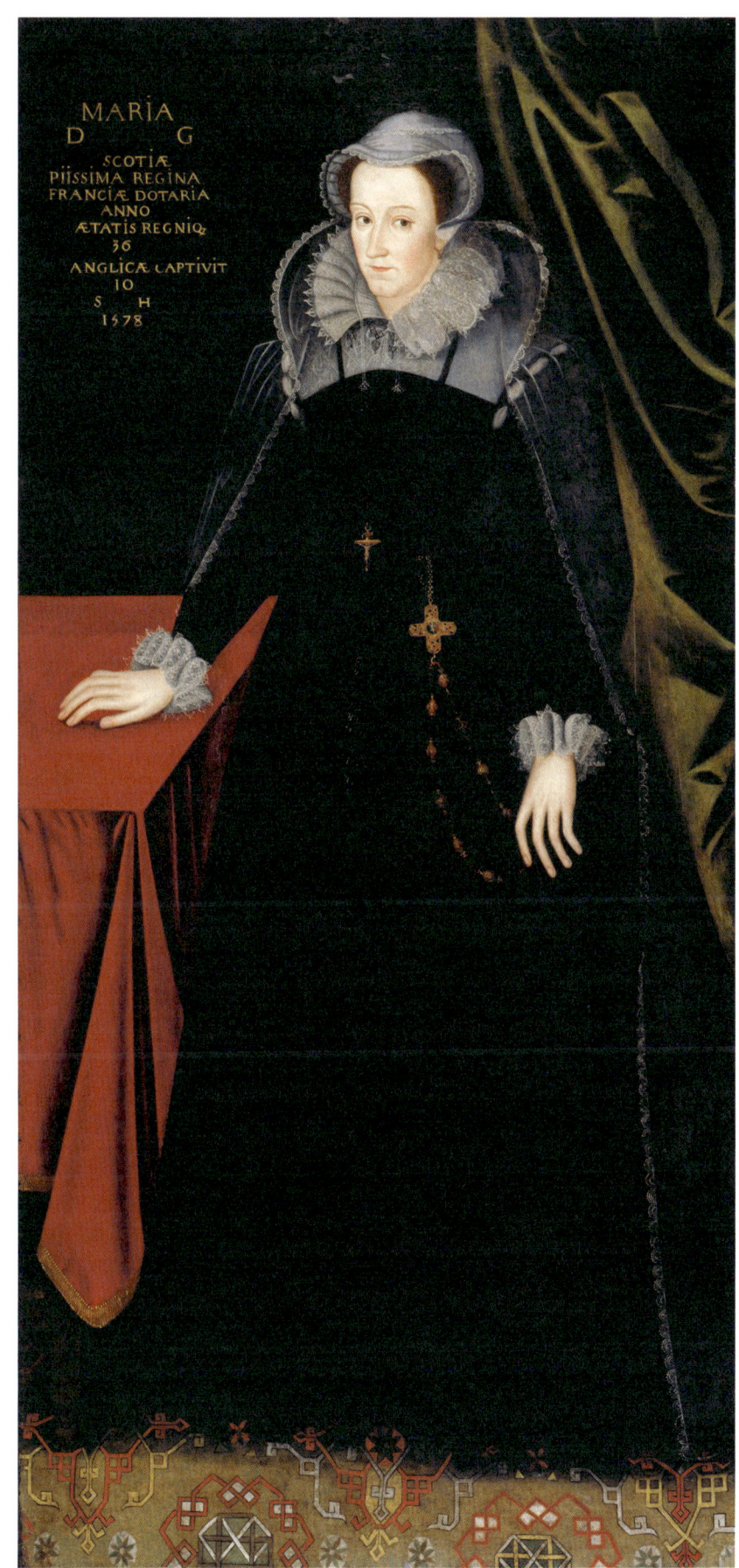

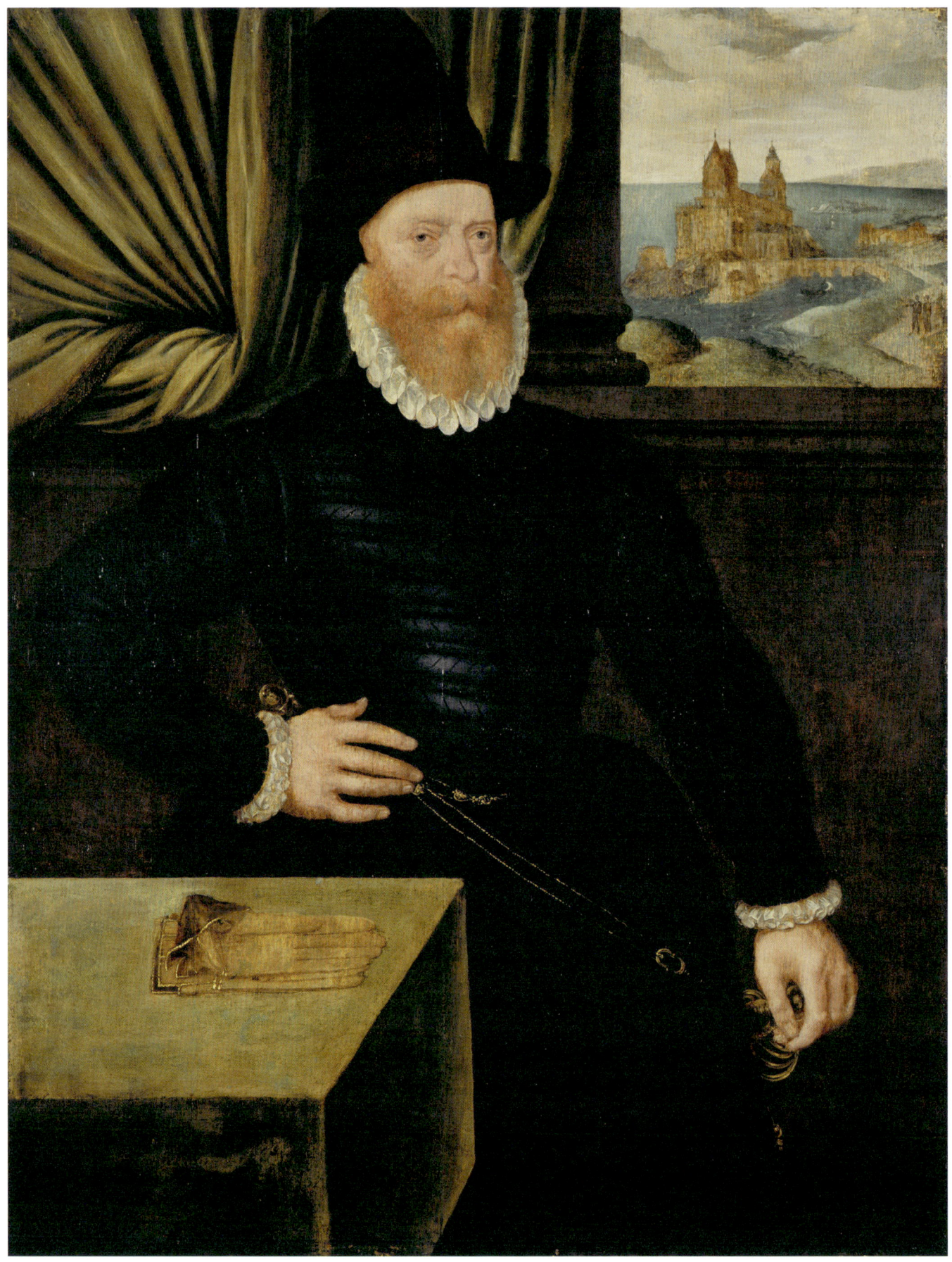

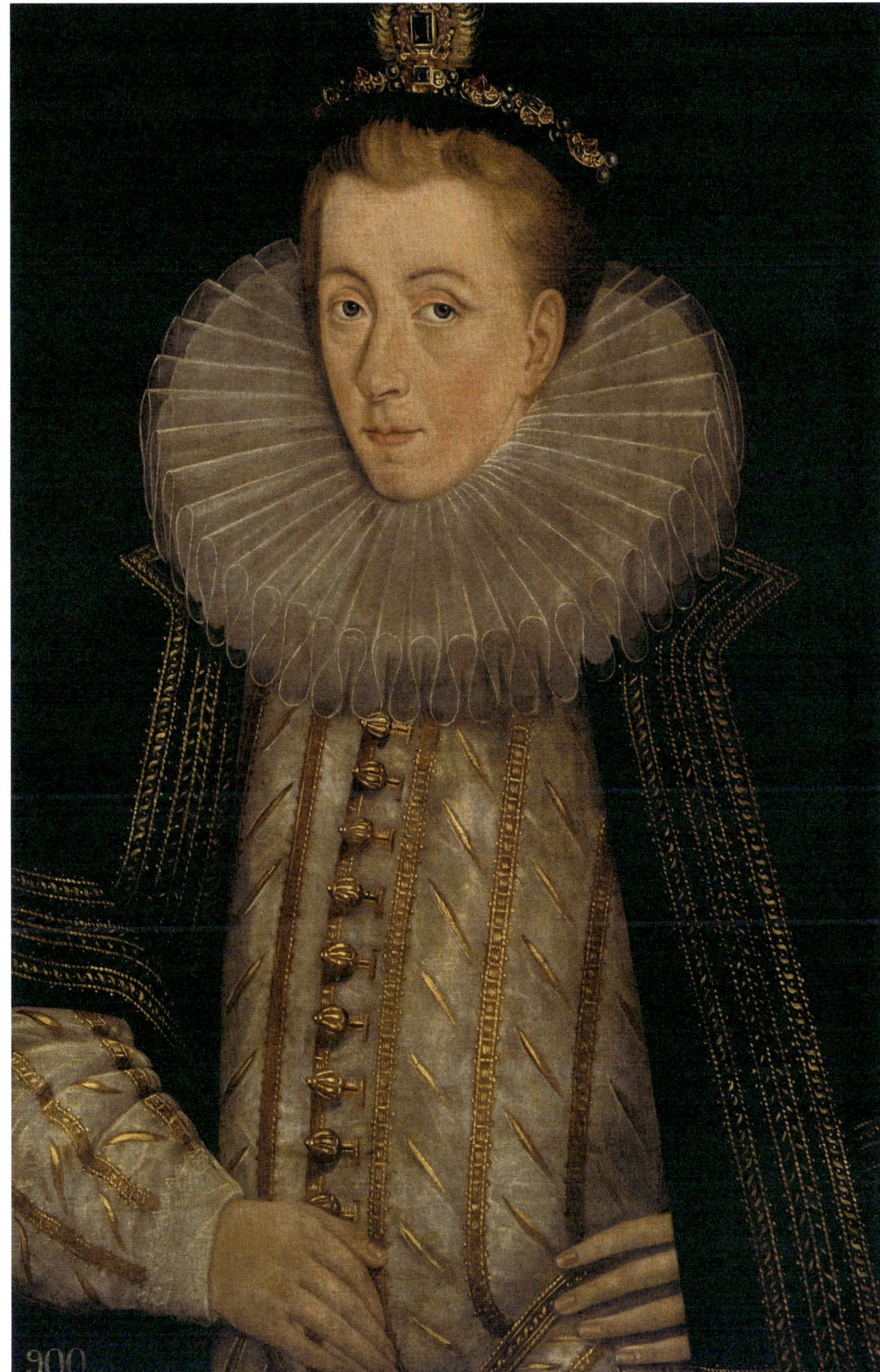

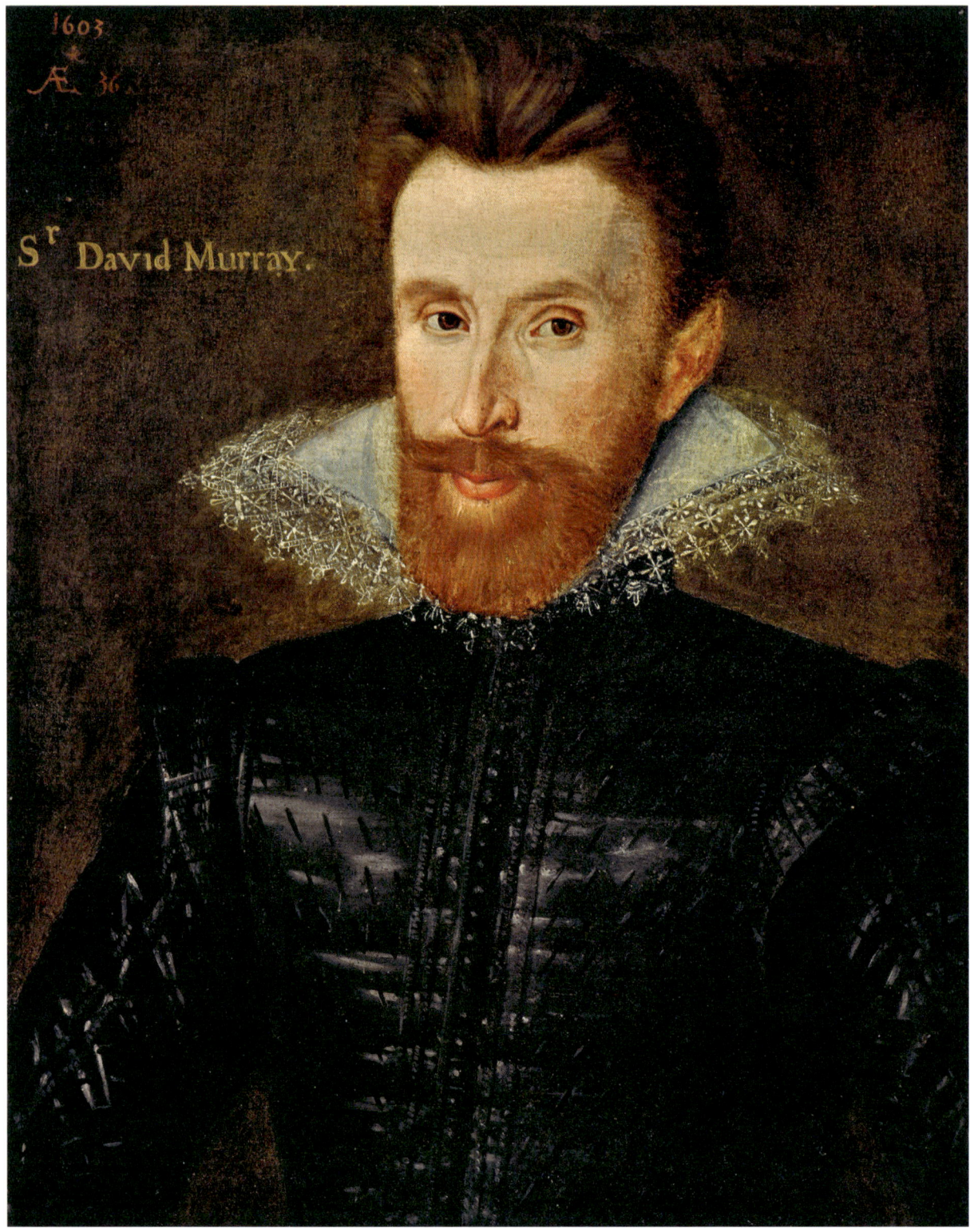

1603

Æ 36

Sr David Murray.

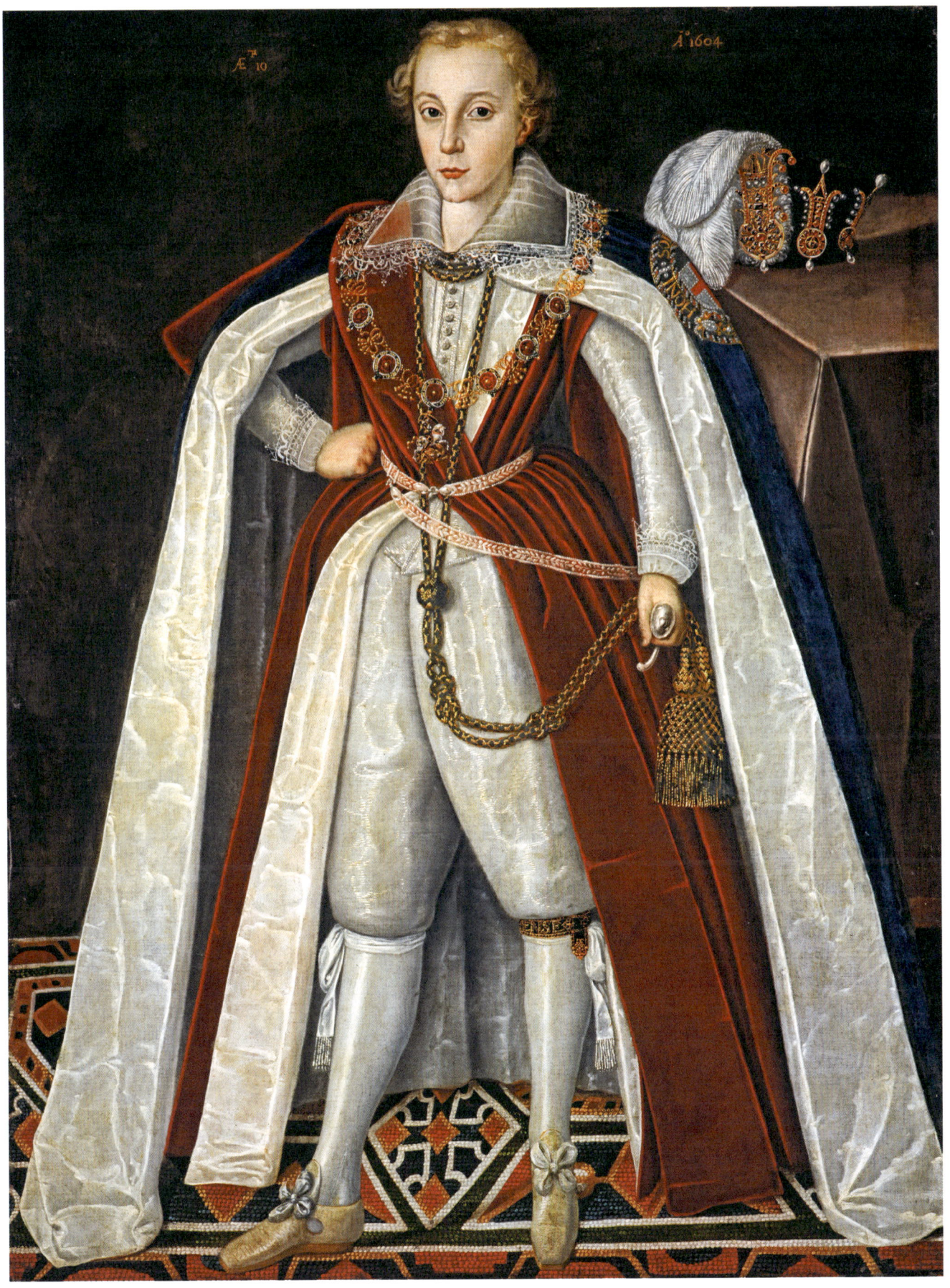

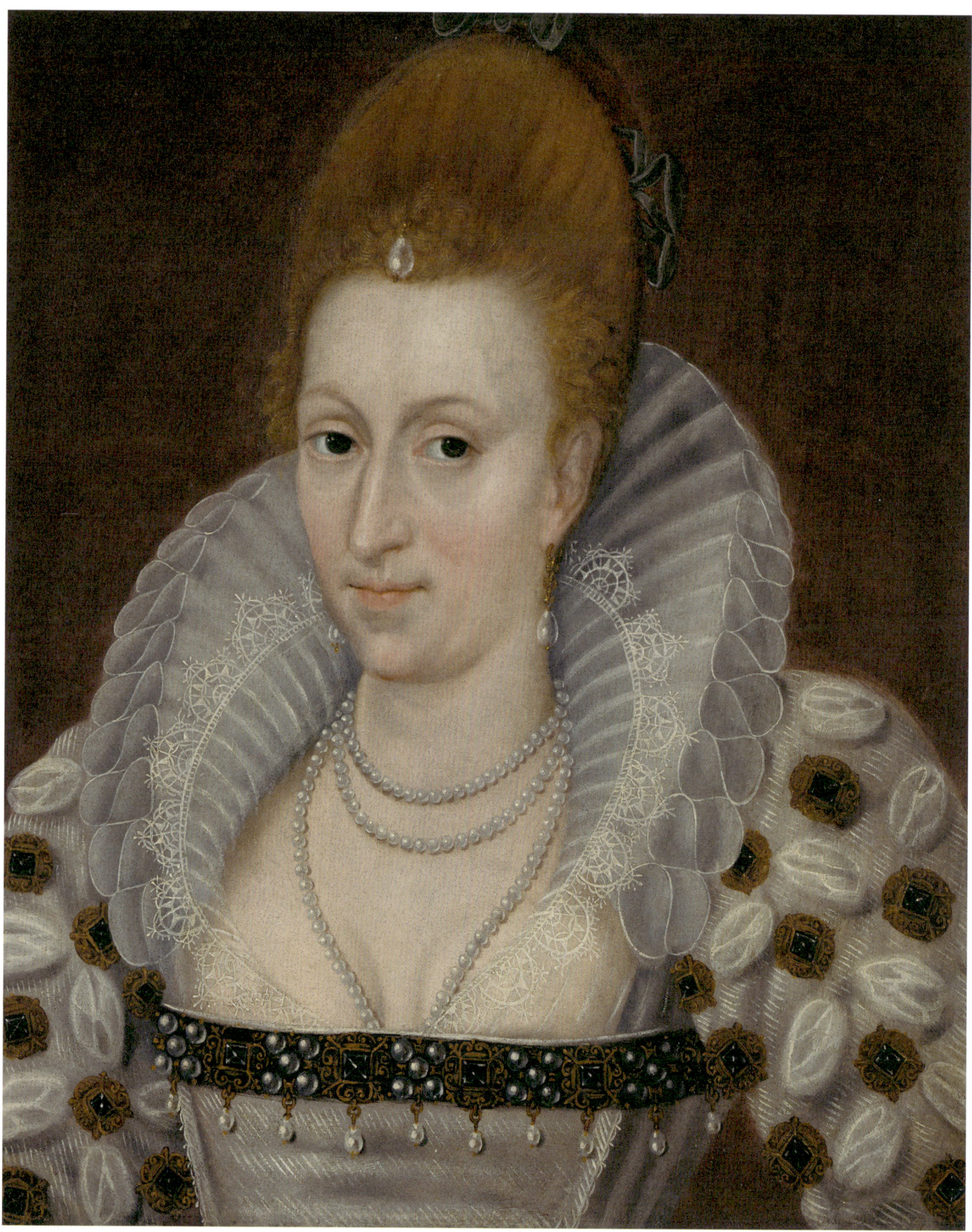

Cat.37 (opposite)
John de Critz the Elder or workshop of John de Critz the Elder (c.1550–1642)
*Anna of Denmark, c.*1605
Oil on panel, 48 × 39 cm
National Galleries of Scotland, Edinburgh (PG 3800)

PROVENANCE: Private collection, England; Private collection, Sweden, 1920s–2007; sold at Bukowski's, Stockholm, sale, 28 November 2007, lot 428; 2007 to 2019, Weiss Gallery London; purchased by National Galleries of Scotland, 2019.

Cat.38 (right)
Robert Peake the Elder (c.1551–1619)
*Charles I, when Duke of York and Albany, c.*1610
Oil on canvas, 127 × 85.7 cm
National Galleries of Scotland, Edinburgh (PG 2212)

PROVENANCE: By descent to Major J.A. Erskine-Murray, 13th Baron Elibank; bequeathed by him, 1973.

REFERENCES: Strong 1969b, p.250, no.231; Edinburgh 1975, p.24, cat.107; Edinburgh 1998, p.30; London 2012a, cat.9, pp.60–61; SNPG 2014, p.23

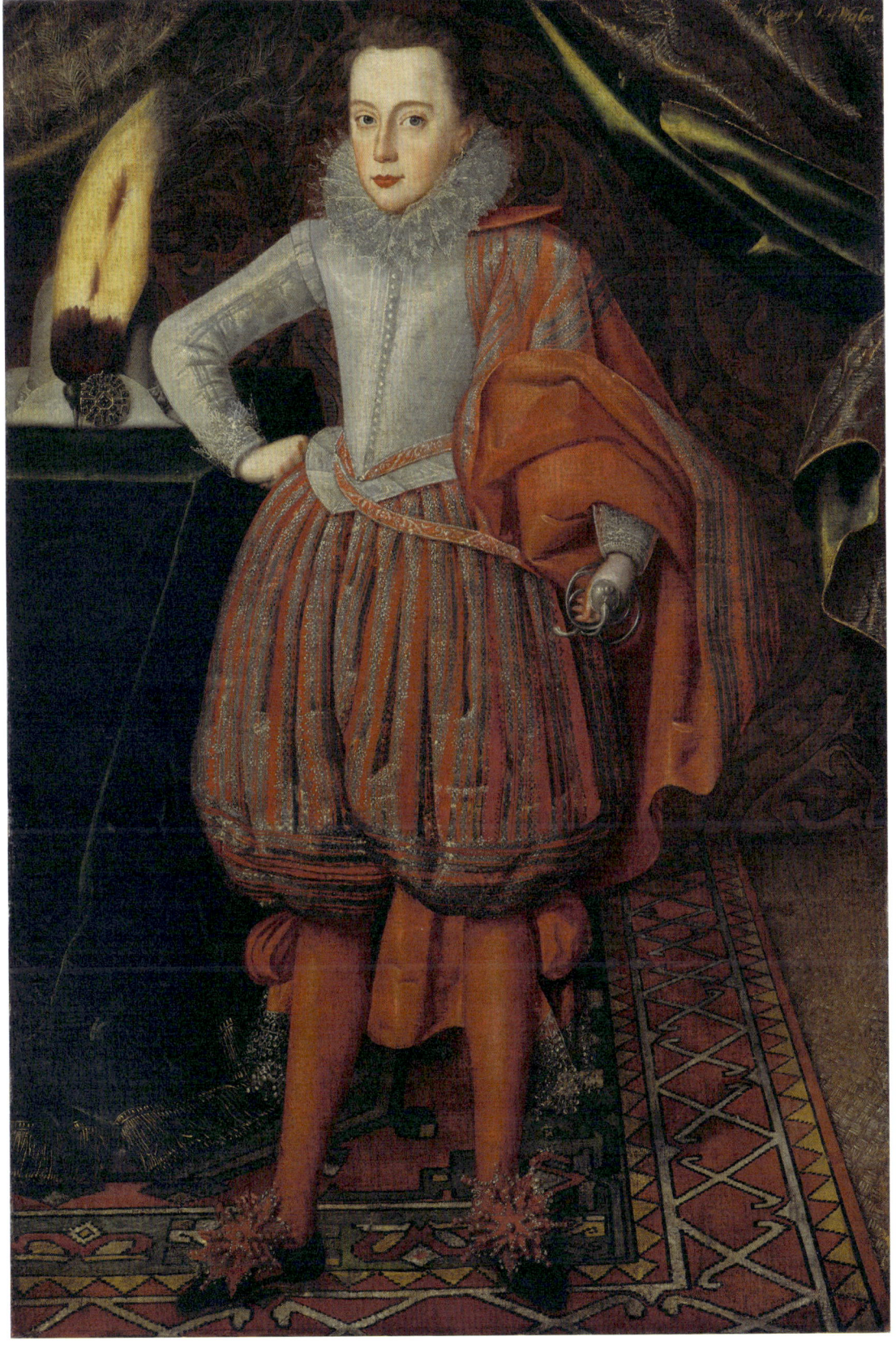

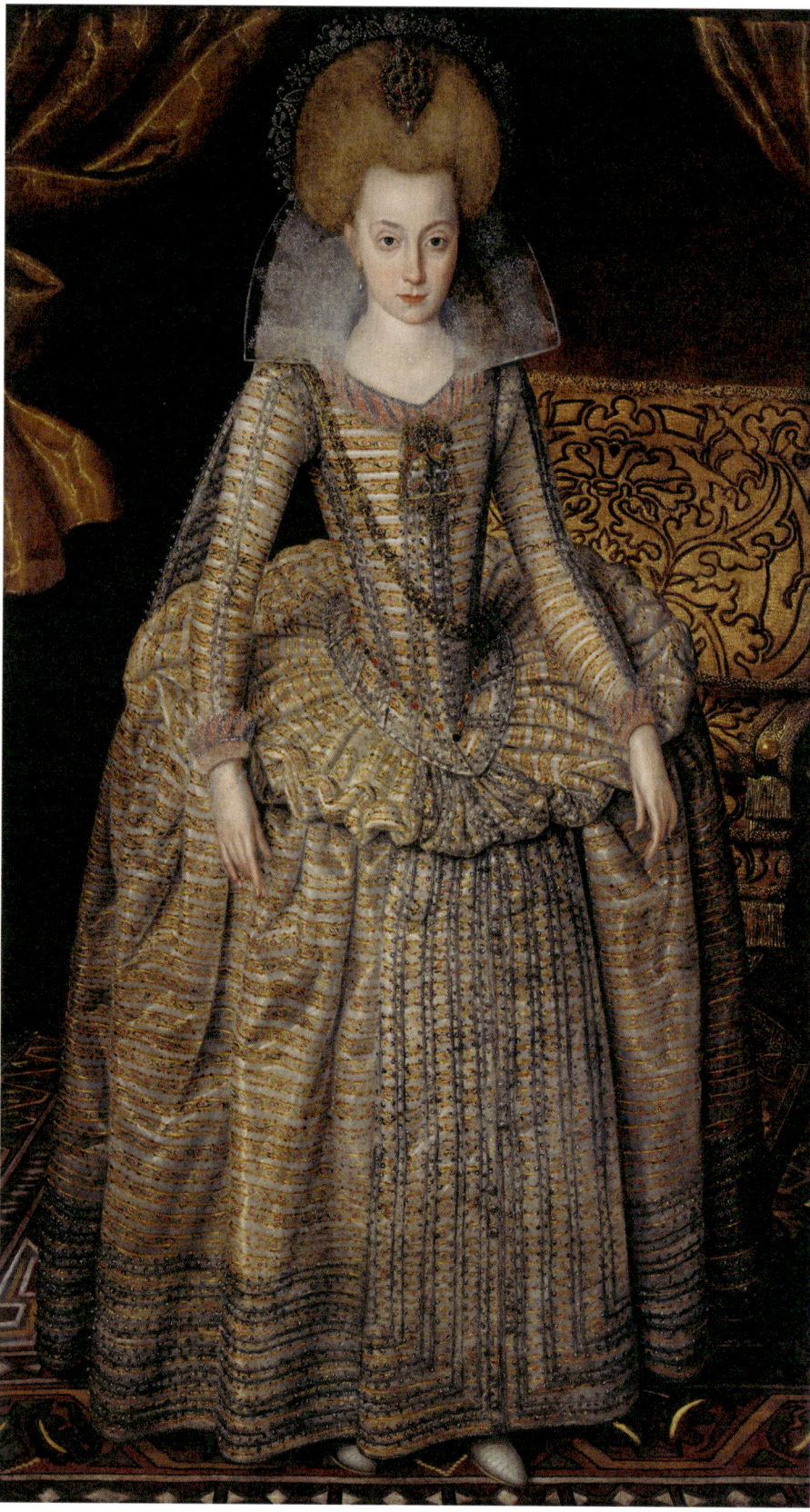

Cat.39 (left)
**Robert Peake the Elder
(c.1551–1619)**
*Princess Elizabeth, Queen
of Bohemia and Electress
Palatine, c.1610*
Oil on canvas, 171.3 × 96.8 cm
National Portrait Gallery, London
(NPG 6113)

PROVENANCE: Formerly at
Hengrave Hall, Suffolk; may have
descended through Sir Charles
Cornwallis (d.1629) whose
daughter married Sir Thomas
Kytson the Younger of Hengrave
(1540–1603); possibly sold at
Hampton's, 5–12 August 1897;
Carolina Lambert, New York 1916;
Boice Thomas, Yonkers; before
being acquired by the Carolina
Museum of Art in 1952, by whom
sold through Christie's; purchased
by the National Portrait Gallery
at Christie's, 16 November 1990,
lot 8.

REFERENCES: Strong 1986, Plate
5; Ribeiro 2000, fig.8, p.59; Cooper
2014, p.68; MacLeod 2015, pp.
288–97; Rae 2015, pp.171–79

Cat.40 (opposite)
**Attributed to Abraham van
Blijenberch (1575/6–1624)**
*William Drummond of
Hawthornden (1585–1649),
Poet and Collector, 1612*
Oil on panel, 60.4 × 48.5 cm
National Galleries of Scotland,
Edinburgh (PG 1096)

PROVENANCE: Formerly in the
collection of the Earl of Home at
The Hirsel, Coldstream; bought
by Sir Hugh Drummond at sale
of Earl of Home's Collection, 20
June 1919 (as attributed to George
Jamesone); bought on behalf
of the Scottish National Portrait
Gallery by Leggatt Brothers,
London, from Christie's, London, 8
June 1928, lot 91 (as attributed to
George Jamesone).

REFERENCES: London 1866,
cat.486, p.83 (attributed to
Cornelius Johnson); Edinburgh
1884, cat.32; Strong 1969a, p.74;
Brown 2000, no.41; Edinburgh
2005, p.20; London 2006, cat.82;
SNPG 2014, p.29

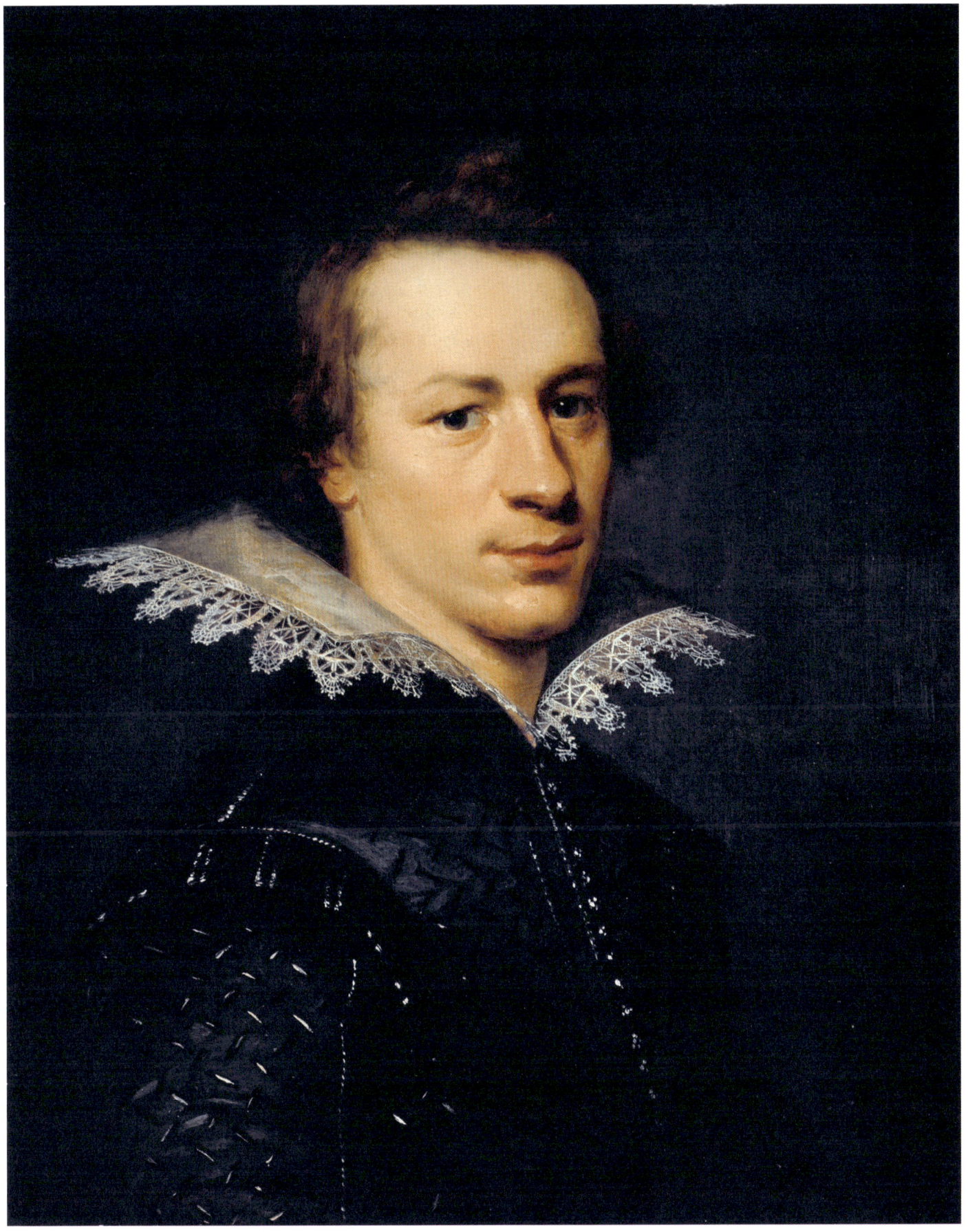

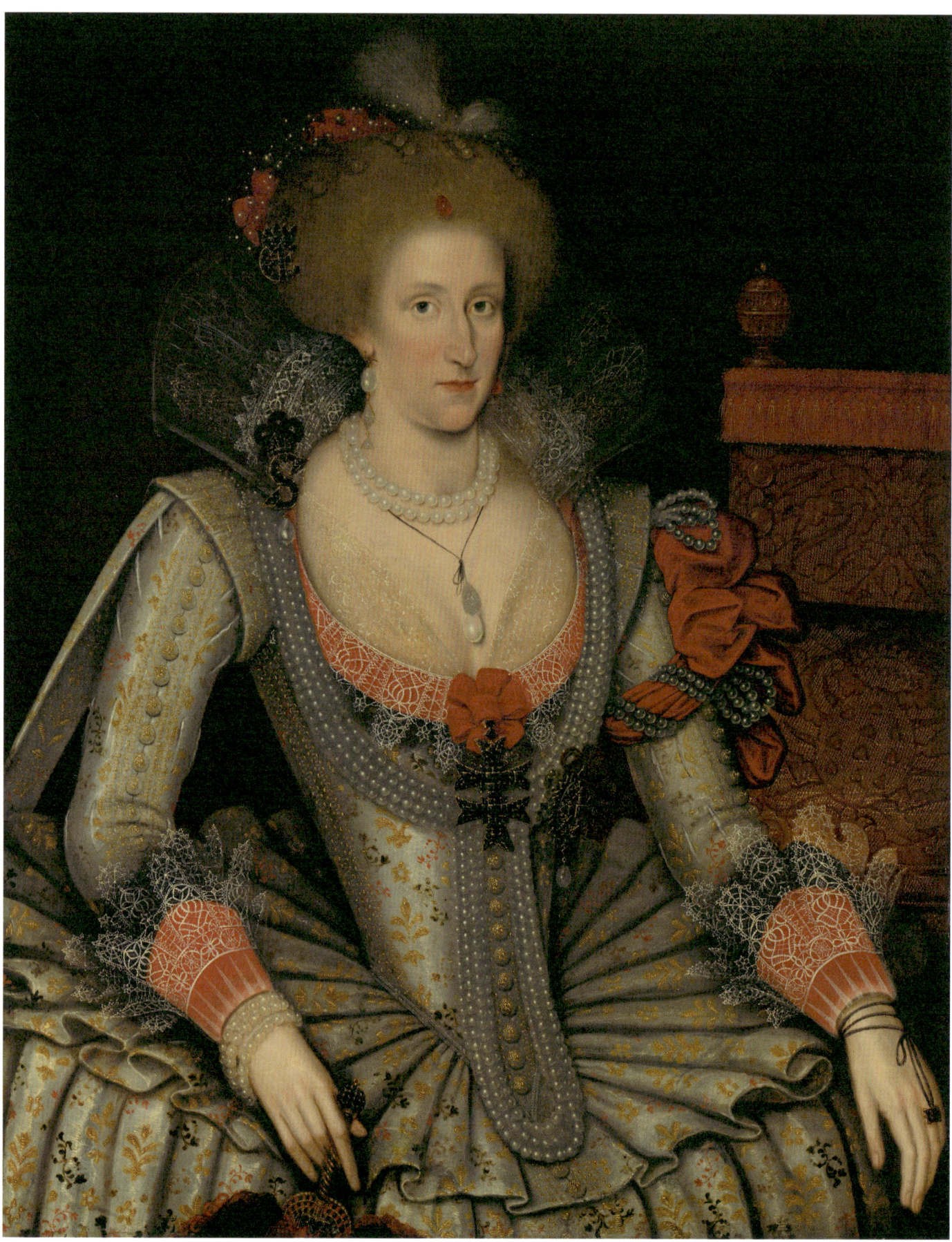

Cat.41 (opposite)
Attributed to Marcus Gheeraerts the Younger (1562–1636)
Anne of Denmark, 1614
Oil on canvas, 110.5 × 87.3 cm
Royal Collection Trust /
His Majesty King Charles III
(RCIN 404437)

PROVENANCE: First recorded in the Royal Collection during the reign of James II at Whitehall, 1687.

REFERENCES: Millar 1963a, no.98, p.79; Millar 1963b, p.534, no.9; Manchester 1964, p.22, cat.5; Edinburgh 1975, p.24, cat.103; London 2013b, p.42

Cat.42 (right)
Attributed to Robert Peake the Elder (c.1551–1619)
Lady Arabella Stuart (c.1577–1615), 1605
Oil on panel, 90.2 × 70.4 cm
National Galleries of Scotland, Edinburgh (PG 9)

PROVENANCE: Purchased from Henry Graves, 1884.

REFERENCES: Edinburgh 1884, cat.47; Edinburgh 1990, p.60; Edinburgh 1998, p.26; SNPG 2014, p.22

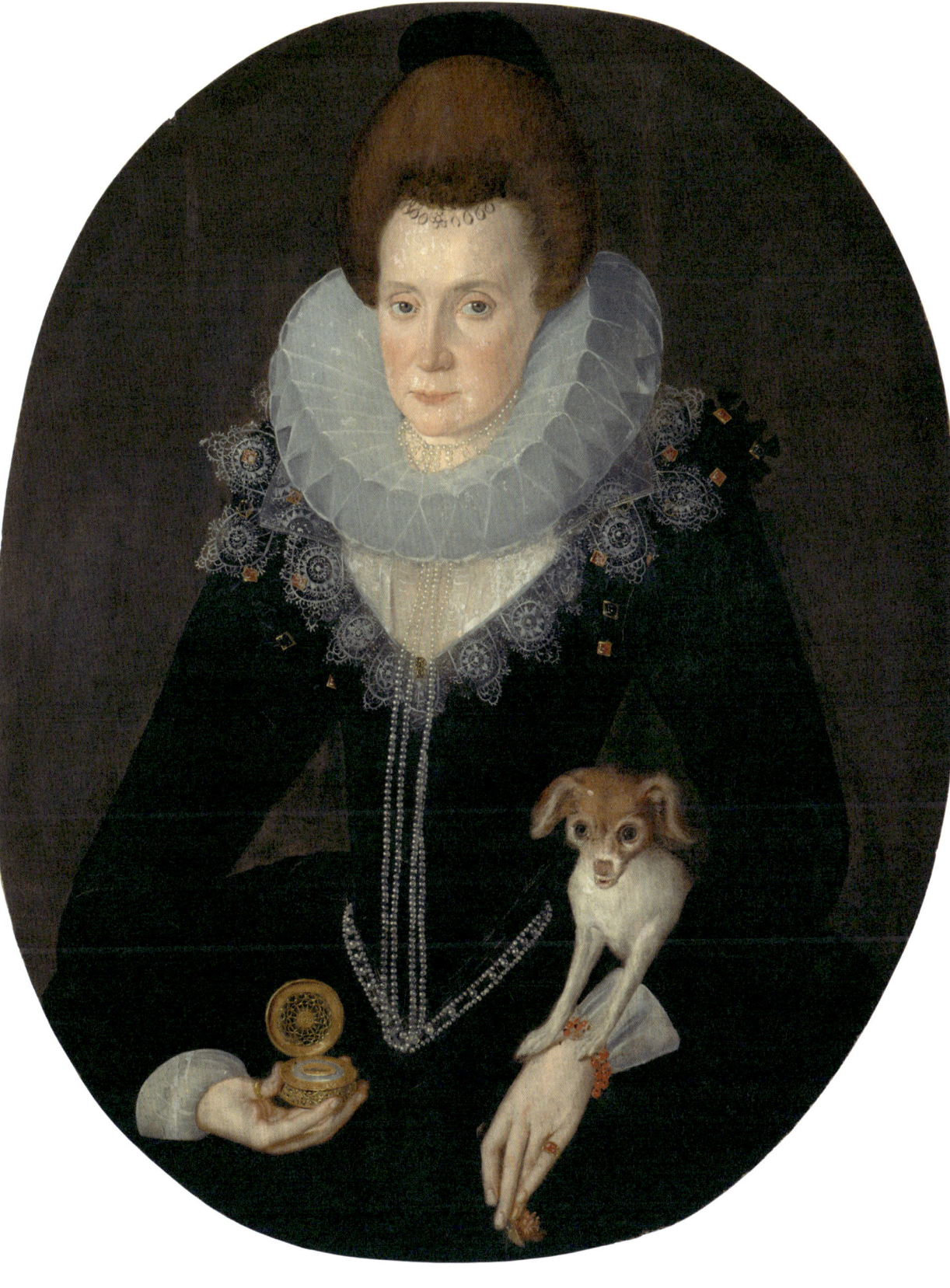

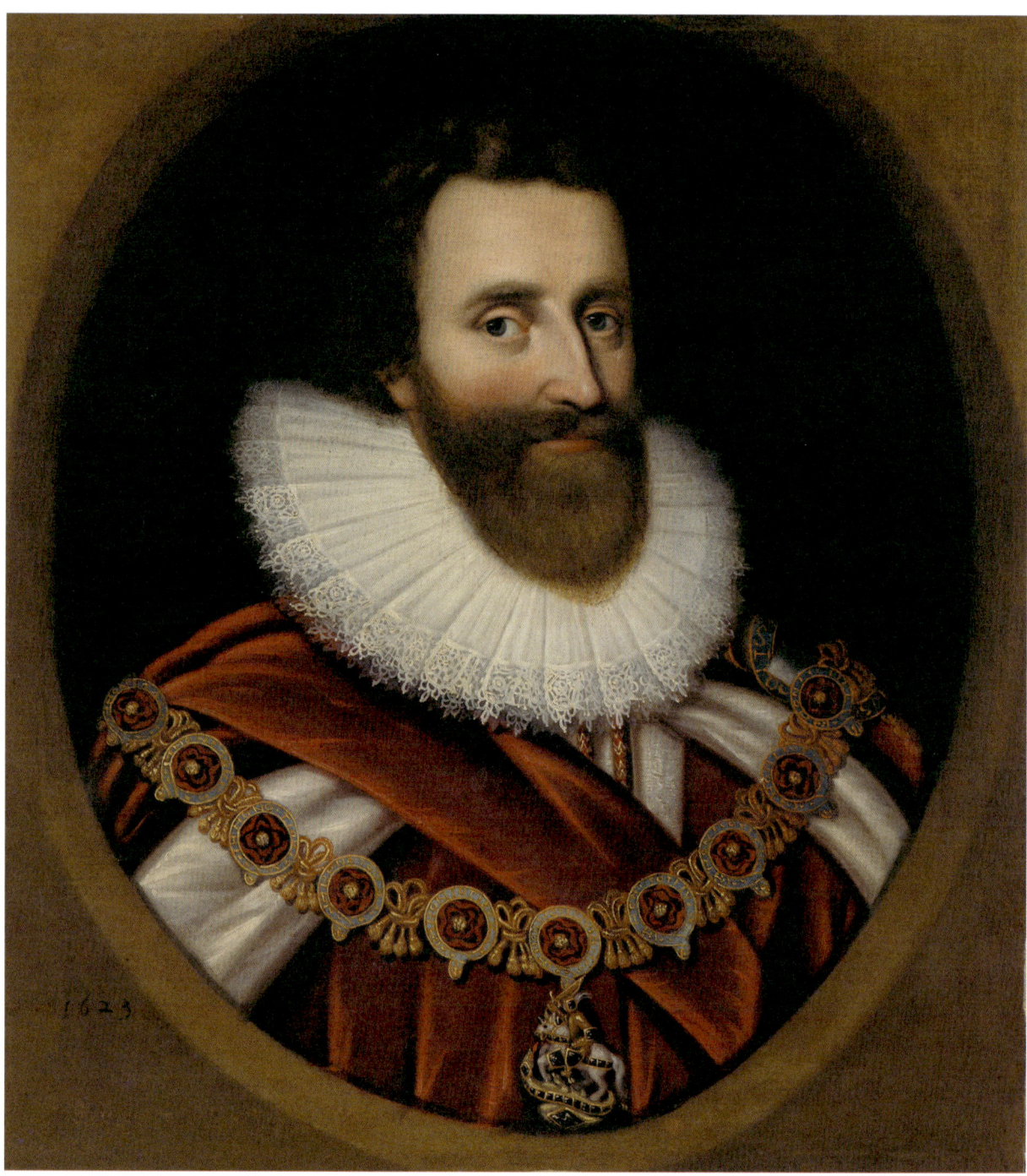

Cat.43 (left)
Unknown artist, after Paul van Somer (1577/8–1621/2)
Ludovic Stuart, 2nd Duke of Lennox (1574–1624), **1623**
Oil on canvas, 68.9 × 63.8 cm
National Galleries of Scotland, Edinburgh (PG 864)

PROVENANCE: Purchased from Lady Halkett, 1916.

Cat.44 (opposite)
Gerrit van Honthorst (1592–1656)
Charles I, **1628**
Oil on canvas, 45.7 × 40.6 cm (cut down, previously 68.5 × 58.4 cm)
Private collection

PROVENANCE: Purchased by Edward Farmer, Watford, from an anonymous sale at Robinson & Foster, as 'Van Dyck, Portrait of a Cavalier', 1948; purchased at Sotheby's, London, 'Old Masters and Early British Paintings' Sale, 20 October 2008, lot 178.

Cat.45
Alexander Keirincx (1600–1652)
*Falkland Palace and the Howe
of Fife, c.1639*
Oil on panel, 45.6 × 68.6 cm
National Galleries of Scotland,
Edinburgh (PG 2409)

PROVENANCE: Painted for Charles I
and recorded as being in the King's
galleries at Oatlands; sold to
Remigius Leemput, 3 May 1650
or 1651; Galerie Pardo, Paris;
purchased from S. Nystad in 1977.

REFERENCES: Millar 1960, p.160;
Millar 1972, p.278; Edinburgh
1990, cat.76, pp.66–67; Edinburgh
1998, cat.2, p.16; Macdonald 2000,
p.49; Townsend 2003, pp.137–50;
SNPG 2014, p.26; Townsend 2018,
no.20F, pp.40–50; Allerston 2023,
no.5, p.32

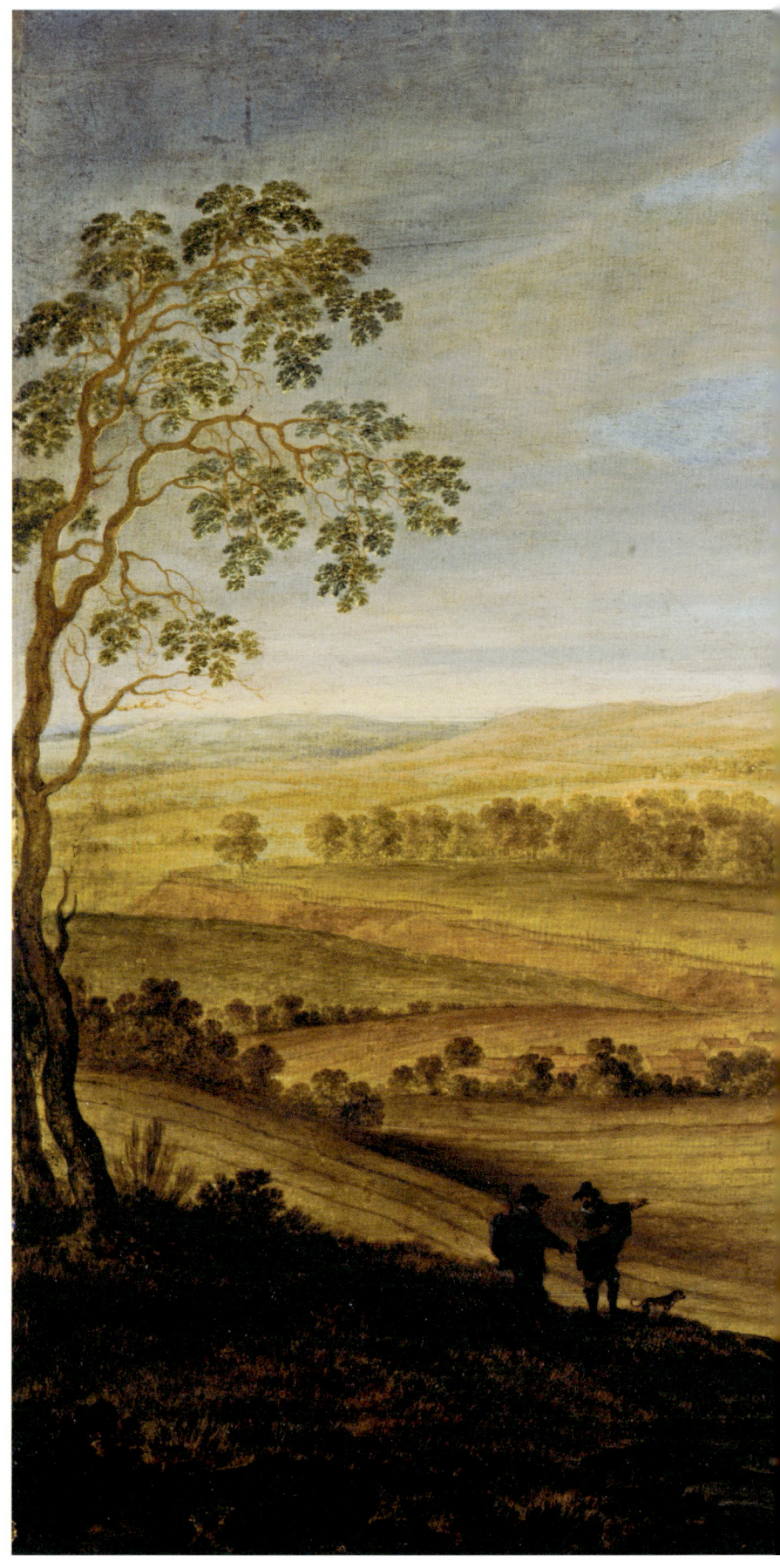

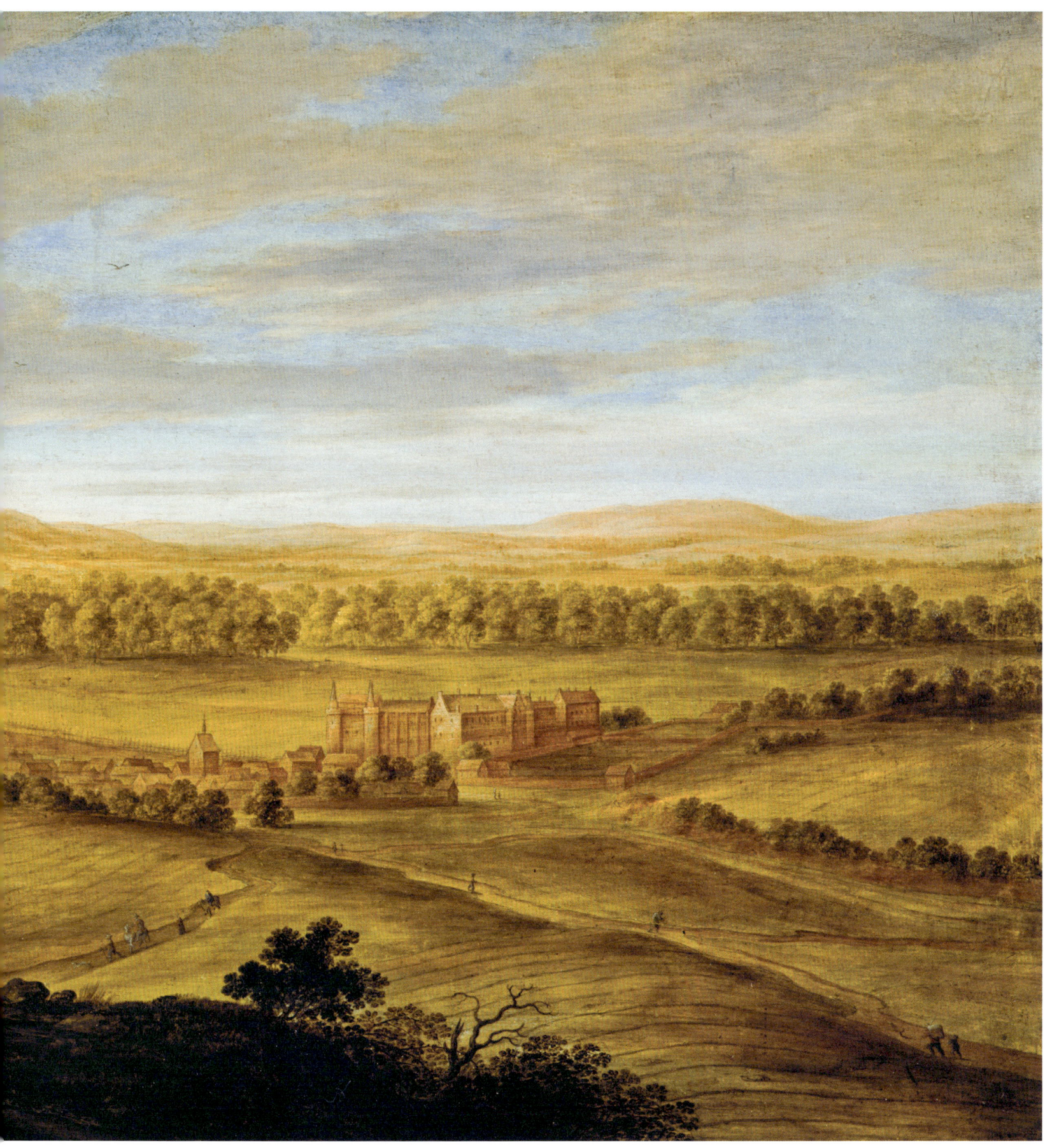

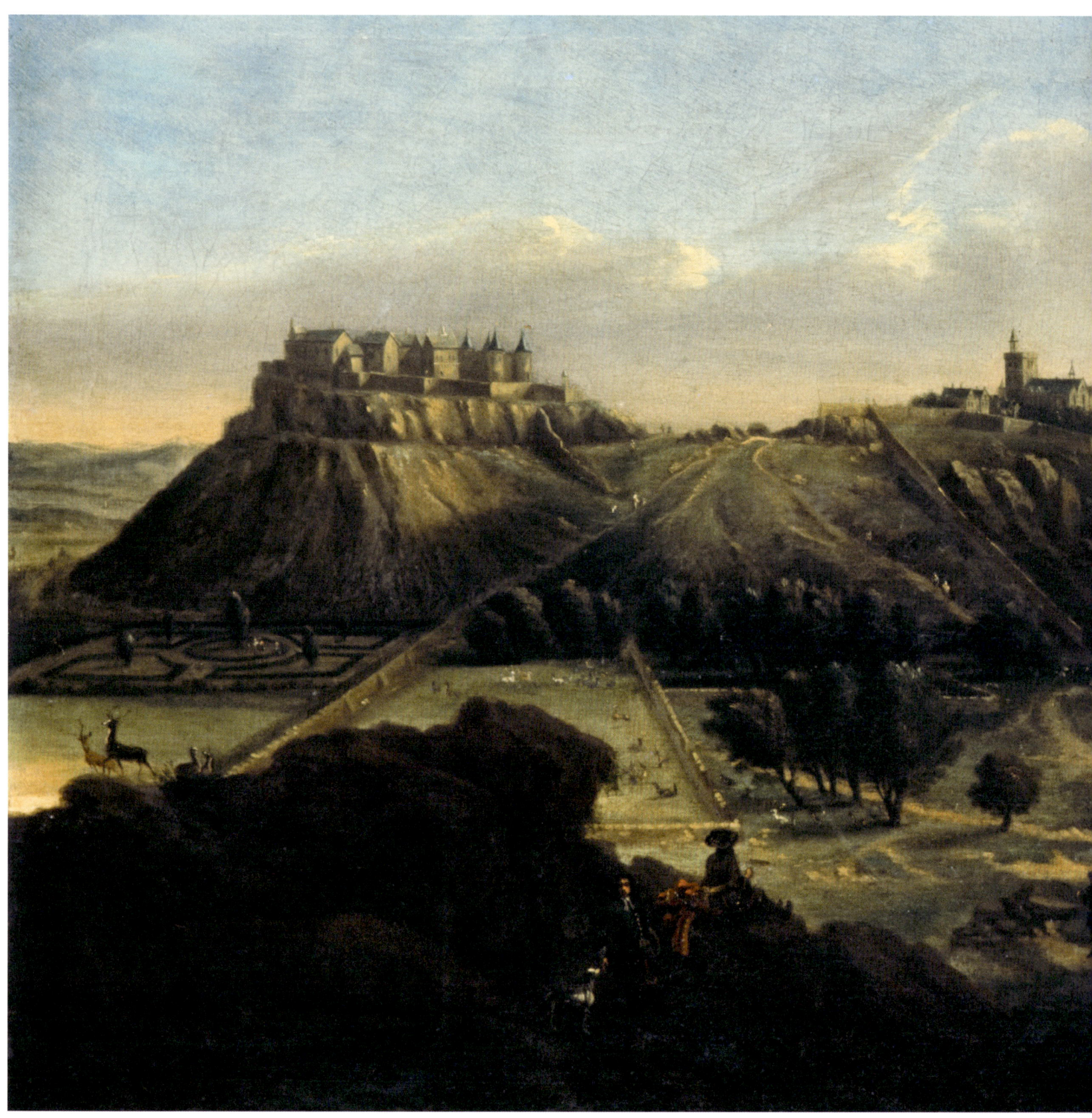

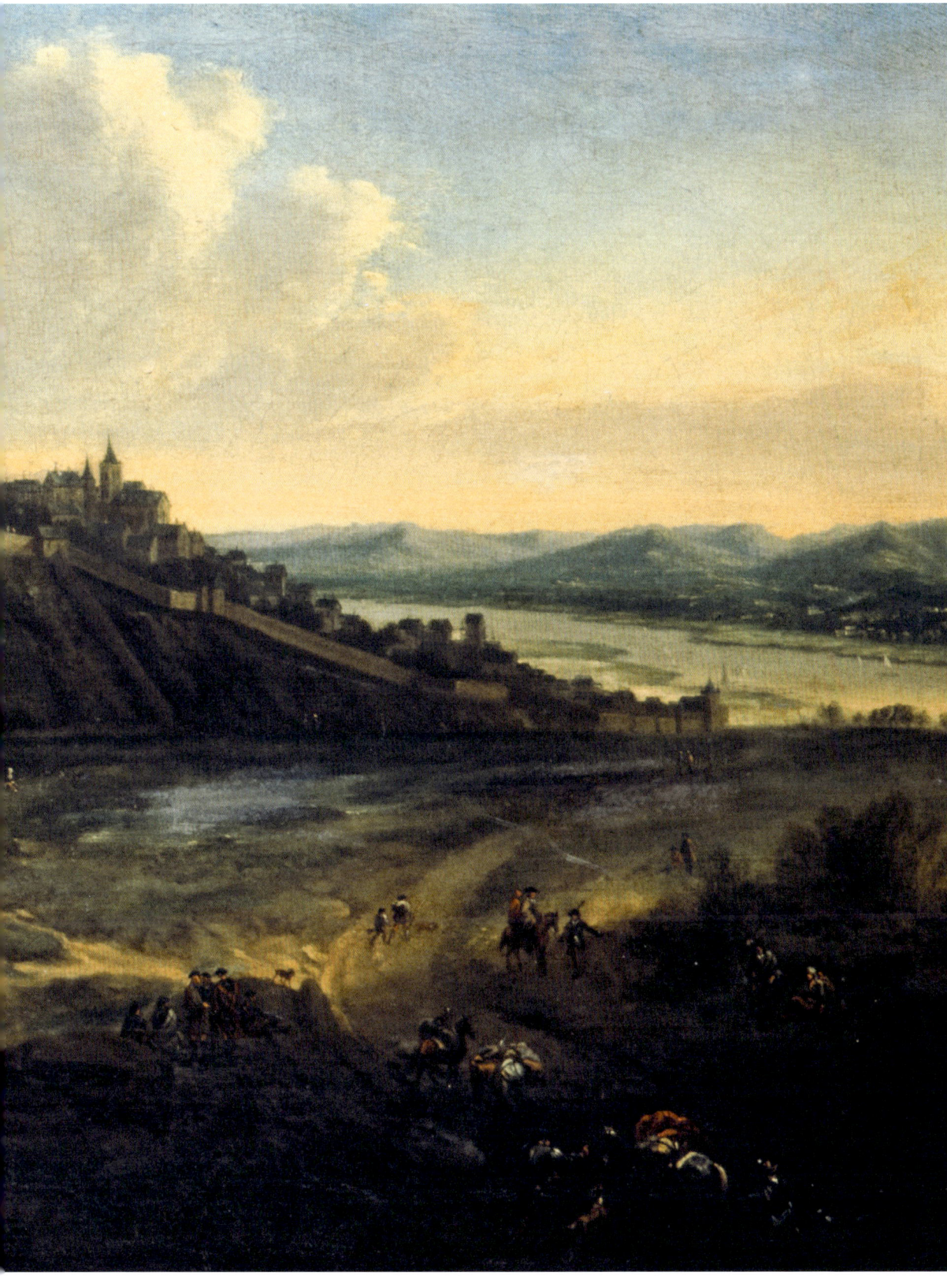

Cat.46
Johannes Vorsterman
(c.1643–1699)
View of Stirling Castle, *c.*1670
Oil on canvas, 62.2 × 109.2 cm
On long-term loan to the National
Galleries of Scotland from The
Duke of Hamilton, Lennoxlove
House (NGL 001.99)

PROVENANCE: Dukes of Hamilton
at Lennoxlove House.

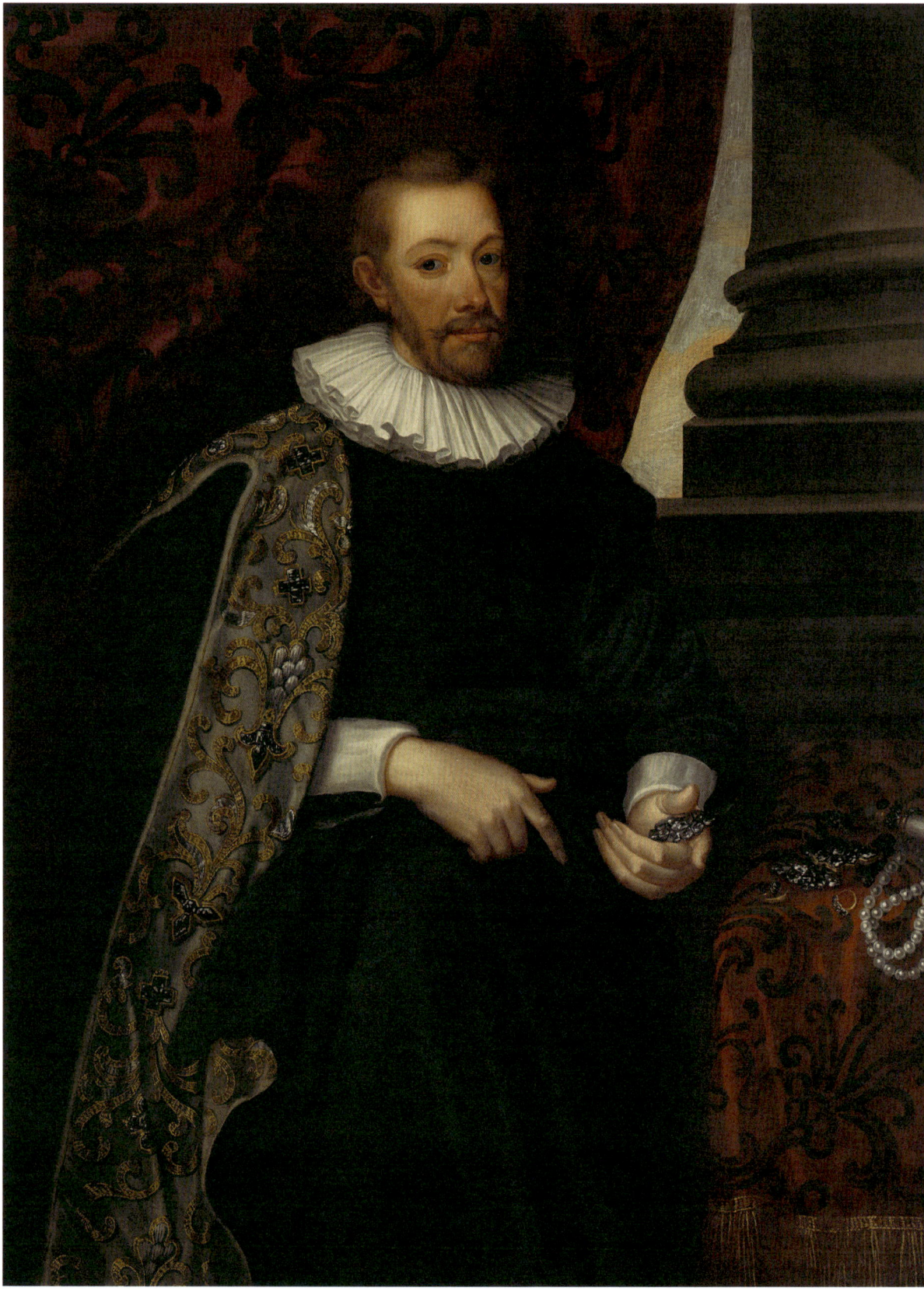

Cat.47 (left)
John Scougall (1657–1737)
George Heriot (1563–1624),
1698
Oil on canvas, 150 × 117 cm
George Heriot's Trust

PROVENANCE: Commissioned
by Governors of George Heriot's
School after 1698.

REFERENCES: Edinburgh 1884,
cat.55; Edinburgh 1975, p.37,
cat.218; Edinburgh 1991, cat.17,
p.30

Cat.48 (opposite)
**John Scougall (1657–1737),
after an unknown sixteenth-
century artist**
*John Erskine, 1st Earl of Mar
(died 1572), Regent of Scotland*,
after 1680
Oil on canvas, 73.7 × 60.7 cm
National Galleries of Scotland,
Edinburgh (PG 653)

PROVENANCE: Purchased from
Mr Montgomery Pearson using
Gray Bequest Fund, 1906.

REFERENCES: Edinburgh 1975,
cat.19, p.11

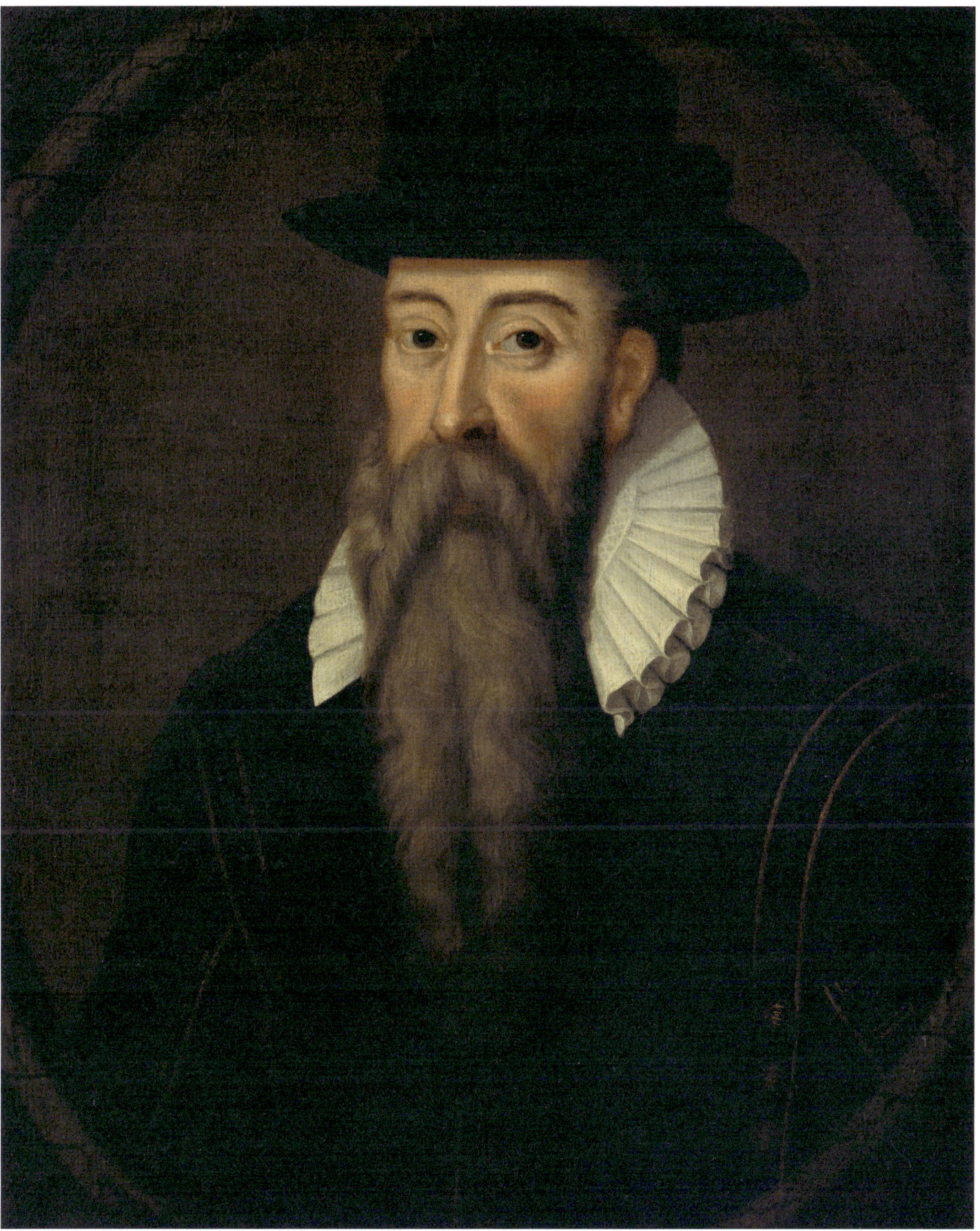

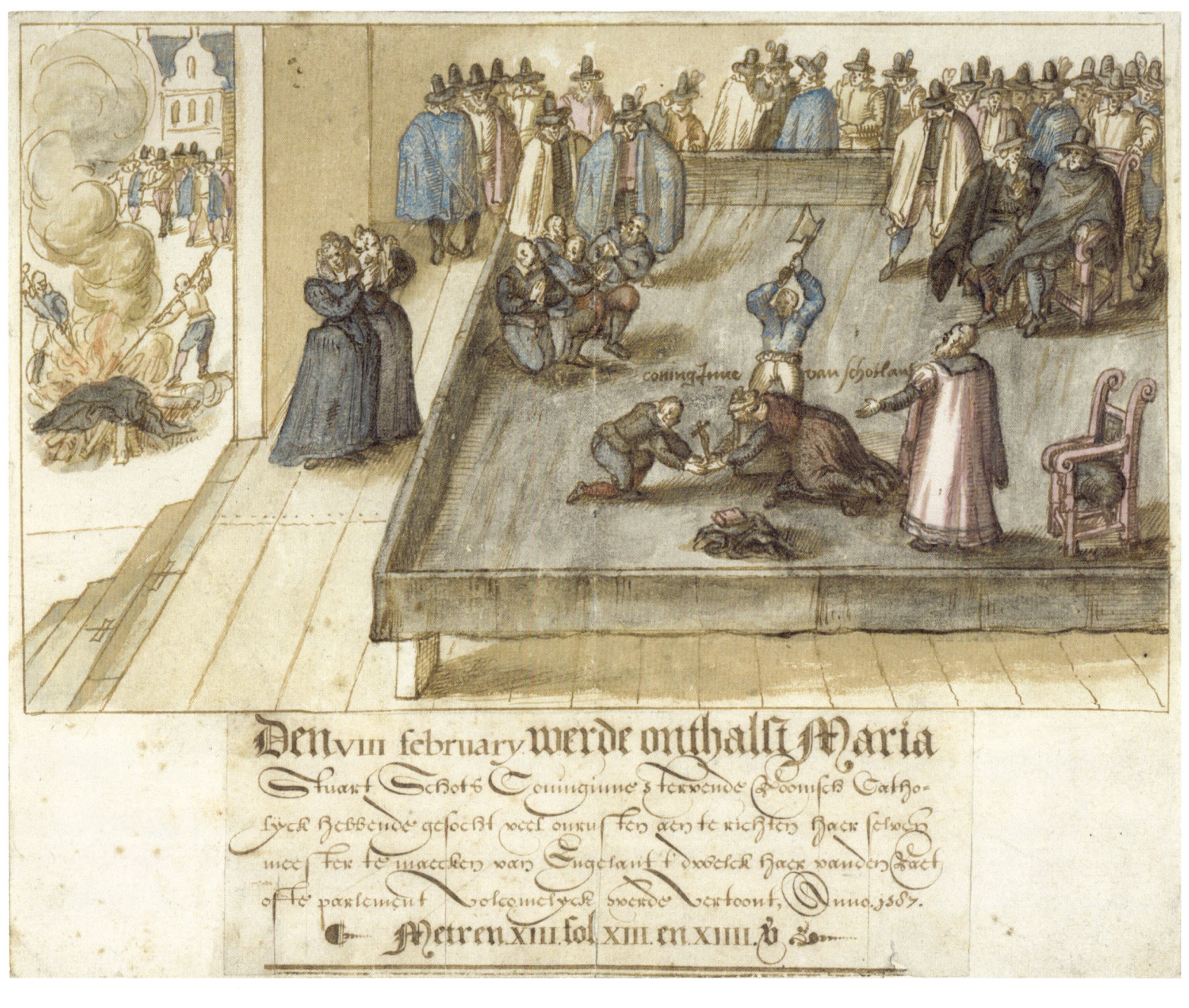

Den VIII february werde onthalst Maria
Stuart Schots Coninginne s'terwende Roomsch Catho-
lyck Hebbende gesocht veel onrusten aen te richten haer scloech
meer ter te maecken van Engelant t'dwelck haer vanden raet
ofte te parlement volcomelyck werde vertoont, Anno 1587.
Metten XIII. fol. XIII. en XIIII. b.

DRAWINGS & WATERCOLOURS

Cat.49 (opposite)
Unknown artist
The Execution of Mary,
*Queen of Scots, c.*1613
Watercolour on paper,
21.9 × 26.4 cm
National Galleries of Scotland,
Edinburgh (PG 1217)

PROVENANCE: Originally part of an
album compiled in 1613 by Willem
Luytsz. van Kittensteyn, Delft;
in the collection of Dr T.J. Walker
by 1887; purchased by Bernard
Halliday, Leicester (dealer) at
Dr Walker's sale, 1918; sold to
Mr T. Hatton; re-purchased by
Bernard Halliday at Hatton's sale,
1933; purchased by the Scottish
National Portrait Gallery, 1934.

REFERENCES: Peterborough 1887,
cat.137, p.33; Edinburgh 1975,
cat.23, pp.6, 11, 14; Edinburgh
1987, cat.31, pp.51–52; Edinburgh
2013, pp.59 and 108, cat.197;
SNPG 2014, p.15

Cat.50 (detail, right)
Esther Inglis (1569–1624)
Cinquante Octonaires sur la
Vanite et Inconstance du Monde
dediez a... Lodowic Duc de
Lenox (Ludovic Stuart, 2nd
Duke of Lennox), 1607
Ink and watercolour on paper, in
green velvet binding, 9.5 × 13.5 cm
Sir Robert Clerk of Penicuik,
National Records of Scotland,
deposited collection
(GD18/4508/5)

PROVENANCE: probably in the
collection of Ludovic Stuart, 2nd
Duke of Lennox; Sir George Clerk
of Penicuik, Bart., 1865; Sir John
Clerk of Penicuik (deposited in
the National Records of Scotland,
1963); Sir Robert Clerk of Penicuik.

REFERENCES: Laing 1865, p.284;
Scott-Elliot & Yeo 1990, pp.58–59

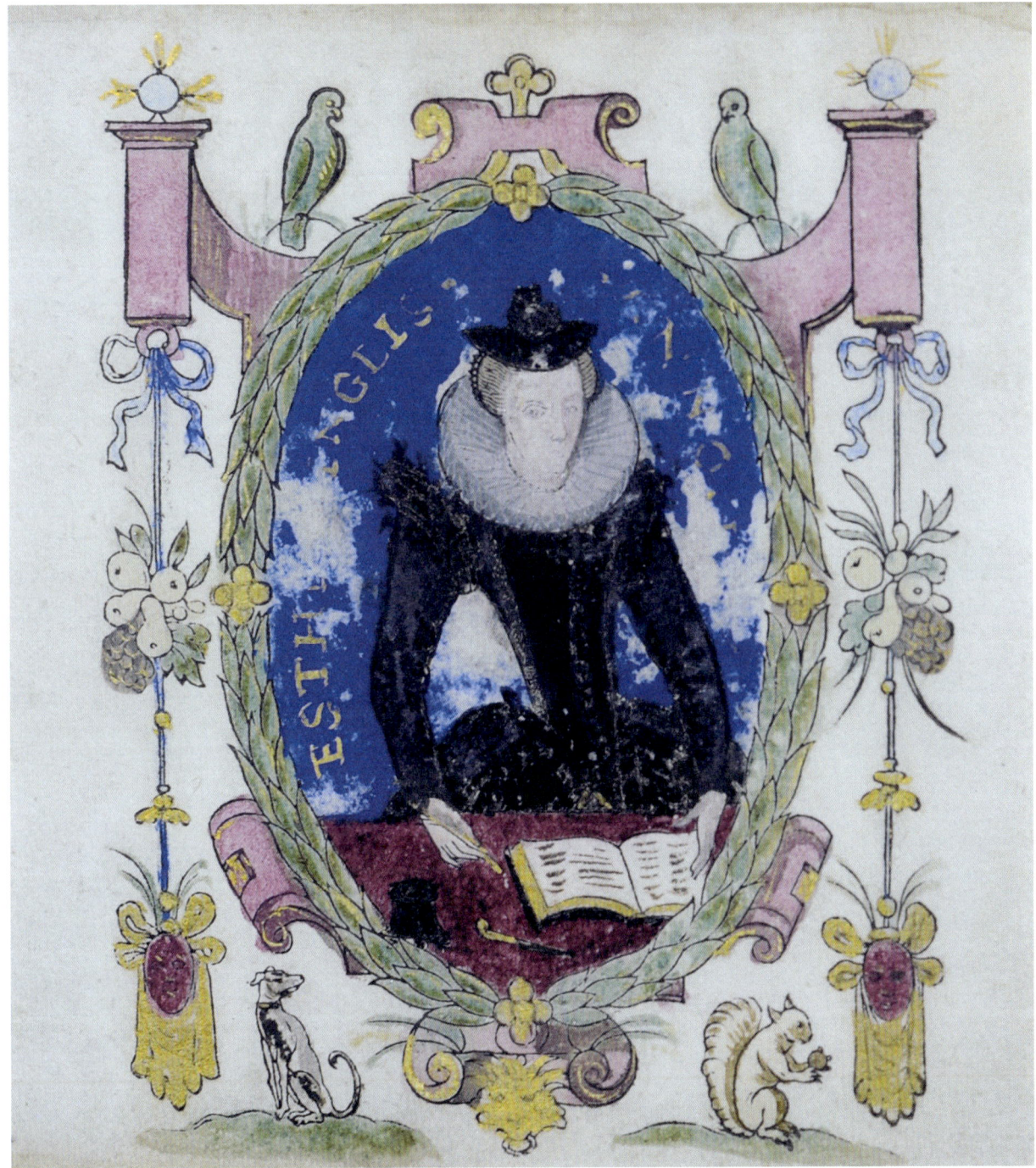

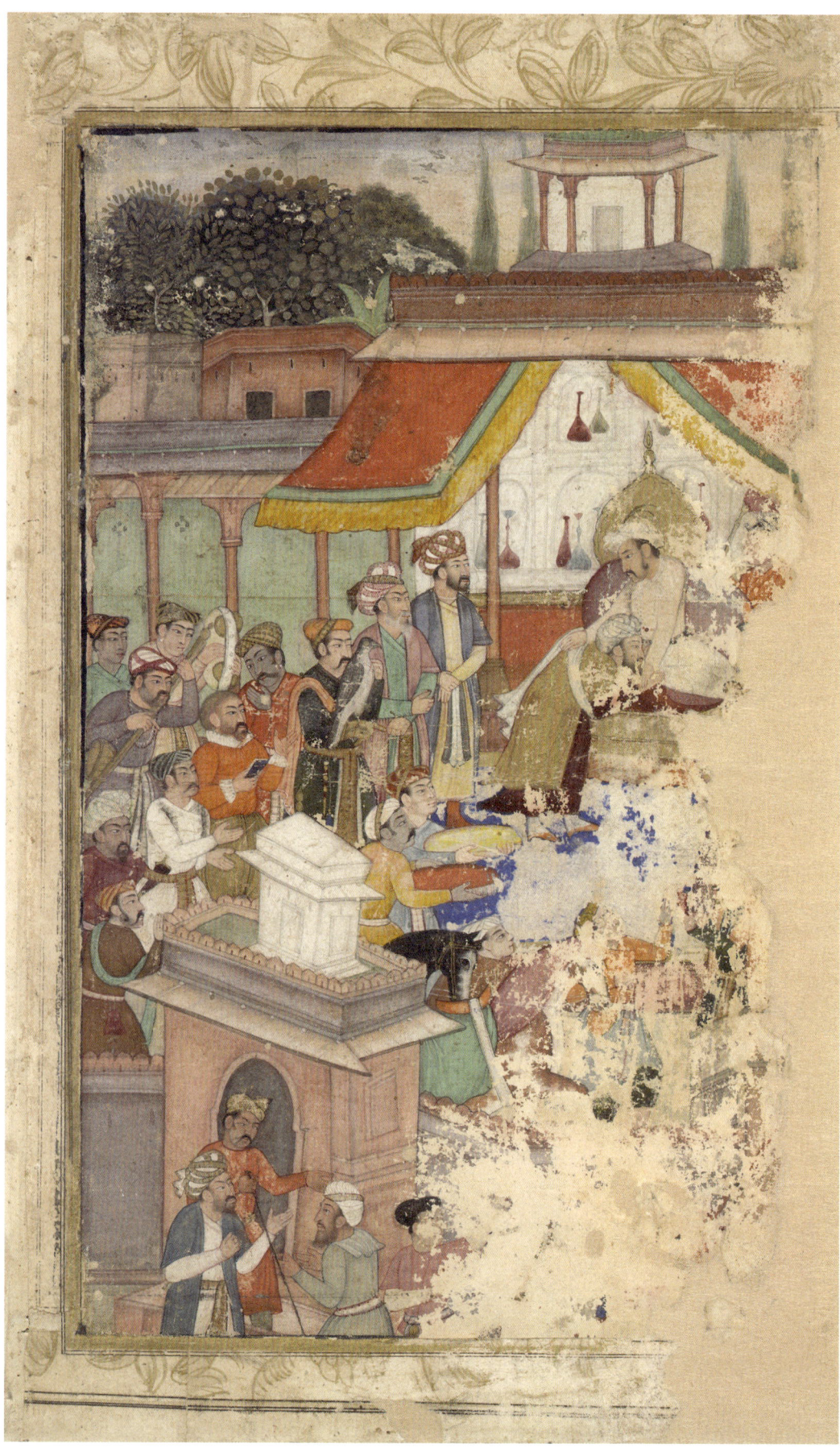

Cat.51
Unknown artist, Mughal Style
Jahangir investing a courtier with a robe of honour watched by Sir Thomas Roe, English ambassador to the court of Jahangir at Agra from 1615–18, and others, c.1616
Watercolour on paper,
27.8 × 16.1 cm
British Museum, London
(1933,0610,0.1)

PROVENANCE: Donated by The Art Fund in 1933.

REFERENCES: Rogers 1993, fig.46, p.72; Das 2023

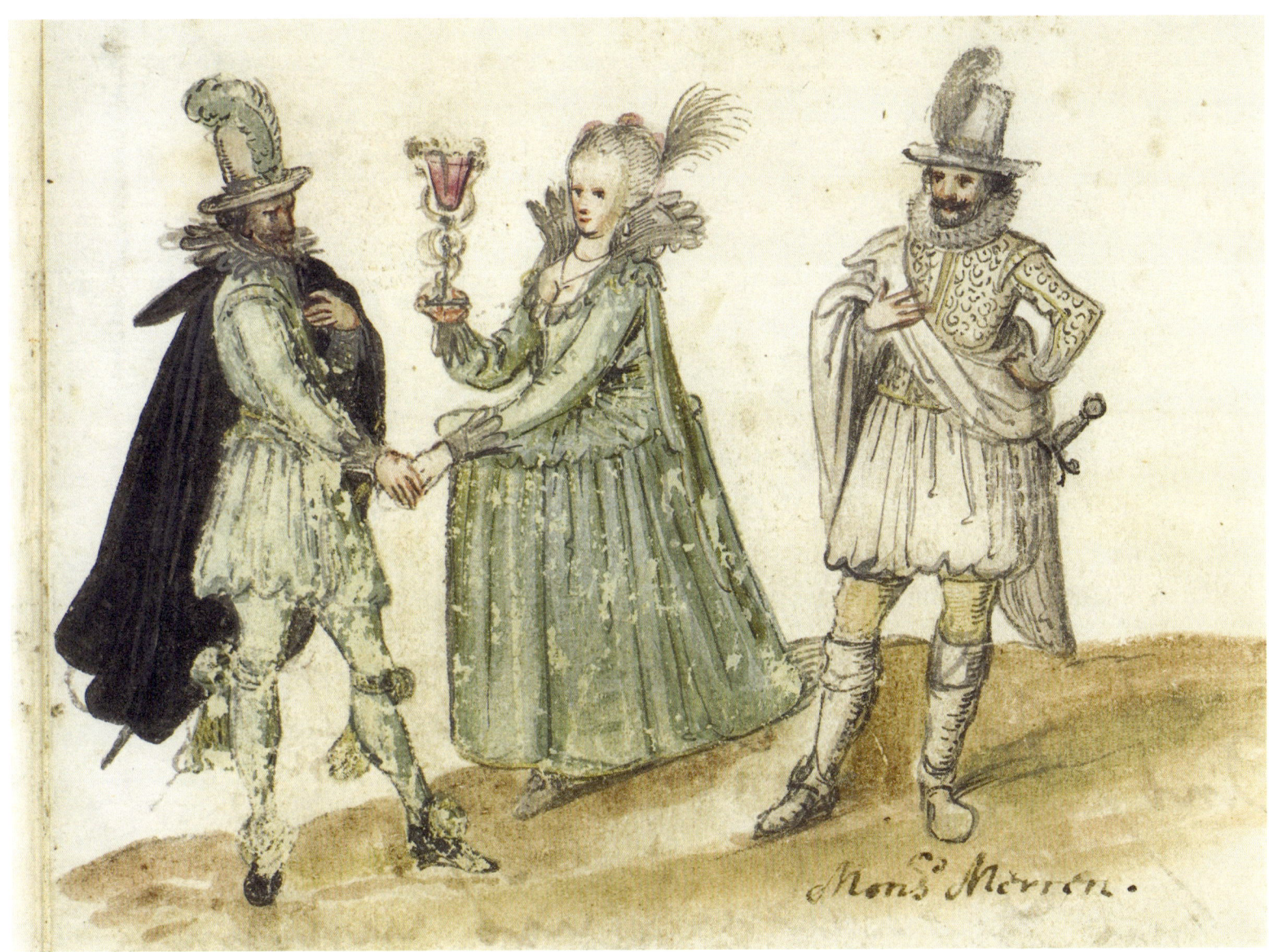

Cat.52
Unknown artist
King James and Anna of Denmark with a Venetian Goblet, from an *Album Amicorum* owned by Michael van Meer, 1614–48
Ink and watercolour on paper, bound in leather, 13 × 19 cm
The University of Edinburgh Heritage Collections (La.III.283, f.152r)

PROVENANCE: David Laing Bequest, 1878.

REFERENCES: Edinburgh 1975, p.9, cat.10; Laroque 1993, pp.66–67; Schlueter 2006, pp.301–14

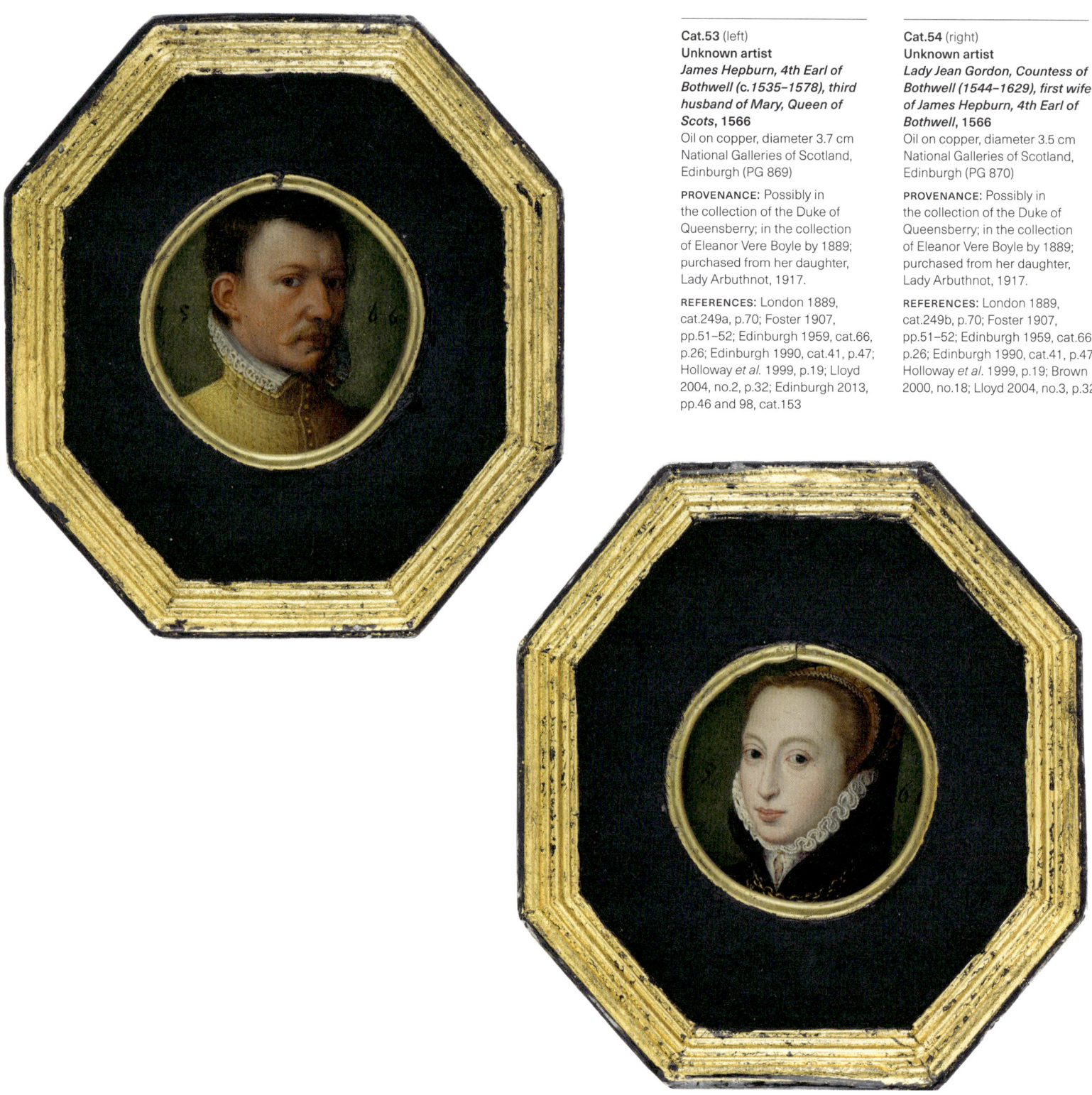

Cat.53 (left)
Unknown artist
James Hepburn, 4th Earl of Bothwell (c.1535–1578), third husband of Mary, Queen of Scots, 1566
Oil on copper, diameter 3.7 cm
National Galleries of Scotland, Edinburgh (PG 869)

PROVENANCE: Possibly in the collection of the Duke of Queensberry; in the collection of Eleanor Vere Boyle by 1889; purchased from her daughter, Lady Arbuthnot, 1917.

REFERENCES: London 1889, cat.249a, p.70; Foster 1907, pp.51–52; Edinburgh 1959, cat.66, p.26; Edinburgh 1990, cat.41, p.47; Holloway *et al.* 1999, p.19; Lloyd 2004, no.2, p.32; Edinburgh 2013, pp.46 and 98, cat.153

Cat.54 (right)
Unknown artist
Lady Jean Gordon, Countess of Bothwell (1544–1629), first wife of James Hepburn, 4th Earl of Bothwell, 1566
Oil on copper, diameter 3.5 cm
National Galleries of Scotland, Edinburgh (PG 870)

PROVENANCE: Possibly in the collection of the Duke of Queensberry; in the collection of Eleanor Vere Boyle by 1889; purchased from her daughter, Lady Arbuthnot, 1917.

REFERENCES: London 1889, cat.249b, p.70; Foster 1907, pp.51–52; Edinburgh 1959, cat.66, p.26; Edinburgh 1990, cat.41, p.47; Holloway *et al.* 1999, p.19; Brown 2000, no.18; Lloyd 2004, no.3, p.32

MINIATURES

Cat.55
Nicholas Hilliard (1547–1619)
James VI & I, 1609
Watercolour on vellum,
5.2 × 4.3 cm
The Buchanan Society, on long-
term loan to the National Galleries
of Scotland, Edinburgh (PGL 153)

PROVENANCE: Messrs John
Yates & Son Antiques, Stirling;
purchased by George Buchanan
of Clairinch, 1935 and presented
to the Buchanan Society, 1936;
on long-term loan to the Scottish
National Portrait Gallery since
1936.

REFERENCES: Reynolds 1952,
p.20; Edinburgh 1990, cat.45, p.49;
Holloway *et al.* 1999, p.22; Lloyd
2004, no.4, p.34; SNPG 2014, p.19

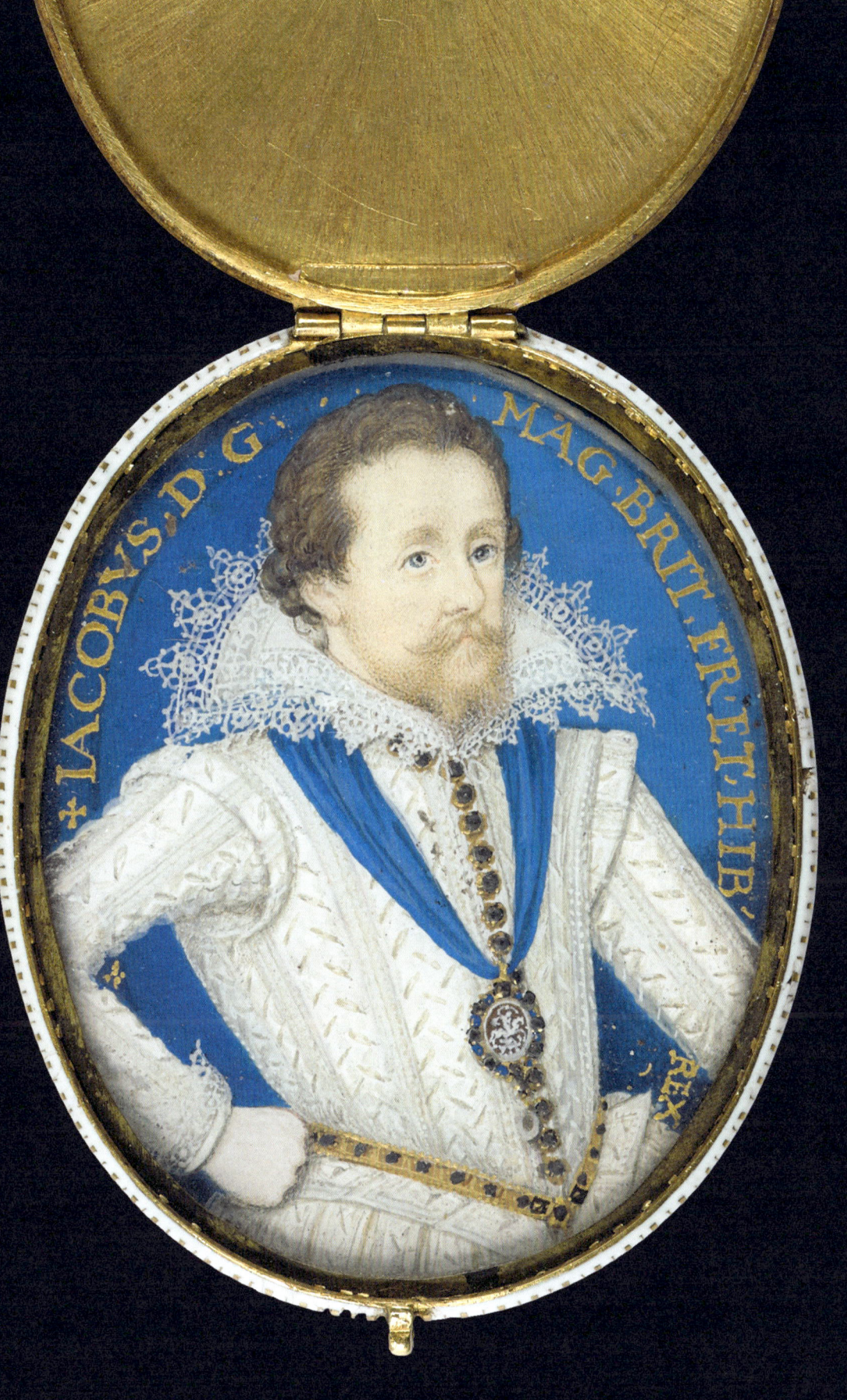

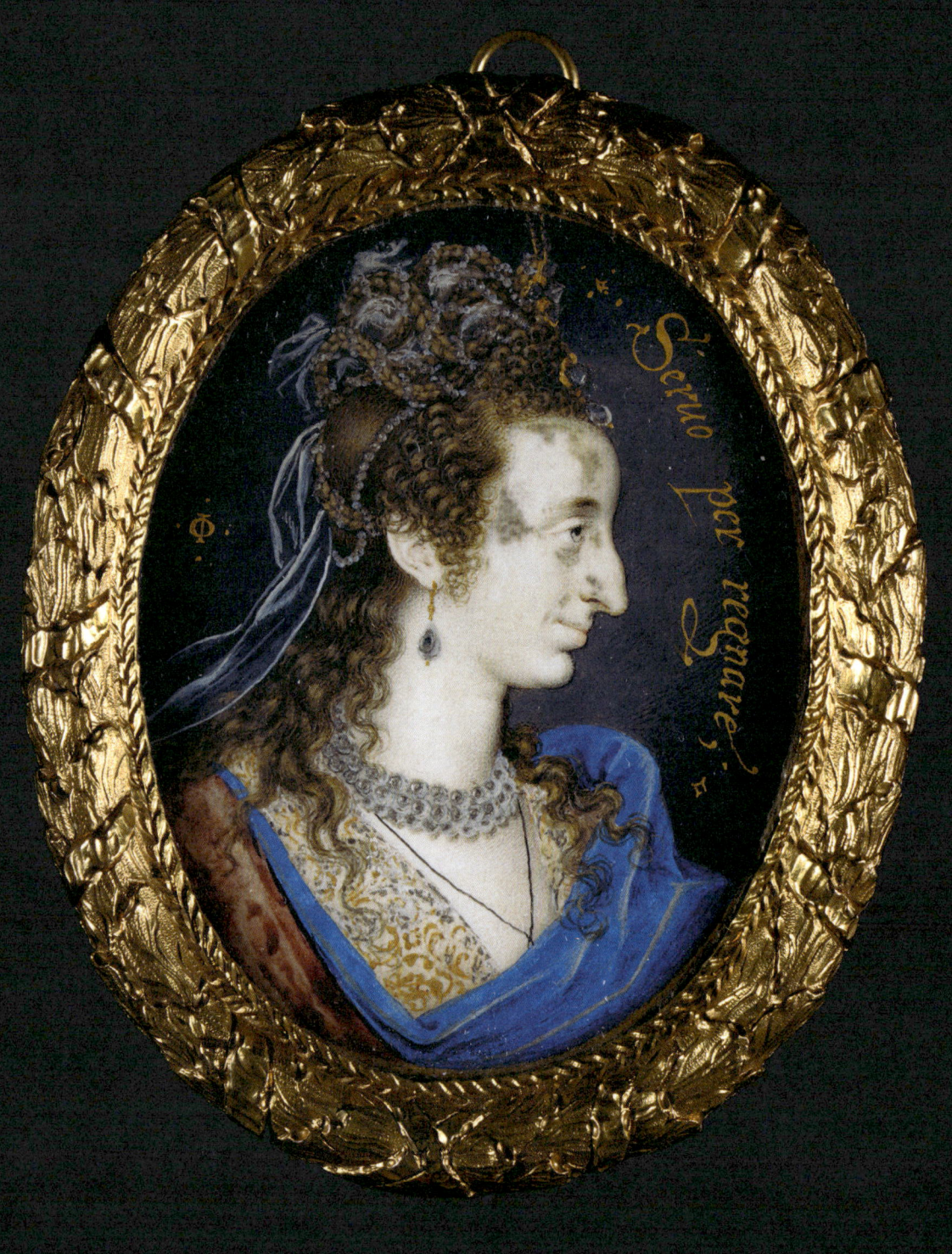

Cat.56
Isaac Oliver (c.1565–1617)
*Anne of Denmark, c.*1610
Watercolour and body colour,
with gold and silver on vellum,
laid on card, 5.2 × 4.2 cm
Royal Collection Trust /
His Majesty King Charles III
(RCIN 420025)

PROVENANCE: Dr Richard Mead;
purchased by Frederick, Prince
of Wales; by descent in the Royal
Collection.

REFERENCES: Auerbach 1961,
p.249; Manchester 1964, p.38,
cat.44; London 1983, cat.225,
pp.139–40; Reynolds 1999, no.52,
pp.89–90; London 1996, pp.84–85;
London 2012a, cat.43, p.116;
London 2019a, cat.83, pp.200–01

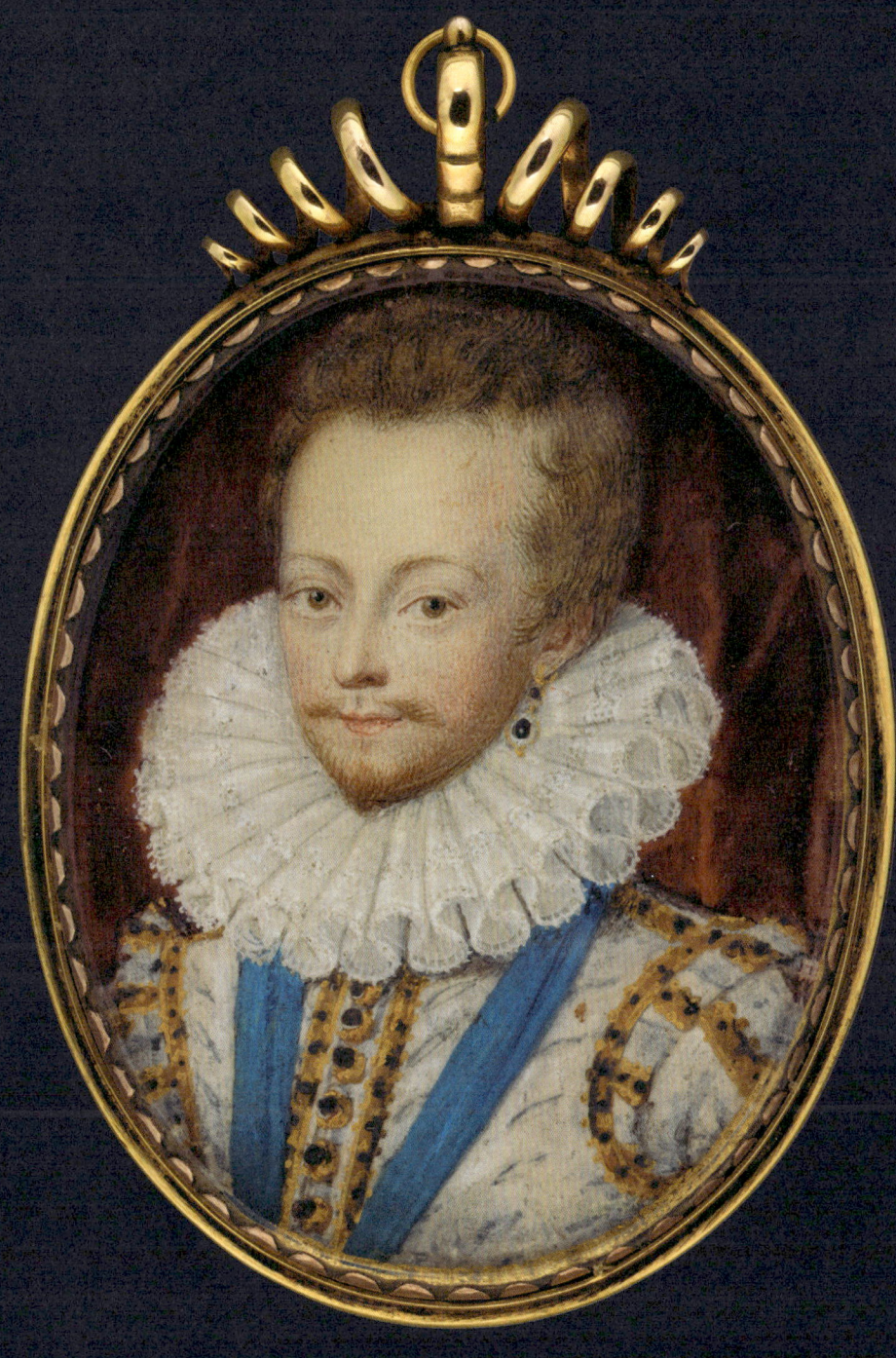

Cat.57
Nicholas Hilliard (1547–1619)
Robert Carr, Earl of Somerset
*(1585/6–1645), c.*1611
Watercolour on vellum laid onto
a playing card, 4.4 × 3.5 cm
National Portrait Gallery,
London (NPG 4260)

PROVENANCE: Collection of Lady
Shelley-Rolls, sold at Christie's,
13 February 1962, lot 58 and
purchased by the National Portrait
Gallery, London.

REFERENCES: Strong 1969a,
p.296; Nicholl 2005, p.20

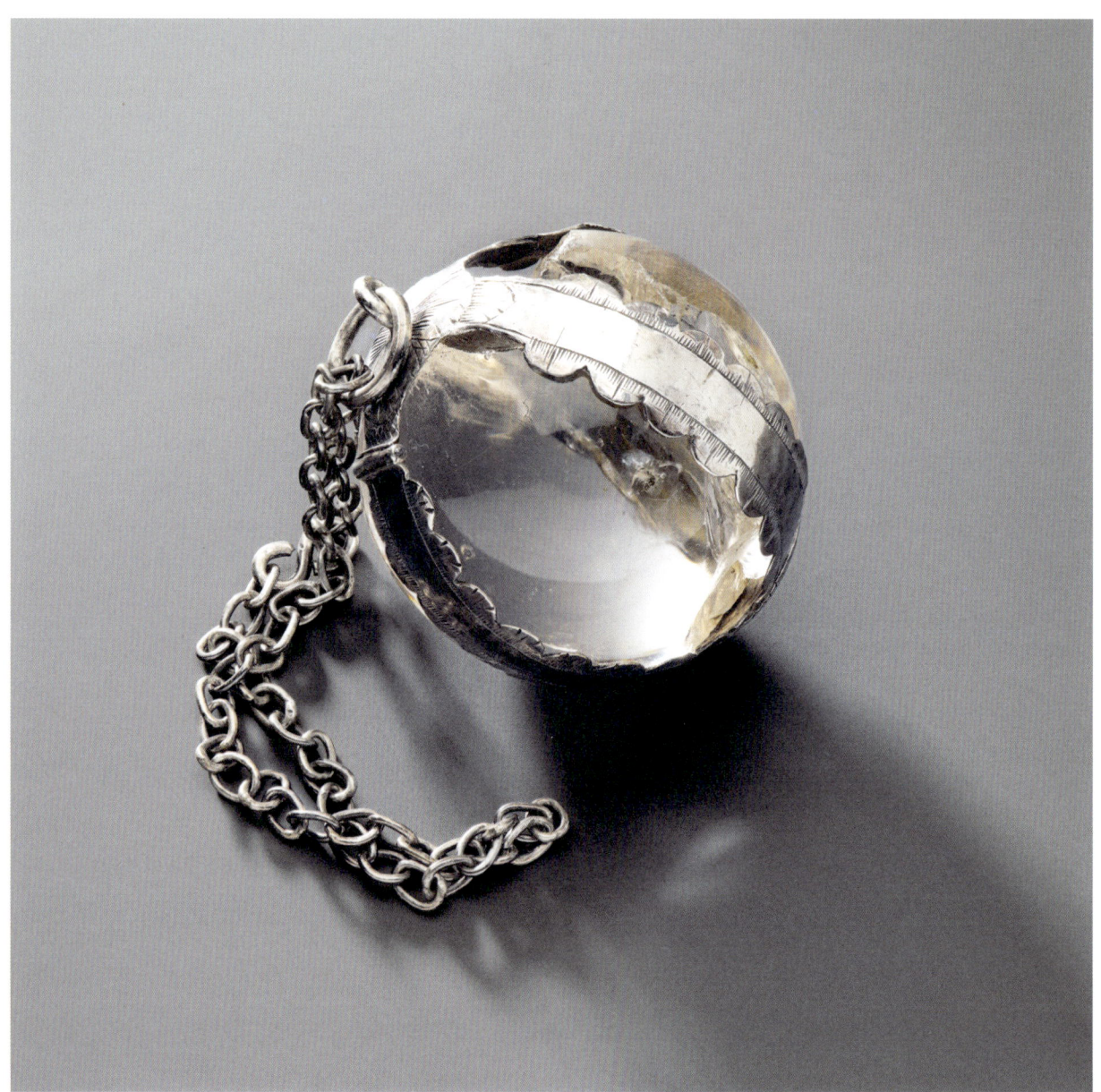

DRESS & JEWELLERY

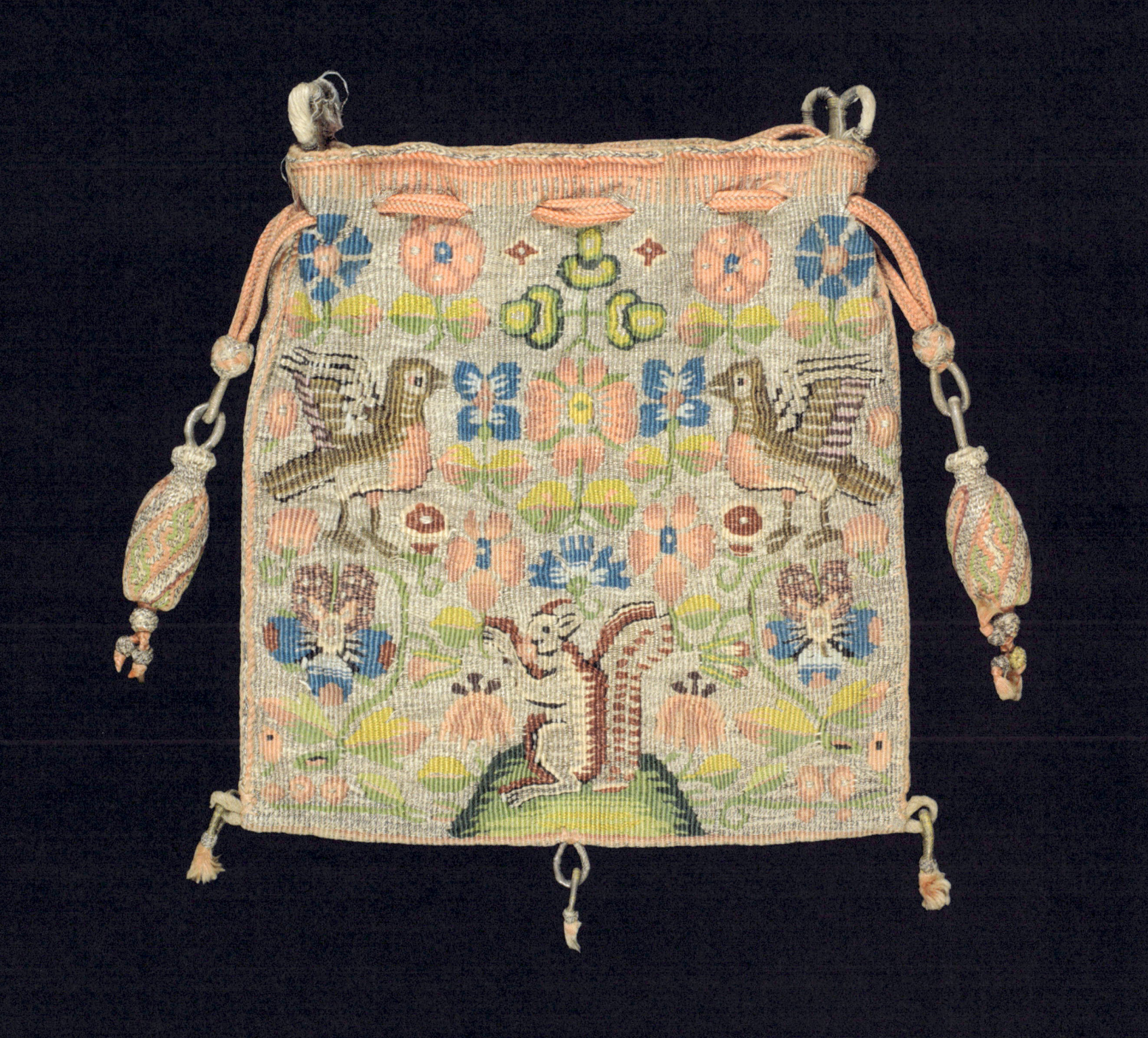

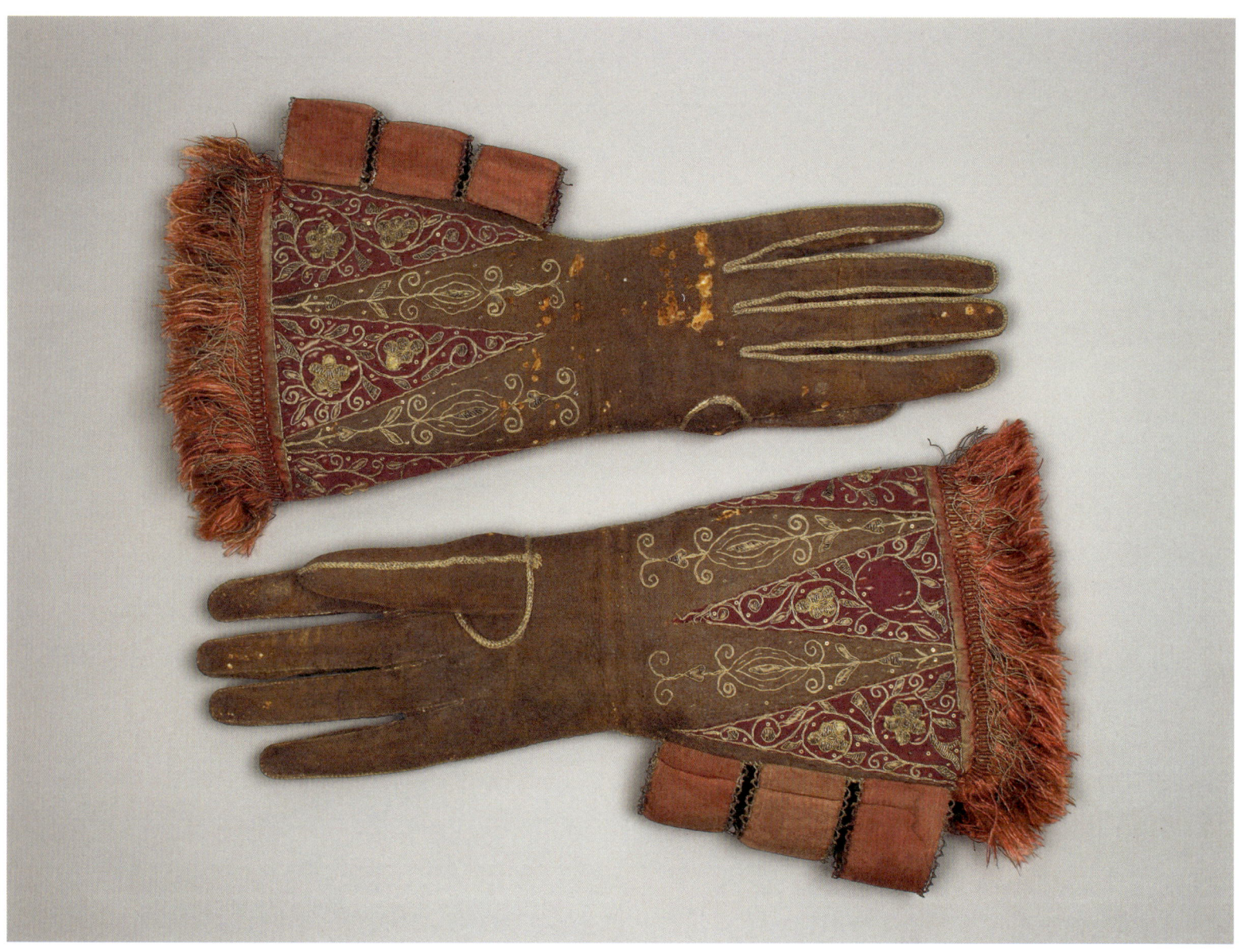

Cat.60 (above)
Unknown maker
Hunting Gloves associated with James VI & I, 1610–25
Doeskin leather, silk, gold and silver metal threads, 44 × 21.5 cm
Fashion Museum Bath, lent by The Glove Collection Trust/ Worshipful Company of Glovers of London ((LOAN) GCT 2337 & A)

PROVENANCE: Given by Robert Spence (1871–1965) as part of 'The Spence Collection' in 1959 to The Worshipful Company of Glovers (owned by The Glove Collection Trust).

Cat.61 (opposite)
Unknown English maker
Women's Embroidered Waistcoat (Bodice), c.1618–20
Linen, silk threads, metal threads and ribbon, waist: 73 cm, bust: 82 cm and nape to hem centre back: 47 cm
Fashion Museum Bath, lent by Richard Porter and Frances Bateman ((LOAN) POR I.13.132)

PROVENANCE: Possibly belonged to Alice Le Strange (1585–1656), wife of Hammon Le Strange (1583–1654) of Hunstanton Hall, Norfolk; by descent through the Le Strange family to Bernard Le Strange (1900–1958); probably acquired as part of the sale of Hunstanton Hall, which was purchased by Mr Eric Porter from Bernard Le Strange in 1948; by descent to the present owners.

REFERENCES: London 2013b, pp.164–68

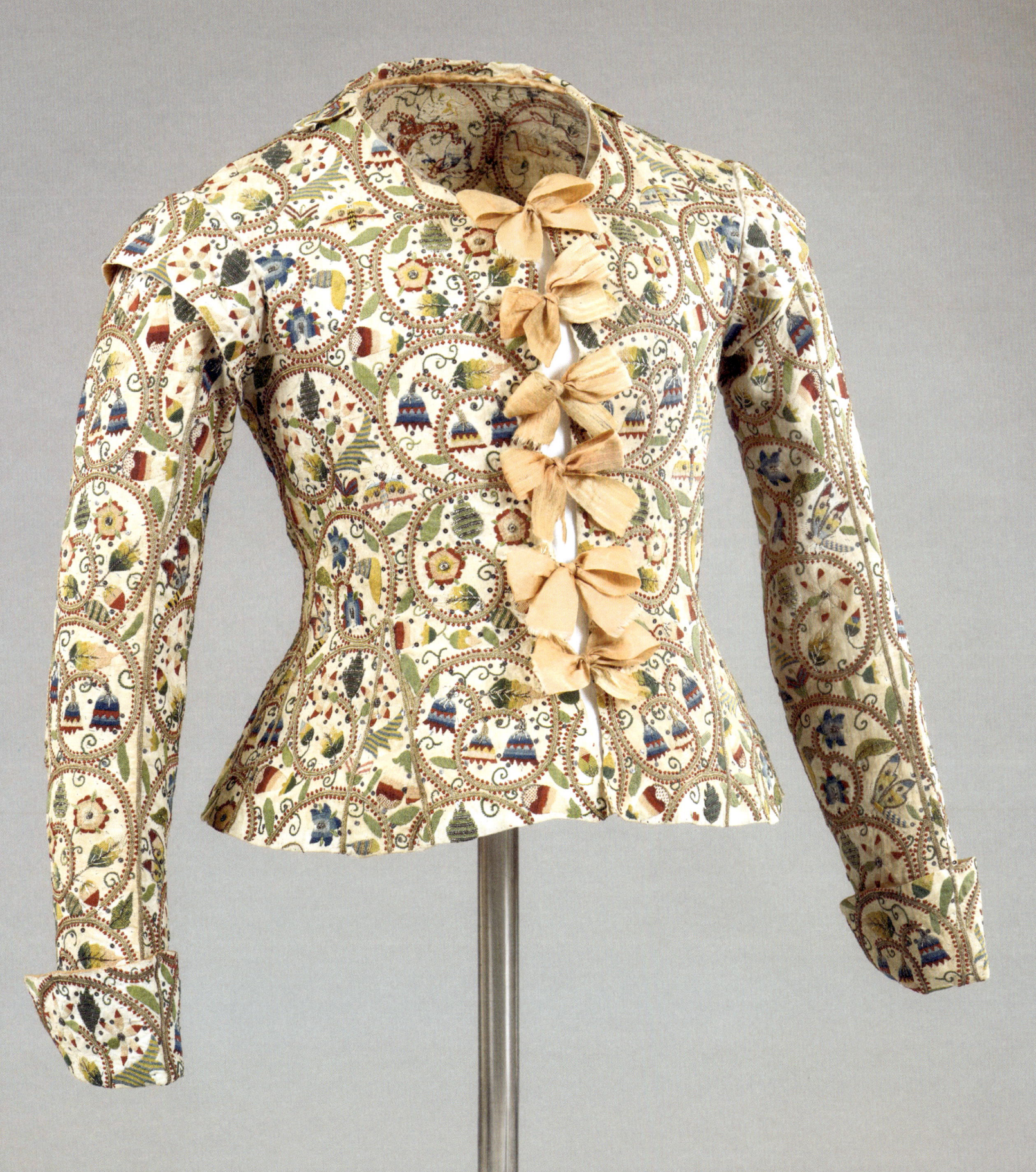

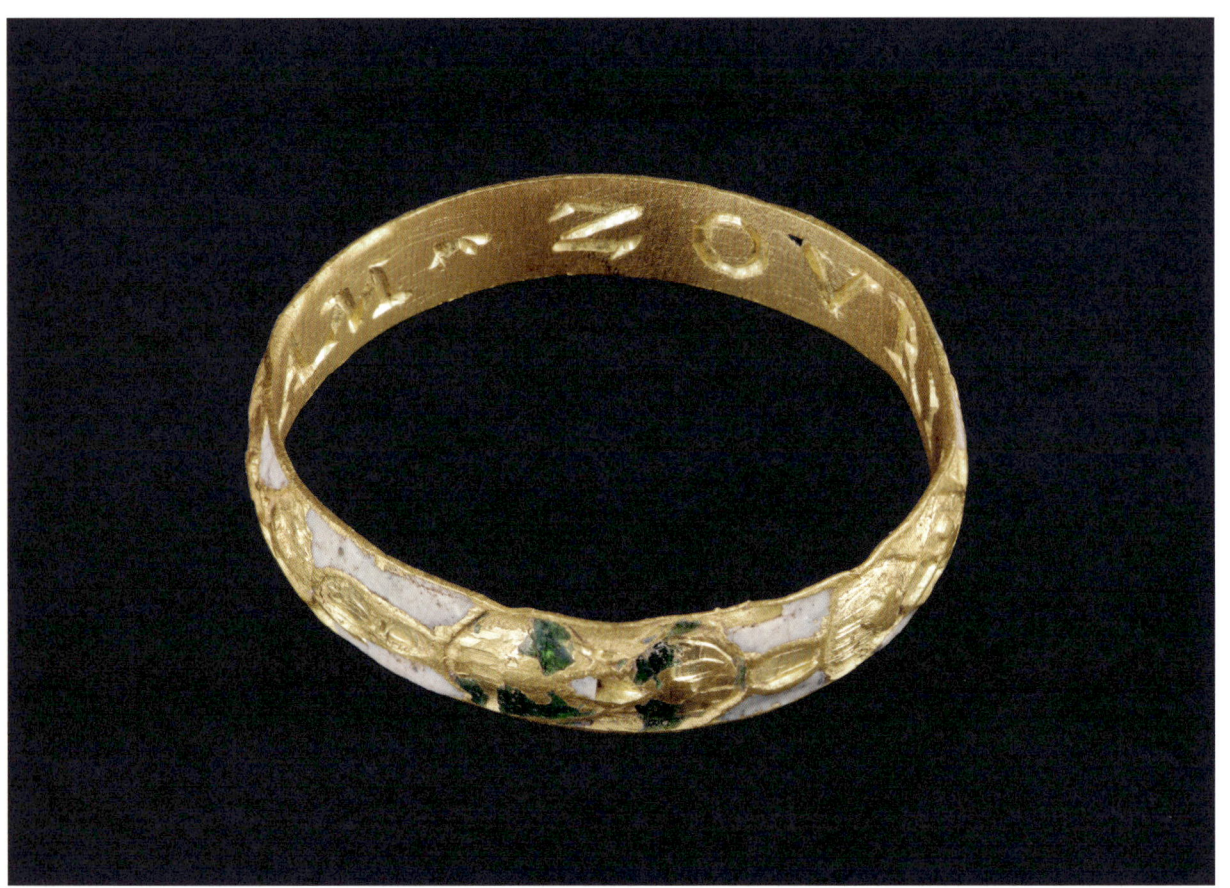

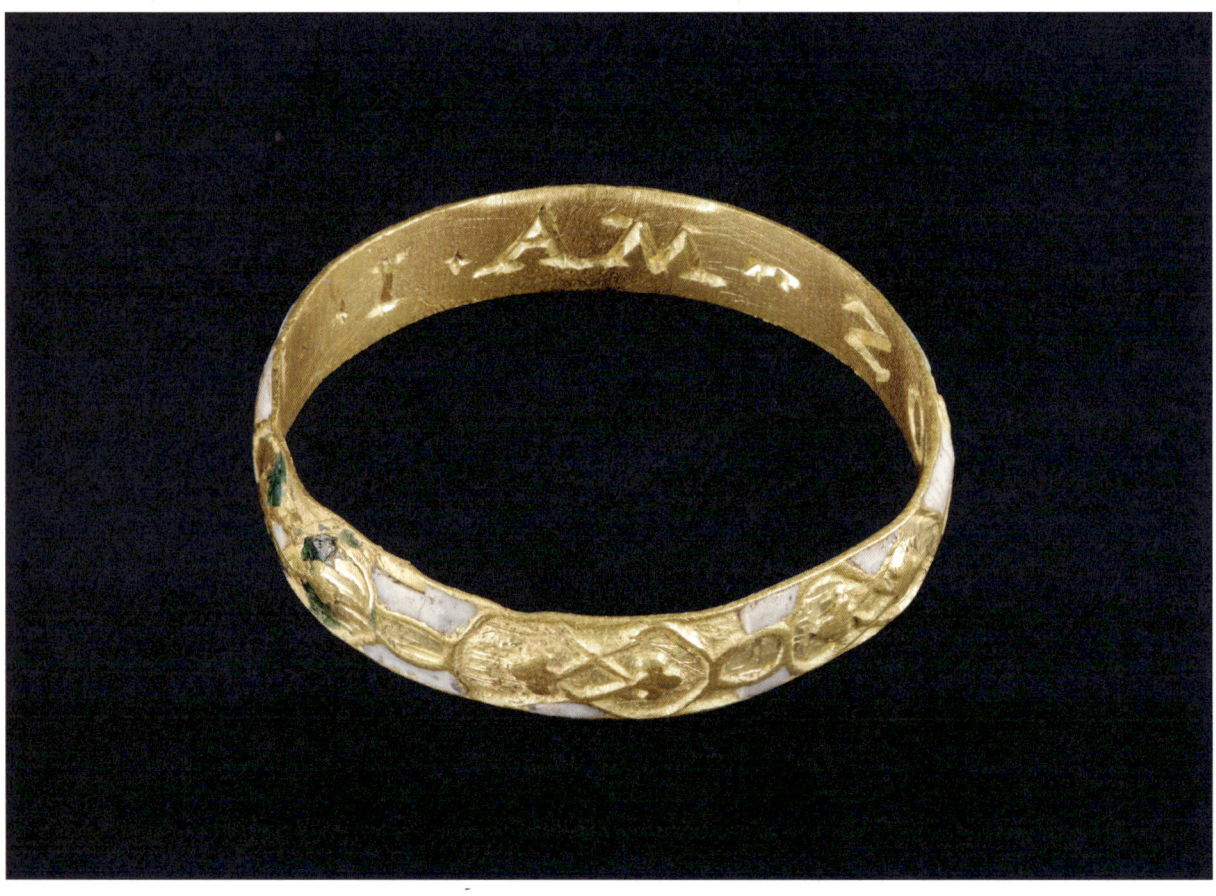

Cat.62
Unknown Scottish maker
Posy Ring, decorated
with foliage and inscribed
'+I+AM-ZOVRIS+' ('I am yours'),
1550–1625
Gold and enamel, 1.9 × 0.37cm
National Museums Scotland,
Edinburgh (X.2021.43)

PROVENANCE: Found through
metal-detecting at Arnprior,
Stirling. Allocated to NMS by the
Queen's and Lord Treasurer's
Remembrancer, 2021.

Cat.63
Unknown, probably
Scottish, maker
Silver Vervel (Hawking Ring)
engraved: 'Ja: Nasmith of Posso'
on obverse, 'in Tueddale' on
reverse, sixteenth century
Silver, diameter 1.8 cm
National Museums Scotland,
Edinburgh (X.2021.42)

PROVENANCE: Found through
metal-detecting, Scottish
Borders. Allocated to NMS by
the Queen's and Lord Treasurer's
Remembrancer, 2021.

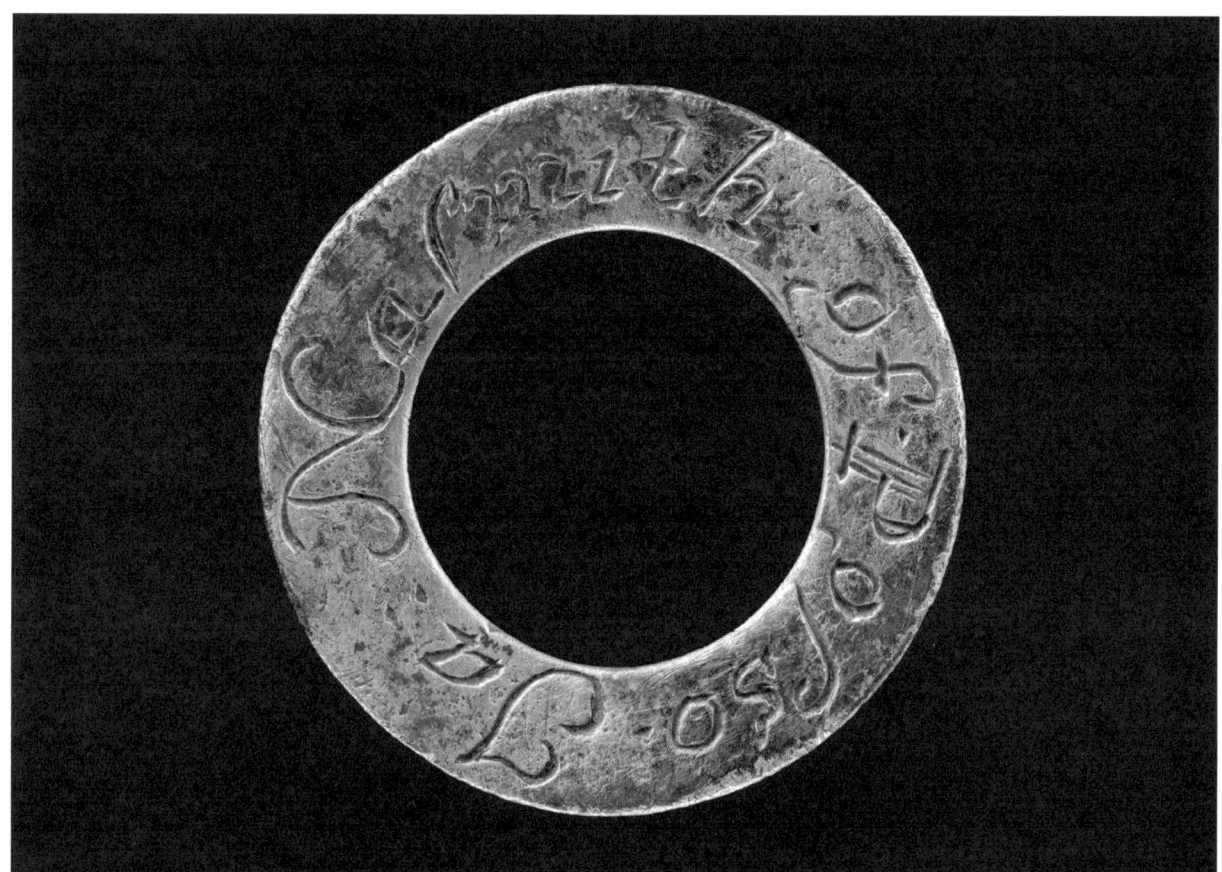

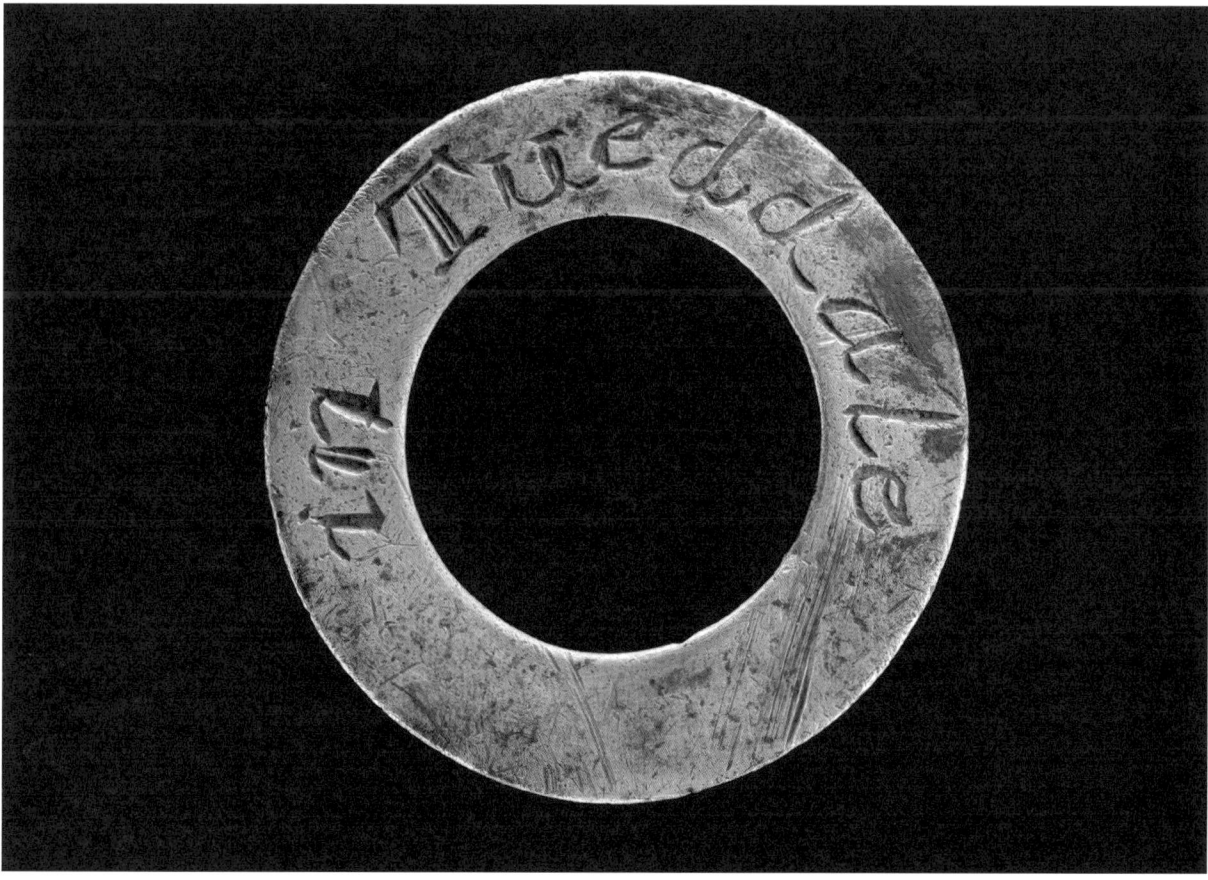

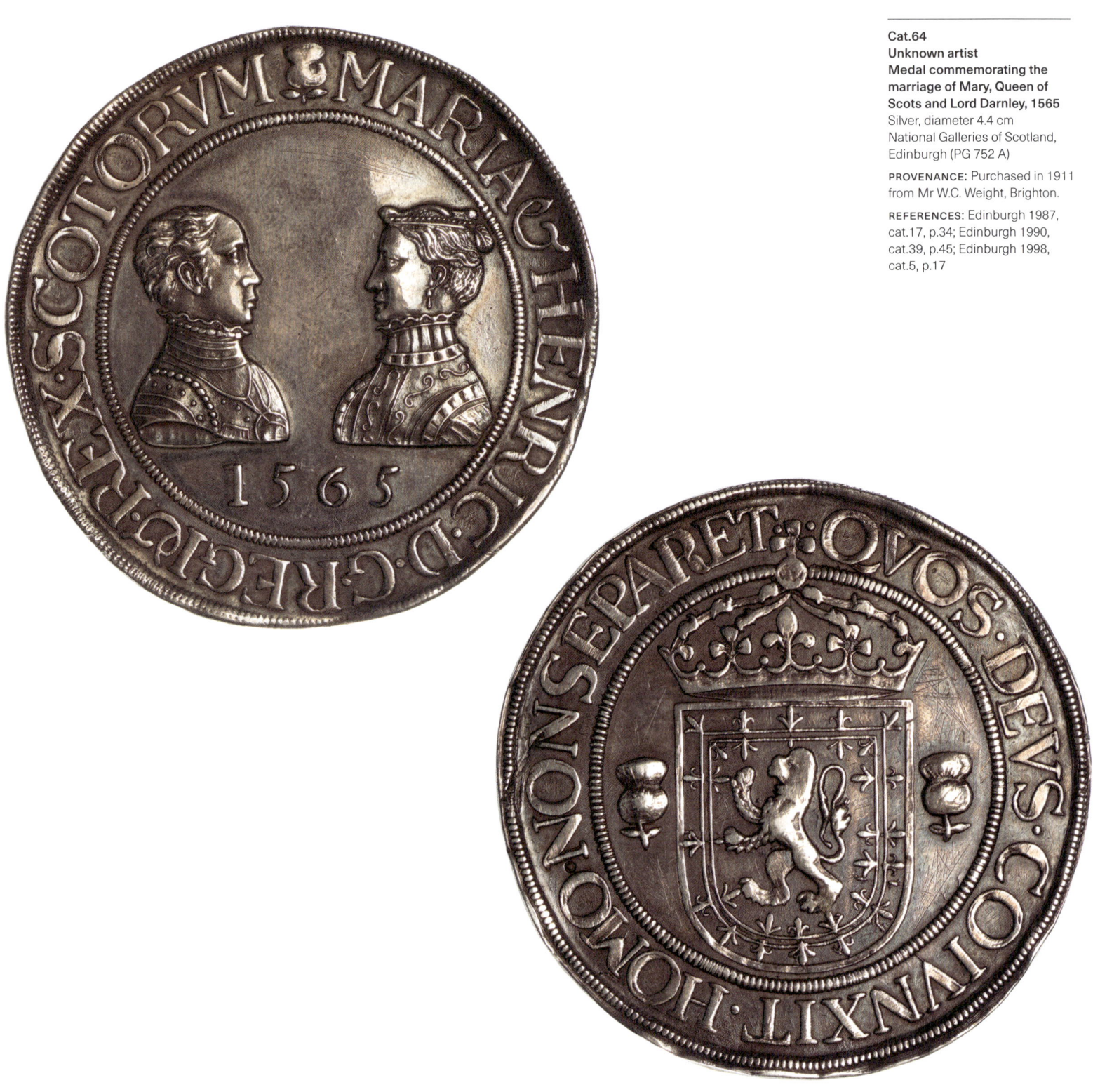

Cat.64
Unknown artist
Medal commemorating the marriage of Mary, Queen of Scots and Lord Darnley, 1565
Silver, diameter 4.4 cm
National Galleries of Scotland, Edinburgh (PG 752 A)

PROVENANCE: Purchased in 1911 from Mr W.C. Weight, Brighton.

REFERENCES: Edinburgh 1987, cat.17, p.34; Edinburgh 1990, cat.39, p.45; Edinburgh 1998, cat.5, p.17

OBJECTS

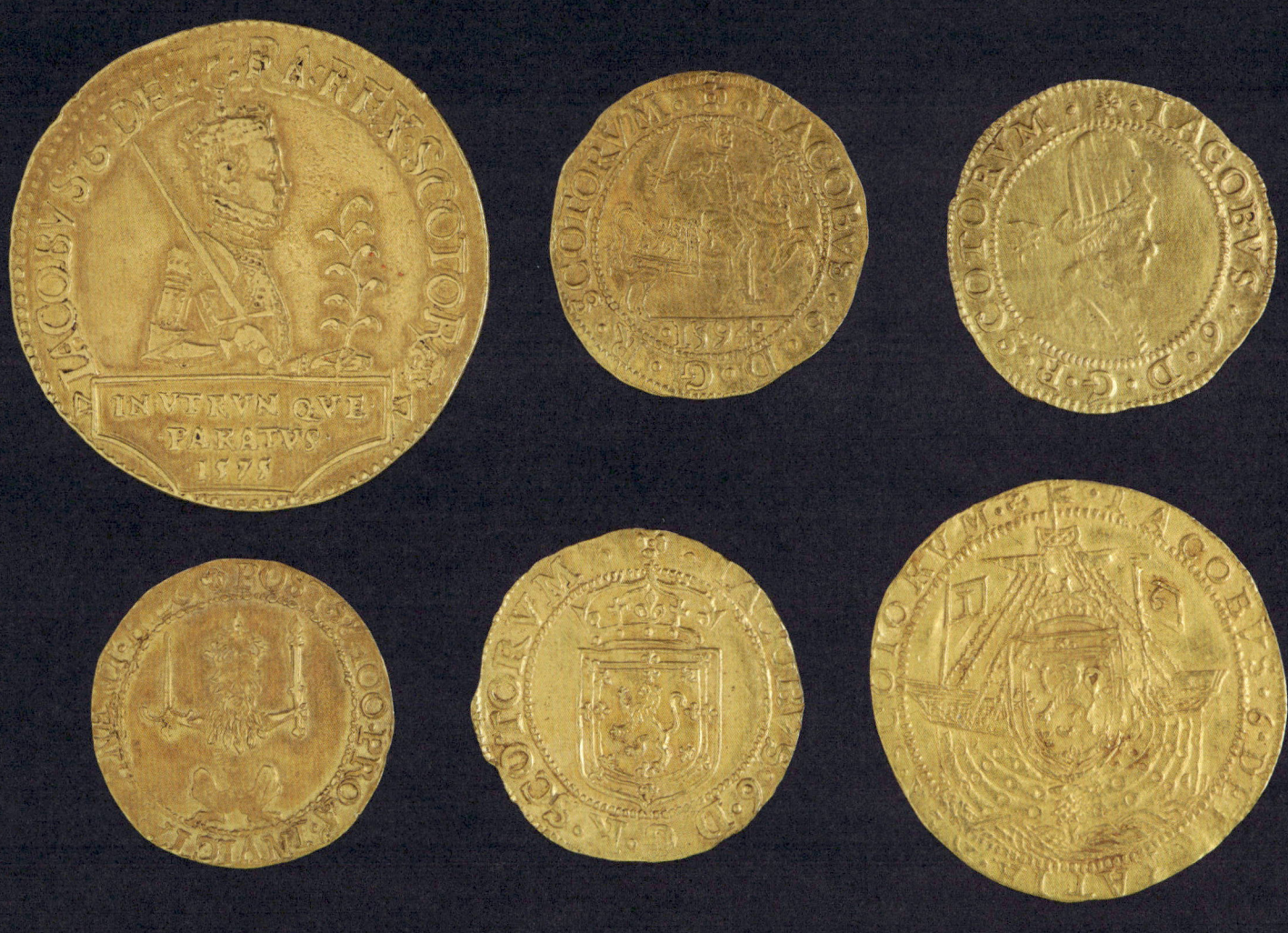

Cat.65 (top left)
Unknown artist
'Twenty Pound Piece' coin, 1575
Gold, 4.1 × 4.2 cm
National Museums Scotland,
Edinburgh (H.C232)

PROVENANCE: Gifted by
A.B. Richardson, 1889.

REFERENCES: Burns 1887,
pp.384–86; Richardson 1901,
no.86, p.258; Stewart 1967,
no.186, p.92; Thomson 1975, p.30

Cat.68 (bottom left)
Unknown artist
'Lion Noble' coin, 1586
Gold, diameter 2.6 cm
National Museums Scotland,
Edinburgh (H.C222)

PROVENANCE: Purchased in
1903, J.G. Murdoch Collection
(1903–1904).

REFERENCES: Stewart 1967,
no.187, p.94

Cat.66 (top centre)
Unknown artist
'Rider' coin, 1594
Gold, diameter 2.8 cm
National Museums Scotland,
Edinburgh (H.C192)

PROVENANCE: Unknown.

REFERENCES: Stewart 1967,
no.196, p.97

Cat.69 (bottom centre)
Unknown artist
**'Sword and Sceptre Piece'
coin, 1603**
Gold, 2.9 × 2.8 cm
National Museums Scotland,
Edinburgh (H.C206)

PROVENANCE: Unknown.

REFERENCES: Stewart 1967, p.97

Cat.67 (top right)
Unknown artist
'Hat Piece' coin, 1593
Gold, diameter 2.8 cm
National Museums Scotland,
Edinburgh (A.1911.506.1180)

PROVENANCE: Bequeathed by
Major Donald Lindsay Carnegie,
1911.

REFERENCES: Burns 1887,
pp.393–94; Stewart 1967, pp.95–96;
Thomson 1975, p.31

Cat.70 (bottom right)
Unknown artist
'Thistle Noble' coin, 1588–90
Gold, diameter 3.5 cm
National Museums Scotland,
Edinburgh (H.C236)

PROVENANCE: Purchased in 1900,
Pollexfen Collection.

REFERENCES: Stewart 1967,
no.191, p.95

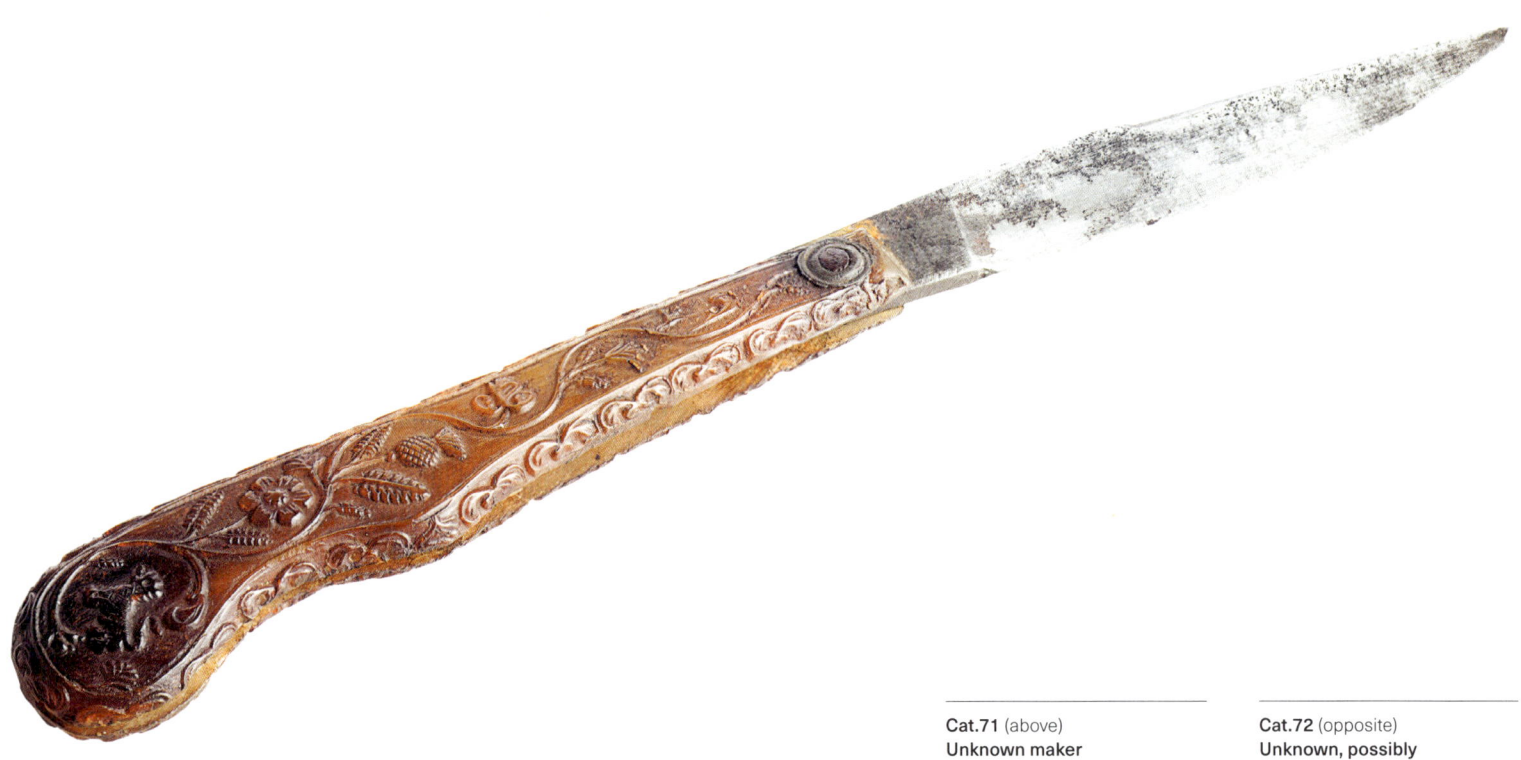

Cat.71 (above)
Unknown maker
Penknife owned by Prince Henry
Frederick, c.1612
Horn and steel 1.5 × 8.5 cm (haft);
1.0 × 5.6 cm (blade)
Blackie House Library and
Museum (AAC0949)

PROVENANCE: Prince Henry
Frederick until 1612; Collection
of Mrs Egiston Bairns; Sold at
Lyon and Turnbull, 'Scottish Silver
& Accessories' Sale, 12 August
2015, lot 197.

Cat.72 (opposite)
Unknown, possibly
Scottish, maker
Chair of the Countess of Mar,
late sixteenth century
Wood (oak), 87.5 × 63.5 × 50 cm
The Earl of Mar and Kellie,
on long-term loan to National
Museums Scotland, Edinburgh
(Q.L.196070)

PROVENANCE: Probably made
for the Earl and Countess of
Mar; by descent through the
Erskine family.

REFERENCES: Edinburgh 1959,
cat.80, p.31; Edinburgh 1975,
cat.239, p.38; Edinburgh 1990,
cat.46, p.50; Brown 2000, pl.25;
Edinburgh 2013, p.94, cat.132

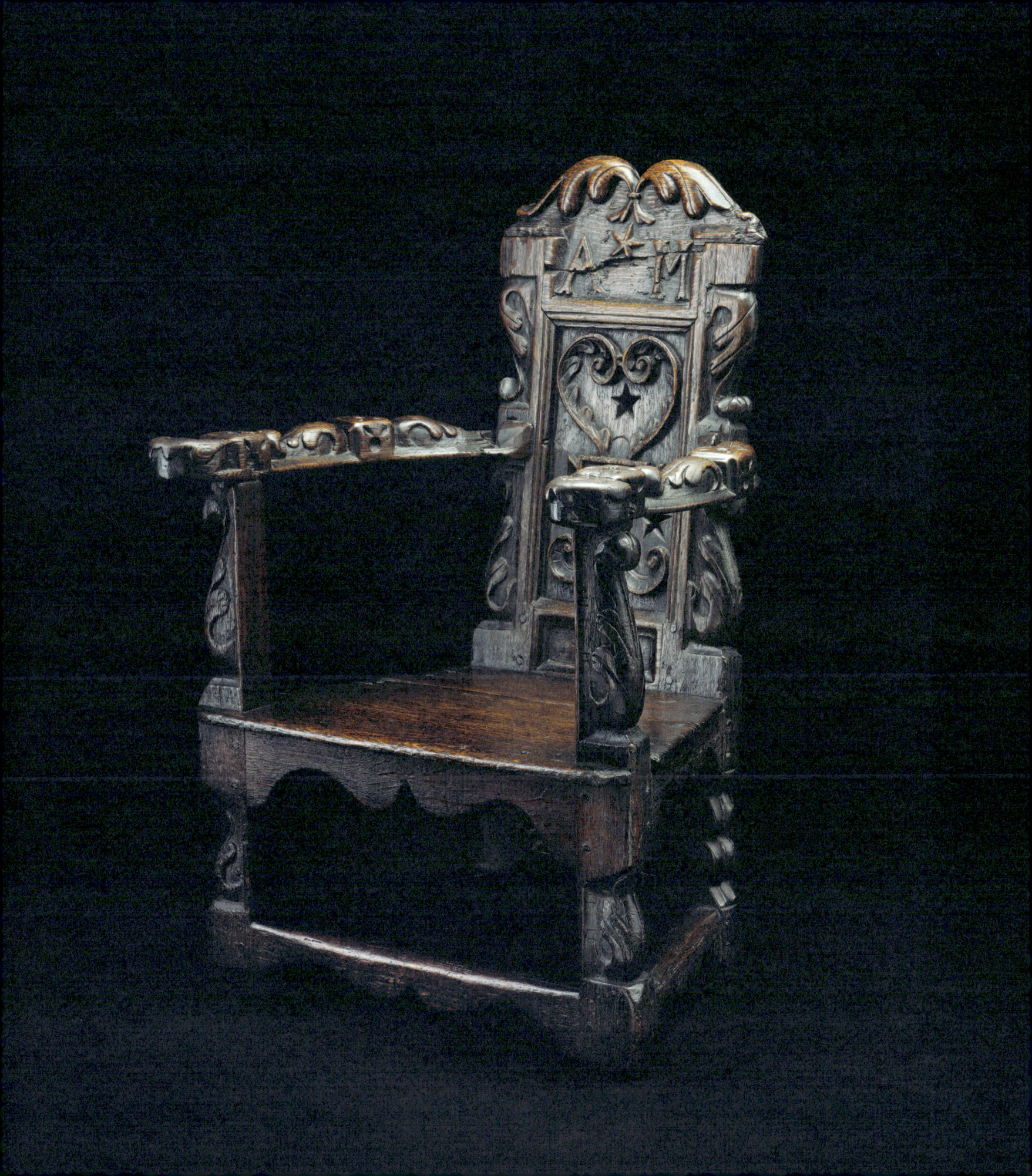

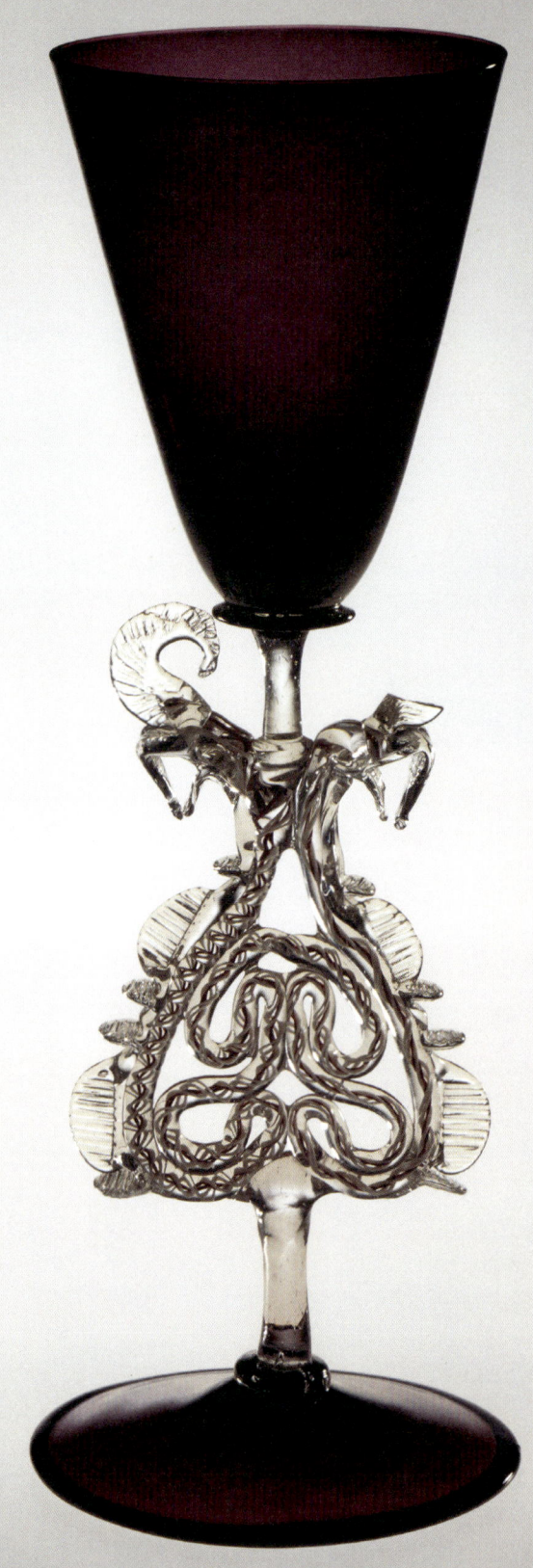

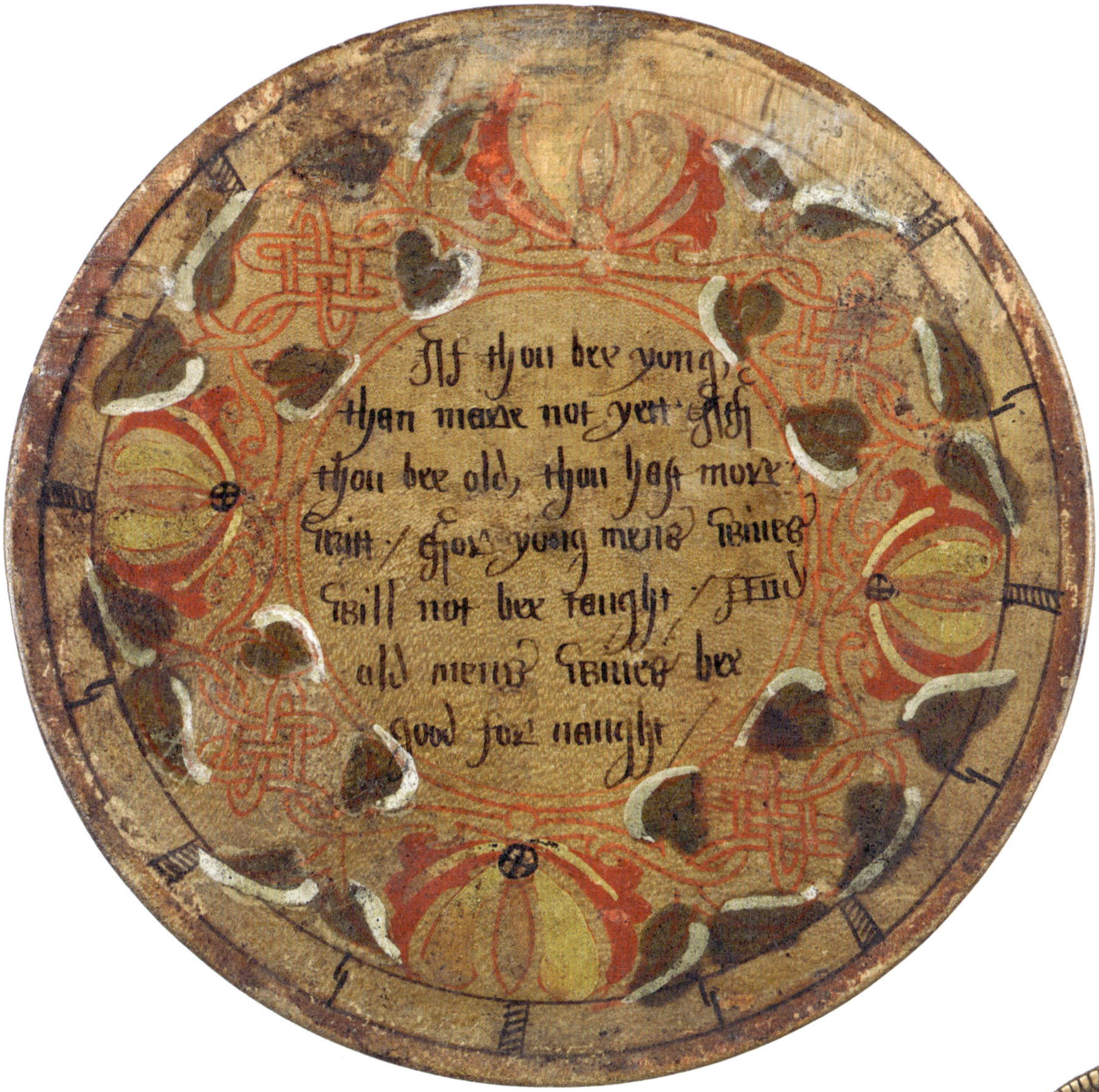

Ilf thou bee yong,
than make not yett ryfh
thou bee old, thou haft more
train / for yong menn ryntes
will not bee taught / and
old menn ryntes bee
good for naught

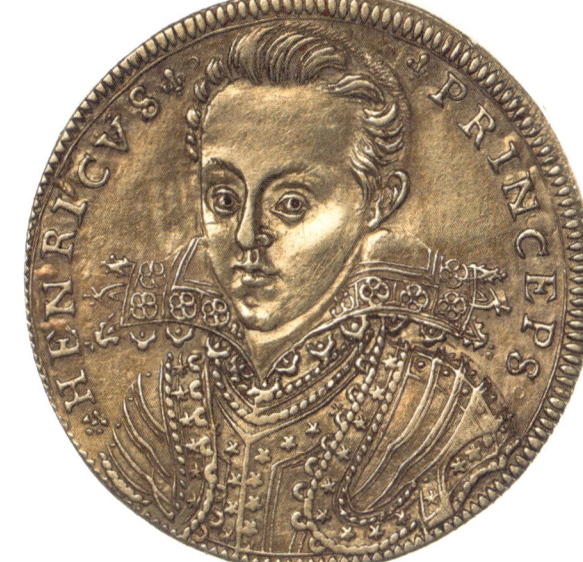

Cat.73 (opposite)
Unknown maker
Façon de Venise (Venetian-style) stirrup cup associated with James VI & I, late sixteenth century
Glass, 25 × 11.1 cm
National Museums Scotland, Edinburgh (H.MEN 69)

PROVENANCE: Bequeathed by Miss Madelaine Halkett, Pitfirrane, Dunfermline, 1951.

REFERENCES: Edinburgh 1975, cat.185, p.29; Edinburgh 1990, p.55; Thomas 2013, p.71

Cat.74 (above)
Unknown, probably English maker
Roundel or plate with painted and printed decoration, between 1570 and 1620
Wood (sycamore), diameter 12.7 cm
National Museums Scotland, Edinburgh (K.1999.528)

PROVENANCE: Purchased at Christie's, London, 1999.

REFERENCES: Akerman 1851, pp.225–30; Evans-Thomas 1932

Cat.75 (right)
Attributed to Charles Anthony (dates unknown)
*Henry Frederick, Prince of Wales, c.*1612
Gold, diameter 2.8 cm
National Galleries of Scotland, Edinburgh (PG 2806)

PROVENANCE: Purchased from Richard Faulkner Ltd, London, 1990.

REFERENCES: Edinburgh 1990, p.59, cat.63

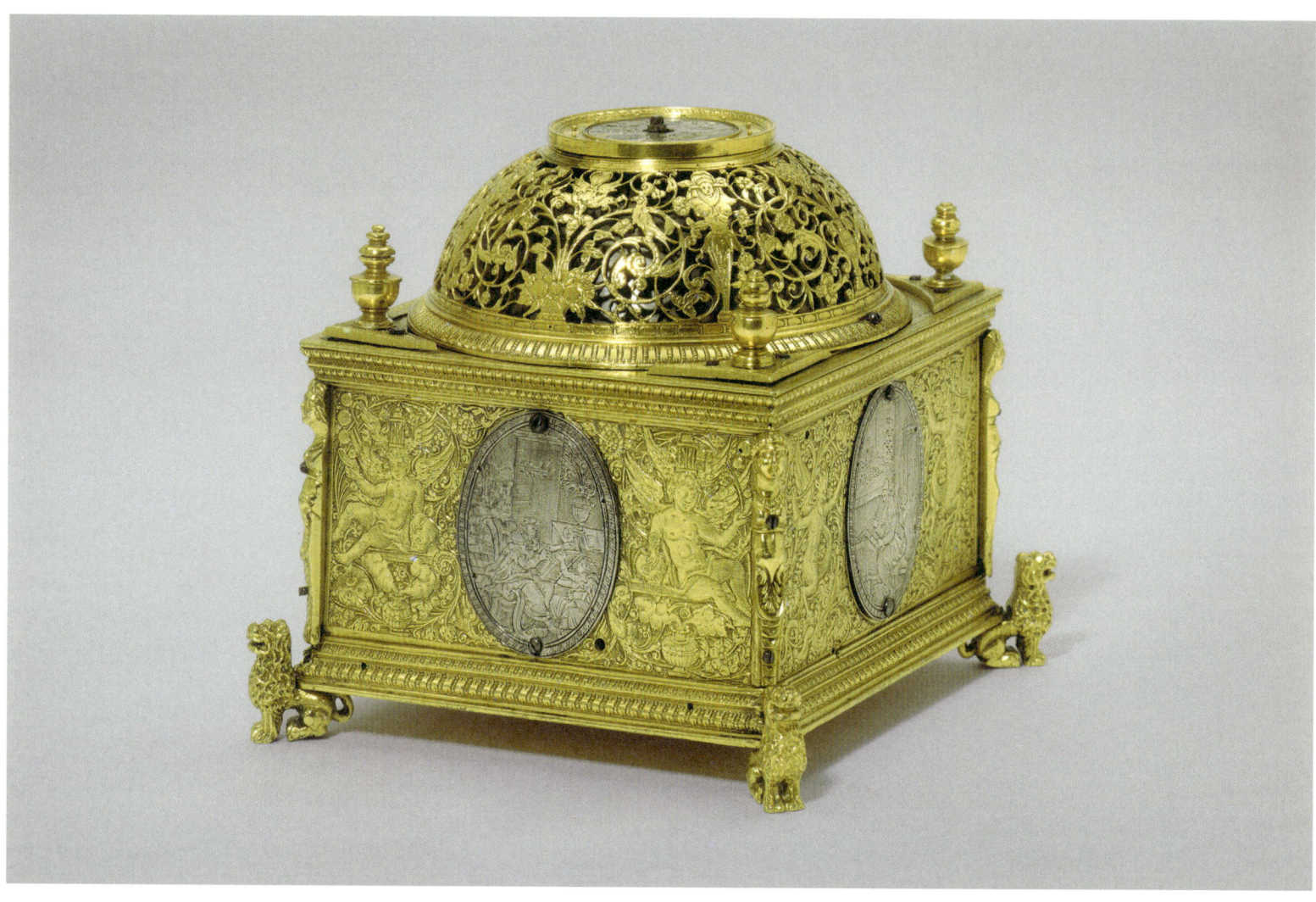

Cat.76 (above)
Movement made by David Ramsay (1585–1653), case made by Louis David (dates unknown)
Table clock, with a silver dial enriched with enamels, 1610–15 (made), late seventeenth century (altered)
Gilt brass, silver and enamel, 10.2 × 11.4 × 11.4 cm
Victoria and Albert Museum, London (M.7-1931)

PROVENANCE: Collection of Prince Peter Soltykoff; acquired by the London dealers S.J. Phillips in the twentieth century; purchased with the assistance of E.J. Phillips, 1931.

REFERENCES: Edinburgh 1959, cat.138, p.48; Edinburgh 1975, cat.227, p.39

Cat.77 (opposite)
David Ramsay (1585–1653)
Watch associated with James VI & I, *c.*1615
Silver, 10 cm open, 6.5 cm closed
National Museums Scotland, Edinburgh (H.NL 63)

PROVENANCE: Bequeathed by Sir Archibald Buchan Hepburn, Bart, FSA Scot, 1930.

REFERENCES: Edinburgh 1959, cat.140, pp.48–49; Edinburgh 1975, cat.229, p.38; Edinburgh 1990, cat.68, p.61; Brown 2000, no.12

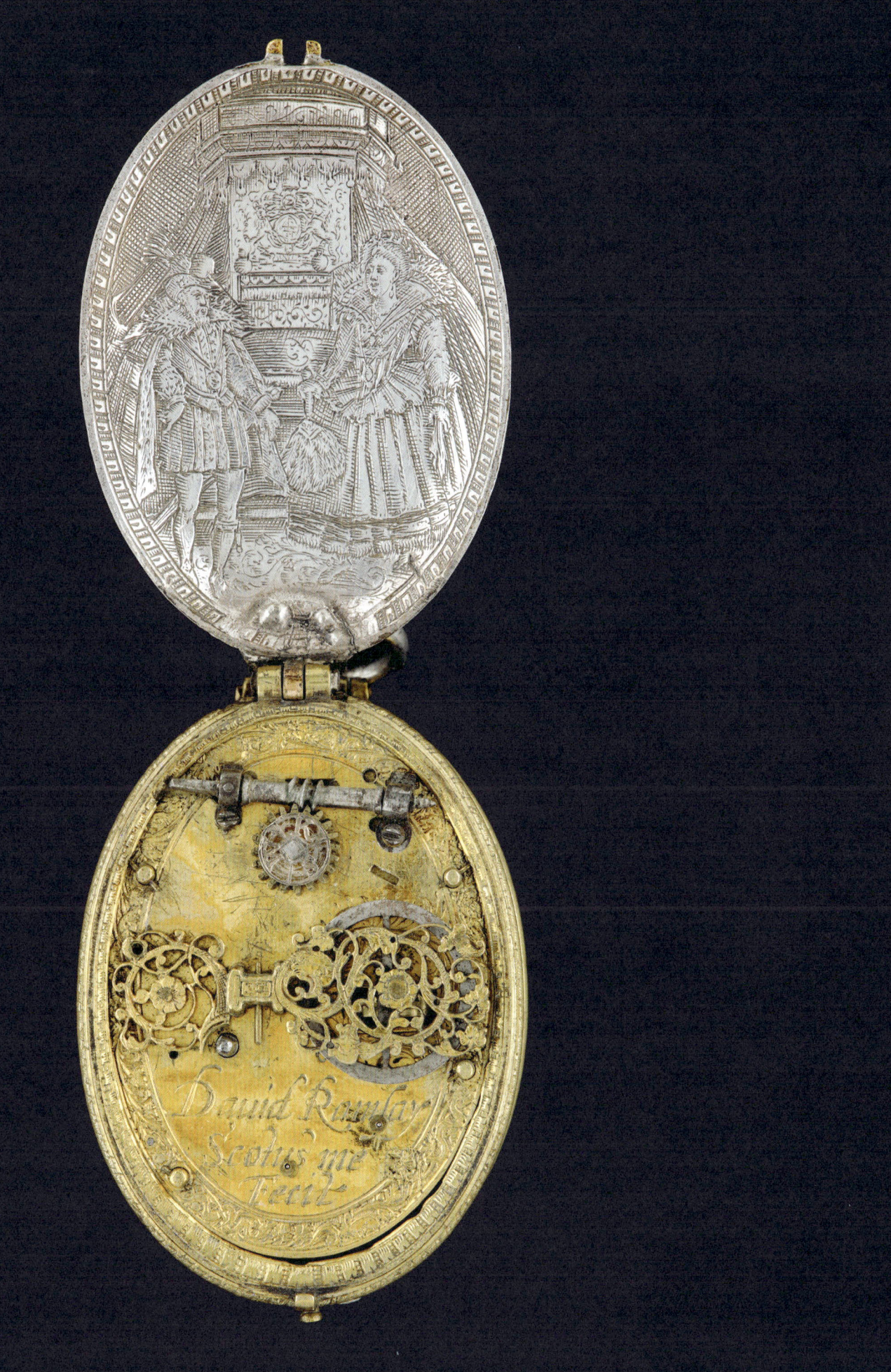

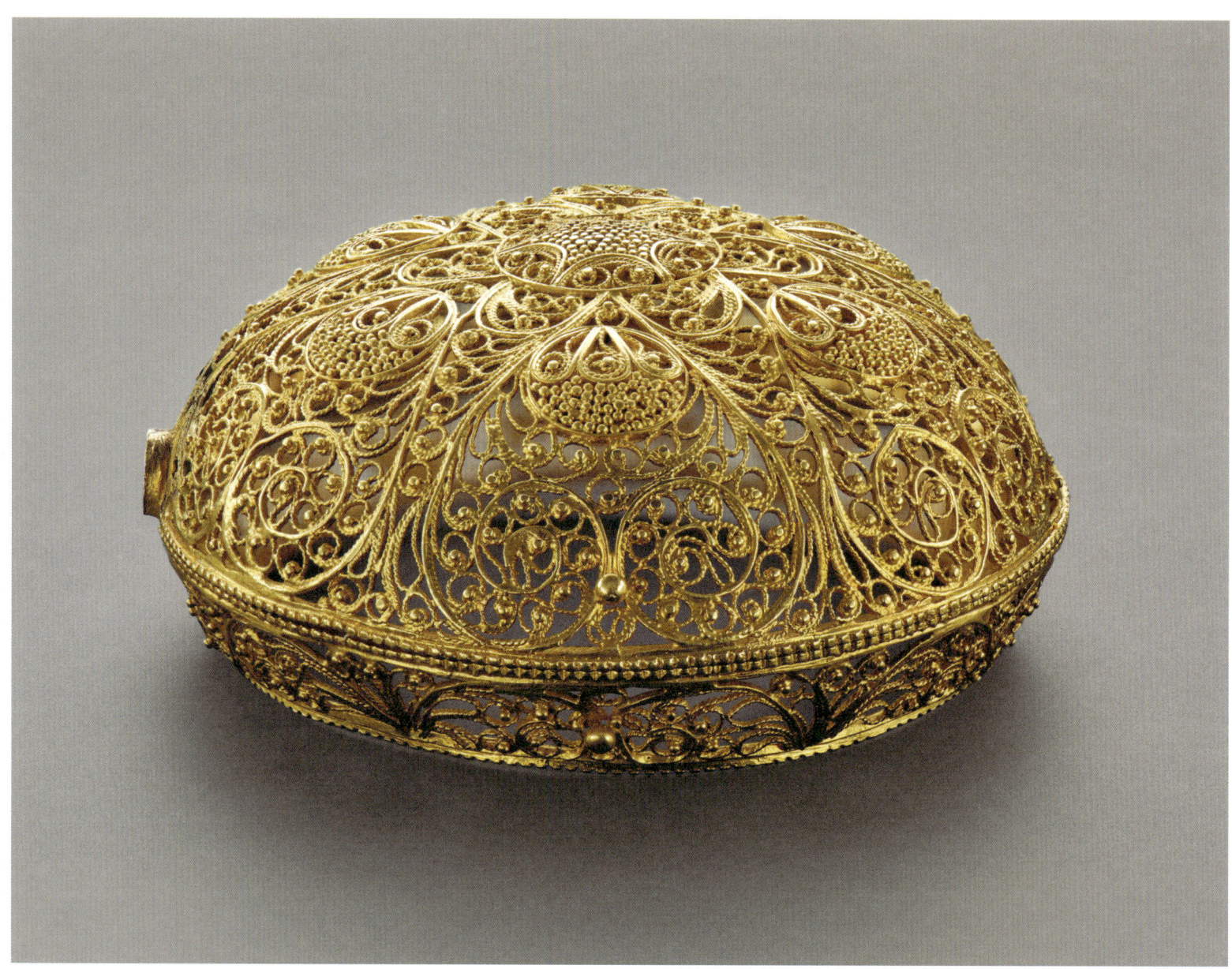

Cat.78 (above)
Unknown, probably Scottish, maker
Gold filigree hinged watch case, said to have belonged to King James VI & I, early seventeenth century
Gold, 5 × 2 cm (closed),
10 × 2 cm (open)
National Museums Scotland, Edinburgh (H.NL 72)

PROVENANCE: Donated by Miss Fraser, 1887.

Cat.79 (opposite)
Gilbert Kirkwood
(active 1609–1645)
Balmaghie Communion Cup,
1617–19
Silver, 19.5 × 12 × 8.3 cm
National Museums Scotland, Edinburgh (X.2015.130.1)

PROVENANCE: Commissioned for the Parish Kirk of Balmaghie, Galloway by minster Mr Hew McGhie; gifted by the Kirk Session of Balmaghie Parish Church, 2015.

REFERENCES: Burns 1892 p.265; Edinburgh 1975, cat.209, p.36

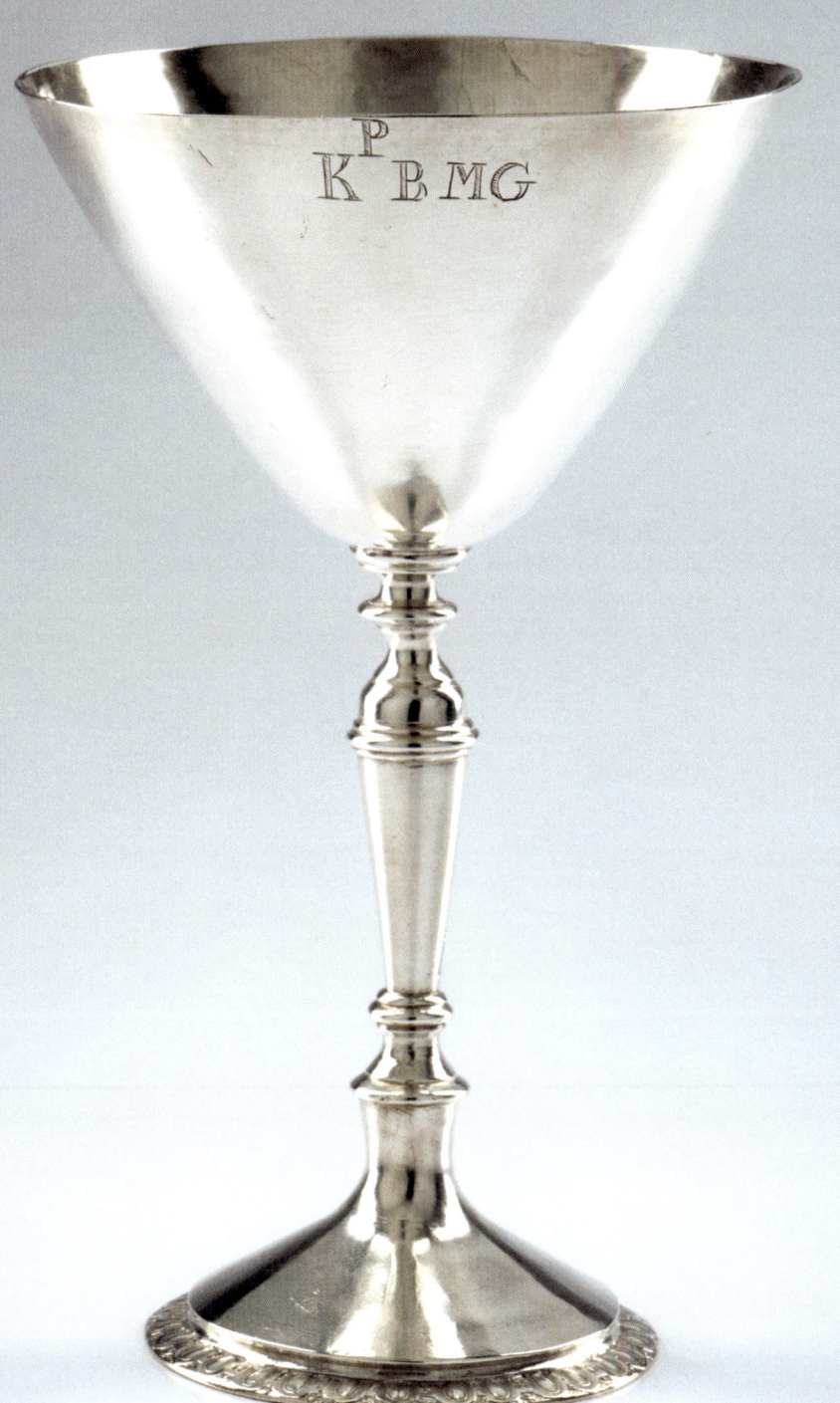

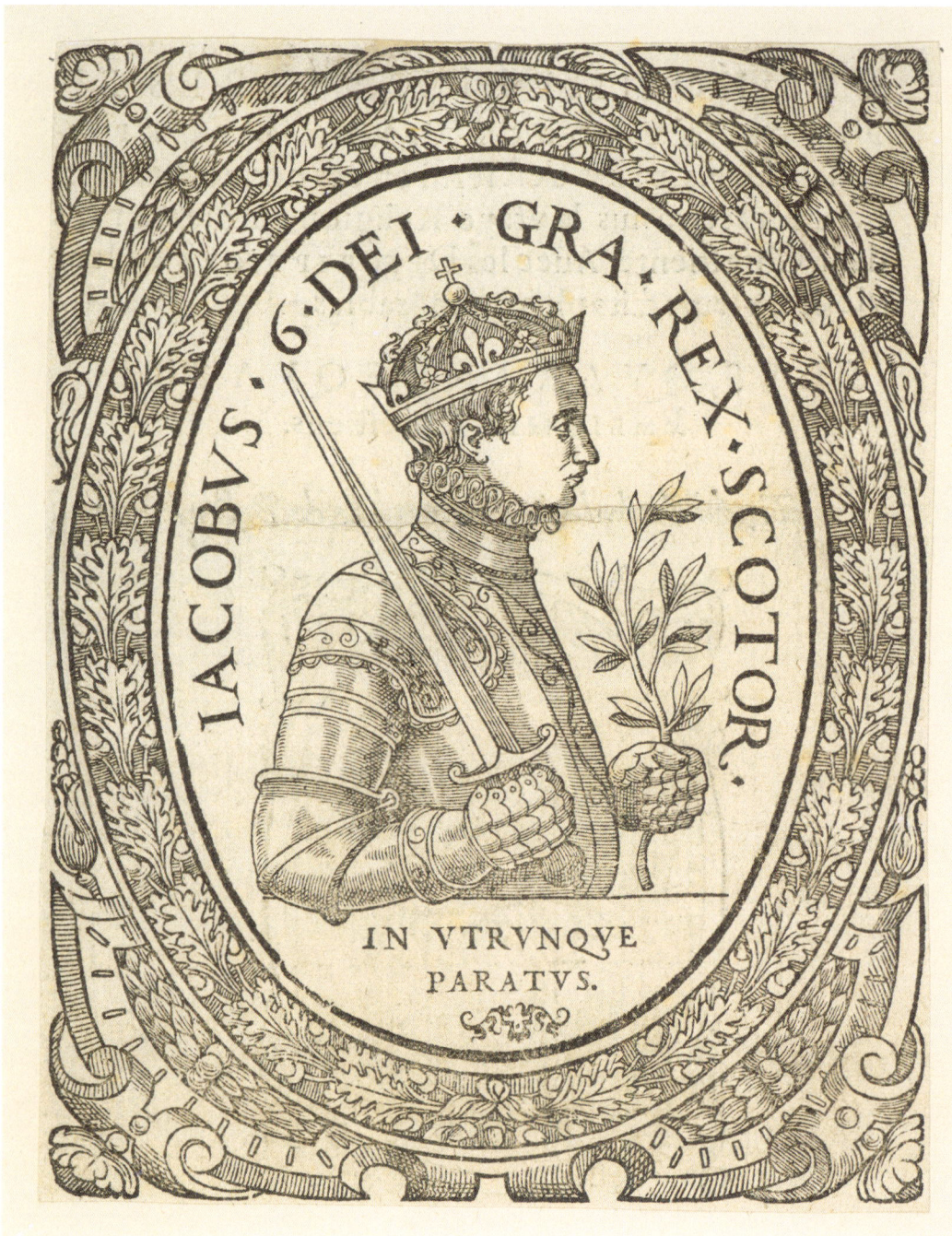

PRINTS

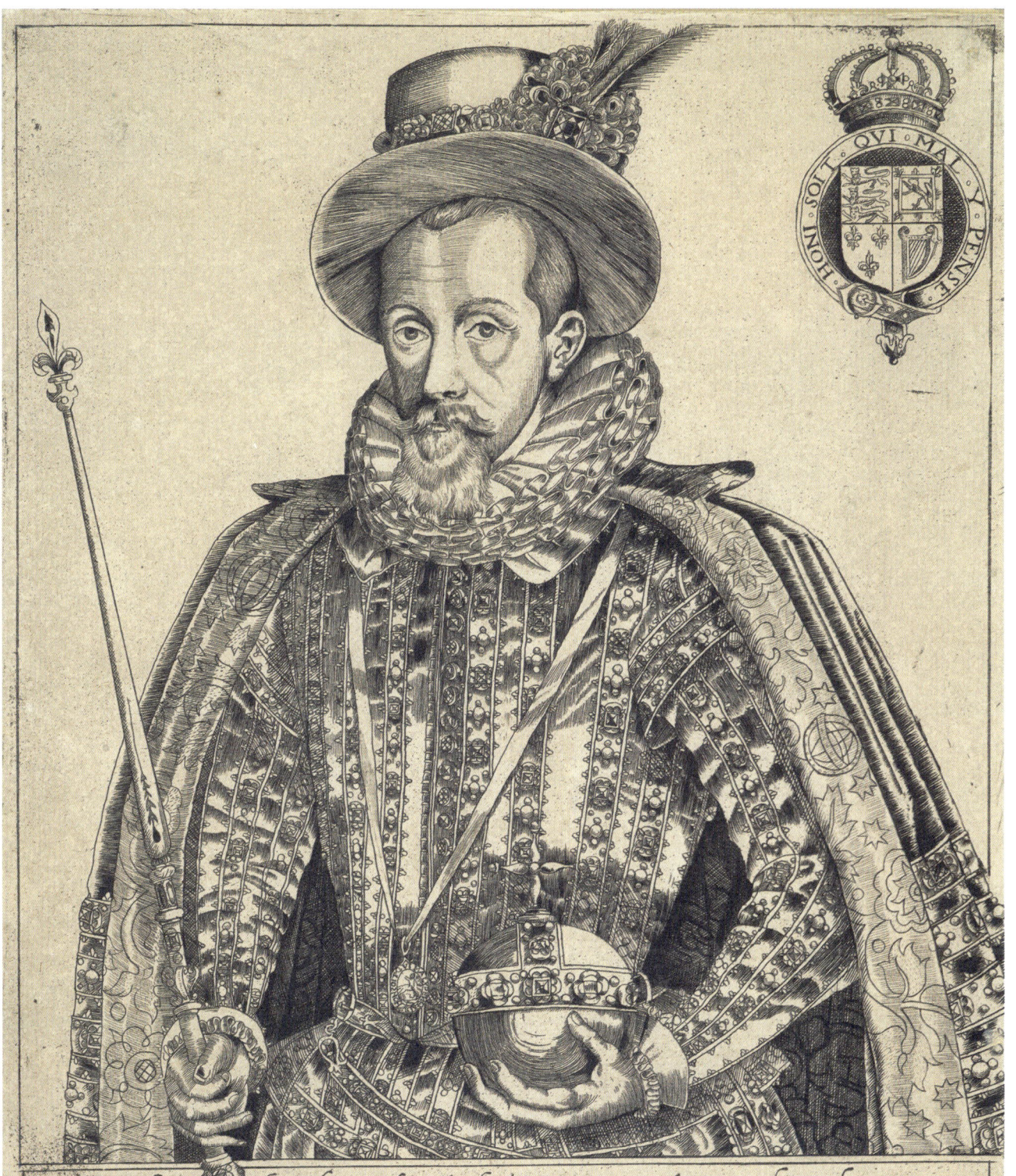

The high and mightie prince James by the grace of god King of England Scotland Fraunce and Ireland defendor of the faith

Laurence Johnson sculpsit. 1603

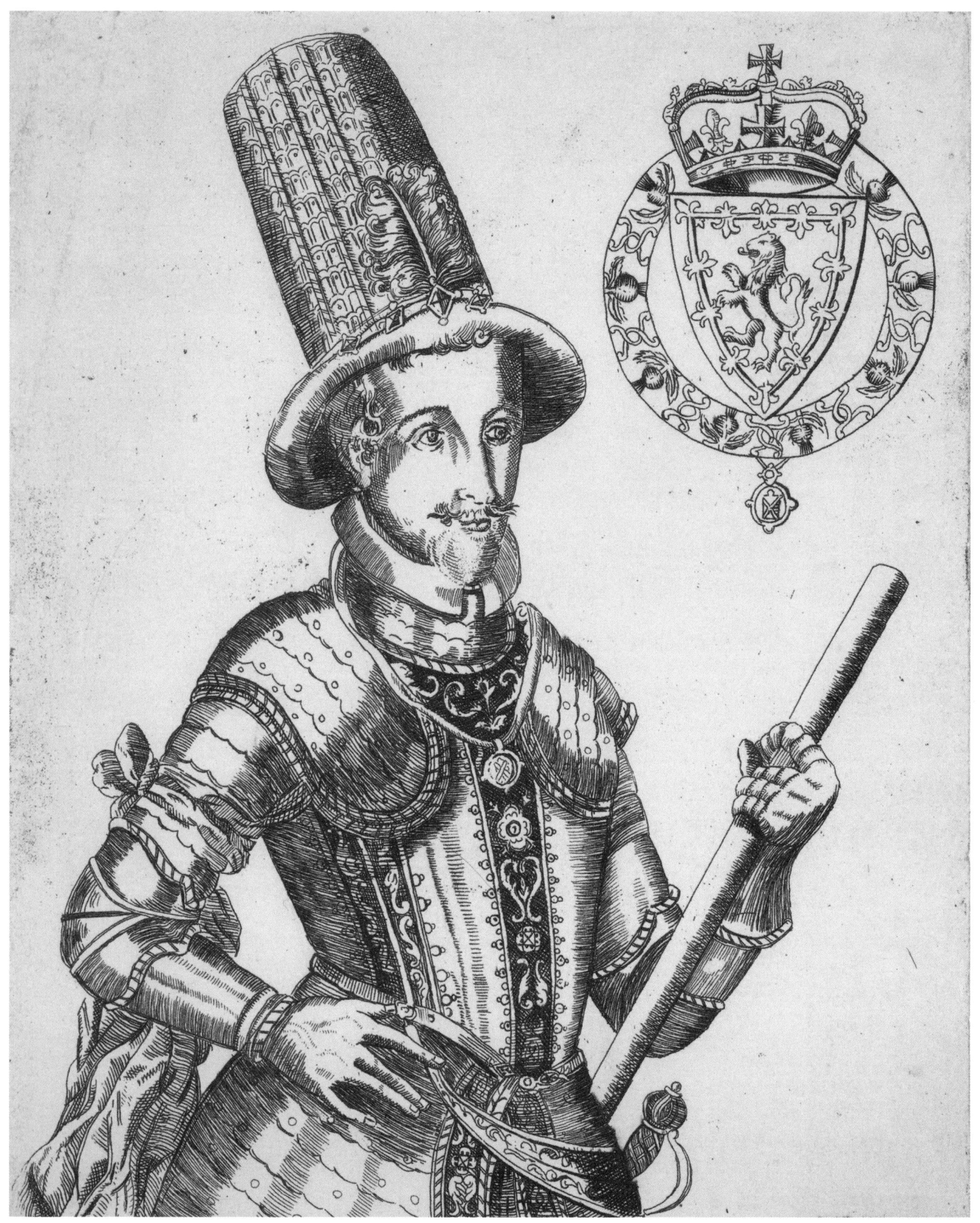

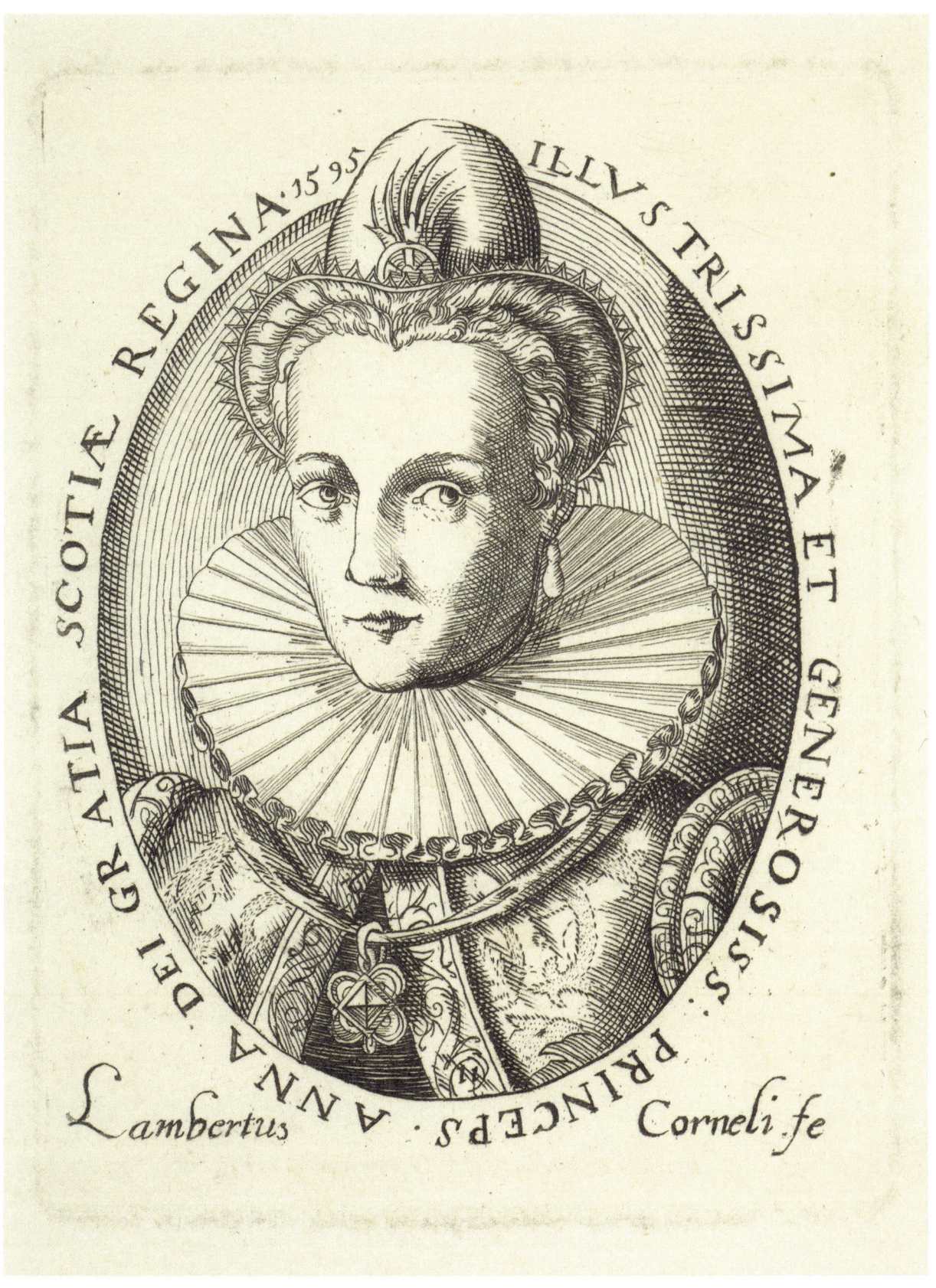

CONCILIVM SEPTEM NOBILIVM ANGLORVM CONIVRANTIVM IN NECEM IACOBI · I ·
MAGNÆ · BRITANNIÆ · REGIS · TOTIVSQ · ANGLICI · CONVOCATI · PARLEMENTI ·

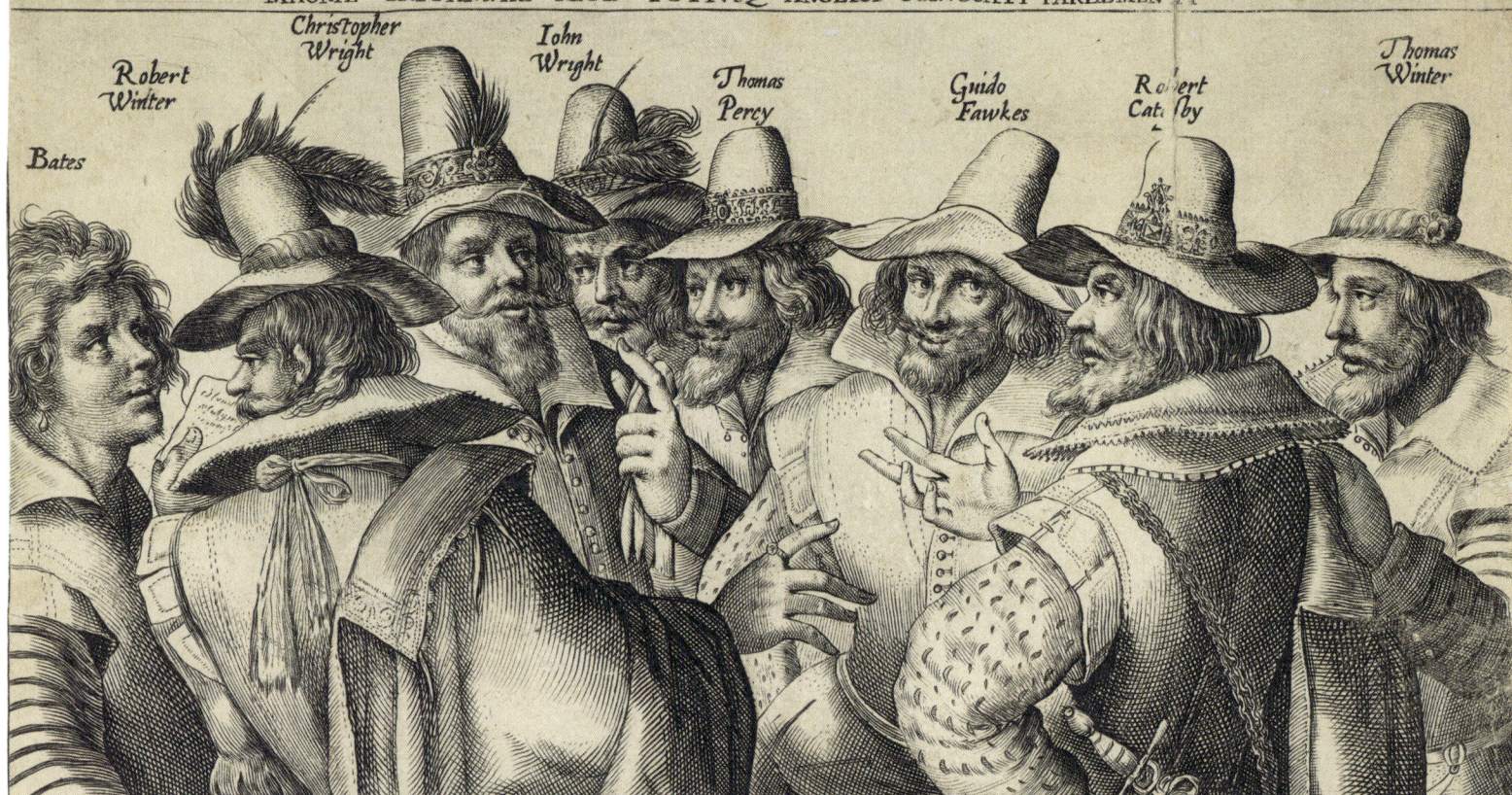

Vides Spectator humanissime, hic expressas effigies septem Anglorum, qui Regem suum cum præcipuis Status Anglici Proceribus ad Parlementum, ut vocant convocatis pulvere tormentario simul horrendo modo in ipsa domo Parlementi euertere voluerunt. Cuius Conurationis nefande Auctores fuere inprimis Robertus Catesby, & Thomas Perci, qui sibi deinde adiunxere alios, Videlicet, Thomam & Robertum Winter, Guidonem Fawkens Iohannem & Christopherum Wright quibus demum accessit Bates Roberti Catesbi Famulus. Sed conuratione hac Diuina prouidentia & clementia decem aut nouis horis ante futuram Cessionem Parlamenti Detecta. & Conuratis persecutis ex ijs Robertus Catesi & Thomas Perci ictu sclopeti periere & eorum Capita domui Parlamenti inperpetuam rei memoriam impofita cæteri, cum multis alijs, qui eandem in rem conspirarant adhuc captiui detinentur, dignam facinore sententiam expectantes.

Icy se voient les effigies des sept Seigneurs Anglois lesquels de façon nouuelle et fort Horrible on attente contre le Roy et son estat aians entre pins p mines et quantité de puldre de faire Saillir sa Maiesté auec les premiers Du Royaulme et principaux officirs estans en parlement à Westminster les premiers auteurs de la diste conspiration Sont, Robert Catesby et Thomas Percy, ausquels depuis ad Ioinctes Thomas et Robert Winter Guido Fawkes Iean et Christophe Wright, et depuis encor le Seruiteur dudist Catesby appelle Bates Mais estante ladist Conspiration descouerte p lagrace et prouidence de Dieu, enuiron dix heures deuant lassemble et assiette dudist parlement et les distes Conspirateurs poursuiuis lesdis premiers auteurs Catesby et Percy sont es se attainct, et tues de Harquebusade leurs testes coupées et portées à Westminster et posées la maison du parlement en memoire de l'acte detes table Restans auec plusieurs aultes trouues Coulpables dudist faict sont encor prisonniers, attendans larrest du Parlement condigne a leurs merites.

Ⓦ

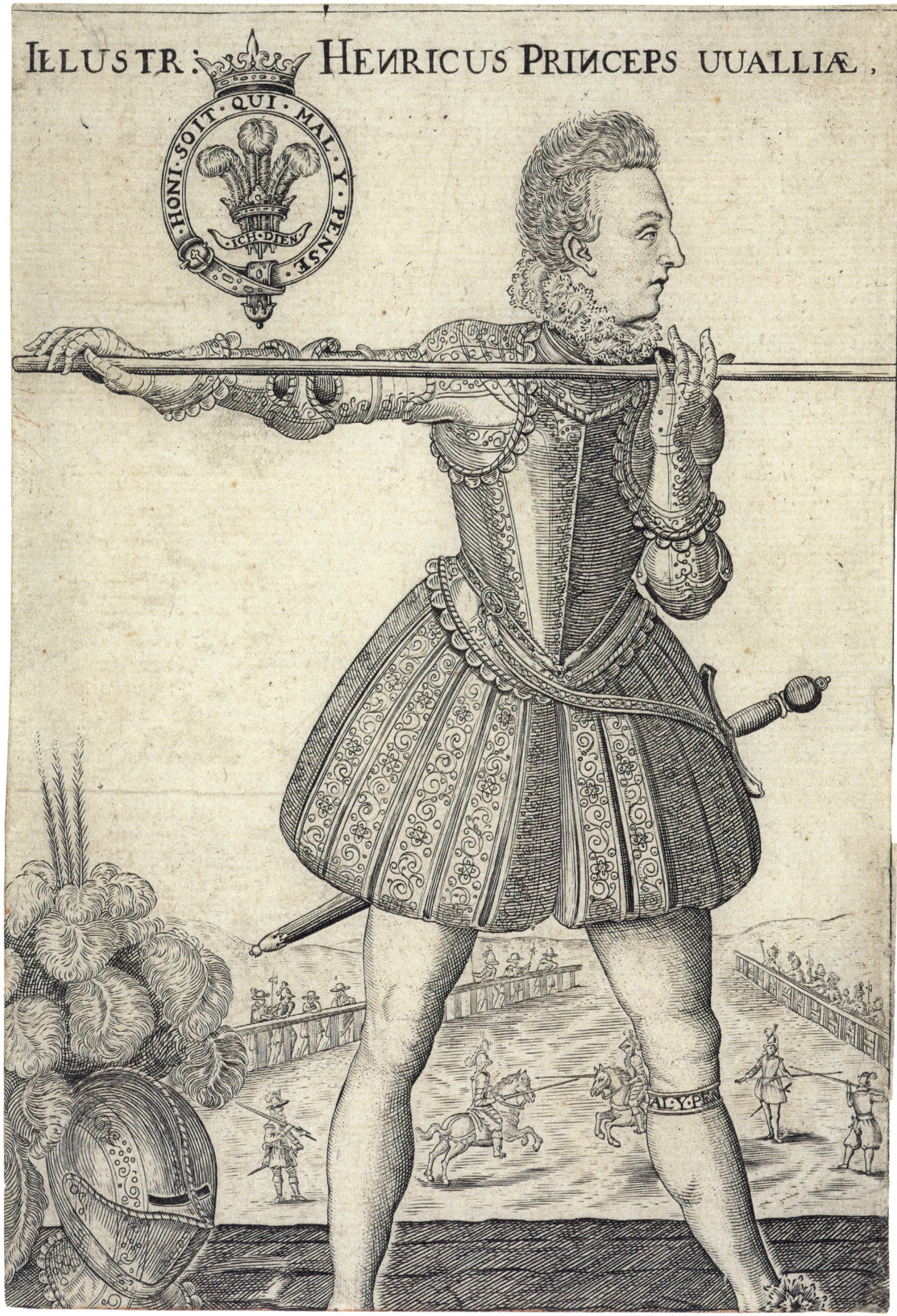

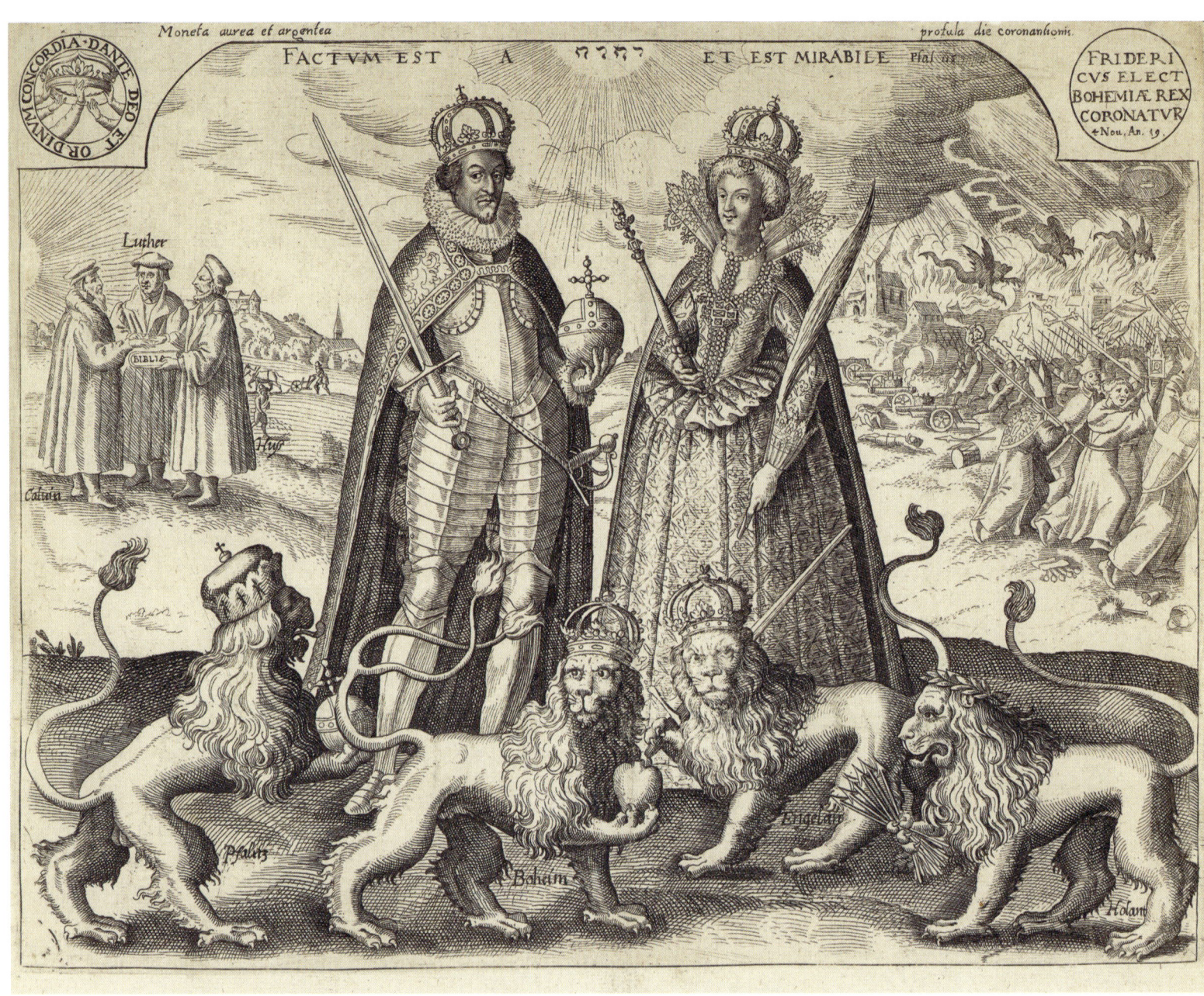

Cat.86 (opposite)
Unknown artist
The Triumph of the Reformation, showing Frederick V, Elector Palatine, King of Bohemia and Elizabeth, Electress Palatine, Queen of Bohemia and the Protestants Victorious over Roman Catholics, 1619
Engraving, trimmed, 23.2 × 29.8 cm
National Galleries of Scotland, Edinburgh (SP II 32.4)

PROVENANCE: Bequeathed by William Finlay Watson, 1886.

REFERENCES: Edinburgh 1975, cat.116, p.24; Edinburgh 1998, p.55

Cat.87 (right)
Possibly workshop of Crispijn de Passe the Elder (*c.*1565–1637)
Frontispiece to Thomas Scott's *Vox Regis,* **published 1624**
Engraving, 16.6 × 12 cm
National Galleries of Scotland, Edinburgh (SP II 53.35)

PROVENANCE: Unknown.

REFERENCES: Edinburgh 1975, cat.11, pp.9, 13

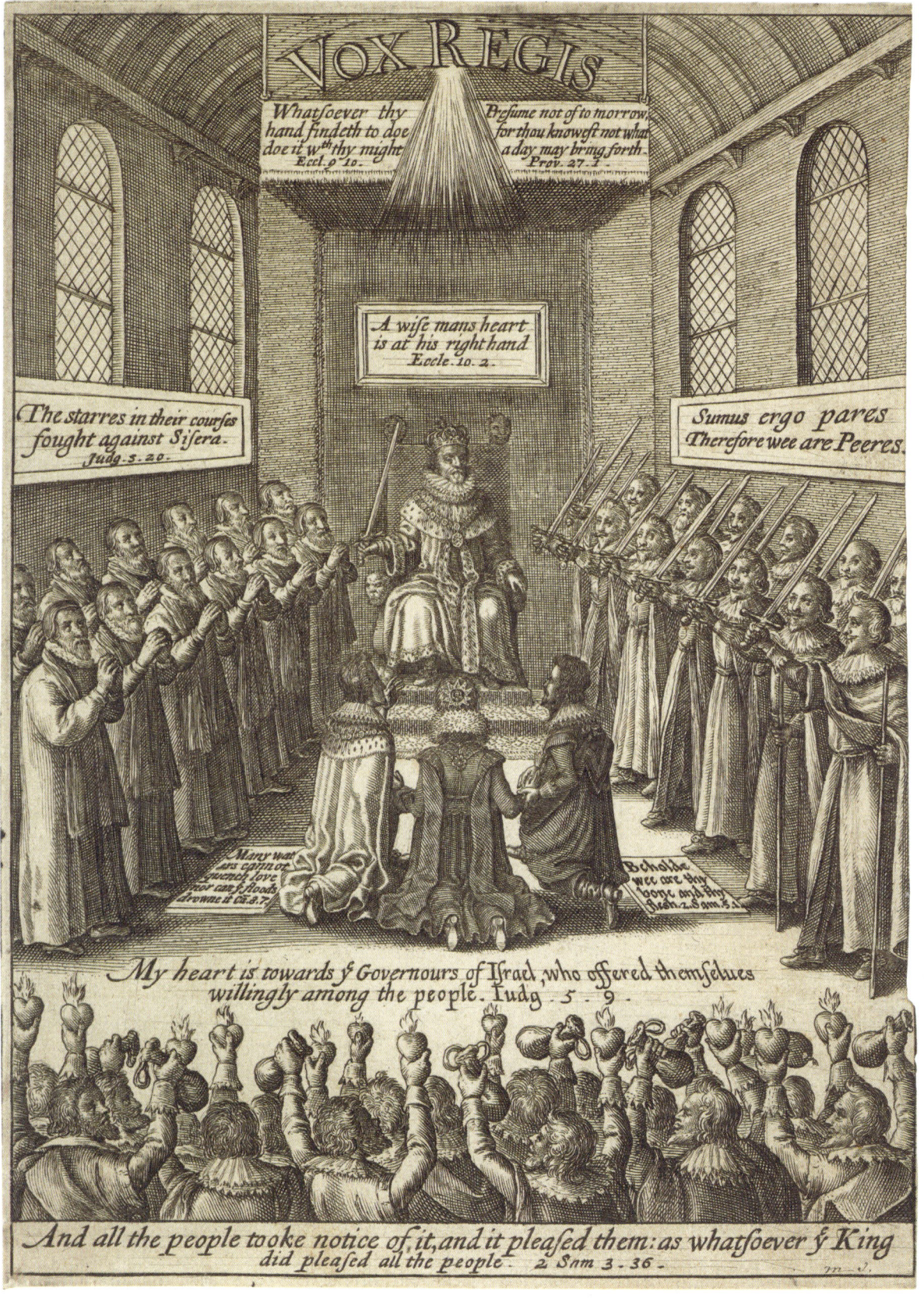

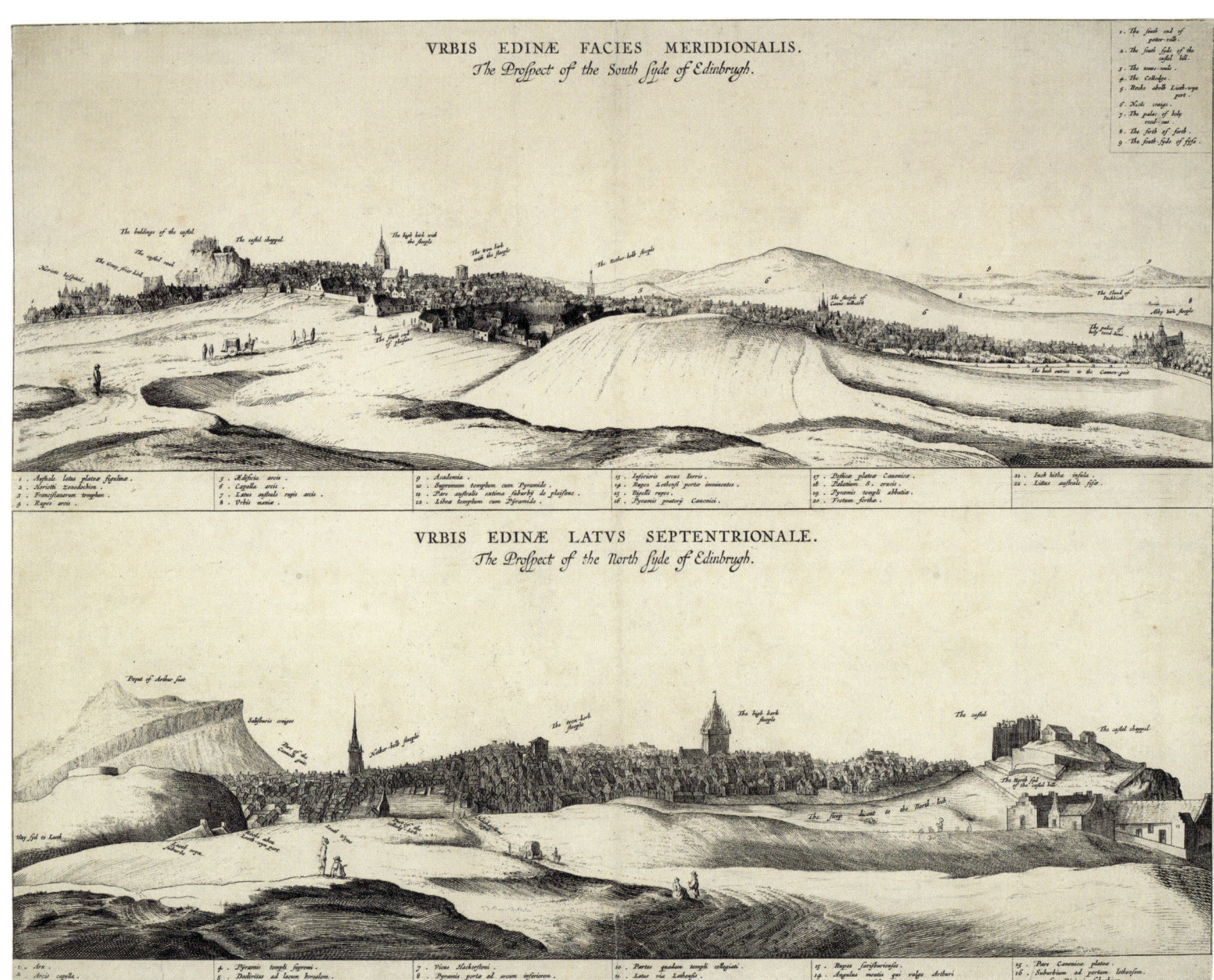

VRBIS EDINÆ FACIES MERIDIONALIS.
The Prospect of the South syde of Edinbrugh.

VRBIS EDINÆ LATVS SEPTENTRIONALE.
The Prospect of the North syde of Edinbrugh.

Cat.88 (opposite)
**Frederick de Wit (1629–1706),
after Rev. James Gordon of
Rothiemay (*c*.1615–1686)**
*The Prospect of the South Side
of Edinburgh and the Prospect
of the North Side of Edinburgh*,
published 1647
Engraving, trimmed, 41.7 × 52.6 cm
National Galleries of Scotland,
Edinburgh (P 8027)

PROVENANCE: Unknown,
possibly bequeathed by William
Finlay Watson in 1886; transferred
from the Scottish National Portrait
Gallery to the Scottish National
Gallery.

Cat.89 (right)
**Crispijn de Passe the Elder
(*c*.1565–1637)**
*Frederick V, Elector Palatine and
King of Bohemia (1596–1632)*,
published *c*.1613–19
Engraving, 17.2 × 13 cm
National Galleries of Scotland,
Edinburgh (TOYNBEE 015)

PROVENANCE: Bequeathed by
Miss Margaret Toynbee, 1986.

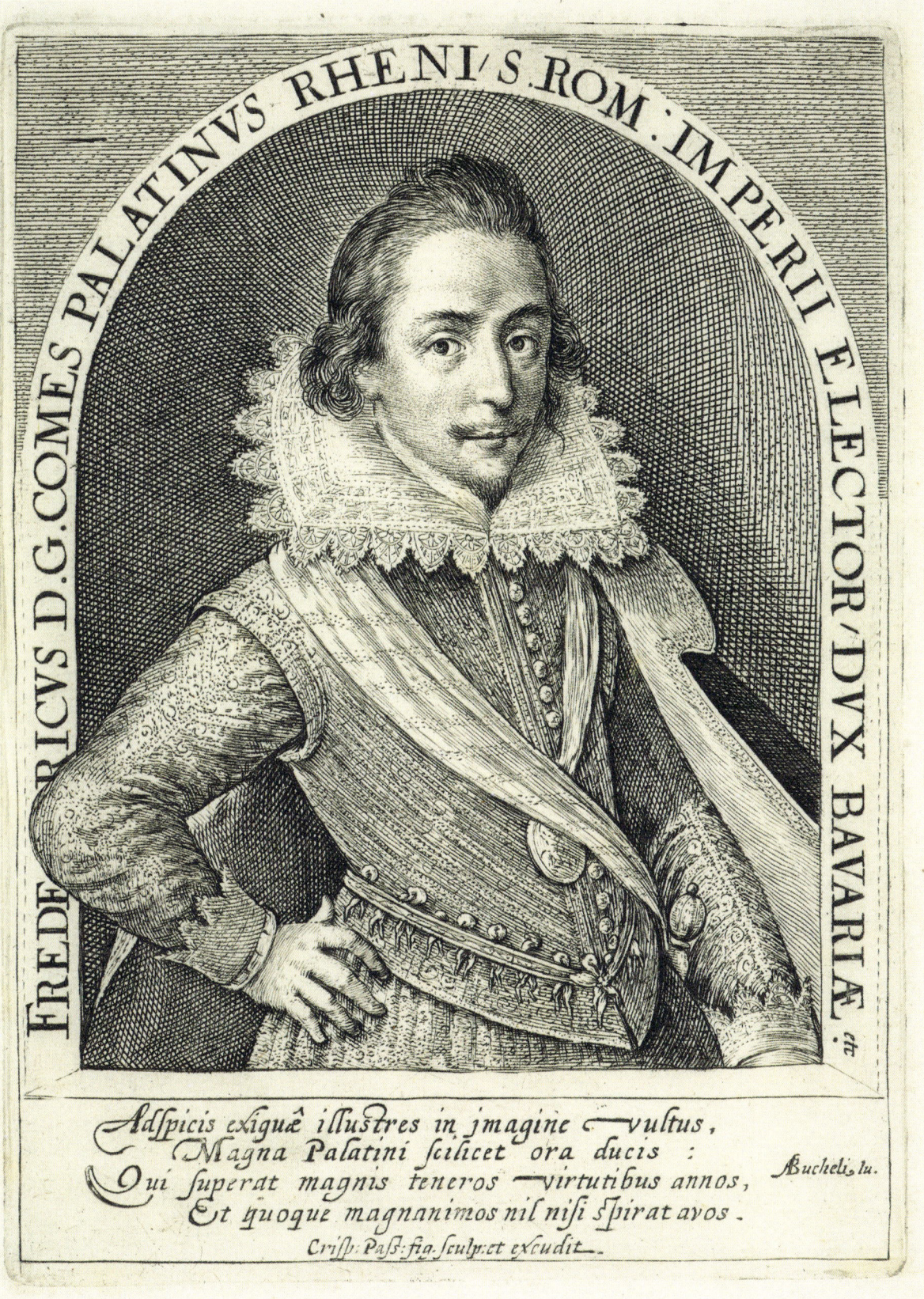

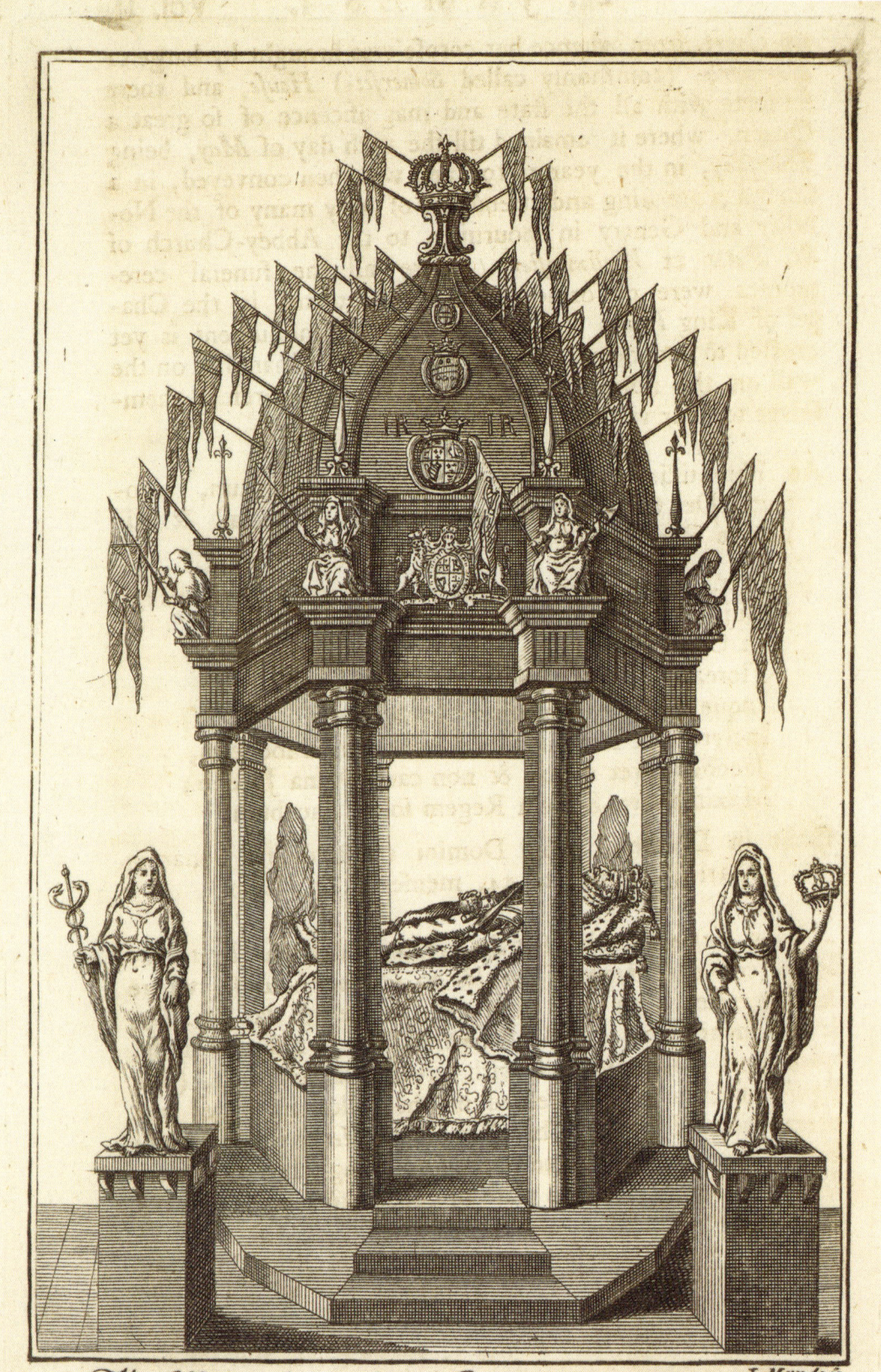

The Mausoleum in Westminster Abbey at the Funeral Obsequies of K. JAMES I.

J. Mynde sc.

Cat.90
James Mynde (active 1740–1770)
The Mausoleum of James VI & I in Westminster Abbey, **between 1740 and 1770**
Engraving, 17 × 10.6 cm
National Galleries of Scotland, Edinburgh (SP II 53.43)

PROVENANCE: Purchased from Dowell's, Edinburgh, December 1932.

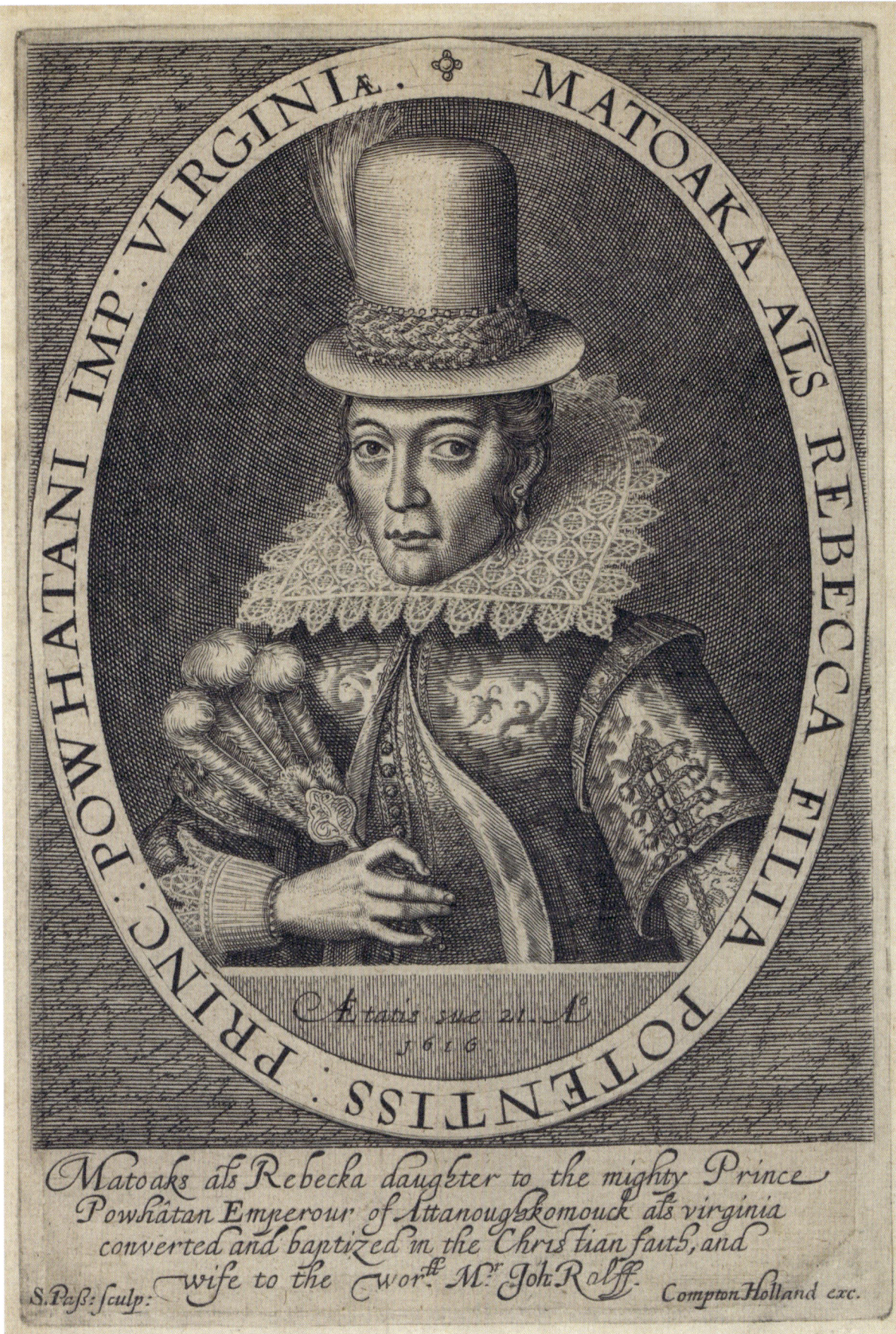

Cat.91
Simon van de Passe (1595–1647), published by Compton Holland (active 1616–1622)
Portrait of Pocahontas, age 21, 1616
Engraving, 17 × 11.7 cm
British Museum, London
(1863,0509.625)

PROVENANCE: John Corrie (1863); Sold at Sotheby's, 24 April 1863; Purchased at this sale by the British Museum.

REFERENCES: O'Donoghue 1908–25, p.605; Hollstein 1949; Hind 1952–64 (II.266.47); London 2012b, pp.240–42, fig.12, p.294

ALSO EXHIBITED

PAINTINGS

Cat.92
Unknown artist
James II (1430–1460), probably late sixteenth century
Oil on panel, 41.3 × 32.9 cm
National Galleries of Scotland, Edinburgh (PG 683)

PROVENANCE: Purchased from D.J.S. Lyell of St Andrews, 1909.

REFERENCES: Caw 1910, pp.116–17; Edinburgh 1959, cat.43, p.19; Thomson 1975, no.3, p.20; Edinburgh 1990, cat.11, p.22

Cat.93
Unknown artist
James III (1451–1488), c.1579
Oil on panel, 40.8 × 32.7 cm
National Galleries of Scotland, Edinburgh (PG 684)

PROVENANCE: Purchased from D.J.S. Lyell of St Andrews, 1909.

REFERENCES: Caw 1910, pp.116–17; Edinburgh 1959, cat.8, p.8; Thomson 1975, no.4, p.21; Edinburgh 1990, cat.13, p.25

Cat.94
Unknown artist
James IV (1473–1513), probably late sixteenth century
Oil on panel, 41.2 × 33 cm
National Galleries of Scotland, Edinburgh (PG 685)

PROVENANCE: Purchased from D.J.S. Lyell of St Andrews, 1909.

REFERENCES: Caw 1910, p.117; Edinburgh 1959, cat.44, pp.19–20; Thomson 1975, no.5, p.21; Edinburgh 1990, cat.16, p.28; Edinburgh 2013, cat.15, p.66

Cat.95
Unknown artist
James V (1512–1542), probably late sixteenth century
Oil on panel, 41.3 × 33 cm
National Galleries of Scotland, Edinburgh (PG 686)

PROVENANCE: Purchased from D.J.S. Lyell of St Andrews, 1909.

REFERENCES: Caw 1910, pp.117–18; Edinburgh 1959, cat.38, p.18; Thomson 1975, no.6, p.21; Edinburgh 1990, cat.18, p.31

Cat.96
Unknown artist, previously attributed to Adrian Vanson (active 1581–1603)
Agnes Douglas, Countess of Argyll (c.1574–1607), 1599
Oil on panel, 86.4 × 77.5 cm
National Galleries of Scotland, Edinburgh (PG 1409)

PROVENANCE: The Earls of Argyll, probably until the execution of the 1st Marquis in 1661; with the Marquesses of Lothian at Newbattle Abbey (probably from the late seventeenth century); bequeathed by the 11th Marquess of Lothian in 1941.

REFERENCES: Edinburgh 1959, cat.99, p.36; Thomson 1974, p.47; Thomson 1975, p.29; Brown 2000, no.14

Cat.97
Unknown artist
Robert Rollock (c.1555–1599), 1599
Oil on canvas, 76.1 × 63.1 cm
National Galleries of Scotland, Edinburgh (PG 635)

PROVENANCE: Bequeathed by H.J. Rollo 1890.

Cat.98
Unknown artist, after Isaac Oliver (c.1565–1617)
Henry Frederick, Prince of Wales, 1612, with an earlier portrait beneath
Oil on panel, 54.6 × 41 cm
National Galleries of Scotland, Edinburgh (PG 846)

PROVENANCE: Collection of Mrs Glassford Bell; purchased at Dowell's, Edinburgh, 27 February 1915.

MINIATURES

Cat.99
Attributed to Leonard Limosin (c.1505–c.1577)
François II of France (1544–1560), c.1560
Limoges enamel on copper, 6 × 7.5 cm
National Galleries of Scotland, Edinburgh (PG 2814)

PROVENANCE: Reputedly from the Debruges Collection which was sold in Paris, January–March 1850; sold at Mentmore sale, Sotheby's, London, 20 May 1977, vol.II, lot 1105; purchased at Christie's, London, 11 April 1990, lot 10; presented by the Patrons of the National Galleries of Scotland, 1990.

REFERENCES: Edinburgh 1990, p.39; Lloyd 2004, p.73, no.1

Cat.100
Unknown, after Arnold Bronckorst (active 1565–1583)
James Hamilton, 2nd Earl of Arran and Duke of Châtelherault (c.1519–1575) and *John Hamilton, 1st Marquess of Hamilton (c.1540–1604)*, c.1575–80
Double-sided portrait miniature in oil on vellum, 3.8 × 4.7 cm
National Galleries of Scotland, Edinburgh (PG 3412)

PROVENANCE: Sir Leonard Twiston-Davies; Lady Twiston-Davies, 1957; sold at Sotheby's, London, 'Winter' Sale, 1968; Bonham's, London, 23 November 2005, lot 1, purchased by the National Galleries of Scotland.

OBJECTS

Cat.101
Unknown, probably Italian, maker
Bezoar stone, mounted in pinchbeck, date unknown
Bezoar (probably goat), pinchbeck, height 6.7 × diameter 4.5 cm
National Museums Scotland, Edinburgh (H.NP 14)

PROVENANCE: Donated by Sir William Fettes Douglas, 1891.

Cat.102
Unknown artist
Medal commemorating the accession of James VI of Scotland to the throne of England, 1603
Silver, diameter 2.9 cm
National Galleries of Scotland, Edinburgh (PG 959)

PROVENANCE: Purchased from Mr W.C. Weight, Letchworth, 1923.

REFERENCES: Edinburgh 1998, p.21

Cat.103
Unknown Newcastle maker (stamped NW)
Clay Pipe from 'The Swan', Duart Point Shipwreck (1653), off the Isle of Mull, Scotland, mid-seventeenth century
Clay, 25 cm
National Museums Scotland, Edinburgh (H.1993.285)

PROVENANCE: Purchased by NMS in 1993 with other material from the wreck.

REFERENCES: Martin 2017

PRINTS

Cat.104
Christoffel van Sichem the Elder (1546–1624)
Elizabeth I, Queen of England (1533–1603), published 1601
Engraving, trimmed, 18.4 × 12.4 cm
National Galleries of Scotland, Edinburgh (EP I 26.1)

PROVENANCE: Bequeathed by William Finlay Watson, 1886.

Cat.105
William Kip (active c.1598–1635), after Stephen Harrison (active c.1603)
The New World
The Pegme of the Dutchmen
The Italians Pegme
The Garden of Plenty
The Temple of Janus
from *'The Arch's [sic] of Triumph' Depicting the Series of Temporary Arches Erected in London on the 15th of March 1604, in Honour of James I's Ceremonial Entrance and Passage Through the City to Parliament*, 1604
Engraving, sheets 35.8 × 25.7 cm
Victoria and Albert Museum, London (14007, 14008, 14010, 14011, 14012)

PROVENANCE: Purchased in 1856.

REFERENCES: Nichols 1831, p.64; Berlin 1939, cat.2978; Hind 1952–64, vol.II, pp.17–34, 210–11

Cat.106
Possibly workshop of Jodocus Hondius (1563–1612), after John Speed (1552–1629)
The Kingdome of Scotland, 1610
Engraving, 38.4 × 51.4 cm
National Galleries of Scotland, Edinburgh (SPL 51.8)

PROVENANCE: Gifted by Major James W. Cursiter, 1934.

Cat.107
Willem de Passe (1598–c.1637) or Magdalena de Passe (1596/1600–1638), after William Hole (before 1600–1624)
Prince Henry Frederick's Hearse, 1620,
after a print from 1612
Engraving, trimmed, 16.3 × 12.1 cm
National Galleries of Scotland, Edinburgh (TOYNBEE 013)

PROVENANCE: Bequeathed by Miss Margaret Toynbee, 1986.

Cat.108
Crispijn de Passe the Elder (c.1565–1637)
Princess Elizabeth, Electress Palatine and Queen of Bohemia, c.1613–19
Engraving, 14.30 × 10.80 cm
National Galleries of Scotland, Edinburgh (TOYNBEE 108)

PROVENANCE: Bequeathed by Miss Margaret Toynbee, 1986.

Cat.109
Unknown artist, after Renold Elstrack (1570–1625 or after)
Sir Thomas Overbury (1581–1613), Poet,
date unknown, after a print from 1615
Ink on paper, 30.5 × 22.1 cm
National Galleries of Scotland, Edinburgh (PG 2095)

PROVENANCE: Bequeathed by David Laing to the Royal Scottish Academy, 1878; transferred to the National Gallery of Scotland, 1910; transferred to the Scottish National Portrait Gallery, 1952.

Cat.110
Unknown artist
Robert Cecil, 1st Earl of Salisbury (1563–1612),
published 1620
Engraving, 14 × 11.7 cm
National Galleries of Scotland, Edinburgh (EP II 174.2)

PROVENANCE: Bequeathed by William Finlay Watson, 1886.

Cat.111
Willem de Passe (1598–c.1637)
The Triumph of King James and His August Progeny, 1624
Engraving, trimmed, 37.8 × 31.5 cm
National Galleries of Scotland, Edinburgh (SP II 53.69)

PROVENANCE: From the collection of G.W. Reid (L.1210); sold to Fawcett at Sotheby's, London, 27 February 1890, lot 362; purchased at Sotheby's, London, 'Old Master, Modern and Contemporary Prints' Sale, 6 December 2000, lot 17.

REFERENCES: Edinburgh 2005, p.19

Cat.112
Robertus van Voerst (1597–1636/7), after Sir Anthony van Dyck (1599–1641)
Inigo Jones (1573–1652), c.1632–35
Engraving, 24.1 × 17.1
National Galleries of Scotland, Edinburgh (EP II 107.1)

PROVENANCE: Bequeathed by William Finlay Watson, 1886.

Cat.113
William Marshall (active c.1617–1650)
William Alexander, 1st Earl of Stirling (c.1567–1640),
published 1637
Engraving, 16.8 × 12.7 cm
National Galleries of Scotland, Edinburgh (SP II 97.1)

PROVENANCE: Bequeathed by William Finlay Watson, 1886.

Cat.114
Wenceslaus Hollar (1607–1677)
Whitehall Palace, c.1637–43
Engraving, 15 × 28.5 cm
National Galleries of Scotland, Edinburgh (P 1703)

PROVENANCE: Purchased in 1949.

Cat.115
Jan Luyken (1649–1712)
The Gowrie Conspiracy, c.1679
Etching on paper, trimmed, 26.7 × 34.3 cm
National Galleries of Scotland, Edinburgh (SP II 53.63)

PROVENANCE: Unknown.

REFERENCES: Edinburgh 1975, cat.29, p.11

Cat.116
François-Germain Aliamet (1734–1790), after a painting attributed to Cornelius Johnson (1593–1661) or Anthony van Dyck (1599–1641)
James Hay, 1st Earl of Carlisle (c.1580–1636), mid- to late eighteenth century, after a seventeenth-century painting
Engraving, 20.2 × 15.8 cm
National Galleries of Scotland, Edinburgh (SP II 19.1)

PROVENANCE: Gifted by Sir William Fettes Douglas, c.1885.

Cat.117
Simon Gribelin (1661–1733), after Peter Paul Rubens (1577–1640)
The Banqueting House Ceiling at Whitehall: The Apotheosis of James I, 1720
Engraving, 32.2 × 47 cm
National Galleries of Scotland, Edinburgh (SP II 53.64)

PROVENANCE: Mrs A.G. Macqueen Ferguson Gift, 1950.

Cat.118
Simon Gribelin (1661–1733), after Peter Paul Rubens (1577–1640)
The Banqueting House Ceiling at Whitehall: The Union of the Crowns of England and Scotland, 1720
Engraving, 32.8 × 47 cm
National Galleries of Scotland, Edinburgh (SP II 53.66)

PROVENANCE: Mrs A.G. Macqueen Ferguson Gift, 1950.

Cat.119
Simon Gribelin (1661–1733), after Peter Paul Rubens (1577–1640)
The Banqueting House Ceiling at Whitehall: The Peaceful Reign of James I, 1720
Engraving, 32.1 × 47 cm
National Galleries of Scotland, Edinburgh (SP II 53.67)

PROVENANCE: Mrs A.G. Macqueen Ferguson Gift, 1950.

Cat.120
Willie Rodger (1930–2018)
James VI & I, 1978
Screenprint, 40.6 × 30.3 cm
National Galleries of Scotland, Edinburgh (UP J 267)

PROVENANCE: Possibly gifted by the artist, 1970s.

Cat.121
Willie Rodger (1930–2018)
Mary, Queen of Scots Holding a Red Heart, 1975
Screenprint, 40.6 × 30.3 cm
National Galleries of Scotland, Edinburgh (UP M 491)

PROVENANCE: Possibly gifted by the artist, 1970s.

BOOKS & MANUSCRIPTS

Cat.122
Written by James VI (1566–1625)
Letter to 'Lady Minny', 1572
Ink on paper, 29 × 20.4 cm
National Records of Scotland, Edinburgh (GD124/10/45)

PROVENANCE: Archives of the Erskine family, Earls of Mar and Kellie. Gifted in 1956 and 1959–77.

Cat.123
Written by Titus Lucretius Carus (mid-90s to mid-50s BC), edition by Denys Lambin (1520/21–1572) printed by Jean Bienné (d.1588), binding by John Gibson (d.1600)
De rerum natura, libri VI. 'The Nature of things, book 6', published Paris, 1570, bound around 1580
Printed book, vellum binding with gilt tooling, 24.2 × 8.5 cm
National Library of Scotland, Edinburgh (Bdg.M.179)

PROVENANCE: James VI & I in the Royal Library; John Rodgers, 18th century; William Gore, later Ormsby-Gore (1779–1860); by descent to William David Ormsby-Gore, 5th Baron Harlech (1918–1985)

REFERENCES: Schweiger 1832, p.574; London 1924, p.291; Gordon 1962, no.102A

Cat.124
Written by Charles V, Holy Roman Emperor (1500–1555); Translated into Italian and transcribed by Giacomo Castelvetro (1546–1616)
Autograph manuscript of 'Ragionamento di Carlo V. Imperatore tenuto al re Philippo suo figliuolo In dargli la libera signoria di tutti gli stati suoi', 'Charles V's advice to his son Phillip II', 1555, copy made 1592
Ink on vellum, vellum binding with gilt tooling, 31.8 × 18 cm
National Library of Scotland, Edinburgh (Adv.MS.23.1.6)

PROVENANCE: Presented to the Advocates' Library in 1708 by Sir Robert Sibbald; Presented by the Faculty of Advocates to the National Library of Scotland in 1925.

REFERENCES: Stübel 1905, pp.181–248; Meikle, Craigie & Purves 1914–40, pp.cxxix–cxxx

Cat.125
Unknown author
Volume of inventories of the royal wardrobe: clothing, silver work, jewels, artillery, 1579
Ink on paper, 32.2 × 23.3 cm
National Records of Scotland, Edinburgh (E35/1)

PROVENANCE: Privy Council Records, Edinburgh.

Cat.126
Written by James VI & I (1566–1625)
Autograph manuscript draft of 'Sonnet Decifring the Perfyte Poete', before 1584
Ink on paper, 22.5 × 20.5 cm
Blackie House Library and Museum (MS0401)

PROVENANCE: James Drummond, 1st Earl of Perth (d.1611); 'J.G.', 1763; sold at Sotheby's (P.J. Croft), 18 December 1985, lot 14; sold at Sotheby's, 'Property from The Collection of Robert S Pirie Volumes I & II: Books and Manuscripts' Sale, 3 December 2015, lot 488.

Cat.127
Written by William Alexander, 1st Earl of Stirling
(c.1567–1640)
*The Monarchicke Tragedies; Croesus, Darius,
The Alexandraean, Iulius Caesar. Newly enlarged
[a nonce edition containing the works advertised
on the title page, the 1604 Paraenesis to the Prince,
and the 1604 Aurora]*, 1604–07
Paper, calfskin on paste boards with gold tooling,
19 × 14.5 cm
Blackie House Library and Museum (CAT8120)

PROVENANCE: Prince Henry Frederick; James
E. Alexander (1838); Emma Alexander (1938);
then by descent.

Cat.128
Written by James VI (1566–1625)
Note about a dog, 1585
Ink on paper, 13 × 24 cm
The University of Edinburgh Heritage Collections
(La.II. 517.2)

PROVENANCE: Bequeathed by David Laing, 1878.

Cat.129
Written by James VI (1566–1625)
*The Essayes of a Prentise, in the Divine Art
of Poesie*, 1585
Ink on paper, 18.5 × 12.5 cm
National Library of Scotland, Edinburgh (H.38.d.36)

PROVENANCE: Presented by Lord Rosebery, 1927.

Cat.130
Unknown author
**Description of form of Coronation of Anna of
Denmark, Queen of Scotland, at Holyroodhouse,
17 May 1590**
Ink on paper, 34.6 × 43 cm
Papers of the Erskine Family, Deposited Collection,
National Records of Scotland, Edinburgh (GD124/10/61)

PROVENANCE: Earls of Mar and Kellie.

Cat.131
Unknown author
**Signet letters narrating that Anna of Denmark
was now pregnant, 1593**
Ink on paper, 40.6 × 30.4 cm
National Records of Scotland, Edinburgh (RH15/19/10)

PROVENANCE: Papers of Home of Eccles.

Cat.132
Written by Christian IV of Denmark (1577–1648)
Letter to James VI, 10 October 1597
Ink on paper, 33.3 × 19.4 cm
National Records of Scotland, Edinburgh (SP13/128/1)

PROVENANCE: State Papers.

Cat.133
Written by William Shakespeare (1564–1616)
Loues Labors Lost (*Love's Labour's Lost*), 1598
Printed book, 17.7 × 13.2 cm, 76 pages
The University of Edinburgh Heritage Collections
(De.3.74)

PROVENANCE: William Drummond of Hawthornden
(1585–1649), who bequeathed his collection to the
Edinburgh University Library.

REFERENCES: Edinburgh 2005, p.14

Cat.134
Written by Esther Inglis (1569–1624)
*Vincula Unions sive scita Britannica, id est de
Unione Insulae Britannicae*, seventeenth century
Ink on paper, 19.5 × 22 cm
The University of Edinburgh Heritage Collections (La.III.249)

PROVENANCE: Bequeathed by David Laing, 1878.

Cat.135
Written by Lady Anna Livingstone (d.1632)
*Lady Anna Livingstone's Account Book as Maiden
in the Household of Princess Elizabeth*, 1603–04
Ink on paper, 26.8 × 9 cm
Papers of the Montgomerie Family, Earls of Eglinton,
Deposited Collection, National Records of Scotland,
Edinburgh (GD3/6/2/4)

PROVENANCE: Archives of the Montgomerie Family,
Earls of Eglinton, deposited 1952.

Cat.136
Unknown author
*Account of Repairs and Work on Jewels for
James VI & I*, 1604
Ink on paper, 33.8 × 22.5 cm
The University of Edinburgh Heritage Collections (La.II.525)

PROVENANCE: Bequeathed by David Laing, 1878.

REFERENCES: Edinburgh 1975, p.37, cat.219

Cat.137
Written by George Heriot (1563–1624) and others
**Itemised account of jewels etc. supplied to the Queen
by George Heriot, 9 March to 20 September 1606**
Ink on paper, 40.3 × 31 cm
Records of George Heriot's Trust, Deposited Collection,
National Records of Scotland, Edinburgh (GD421/1/3/32)

PROVENANCE: George Heriot; George Heriot's Trust.

REFERENCES: Hunt, Thornton & Dalgleish 2016, pp.189–92

Cat.138
Written by James VI & I (1566–1625)
The King Maiesties Speech, 1603, published 1609
Printed book, bound in leather with gold tooling,
19 × 14 cm, 68 pages
The University of Edinburgh Heritage Collections (De.3.39)

PROVENANCE: Halliwell-Phillipps Collection.

Cat.139
Commissioned by James VI & I (1566–1625)
*The Holy Bible, conteyning the Old Testament,
and the New. King James Bible first edition*, 1611
Printed book, 43 × 30.5 cm, 289 pages
National Library of Scotland, Edinburgh (H.S.385)

PROVENANCE: Unknown.

Cat.140
Written by William Drummond of Hawthornden
(1585–1649)
Tears on the Death of Moeliades, 1614
Printed book, 27.2 × 20.5 cm, 16 pages
The University of Edinburgh Heritage Collections (De.4.54/2)

PROVENANCE: Presented by the author to King James's
College, now the University of Edinburgh, 1630.

REFERENCES: MacDonald 1976, pp.3–7; Williamson 1978,
pp.185–86; Edinburgh 2005, p.9; London 2012a, cat.78d,
pp.170–71

Cat.141
Written by William Drummond of Hawthornden
(1585–1649)
*Forth Feasting, A Panegyricke to the Kings most
Excellent Majestie*, 1617
Printed pamphlet, 19 × 12.5 cm, 16 pages
National Library of Scotland, Edinburgh (H.29.c.12)

PROVENANCE: Presented by Lord Rosebery, 1927.

REFERENCES: Edinburgh 1975, p.30, cat.148

Cat.142
Edited by John Adamson (1576–1651?)
*The Muses Welcome to the High and Mighty
Prince James*, 1618
Printed book, bound in leather with gold tooling,
29 × 16 cm, 331 pages
National Library of Scotland, Edinburgh (L.C. 1220)

PROVENANCE: Part of the Lauriston Castle Collection
bequeathed to the Library in 1926 by William Robert Reid
(1854–1919) and Mrs Reid.

Cat.143
Unknown author
Account of the Prince's Apothecary, 1619
Ink on paper, 20 × 15.5 cm
The University of Edinburgh Heritage Collections (La.II.63.7)

PROVENANCE: Bequeathed by David Laing, 1878.

Cat.144
Written by George Villiers, Duke of Buckingham
(1592–1628)
Letters to James VI & I, 1620s
Ink on paper, 30.5 × 20.5 cm, 30 × 18.5 cm and 30 × 20.5 cm
National Library of Scotland, Edinburgh (Adv. MS 33.1.7
vol.22, fols 70, 79)

PROVENANCE: James Balfour of Denmilne; purchased by
the Advocates Library in 1698.

REFERENCES: Bergeron 1999, pp.147–219; Bergeron 2002,
pp.344–68

Cat.145
Written by Sir Anthony Weldon (1583–1648)
*The Court and Character of King James / Written and
Taken by Sir. A: W being an Eye, and Eare Witnesse*, 1650
Printed book, 14 × 9 cm, 194 pages
National Galleries of Scotland Special Collections,
Edinburgh (S.C. 66.Ja)

PROVENANCE: Unknown.

Detail of cat.87 (opposite)

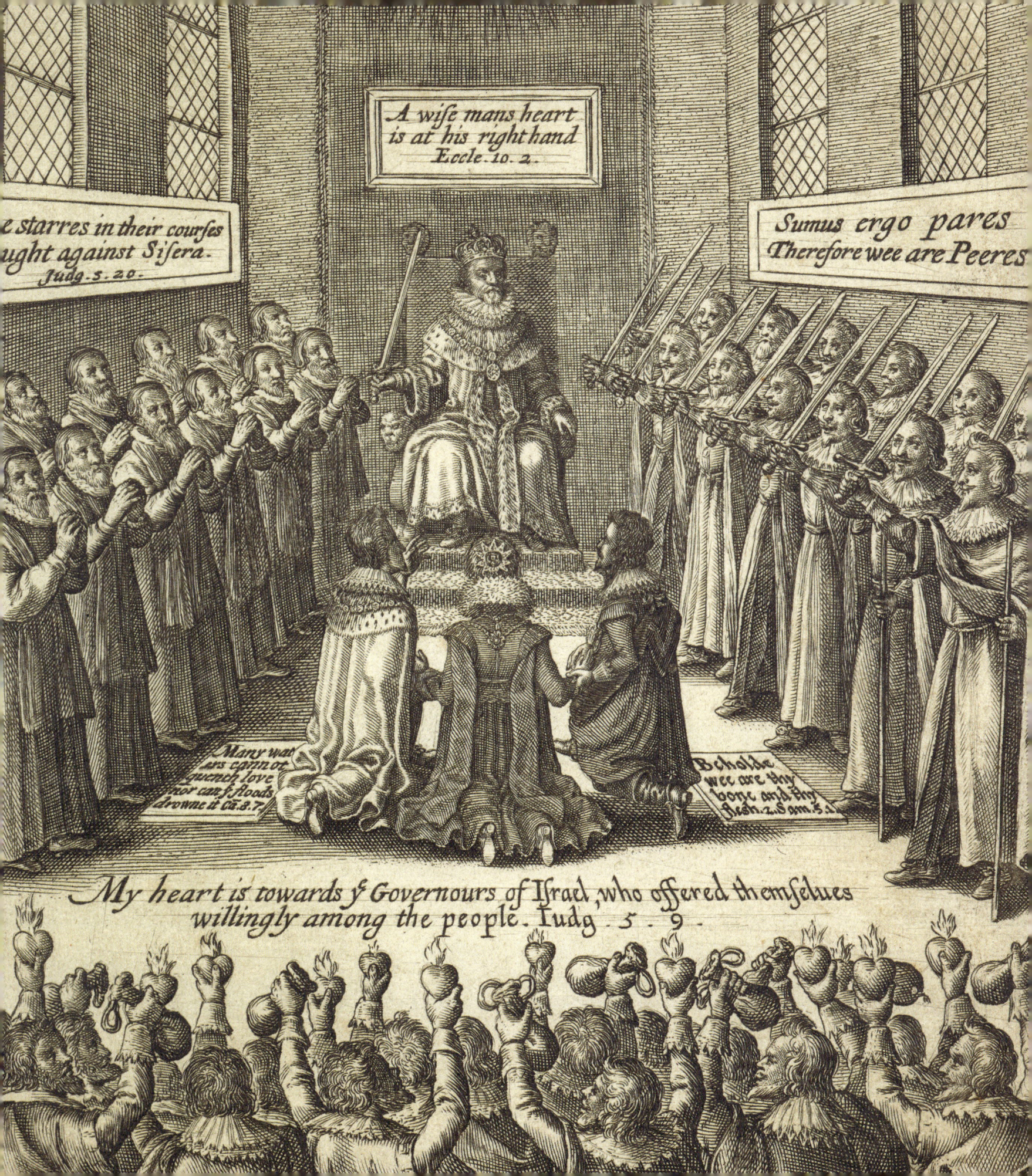

CHRONOLOGY

1566 (JUNE)
James is born at Edinburgh Castle, son of Mary, Queen of Scots and Henry Stuart, Lord Darnley

1567 (JULY)
Mary, Queen of Scots is forced to abdicate the Scottish throne. James is crowned King James VI of Scotland in the church of the Holy Rude at Stirling Castle

1567–78
Scotland is ruled by a succession of Regents – James Stewart, 1st Earl of Moray; Matthew Stewart, 4th Earl of Lennox; John Erskine, 1st Earl of Mar; James Douglas, 4th Earl of Morton

1578 (MARCH)
Regent Morton resigns. James accepts adult rule

1579 (OCTOBER)
James makes his royal entry in Edinburgh

1580 (JUNE)
Royal progress around Scotland. James visits many royal burghs including Dundee, Aberdeen and St Andrews

1582–83 (AUGUST '82–MAY '83)
The Ruthven Raid – a group of Presbyterian nobles led by William Ruthven, Lord Ruthven and 1st Earl of Gowrie kidnap James and place him under house arrest at Ruthven Castle and rule against the king's will

1585
James takes full control of his reign

1586 (JULY)
The 'Treaty of Berwick' brings peace between Scotland and England

1587 (FEBRUARY)
Execution of Mary, Queen of Scots at Fotheringhay Castle

1589
James marries Anna of Denmark

1589–90
James and Anna take an extended honeymoon in Scandinavia

1590 (MAY)
Anna of Demark is crowned at Holyrood Abbey

1594 (FEBRUARY)
Birth of Prince Henry, followed in August by his baptism, both at Stirling Castle

1596 (AUGUST)
Birth of Princess Elizabeth at Falkland Palace

1600 (AUGUST)
Gowrie Conspiracy – a supposed plot to kill James in which the leaders, John Ruthven, 3rd Earl of Gowrie and his brother Alexander, master of Ruthven, are killed in mysterious circumstances

1600 (NOVEMBER)
Birth of Prince Charles at Dunfermline Palace

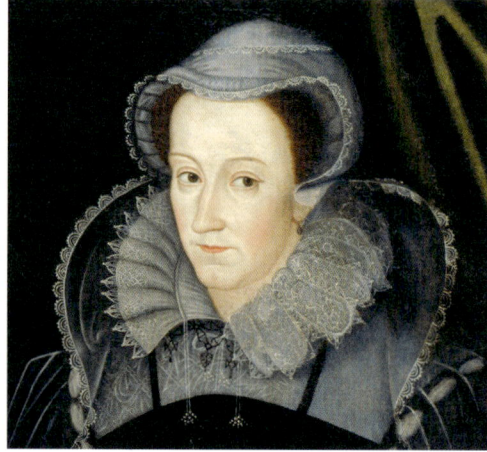

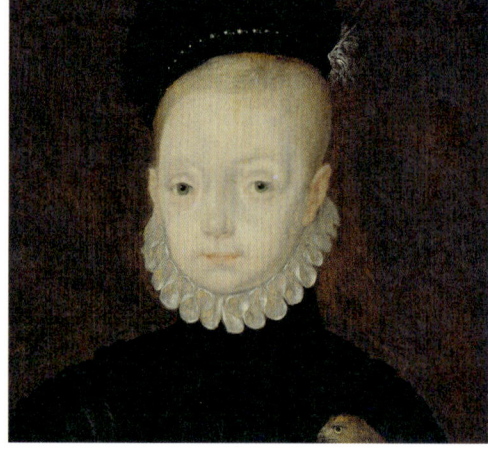

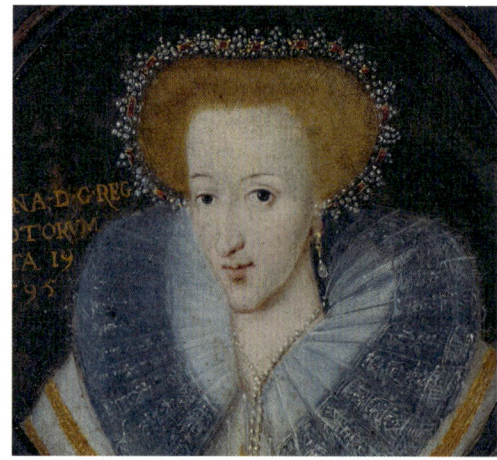

1603 (MARCH)

Death of Elizabeth I and accession of James VI of Scotland to the throne, becoming James I of England and Ireland

1603 (JUNE)

Royal progress of Anna, Prince Henry and Princess Elizabeth from Scotland to London

1603 (JULY)

Coronation of James and Anna at Westminster Abbey

1603 (JULY)

The 'Bye' and 'Main' Plots to remove James from the throne in favour of Arabella Stuart are uncovered

1604 (MARCH)

Official processional entry of James into London (delayed from the previous year by the plague)

1604 (MAY–JULY)

The Somerset House Conference, leading in August to the signature of the Treaty of London which brings peace between England and Spain

1605 (NOVEMBER)

Gunpowder Plot

1611

Publication of the *King James Bible*

1612 (NOVEMBER)

Death of Henry, Prince of Wales aged eighteen. Charles becomes heir apparent

1613 (FEBRUARY)

Princess Elizabeth marries Frederick V, Elector Palatine, and leaves England. Masques were performed as part of the wedding celebrations

1617 (MARCH)

James makes his only return visit to Scotland

1619 (MARCH)

Death of Anna of Denmark

1623 (FEBRUARY)

'The Spanish Match': after years of negotiation, Prince Charles travels incognito to Spain with George Villiers, 1st Duke of Buckingham, in an attempt to woo the Spanish Infanta Maria Anna

1625 (MARCH)

Death of James. Succeeded by his son Charles, as Charles I. Charles marries the French Princess Henrietta Maria in the same year

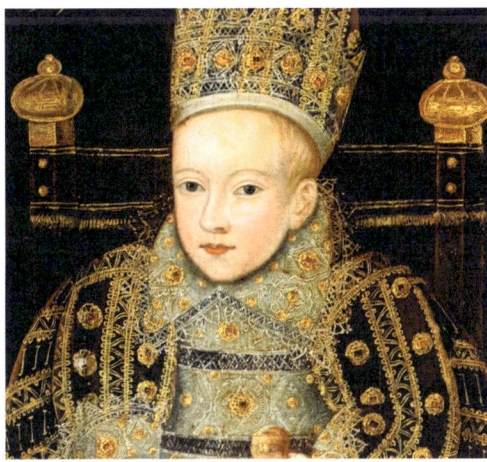
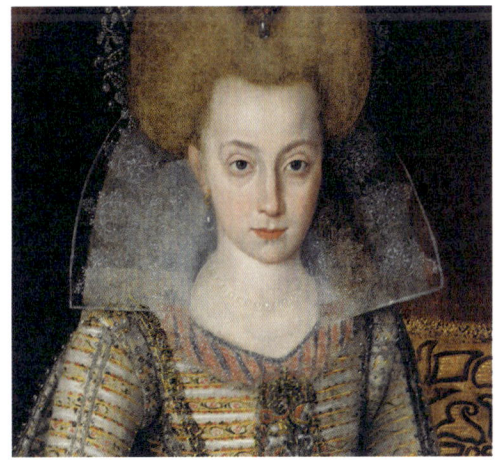
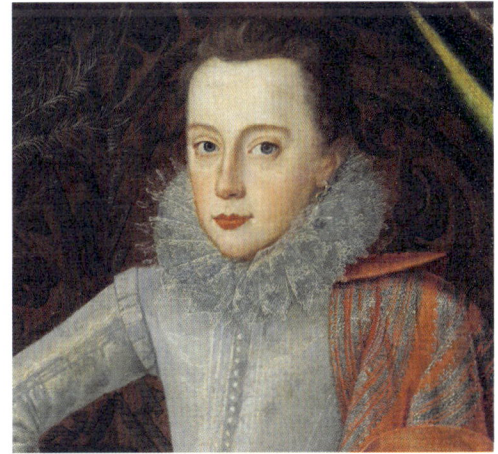

NOTES

Introduction

1 Ralph Houlbrooke, 'James's reputation, 1625–2005' in Houlbrooke 2006, p.171.
2 *CSP Scot* 1936, p.174; Moysie 1830, p.113.
3 Millar 1960, no.16, p.65.
4 I am grateful to Michael Pearce, who pointed out this entry in the National Records of Scotland, Edinburgh (hereafter NRS): NRS, E35/11/15. In 1567, £4 10s Scots equalled £1 sterling. When James acceded to the throne of England, the exchange rate for Scots pounds to sterling was fixed at 12:1.
5 In 1580, payments were made to Bronckorst, including £64 Scots for 'Certaine Pourtraitures maid be me at his Majesties Command'. This included the portrait of James, one 'fra the belt upward' and the other of 'his majestie full length'. A portrait of 'Mr George Buchanane' was also paid for. NRS, E21/61 fol.43r and voucher NRS, E23/5/6.
6 Analysis was carried out during the *Making Art and Tudor Britain* research project led by the National Portrait Gallery, London, 2012.
7 Dendrochronological analysis carried out in 2015 dates the panel to after 1589. Buchanan died in 1582, and by this point Bronckorst was back in London and is registered with his wife as living in the parish of St Nicholas Acons in Langborn ward. I am grateful to Edward Town (Yale Center for British Art) for sharing this research on Bronckorst.
8 James's first entry into a royal burgh had taken place in August 1571 when he was five years old. He rode from Stirling Castle to the Tolbooth at Stirling, where he made his first public speech. See Juhala 2000.
9 Michael Lynch, 'Court ceremony and ritual', in Goodare & Lynch 1999, p.75. The Over Bow was in the vicinity of present-day Victoria Street. The Salt Tron was on the Royal Mile.
10 Thomson 1975, pp.20–21.
11 Lynch, 'Court ceremony and ritual', in Goodare & Lynch 1999, p.75.
12 Goodare & Lynch 1999, p.3. Dr Steven Reid, University of Glasgow, suggests that James wielded royal power from 1585, when he was free from noble faction.
13 Lynch, 'Court ceremony and ritual', in Goodare & Lynch 1999, p.80.
14 Ibid., p.81. NRS, E21/61, Dec 1580. It should be emphasised that the phrase 'extrardinar pains' indeed refers to the unusually high sum of money paid to Hudson for the task, as opposed to the difficulty that Hudson had in instructing the king. With thanks to Dr Alison Rosie

15 NRS, PS1/60, 16 October 1589.
16 NRS, E23/6/17, 6 September 1581 (a faded exchequer voucher; £46 to Arnold for pictures, £30 for the portrait to be sent with William to the princess).
17 For a full account of the negotiations leading up to the journeys to and from Scotland and Denmark and for both wedding ceremonies, see Stevenson 1997.
18 Lynch, 'Court ceremony and ritual', in Goodare & Lynch 1999, p.84.
19 For more on the court at Holyroodhouse, see Juhala 2000.
20 NRS, SP13/128, 1597.
21 This small portrait gives us an idea of how the larger portrait of Anna may have looked. Another pair of portraits of James and Anna that take a similar format to the Vanson portraits were previously in the stock of Philip Mould, London.
22 NRS, PC1/17: King's warrant to a visiting English company which had performed at court, to perform in public at a house in Blackfriars Wynd to the annoyance of the clergy, incurring a further monition from James to stop them from preventing their parishioners attending, 1599.
23 In Aberdeen, Fletcher is awarded 'The Freedom of the Burgh', listed as 'Laurence Fletcher comediane to his majestie': Registers of the Town Council of Aberdeen, vol.40.
24 The National Archives, Kew, Richmond, Surrey (hereafter TNA), C 82/1690, no.78: Warrant under the privy seal for the issue of letters patent authorising Shakespeare and his companions to perform plays throughout the realm under royal patronage, 18 May 1603. For more on Lawrence Fletcher's role within the 'King's Men', see Syme 2019.
25 TNA, LC 2/4/5, p.77. Although James and Anna were crowned on 25 July 1603, the official coronation ceremony and entry into London was postponed due to an outbreak of the plague and took place the following year on 15 March 1604.
26 George Heriot's accounts to Anna of Denmark (the customer accounts) are preserved in the National Archives (TNA, LR2); the parallel accounts (the vendor accounts) are in the National Records of Scotland (NRS, GD421) deposited collection from George Heriot's Trust.
27 Maureen Meikle, 'A meddlesome princess: Anna of Denmark and Scottish court politics, 1589–1603', in Goodare & Lynch 1999, p.126.
28 In a Royal Proclamation dated 20 October 1604, James claimed the name and style

'King of Great Brittaine'. The title was not made official until the Act of Union 1707.
29 James Loxley, paper delivered as part of the session 'Fashioning the Royal Body: Intimacy and Display' in the 'Bright Star of the North: James VI & I Knowledge Exchange Workshop', 27 June 2019, Scottish National Portrait Gallery.
30 Portrait pendants of Anna and James can be found in the Museo del Prado, Madrid and the Pitti Palace, Florence. A portrait of the king was recorded in the 1608 accounts of the Treasurer of the Chamber as being sent to Ferdinando I de' Medici, Grand Duke of Florence: TNA, E351/543 fol.199; see Town 2012, pp.482–86.
31 The Sancy diamond had extraordinary lineage, having belonged to French kings before it was sold to James in 1604: London 2013b, pp.116–17.
32 Verner 1950. I'd like to thank Dr Lauren Working (University of York) for her guidance on the preferred terminology when discussing the histories of the Indigenous peoples of America and their lands.
33 Working 2020, p.26. The image in the *Album Amicorum* is probably derived from the broadside which advertised a Virginia Company lottery, which aimed to raise money for the colony and featured an engraving of Eiakintomino and another Powhatan man called Matahan. Currently we have no evidence to ascertain whether Eiakintomino's was a forced or voluntary migration.
34 Nubia and Kupperman nd.
35 Working 2022.
36 Chida-Razvi 2014.
37 In November 1620, Protestant forces were defeated by Emperor Ferdinand II's army at the Battle of White Mountain. Elizabeth, Frederick and their family were forced to flee Bohemia. For James's reaction to the situation, see Croft 2003, pp.105–16.

James VI & I and the Pageantry of Fatherhood

1 James 1599, p.121.
2 Sharpe 2009, p.156.
3 Margaret (1598–1600), Robert (b. and d.1602), Sophia (b. and d.1606) and Mary (1605–1607) all died in infancy.
4 Fowler 1594, pp.2–2v.
5 Ibid., p.2v.
6 Murray 2017, p.20.
7 Fowler 1594, p.4v.
8 Ibid., p. 8v. The published report of the baptism, as well as the account of the Dutch representatives, records that the

prince was actually given the names 'Frederick Henry' – see Ferguson 1899, vol.I, pp.163–64. An early portrait (fig.5) also styles the prince 'Frederick Henry'. James's treatise on kingship, *Basilikon Doron*, however, is dedicated to 'Henrie my dearest sonne' – see James 1599, Sig.A4r. It is likely that 'Henry' became the favoured designation in order to emphasise connections with English Tudor royalty.
9 Fowler 1594, p.12v.
10 Ibid., pp.11v–12.
11 Stevenson 1997, p.72.
12 British Library, Harleian MS 1423, fol.133; Birch 1760, p.18.
13 British Library, Harleian MS 1423, fol.133.
14 Fowler 1594, p.6v.
15 Nichols 1828, vol.2, p.467.
16 Anon. 1613, Sig.A4v.
17 Ibid., Sig.A4v; TNA, SP14/72, fol.52r; McClure 1939, vol.1, p.424.
18 Green 1854, p.199.
19 Akkerman 2013, p.159.
20 McClure 1939, vol.1, p.404.
21 Curran 2016, p.94.
22 British Library, Royal MS 17 C XXXV, fol.1r; British Library, MS RP 686/2, fol.1r.
23 British Library, Royal MS 17 C XXXV.
24 Anon. 1613, Sig.A2v.
25 Taylor 1613, Sig.B3v.
26 Werrett 2011, pp.169–70.
27 Daniel 1610, Sig.B1r.
28 Middleton 1616, Sig.A4v.
29 Ibid., Sig.A4v–B1r.
30 Ibid., Sig.B1v.
31 Murray 2017, p.36.
32 Gregg 1984, p.70.
33 Brotton 2006, p.11.
34 Gregg 1984, p.84.
35 Ibid., p.85.
36 TNA, SP 14/153, f.25.
37 McClure 1939, vol.2, p.516; TNA, SP 14/153, fol.36.
38 Anon. 1623, single sheet.
39 Bellany & Cogswell 2015, p.3.
40 Gregg 1984, p.91.
41 *CSPV* 1900, p.510.

Dressing the Stuart Court

1 *CSPV* 1905, no.672: 26 October 1612 – Antonio Foscarini, Venetian Ambassador in England, to the Doge and Senate.
2 *CSPV* 1905, nos 680, 775: 9 November 1612; 1 March 1613 – the same to the same.
3 NRS, E35/13, vol.2, p.7.
4 NRS, E35/14, fol.14v.
5 Ibid., vol.7, p.9. This included a charge of £8,238 18s 5d Scots for the queen's servitors.

6 NRS, E35/13, vol.1, p.1; vol.3, pp.2, 3.
   On these accounts, and Anna's Scottish
   wardrobe more generally, see Field 2019.
   See also Pearce 2019.
7 NRS, E35/13, vol.3, pp.9–18.
8 Ibid., vol.4, pp.4–9.
9 Cole 2010, pp.6, 360–416; Juhala 2000,
   p.121.
10 Juhala 2000, pp.61, 121, 127–28, 130,
   132–35; Cole 2010, p.21.
11 Cole 2010, pp.8–10; Barroll 2001, pp.38–
   39; Croft 1991, pp.136–37. See also Colvin
   1982, pp.175, 144, 237–39, 278, 321–22.
12 TNA, E351/543, fols 246v, 247r–v,
   260r–263r; TNA, E351/544, fols 8r,
   10r–11v, 26r–27v, 43v–44r, 58r–59v,
   78v–79r, 91r–92r, 99v, 100r–v.
13 NRS, E35/13, vol.1, pp.12–13.
14 Ibid., p.13.
15 Field 2019.
16 A safeguard was an outer-skirt or petticoat
   worn by women for protective reasons
   during riding: 'safeguard, n.', OED Online.
17 NRS, E35/13, vol.2, p.3. Similarly, Queen
   Elizabeth's riding clothes were coordinate
   suites: see Arnold 1988, p.142.
18 CSP Scot 1936, p.306.
19 NRS, E35/13, vol.1, pp.8–9.
20 E35/13, vol.1, pp.74–75.
21 NRS, E21/74, fols 56, 57: July 1600.
22 NRS, E21/68, fol.170. 'S(c)hank n.',
   Dictionary of the Scots Language.
23 TNA, LC5/50: 20 September 1603.
24 For gift-exchange in Scotland and England
   see, for example, Peck 1981; Peck 1993,
   pp.30–46; Heal 2014a; Heal 2014b;
   Ungerer 1998.
25 Cambridge University Library (hereafter
   CUL), MS Dd.I.26, fols 18r–v, 21r.
26 Quinton 2013, pp.66–73.
27 Field 2017. A full transcription of the
   inventory is published as supplementary
   material.
28 Scarisbrick 1991, pp.200, 212, 213, 226,
   nos 64, 196, 200, 321.
29 Ibid., p.194.
30 Devon 1836, pp.104–05.
31 NRS, E35/14, fol.15v.
32 NRS, E35/13, vol.2, pp.61–63.
33 Ibid., vol.6, pp.2–4; NRS, E35/13, vol.8,
   pp.76–77. For the apparelling of Anna's
   servitors in Scotland, see also Field 2019.
   See also Pearce 2019.
34 NRS, E35/14, fol.19r.
35 TNA, LR2/122, fol.24r.
36 These portraits are now in a private
   collection, Scotland; Dunedin Public
   Gallery, New Zealand (1-1974); and Tate,
   London (T00398).
37 Hunt, Thornton & Dalgleish 2016.
38 Devon 1836, p.16.
39 CSPV 1900, p.179, no.267.
40 Hunt, Thornton & Dalgleish 2016,
   pp.188–90.

Writing Monarchy, Union, Fatherhood and Tobacco

1 James, speech to English parliament, 21
   March 1610, in James 1616, pp.527–48, at
   p.529.
2 James, speech to English parliament, 1605,
   in James 1616, pp.499–508, at p.500.
3 James, speech, 1610, in James 1616, p.531.
4 James, The True Lawe of Free Monarchies,
   in James 1616, pp.191–210, at pp.194, 203,
   208.
5 Buchanan 1579, p.92.
6 James, True Lawe, in James 1616, p.192.
7 Ibid., p.202.
8 James, Basilikon Doron, in James 1616,
   pp.137–92, at p.156.
9 Ibid., p.164; James, True Lawe, in James
   1616, p.204.
10 Ibid., p.204.
11 Scottish Privy Council, proclamation, 24
   March 1603, Buron & Masson 1877–79,
   p.553.
12 James, speech to English parliament, 31
   March 1607, in James 1616, pp.509–26, at
   p.511.
13 James, speech to English parliament, 19
   March 1604, in James 1616, pp.485–97, at
   p.488.
14 Ibid., p.486.
15 James, speech, 1607, in James 1616, p.524.
16 James, speech, 1604, in James 1616,
   p.488.
17 James, speech, 1607, in James 1616,
   pp.520–21.
18 Lo here (my Son) a mirror view and fair;
   Which shows the shadow of a worthy
   King; Your father bids you study here
   and read; How to become a perfect King
   indeed.
19 James, Basilikon Doron, in James 1616,
   pp.184, 185, 187.
20 Ibid., pp.182–83.
21 Ibid., pp.187, 172.
22 Ibid., p.160.
23 James, Daemonologie, in James 1616,
   pp.91–136, at pp.91, 112.
24 Ibid., p.116.
25 Ibid., p.119.
26 Ibid., p.136.
27 James, A Discovrse of the Maner of the
   Discoverie of the Powder Treason, Joyned
   With the Examination of Some of the
   Prisoners, in James 1616, pp.223–46, at
   pp.224, 229, 230.
28 Ibid., pp.224, 231.
29 James, A Counterblast to Tobacco, in James
   1616, pp.211–22, at pp.212, 213, 214, 222.
30 Ibid., pp.217, 218, 220, 221.
31 Sommerville 1994, pp.268–69, n.1.

Painters and Scottish Patrons at the London Court of James VI & I, 1603–25

1 London 2018.
2 See Martin 2005; Hearn 2011 focuses on
   Rubens's first surviving painted sketch
   (fig.18), produced in 1628–30, towards
   the ceiling design.
3 See, for example, Chaney 2003 and
   Bracken 2015.
4 Rae & Burnstock 2014, pp.54–66.
5 Millar 1963a, pp.13–15.
6 The portrait of Albert is now lost; the
   portrait of Infanta Isabella Clara Eugenia
   is now attributed to Frans Pourbus the
   Younger (1569–1622), c.1598–1600
   (Royal Collection Trust).
7 Juan Pantoja de la Cruz (1553–1608),
   Philip III, King of Spain, signed and dated
   1605 (Royal Collection Trust).
8 Attributed to Jacob Bunel (1558–1614),
   Henry IV, c.1600–10 (Royal Collection
   Trust).
9 Millar 1963a, p.15.
10 Hearn 2012; for an international account
   of the full-length portrait format, see
   Bikker 2018.
11 For recent accounts of Jacobean
   miniatures, see London 2019a and
   Goldring 2019.
12 See Hearn 2015.
13 For Lucas de Heere, see Town 2014,
   pp.68–69, and Goldring 2019, pp.79–82,
   136–37.
14 Town 2014, pp.65–68.
15 For detailed information on both of these
   paintings, see Hearn 2004. See also
   MacLean 2017.
16 Ibid.
17 For a surviving portrait miniature of
   Charles Howard, 2nd Baron Howard
   of Effingham (1536–1624), attributed
   to Rowland Lockey, c.1605, see Royal
   Museums Greenwich, acc.MNT0136.
18 For the two Harington portraits, see
   London 1995, cat.126, pp.185–86, and
   London 2009, cat.1, pp.42–43. For Peake,
   see Town 2014, pp.152–53, and MacLeod
   2015.
19 MacLeod 2018, p.78.
20 For Gheeraerts II, see London 2002 and
   Town 2014, pp.87–88.
21 MacLeod 2018, pp.78–82.
22 See London 1995, cat.131, pp.194–95;
   Anna subsequently also commissioned
   a portrait of Derry from Paul van Somer
   (now lost).
23 Town 2014, p.88.
24 ODNB 2004, vol.49, pp.798–801, entry for
   'Alexander Seton, 1st Earl of Dunfermline',
   by Maurice Lee, Jr.
25 London 2002, pp.24–26.
26 Bath 2003, chapter 4, pp.79–103.
27 ODNB 2004, vol.25, pp.1006–09, entry
   for 'James Hay, 1st Earl of Carlisle', by Roy
   E. Schreiber.
28 They are thought to be studio versions
   of a now lost original. One is fig.21 (The
   Weiss Gallery; see London 2019b, fig.21,
   pp.100–03); the other, with a provenance
   from the Campion family of Danny,
   Hurstpierpoint, Sussex, was offered at
   Sotheby's, London, 14 March 1984, lot 15.
29 A full-length portrait of Hay, signed and
   inscribed, lower right, 'Michael Miereveld
   fecit … / … interrellatum pinxit / Anno
   Dom M.D.C.XX AEt:XL' was offered at
   Sotheby's, London, 5 December 2019,
   lot 126. A Van Miereveld-style head-
   and-shoulders portrait of the same
   sitter, differently attired, was offered at
   Sotheby's, London, 14 July 1993, lot 10.
30 Ekkart, Jansen & Verhave 2011.
31 On Van Miereveld's British clients, see
   Jansen & Verhave 2015.
32 See Town 2014, p.178.
33 See London 1995, cat.138, pp.204–05.
34 For Ancram, see ODNB 2004, vol.31,
   pp.392–93, entry for 'Robert Ker, 1st Earl
   of Ancram' by David Stevenson. For Van
   Blijenberch's portrait of him, see London
   1972, cat.14, p.20.
35 Millar 1960, p.1: 'Done by/ Abraham /
   Blyenburch/ pijntit opan de lijeht / Item ju
   M Picture at length done when / j M was
   Princ In a guilded Carved frame'.
36 For Van Somer, see ODNB 2004, vol.51,
   pp.559–60, entry for 'Paul van Somer' by
   Karen Hearn; also Town 2014, pp.182–83.
37 For a short account of this portrait, see
   MacLeod 2018, p.82.
38 ODNB 2004, on Van Somer, vol.51, p.560.
39 For Daniel Mytens, the principal source
   remains Ter Kuile 1969; see also ODNB
   2004, vol.40, pp.91–93, entry for 'Daniel
   Mytens [Mijtens]' by Anne Thackray.
40 Ibid.
41 ODNB 2004, vol.24, pp.838–39, entry
   for 'James Hamilton, 2nd Marquess of
   Hamilton' by David Stevenson.
42 McEvansoneya 1992; see also Hearn 2003,
   pp.227–28.
43 See London 2009, cat.7, p.50.
44 See, for example, Barnes et al. 2004, p.2.

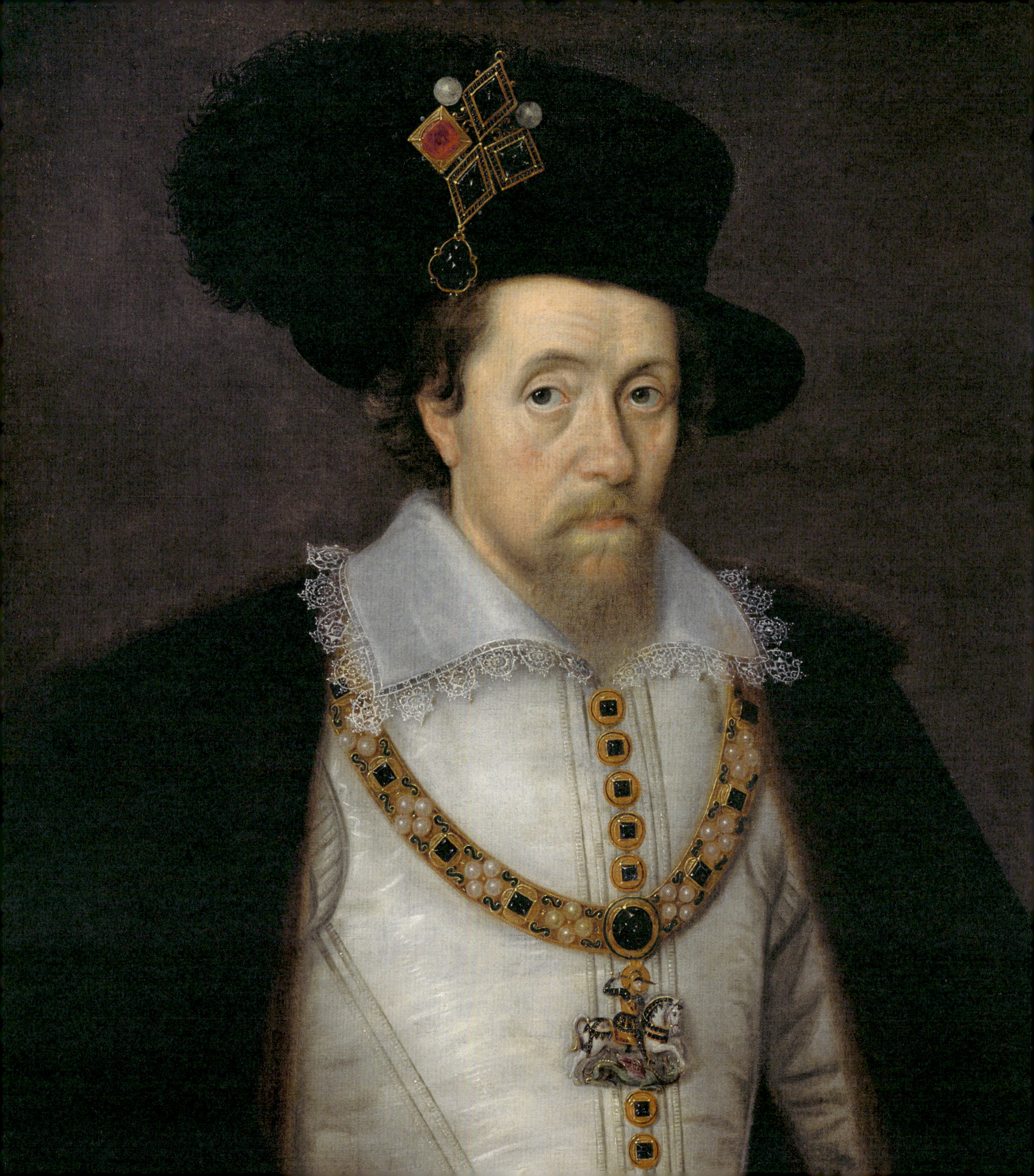

BIBLIOGRAPHY

Manuscript Sources

British Library: Harleian MS 1423; MS RP 686/2; Royal MS 17 C XXXV

Cambridge University Library: MS Dd.I.26

National Records of Scotland: E21/61 fol.43r; E21/61 Dec 1580; E21/68; E21/74; E23/5/6; E23/6/17; E35/11/15; E35/13; E35/14; GD421; PC1/17; PS1/60, 16 October 1589; SP13/128, 1597

The National Archives: C 82/1690, no.78; LC 2/4/5, p.77, 15 May 1604; E351/543; E351/544; LC5/50; LR2; LR2/122; SP14/72; SP 14/153

Published Sources

Akerman 1851
J.Y. Akerman, *Archaeologia*, vol.xxxiv, 1851

Akkerman 2013
Nadine Akkerman, *The Letters of Elizabeth Stuart, Queen of Bohemia*, vol.1, Oxford, 2013

Aldis 1904
Harry G. Aldis, *List of Books Printed in Scotland Before 1700*, Edinburgh, 1904

Allerston 2023
Patricia Allerston (ed.), *Scottish Art in 100 Works*, Edinburgh, 2023

Anon. 1613
Anon., *The Mariage [sic] of Prince Fredericke and the King's Daughter, the Lady Elizabeth*, London, 1613

Anon. 1623
Anon., *The High and Mighty Prince Charles, Prince of Wales, &c. the Manner of his Arrival at the Spanish Court, the Magnificence of his Royall Entertainment There, his Happy Returne and Hearty Welcome*, London, 1623

Arnold 1988
Janet Arnold, *Queen Elizabeth's Wardrobe Unlock'd*, Leeds, 1988

Auerbach 1961
Erna Auerbach, *Nicholas Hilliard*, London, 1961

Awais-Dean 2017
Natasha Awais-Dean, *Bejewelled: Men and Jewellery in Tudor and Jacobean England*, London, 2017

Barnes *et al.* 2004
Susan J. Barnes *et al.*, *Van Dyck: Complete Catalogue of the Paintings*, New Haven and London, 2004

Barroll 2001
Leeds Barroll, *Anna of Denmark, Queen of England: A Cultural Biography*, Philadelphia, 2001

Bath 2003
Michael Bath, *Renaissance Decorative Painting in Scotland*, Edinburgh, 2003

Bayne-Powell 1985
Robert Bayne-Powell, *Catalogue of the Portrait Miniatures in the Fitzwilliam Museum Cambridge*, Cambridge, 1985

Bellany & Cogswell 2015
Alastair Bellany and Thomas Cogswell, *The Murder of King James I*, New Haven and London, 2015

Bergeron 1999
David Moore Bergeron, *King James and Letters of Homoerotic Desire*, Iowa, 1999

Bergeron 2002
David Moore Bergeron, 'Writing King James's sexuality,' in Daniel Fischlin and Mark Fortier (eds), *Royal Subjects: Essays on the Writings of James VI and I*, Detroit, 2002, pp.344–68

Berlin 1939
Staatliche Kunstbibliothek (Berlin), *Katalog der Ornamentstichsammlung der Staatlichen Kunstbibliothek Berlin*, Berlin and Leipzig, 1939

Bikker 2018
Jonathan Bikker, *High Society*, Amsterdam, 2018

Birch 1760
Thomas Birch, *The Life of Henry Prince of Wales, Eldest Son of King James I*, Dublin, 1760

Bolland 2018
Charlotte Bolland, *Tudor and Jacobean Portraits: National Portrait Gallery*, London, 2018

Bracken 2015
Susan Bracken, 'Collectors in England: evolutions in taste 1580–1630', in Tarnya Cooper *et al.* (eds), *Painting in Britain 1500–1630: Production, Influences, and Patronage*, Oxford, 2015, pp.384–91

Brotton 2006
Jerry Brotton, 'Buying the Renaissance prince: Prince Charles's art purchases in Madrid, 1623', in Alexander Samson (ed.), *The Spanish Match: Prince Charles's Journey to Madrid, 1623*, Aldershot and Burlington, 2006

Brown 2000
Keith M. Brown, *Noble Society in Scotland: Wealth, Family and Culture, from Reformation to Revolution*, Edinburgh, 2000

Buchanan 1579
George Buchanan, *De Jure Regni Apud Scotos Dialogus; or, a dialogue, concerning the due priviledge of government in the kingdom of Scotland, betwixt George Buchanan and Thomas Maitland*, Edinburgh, 1579, transl. 1680

Burns 1887
Edward Burns, *The Coinage of Scotland*, vol.2, Edinburgh, 1887

Burns 1892
Thomas Burns, *Old Scottish Communion Plate*, Edinburgh, 1892

Buron & Masson 1877–79
J. Buron and D. Masson (eds), *The Register of the Privy Council of Scotland, 1545–1625*, vol.6, Edinburgh, 1877–79

Caw 1903
James L. Caw, *Scottish Portraits*, 2 vols, Edinburgh, 1903, vol.1

Caw 1910
James L. Caw, 'Portraits of the first five Jameses', *The Scottish Historical Review*, vol. VII, no.26, January 1910, pp.113–18

Caw 1936
James L. Caw, *Catalogue of Pictures at Pollok House*, Glasgow, 1936

Chaney 2003
Edward Chaney, 'The Italianate evolution of English collecting', in Edward Chaney (ed.), *The Evolution of English Collecting*, New Haven and London, 2003, pp.1–124

Chida-Razvi 2014
Mehreen M. Chida-Razvi, 'The Perception of Reception: The Importance of Sir Thomas Roe at The Mughal Court of Jahangir', *The Journal of World History*, vol.25, no.2/3, June/September 2014, pp.263–84

Cole 2010
Emily Cole, 'The state apartment in the Jacobean country house, 1603–1625', unpublished DPhil thesis, University of Sussex, Brighton, 2010

Detail of cat.8 (opposite)

Colvin 1982
    Howard Colvin, *The History of the King's Works*, vol.4, London, 1982
Cooper 2014
    Tarnya Cooper (ed.), *National Portrait Gallery: A Portrait of Britain*, London, 2014
Croft 1991
    Pauline Croft, 'Robert Cecil and the early Jacobean court', in Linda Levy Peck (ed.), *The Mental World of the Jacobean Court*, Cambridge, 1991, pp.134–48
Croft 2003
    Pauline Croft, *King James*, Basingstoke, 2003
CSP Scot 1936
    Calendar of State Papers Relating to Scotland and Mary Queen of Scots, 1457–1603, vol.10 (1589–1593), edited by William K. Boyd and Henry W. Meikle, Edinburgh, 1936
CSPV 1900
    Calendar of State Papers and Manuscripts, Relating to English Affairs, Existing in the Archives and Collections of Venice (CSPV), vol.10 (1603–1607), edited by Horatio F. Brown, London, 1900
CSPV 1905
    Calendar of State Papers and Manuscripts, Relating to English Affairs, Existing in the Archives and Collections of Venice (CSPV), vol.12 (1610–1613), edited by Horatio F. Brown, London, 1905
Curran 2006
    Kevin Curran, 'James I and fictional authority at the Palatine wedding celebrations', *Renaissance Studies*, vol.20, 2006, pp.51–67
Curran 2016
    Kevin Curran, *Marriage, Performance and Politics at the Jacobean Court*, Aldershot and Burlington, 2016
Daniel 1610
    Samuel Daniel, *The Order and Solemnitie of the Creation of the High and Mightie Prince Henrie*, London, 1610
Das 2023
    Nandini Das, *Courting India: England, Mughal India and the Origins of Empire*, London, 2023
Devon 1836
    Frederick Devon, *Issues of the Exchequer, Being Payments Made out of His Majesty's Revenues During the Reign of King James I*, London, 1836
Dictionary of the Scots Language
    http://www.dsl.ac.uk (accessed 21 April 2019)
Dundee 1867
    Dundee Fine Art Exhibition, 1867
Edinburgh 1883
    Board of Manufactures, *Catalogue of Loan Exhibition, Works of Old Masters and Scottish National Portraits*, exh. cat., Edinburgh, 1883

Edinburgh 1884
    John Miller Gray, *Scottish National Portraits: Catalogue of Loan Exhibition*, exh. cat., Board of Manufactures, Royal Institution, Edinburgh, 1884
Edinburgh 1959
    Renaissance Decorative Arts in Scotland 1480–1650, exh. cat., National Museum of Antiquities of Scotland (NMAS) and the Scottish National Portrait Gallery (SNPG), Edinburgh, 1959
Edinburgh 1975
    Basil Skinner, *King James VI & I*, exh. cat., Royal Scottish Museum, Edinburgh, 1975
Edinburgh 1976
    Rosalind K. Marshall, *Childhood in Seventeenth Century Scotland*, exh. cat., Scottish National Portrait Gallery, Edinburgh, 1976
Edinburgh 1987
    Helen Smailes and Duncan Thomson, *The Queen's Image*, exh. cat., Scottish National Portrait Gallery, Edinburgh, 1987
Edinburgh 1990
    Rosalind K. Marshall *et al.*, *Dynasty: The Royal House of Stewart*, exh. cat., National Galleries of Scotland and National Museums of Scotland, Edinburgh, 1990
Edinburgh 1991
    Rosalind K. Marshall and George R. Dalgleish, *The Art of Jewellery in Scotland*, exh. cat., Scottish National Portrait Gallery, Edinburgh, 1991
Edinburgh 1998
    Rosalind K. Marshall, *The Winter Queen: The Life of Elizabeth of Bohemia 1596–1662*, exh. cat., Scottish National Portrait Gallery, Edinburgh, 1998
Edinburgh 2005
    John Scally and Julie Lawson, *'A Labyrinth of Delight': The World of William Drummond of Hawthornden 1585–1649*, exh. cat., Edinburgh University Library, Museums and Galleries and the Scottish National Portrait Gallery, Edinburgh, 2005
Edinburgh 2013
    Rosalind K. Marshall, *Mary Queen of Scots: 'In The End Is My Beginning'*, exh. cat., National Museum of Scotland, Edinburgh, 2013
Ekkart, Jansen & Verhave 2011
    Rudi Ekkart, Anita Jansen and Johanneke Verhave, *De Portretfabriek van Michiel van Mierevelt (1566–1641)*, Zwolle, 2011
Evans-Thomas 1932
    Owen Evans-Thomas, *Domestic Utensils of Wood XVIth to XIXth Century: A Short History of Wooden Articles in Domestic Use from the Sixteenth to the Middle of the Nineteenth Century*, London, 1932
Ferguson 1899
    James Ferguson (ed.), *Papers Illustrating the History of the Scots Brigade in the Service of the*

United Netherlands, Scottish History Society, vol.1, Edinburgh, 1899
Field 2017
    Jemma Field, 'The wardrobe goods of Anna of Denmark, Queen Consort of Scotland and England (1574–1619)', *Costume*, vol.51, no.1, 2017, pp.3–27
Field 2019
    Jemma Field, 'Dressing a queen: the wardrobe of Anna of Denmark at the Scottish court of King James VI, 1590–1603', *The Court Historian*, vol.24, no.2, 2019, pp.152–67
Foster 1907
    J.J. Foster, *The Stuarts: Being Outlines of the Personal History of the Family*, London, 1907
Fowler 1594
    William Fowler, *A True Reportarie of the Most Triumphant, and Royal Accomplishment of the Baptisme of the Most Excellent, Right High and Mightie Prince Frederik Henry*, Edinburgh, 1594
Glasgow 1901
    International Exhibition Glasgow 1901: Official Catalogue of the Fine Art Section, exh. cat., Glasgow, 1901
Glasgow 1968
    The Stirling Maxwell Collection Pollok House, Glasgow, c.1968
Goldring 2019
    Elizabeth Goldring, *Nicholas Hilliard: Life of an Artist*, New Haven and London, 2019
Goodare & Lynch 1999
    Julian Goodare and Michael Lynch (eds), *The Reign of James VI*, East Linton, 1999
Gordon 1962
    Cosmo Alexander Gordon, *A Bibliography of Lucretius*, London, 1962
Green 1854
    Mary Anne Everett Green, *Lives of the Princesses of England*, vol.5, London, 1854
Gregg 1984
    Pauline Gregg, *King Charles I*, Berkeley and Los Angeles, 1984
Groundwater 2024
    Anna Groundwater (ed.), *Decoding the Jewels: Renaissance Jewellery in Scotland*, Edinburgh, 2024
Hayward 2020
    Maria Hayward, *Stuart Style*, London, 2020
Heal 2014a
    Felicity Heal, 'Royal gifts and gift-exchange in sixteenth-century Anglo-Scottish politics', in Steve Boardman and Julian Goodare (eds), *Kings, Lords and Men in Scotland and Britain, 1300–1625: Essays in Honour of Jenny Wormald*, Edinburgh, 2014, pp.283–300

Heal 2014b
Felicity Heal, *The Power of Gifts: Gift-Exchange in Early Modern England*, Oxford, 2014

Hearn 2003
Karen Hearn, 'A question of judgement: Lucy Harington, Countess of Bedford, as art patron and collector', in Edward Chaney (ed.), *The Evolution of English Collecting*, New Haven and London, 2003, pp.221–39

Hearn 2004
Karen Hearn, *Talking Peace 1604: The Somerset House Conference Paintings*, London, 2004

Hearn 2011
Karen Hearn, *Rubens and Britain*, London, 2011

Hearn 2012
Karen Hearn, 'The full-length portrait in early 17th-century Britain', in Laura Houliston (ed.), *The Suffolk Collection*, Swindon, 2012, pp.28–39

Hearn 2015
Karen Hearn, '"Picture drawer born at Antwerp": migrant artists in Jacobean London', in Tarnya Cooper *et al.* (eds), *Painting in Britain, 1500–1630: Production, Influences, and Patronage*, Oxford, 2015, pp.278–87

Hind 1952–64
A.M. Hind, *Engraving in England in the Sixteenth and Seventeenth Centuries*, 3 vols, Cambridge, 1952–64

Holloway *et al.* 1999
James Holloway *et al.*, *Companion Guide to the National Portrait Gallery*, Edinburgh, 1999

Hollstein 1949
F.W.H. Hollstein, *Dutch and Flemish etchings, engravings and woodcuts c.1450–1700*, Amsterdam, 1949

Houlbrooke 2006
Ralph Houlbrooke (ed.), *James VI & I: Ideas, Authority and Government*, Aldershot, 2006

Hunt, Thornton & Dalgleish 2016
Arnold Hunt, Dora Thornton and George Dalgleish, 'A Jacobean reliquary reassessed: Thomas Lyte, the Lyte genealogy and the Lyte Jewel', *The Antiquaries Journal*, vol.96, 2016, pp.169–205

Ingamells 2008
John Ingamells, *Dulwich Picture Gallery*, London, 2008

James 1599
James VI & I, *Basilikon Doron*, Edinburgh, 1599

James 1616
James VI & I, *The Workes of the Most High and Mightie Prince, Iames by the Grace of God, King of Great Britaine, France and Ireland, Defender of the Faith, &c.*, London, 1616

Jansen & Verhave 2015
Anita Jansen and Johanneke Verhave, 'The ambassador and the painter: Sir Dudley Carleton and Michiel van Mierevelt', in Tarnya Cooper *et al.* (eds), *Painting in Britain 1500–1630: Production, Influences, and Patronage*, Oxford, 2015, pp.298–309

Juhala 2000
Amy Juhala, 'The household and court of King James VI of Scotland, 1567–1603', PhD thesis, University of Edinburgh, 2000, https://era.ed.ac.uk/handle/1842/1727 (accessed 17 December 2019)

Kerr-Peterson & Reid 2017
Miles Kerr-Peterson and Steven J. Reid (eds), *James VI and Noble Power in Scotland 1578–1603*, London, 2017

Laing 1865
David Laing, 'Notes Relating to Mrs Esther (Langlois or) Inglis, The Celebrated Calligraphist, with an Enumeration of Manuscript Volumes Written by her Between the Years 1586 and 1624', *The Proceedings of the Society of Antiquaries of Scotland*, vol.6, December 1865, pp.284–309

Laing 1867
David Laing, *Adversaria: Notices Illustrative of Some of the Earlier Works Printed for the Bannatyne Club*, Edinburgh, 1867

Laroque 1993
Françoise Laroque, *The Age of Shakespeare*, New York and London, 1993

Leighton 2015
John Leighton, *100 Masterpieces: National Galleries Scotland*, Edinburgh, 2015

Lloyd 2004
Stephen Lloyd, *Portrait Miniatures from the National Galleries of Scotland*, Edinburgh, 2004

London 1866
Catalogue of the First Special Exhibition of National Portraits Ending With the Reign of King James, the Second, On Loan to the South Kensington Museum, April 1866, exh. cat., South Kensington Museum, London, rev. edn, 1866

London 1889
Exhibition of the Royal House of Stuart, exh. cat., New Gallery, London, 1889

London 1924
Short-title catalogue of books printed in France and of French books printed in other countries from 1470 to 1600 in the British Museum, London, 1924

London 1972
Oliver Millar, *The Age of Charles I: Painting in England 1620–1649*, exh. cat., Tate Gallery, London, 1972

London 1981
Anna Somers Cocks (ed.), *Princely Magnificence: Court Jewels of the Renaissance, 1500–1630*, exh. cat., Victoria and Albert Museum, London, 1981

London 1983
Roy Strong, *Artists of the Tudor Court: The Portrait Miniature Rediscovered 1520–1620*, exh. cat., Victoria and Albert Museum, London, 1983

London 1995
Karen Hearn (ed.), *Dynasties: Painting in Tudor and Jacobean England 1530–1630*, exh. cat., Tate Gallery, London, 1995

London 1996
Christopher Lloyd and Vanessa Remington, *Masterpieces in Little: Portrait Miniatures from the Collection of Her Majesty Queen Elizabeth II*, exh. cat., Royal Collection Trust, London, 1996

London 2002
Karen Hearn, *Marcus Gheeraerts II: Elizabethan Artist in Focus*, exh. cat., Tate Britain, London, 2002

London 2006
Tarnya Cooper, *Searching for Shakespeare*, exh. cat., National Portrait Gallery, London, 2006

London 2009
Karen Hearn (ed.), *Van Dyck and Britain*, exh. cat., Tate Britain, London, 2009

London 2012a
Catharine MacLeod, *The Lost Prince: The Life and Death of Henry Stuart*, exh. cat., National Portrait Gallery, London, 2012

London 2012b
Jonathan Bate and Dora Thornton, *Shakespeare: Staging the World*, exh. cat., British Museum, London, 2012

London 2013a
Tarnya Cooper, *Elizabeth I and Her People*, exh. cat., National Portrait Gallery, London, 2013

London 2013b
Anna Reynolds, *In Fine Style: The Art of Tudor and Stuart Fashion*, exh. cat., Royal Collection Trust, London, 2013

London 2018
Desmond Shawe-Taylor and Per Rumberg (eds), *Charles I: King and Collector*, exh. cat., Royal Academy of Arts, London, 2018

London 2019a
Catharine MacLeod, *Elizabethan Treasures: Miniatures by Hilliard and Oliver*, exh. cat., National Portrait Gallery, London, 2019

London 2019b
Facing History: Northern European Portraiture 1570–1735, exh. cat., Weiss Gallery, London, 2019

London 2021
Susan Doran (ed.), *Elizabeth and Mary: Royal Cousins, Rival Queens*, exh.cat., British Library, London, 2021

MacDonald 1976
Robert H. MacDonald (ed.), *William Drummond of Hawthornden: Poems and Prose*, Edinburgh, 1976

Macdonald 2000
Murdo Macdonald, *Scottish Art*, London, 2000

MacLean 2017
Gerald MacLean, 'Ottoman Things in Early-Modern England', in Caroline Lehni *et al.* (eds), *Geographies of Contact: Britain, the Middle East and the Circulation of Knowledge*, Strasbourg, 2017, pp.92–107 (published on OpenEdition Books, 14 October 2019, https://books.openedition.org/pus/6035).

MacLeod 2015
Catharine MacLeod, 'Robert Peake: portraits, patrons and technical evidence', in Tarnya Cooper *et al.* (eds), *Painting in Britain 1500–1630: Production, Influences, and Patronage*, Oxford, 2015, pp.288–97

MacLeod 2018
Catharine MacLeod, 'Facing Europe: the portraiture of Anne of Denmark (1574–1619)', in Jill Bepler and Svante Norrhem (eds), *Telling Objects: Contextualizing the Role of the Consort in Early Modern Europe*, Wolfenbüttel, 2018, pp.63–87

Manchester 1857
John Peck, *Catalogue of the Art Treasures of the United Kingdom*, exh. cat., Manchester, 1857

Manchester 1964
The Age of Shakespeare, exh. cat., Whitworth Art Gallery, Manchester, 1964

Martin 2005
Gregory Martin, *The Ceiling Decoration of the Banqueting Hall, Corpus Rubenianum Ludwig Burchard Part XV*, Antwerp, 2005

Martin 2017
Colin J.A. Martin, *A Cromwellian Warship wrecked off Duart Castle, Mull, Scotland, in 1653*, Edinburgh, 2017

McClure 1939
N.E. McClure (ed.), *The Letters of John Chamberlain*, 2 vols, Philadelphia, 1939, vol.2

McEvansoneya 1992
Philip McEvansoneya, 'An unpublished inventory of the Hamilton collection in the 1620s and the Duke of Buckingham's pictures', *Burlington Magazine*, vol.134, 1992, pp.524–26

Meikle, Craigie & Purves 1914–40
Henry W. Meikle, James Craigie and John Purves (eds), 'Works of William Fowler', *Edinburgh: Scottish Text Society*, 1914–40, Third Series, Vol.III, pp.cxxix–cxxx

Middleton 1616
Thomas Middleton, *Civitatis Amor: The Cities Love*, London, 1616

Millar 1960
Oliver Millar (ed.), 'Abraham van der Doort's Catalogue of the collections of Charles I', *Walpole Society*, vol.37, 1960

Millar 1963a
Oliver Millar, *The Tudor, Stuart and Early Georgian Pictures in the Collection of Her Majesty the Queen*, London, 1963

Millar 1963b
Oliver Millar, 'Marcus Gheeraerts, the Younger', *Burlington Magazine*, vol.105, no.729, 1963, pp.533–41

Millar 1969
Oliver Millar, *Later Georgian Pictures in the Collection of Her Majesty the Queen*, London, 1969

Millar 1972
Oliver Millar (ed.), 'The inventories and valuations of the King's goods, 1649–1651', *Walpole Society*, vol.43, 1972

Moysie 1830
David Moysie, *Memoirs of the Affaires of Scotland, 1577–1603*, ed. by J. Dennistoun, Edinburgh, 1830

Murray 2017
Catriona Murray, *Imaging Stuart Family Politics: Dynastic Crisis and Continuity*, Abingdon and New York, 2017

Nicholl 2005
Charles Nicholl, *Shakespeare and his Contemporaries*, London, 2005

Nichols 1828
John Nichols, *The Progresses, Processions and Magnificent Festivities of King James the First*, 3 vols, London, 1828, vol.2

Nichols 1831
John Nichols, *London Pageants: I. Accounts of Sixty Royal Processions and Entertainments in the City of London*, London, 1831

Nubia & Kupperman nd
Onyeka Nubia and Karen Ordhal Kupperman, 'An American Princess in London', *Our Migration Story: The Making of Britain Website, Early Modern Migrations 1500–1750*, https://www.ourmigrationstory.org.uk/oms/an-american-princess-in-london (accessed 13 August 2024)

O'Donoghue 1908–25
Freeman M. O'Donoghue, *Catalogue of Engraved British Portraits preserved in the Department of Prints and Drawings in the British Museum* (Volume III), 1908–25, London

ODNB 2004
Oxford Dictionary of National Biography, Oxford, 2004

OED online
Oxford English Dictionary, https://www.oed.com (accessed 10 March 2019)

Ogden 2018
Jack Ogden, *Diamonds: An Early History of the King of Gems*, New Haven, 2018

Payne 2001
M.T.W. Payne, 'An inventory of Queen Anne of Denmark's "ornaments, furniture, householde stuffe, and other parcells" at Denmark House, 1619', *Journal of the History of Collections*, vol.13, no.1, 2001, pp.23–44

Pearce 2019
Michael Pearce, 'Anna of Denmark: Fashioning a Danish Court in Scotland', *Court Historian*, vol.24, no.2, 2019, pp.138–51

Peck 1981
Linda Levy Peck, 'Court patronage and government policy: the Jacobean dilemma', in Guy Fitch Lytle and Stephen Orgel (eds), *Patronage in the Renaissance*, Princeton, 1981, pp.27–46

Peck 1993
Linda Levy Peck, *Court Patronage and Corruption in Early Stuart England*, London, 1993

Peterborough 1887
Catalogue of the Tercentenary of Mary, Queen of Scots Exhibition, exh. cat., Peterborough, 1887

Quinton 2013
Rebecca Quinton, *Glasgow Museums Seventeenth-Century Costume*, London, 2013

Rae 2015
Caroline Rae, 'Marcus Gheeraerts the Younger, John de Critz, Robert Peake and William Larkin: A comparative study', in Tarnya Cooper, Aviva Burnstock, Maurice Howard and Edward Town (eds), *Painting in Britain 1500–1630: Production, Influences and Patronage*, Oxford, 2015, pp.171–79

Rae & Burnstock 2014
Caroline Rae and Aviva Burnstock, 'A technical study of portraits of James VI and I attributed to John de Critz the Elder (d.1642): artist, workshop and copies', in Erma Hermans (ed.), *European Paintings 15th–18th Century: Copying, Replicating and Emulating*, New York, 2014, pp.58–66

Reynolds 1952
Graham Reynolds, 'Portraits by Nicholas Hilliard and his assistants of King James I and his family', *Walpole Society*, vol.34, 1952, pp.14–26

Reynolds 1999
Graham Reynolds, *The Sixteenth and Seventeenth Century Portrait Miniatures in the Collection of Her Majesty the Queen*, London, 1999

Ribeiro 2000
Aileen Ribeiro, *The Gallery of Fashion*, London, 2000

Ribeiro 2005
Aileen Ribeiro, *Fashion and Fiction: Dress in Art and Literature in Stuart England*, New Haven and London, 2005

Richardson 1901
A.B. Richardson, *Catalogue of the Scottish Coins in the National Museum of Antiquities*, Edinburgh, 1901

Rogers 1993
J.M. Rogers, *Mughal Miniatures (Eastern Art)*, London, 1993

Scarisbrick 1986
Diana Scarisbrick, 'Anne of Denmark's jewellery, old and new', *Apollo*, vol.123, 1986, pp.228–36

Scarisbrick 1991
Diana Scarisbrick, 'Anne of Denmark's jewellery inventory', *Archaeologia*, vol.109, 1991, pp.193–238

Scarisbrick 1994
Diana Scarisbrick, *Jewellery in Britain 1066–1837*, Norwich, 1994

Scarisbrick 1995
Diana Scarisbrick, *Tudor and Jacobean Jewellery*, London, 1995

Schlueter 2006
June Schlueter, 'Michael van Meer's *Album Amicorum*, with illustrations of London, 1614–15', *Huntington Library Quarterly*, vol.69, no.2, June 2006, pp.301–14

Schweiger 1832
Franz Ludwig Anton Schweiger, *Handbuch der classischen Bibliographie*, Volume II, Leipzig, 1832

Scott-Elliot & Yeo 1990
A.H. Scott-Elliot and Elspeth Yeo, 'Calligraphic manuscripts of Esther Inglis (1571–1624): a catalogue', *Papers of the Bibliographical Society of America*, vol.84, 1990, pp.10–86

Seaby & Purvey 1984
Peter Seaby and P. Frank Purvey, *Standard Catalogue of British Coins, Volume 2: Coins of Scotland, Ireland and the Islands*, London, 1984

Sharpe 2009
Kevin Sharpe, *Selling the Tudor Monarchy: Authority and Image in Sixteenth-Century England*, New Haven and London, 2009

SNPG 2014
Scottish National Portrait Gallery Guide, Edinburgh, 2014

Sommerville 1994
Johann P. Sommerville (ed.), *King James VI and I: Political Writings*, Cambridge, 1994

Stevenson 1997
David Stevenson, *Scotland's Last Royal Wedding: The Marriage of James VI and Anna of Denmark*, Edinburgh, 1997

Stewart 1967
I.H. Stewart, *The Scottish Coinage*, 2nd edn, London, 1967

Strong 1966
Roy Strong, 'Three royal jewels: the Three Brothers, the Mirror of Great Britain and the Feather', *Burlington Magazine*, vol.108, 1966, pp.350–53

Strong 1969a
Roy Strong, *Tudor and Jacobean Portraits in the National Portrait Gallery*, London, 1969

Strong 1969b
Roy Strong, *The English Icon: Elizabethan and Jacobean Portraiture*, London, 1969

Strong 1986
Roy Strong, *Henry, Prince of Wales and England's Lost Renaissance*, London, 1986

Stübel 1905
Bruno Stübel, 'Instruktion Karls V. für Philipp II. vom 25. Oktober 1555', *Archiv für österreichische Geschichte*, vol.93, 1905

Syme 2019
Holger Schott Syme, 'The Jacobean King's men: a reconsideration', *Review of English Studies*, New Series, vol.70, no.294, 2019, pp.231–51

Taylor 1613
John Taylor, *Heavens Blessing and Earths Joy*, London, 1613

Taylor 2015
David A.H.B. Taylor, 'Gesture recognition: Adam de Colone and the transmission of portrait types from the Low Countries and England to Scotland', in Tarnya Cooper *et al.* (eds), *Painting in Britain, 1500–1630: Production, Influences and Patronage*, Oxford, 2015, pp.310–23

Ter Kuile 1969
Onno ter Kuile, 'Daniel Mijtens: "His Majesties Picture Drawer"', *Nederlands Kunsthistorisch Jaarboek*, vol.20, 1969, pp.1–106

Thomas 2013
Andrea Thomas, *Glory and Honour: The Renaissance in Scotland*, Edinburgh, 2013

Thomson 1974
Duncan Thomson, *The Life and Art of George Jamesone*, Oxford, 1974

Thomson 1975
Duncan Thomson, *Painting in Scotland 1570–1650*, Edinburgh, 1975

Thurley 2009
Simon Thurley, *Somerset House: The Palace of England's Queens, 1551–1692*, London, 2009

Town 2012
Edward Town, '"Whilst he had his perfect sight" – new light on the life and career of John de Critz the Elder', *Burlington Magazine*, vol.154, 2012, pp.482–86

Town 2014
Edward Town, 'Biographical dictionary of London painters 1547–1625', *Walpole Society*, vol.76, 2014, pp.1–235

Townsend 2003
Richard P. Townsend, 'Alexander Keirincx's royal commission of 1639–1640', in Juliette Roding *et al.* (eds) *Dutch and Flemish Artists in Britain 1550–1800*, Leiden, 2003, pp.137–50

Townsend 2018
Richard P. Townsend, 'Alexander Keirincx' Aufenthalt in Großbritannien', in Ursula Härting *et al.*, *Alexander Keirincx (1600–1652). Der Baummaler – Die Gemälde*, Schoten, 2018, pp.40–50

Ungerer 1998
Gustav Ungerer, 'Juan Pantoja de la Cruz and the circulation of gifts between the English and Spanish courts, 1604–5', *Shakespeare Studies*, vol.26, 1998, pp.145–86

Verner 1950
Coolie Verner, 'The First Maps of Virginia, 1590–1673', *The Virginia Magazine of History and Biography 58*, no.1, January 1950, pp.3–15

Werrett 2011
Simon Werrett, 'Watching the fireworks: early modern observation of natural and artificial spectacles', *Science in Context*, vol.24, no.2, 2011, pp.162–82

Wheelock et al. 2008
Arthur Wheelock *et al.*, *Jan Lievens: A Dutch Master Rediscovered*, New Haven and London, 2008

Williamson 1978
Jerry Wayne Williamson, *The Myth of the Conqueror: Prince Henry Stuart – A Study of Seventeenth-century Personation*, New York, 1978

Working 2020
Lauren Working, *The Making of an Imperial Polity: Civility and America in the Jacobean Metropolis*, Cambridge, 2020

Working 2022
Lauren Working, *Lives in Transit in Early Modern England: Identity and Belonging*, 2022, pp.185–92

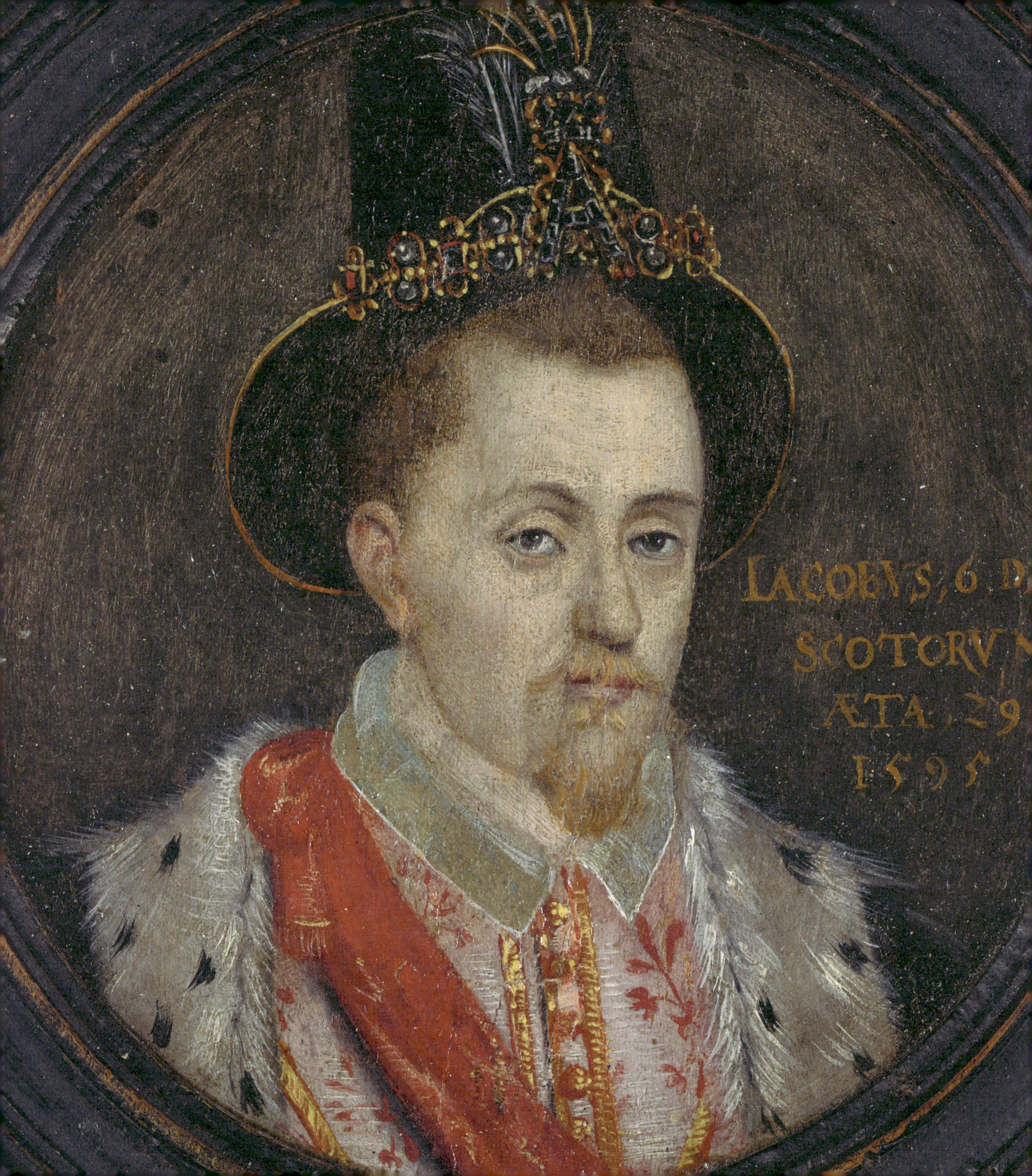

IACOBVS, 6 D
SCOTORV
ÆTA. 29
1595

INDEX

IMAGE CREDITS

ACKNOWLEDGEMENTS

In addition to those acknowledged in the foreword I would like to thank all those who contributed to the publication and the exhibition. Special thanks are given to the contributing authors of this publication: Jemma Field, Anna Groundwater, Karen Hearn and Catriona Murray. Catriona and Anna not only contributed essays to the book but were academic advisors for the project, and from the outset were incredibly generous with their time, creative ideas and support, for which I thank them wholeheartedly. I am indebted to a number of colleagues and academics from across the UK and the USA who shared their expertise and advice, including Michael Bath, Deborah Clarke, James Cook, David Forsyth, Hazel Forsyth, John Gilbert, Anette Hagan, Maria Hayward, Ulrike Hogg, Rachel Hosker, Amy Juhala, Catharine MacLeod, James Loxley, Maureen Meikle, Michael Pearce, Jamie Reid-Baxter, Steven Reid, and Alison Rosie.

A project of this complexity and scale requires a team of dedicated individuals and I would like to thank my National Galleries of Scotland colleagues, in particular Liz Louis, whose research skills and eye for detail were invaluable, Christopher Baker, James Berry, Louise Rowlands, Lesley Stevenson, and the project delivery team. I am grateful to my colleagues in the NGS publishing department, Catherine Aitken and Ann Crawford, and, outwith the galleries, Ocky Murray for the beautiful book design.

My final thanks are to Gordon, Logan, Sheena and John who have lived with King James for as long as I have.

Kate Anderson

Detail of cat.81 (opposite)

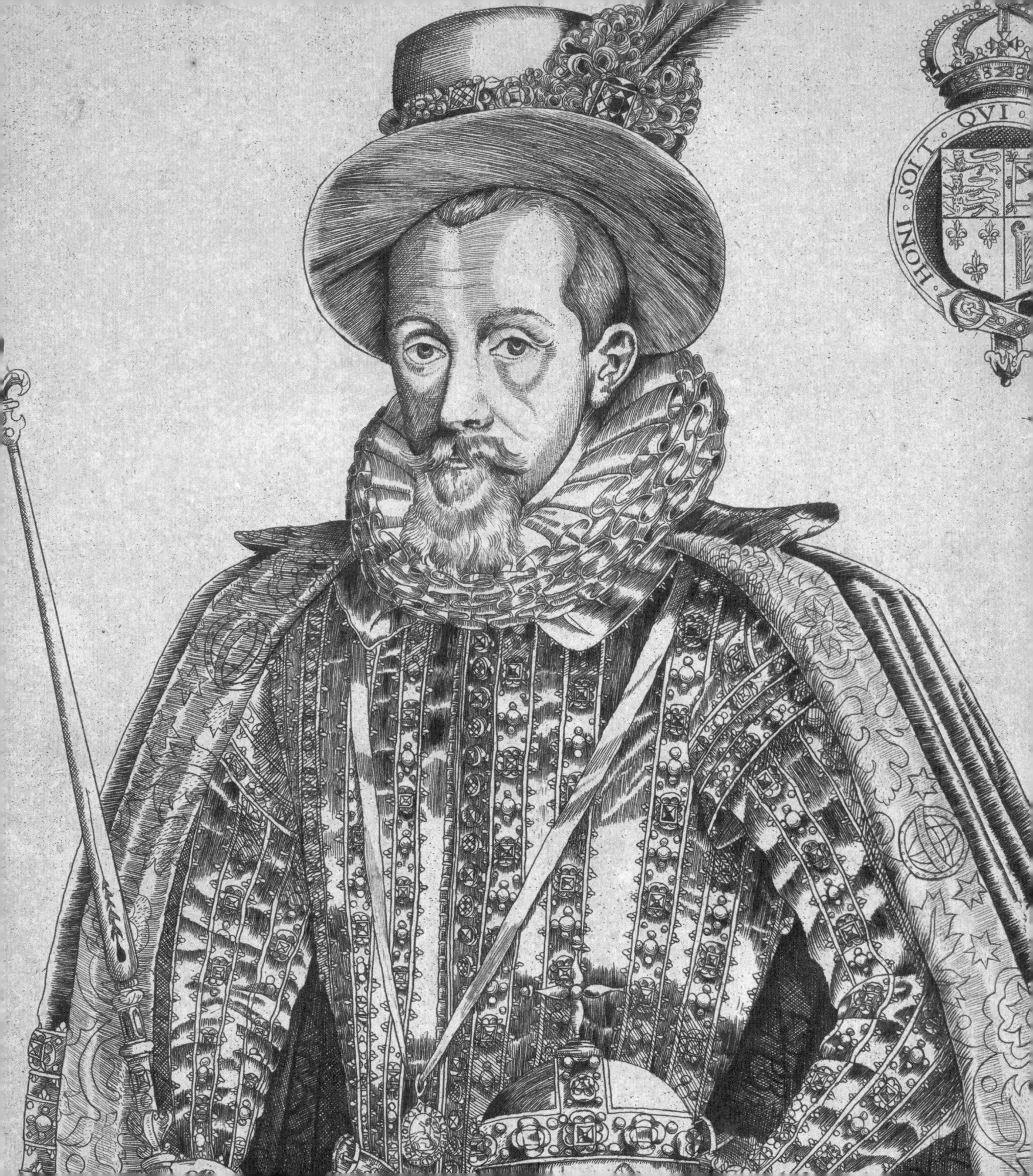

Published by the Trustees of the National Galleries of Scotland to accompany the exhibition
The World of King James VI and I, held at the National Galleries of Scotland: Portrait,
from 26 April to 14 September 2025

© The Trustees of the National Galleries of Scotland, 2025

ISBN 978 1 911054 70 2

Project Manager for this title: Catherine Aitken
Copy-editor: Abigail Grater
Proof-reader: Ivor Normand, Howard Watson
Indexer: Emma Caddy

Publishing Team
Publisher: Ann Crawford
Publishing Project Editor: Catherine Aitken
Publishing Co-ordinator: Jennifer McIlreavy, Jonny Clowes, Megan Boyle
Publishing Assistant: Hannah Killoh, Caitlin Mellon

Designed and typeset in Sabon by Ocky Murray
Printed in Belgium by Albe de Coker

Front cover: Nicholas Hilliard, *James VI & I*, 1609 (detail of cat.55), The Buchanan Society,
on long-term loan to the National Galleries of Scotland, Edinburgh

Back cover: Unknown artist, *King James riding to Parliament with three noblemen*, from
an Album Amicorum owned by Michael van Meer, 1614–48 (cat.6), The University of
Edinburgh Heritage Collections

Frontispiece: Attributed to John de Critz the Elder, *James VI & I*, c.1606 (detail of cat.7),
Dulwich Picture Gallery, London

This exhibition has been assisted by the Scottish Government and the Government
Indemnity Scheme.

The proceeds from the sale of this book go towards supporting the National Galleries
of Scotland. For a complete list of current publications, please write to:
NGS Publishing, 70 Belford Road, Edinburgh EH4 3DE
or visit our website: www.nationalgalleries.org

National Galleries of Scotland is a charity registered in Scotland (No.SC003728)

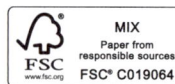

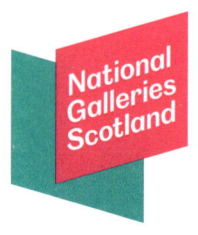

Supported by  Friends

Supported by 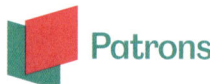 Patrons